Advanced AI and Prompt Engineering Techniques and Resources

Houssem Chemingui
Brest Business School, France

Munir Ahmad
Survey of Pakistan, Pakistan

IGI Global
Scientific Publishing
Publishing Tomorrow's Research Today

Vice President of Editorial Melissa Wagner
Director of Acquisitions Mikaela Felty
Director of Book Development Jocelynn Hessler
Production Manager Mike Brehm
Cover Design Jose Rosado

Published in the United States of America by
IGI Global Scientific Publishing
701 East Chocolate Avenue
Hershey, PA, 17033, USA
Tel: 717-533-8845 | Fax: 717-533-7115
Website: https://www.igi-global.com E-mail: cust@igi-global.com

Library of Congress Cataloging-in-Publication Data

Names: Chemingui, Houssem, 1990- editor http://id.loc.gov/rwo/agents/n2024051984 | Ahmad, Munir, 1978- editor http://id.loc.gov/rwo/agents/n2025008753
Title: Advanced AI and prompt engineering techniques and resources / edited by: Houssem Chemingui, Munir Ahmad.
Description: Hershey, PA : IGI Global Scientific Publishing, [2026] | Includes bibliographical references. | Summary: "In this book, we explore advanced techniques for prompt engineering, diving deep into strategies and methodologies that push the boundaries of AI capabilities. The goal is to provide readers with the tools to craft sophisticated prompts that lead to enhanced AI performance, whether for creative tasks, problem-solving, or data analysis. From understanding model behavior to leveraging contextual clues, this book serves as a comprehensive resource for anyone looking to master the art of interacting with AI at an advanced level"-- Provided by publisher.
Identifiers: LCCN 2025001652 (print) | LCCN 2025001653 (ebook) | ISBN 9798337302508 hardcover | ISBN 9798337302515 paperback | ISBN 9798337302522 ebook
Subjects: LCSH: Natural language generation (Computer science) http://id.loc.gov/authorities/subjects/sh2017004703 | Natural language processing (Computer science) http://id.loc.gov/authorities/subjects/sh88002425
Classification: LCC QA76.9.N38 A337 2025 (print) | LCC QA76.9.N38 (ebook) | DDC 006.3/5--dc23/eng/20250421
LC record available at https://lccn.loc.gov/2025001652
LC ebook record available at https://lccn.loc.gov/2025001653

British Cataloguing in Publication Data
A Cataloguing in Publication record for this book is available from the British Library.

Table of Contents

Detailed Table of Contents

Prompt engineering is evolving into both an art and a science, essential for effective interaction with AI models like GPT. As generative AI advances, crafting prompts demands greater precision, relevance, and creativity. This chapter from Advanced Prompt Engineering Techniques and Resources explores how AI interprets human input, detailing methods such as zero-shot, few-shot, chain-of-thought, scaffolding, and persona-based prompting. It provides strategies to reduce hallucinations, improve clarity, and tailor outputs across domains like content creation, research, and business automation. Practical tools, prompt templates, and benchmarking techniques are introduced to support continuous refinement. Ethical aspects like bias, fairness, and human-AI collaboration are also examined, positioning prompt engineering as both a practical necessity and an emerging academic discipline. Readers gain foundational knowledge and actionable frameworks to design more impactful and responsible AI prompts.

The chapter provides a comprehensive approach to learning contextual and task-specific prompting, two essential components for enhancing interactions with AI

The chapter discusses the importance of ethics in the development and use of AI. As AI becomes a bigger part of our daily lives, it is necessary to ensure that it is used in ways that are fair, safe, and respectful of human values. The article explains key ethical concerns such as bias, lack of fairness, loss of privacy, job loss, and lack of accountability. It also introduces major global efforts, such as the EU AI Act, OECD AI Principles, and UNESCO's guidelines, which aim to guide the safe and responsible use of AI. It highlights the need for collaboration between experts from various fields to develop trustworthy AI. As technology continues to evolve, the role of ethics will become increasingly important. The main goal is to ensure that AI supports human well-being and helps create a better future for all.

Bias in AI-generated responses presents significant ethical and societal challenges, often stemming from imbalanced training data and systemic inequities. This study investigates advanced prompt engineering techniques, including contextual prompting, iterative refinement, bias-aware framing, and dynamic prompting, as proactive solutions for mitigating bias in AI text generation. Through quantitative and qualitative analyses, the research demonstrates that these techniques effectively reduce bias, enhance fairness, and maintain response quality across diverse domains. Dynamic prompting emerges as the most effective, achieving substantial reductions in the Bias Amplification Index (BAI) and improvements in the Fairness Index (FI). While these techniques show scalability and adaptability, challenges remain in addressing intersectional biases and architectural limitations. This study positions prompt engineering as a critical tool for ethical AI development, offering actionable insights for researchers and practitioners.

Fish diversity is correlated with the biotic and abiotic factors in the aquatic environment. Fish samples from the Vembanad lake were collected for three consecutive years. Sodium, Potassium, Magnesium, Manganese, Copper, Iron, Calcium, Dissolved Oxygen, BOD, pH, salinity, and temperature in the water samples were analyzed using APHA (1998). Fish diversity was analyzed using diversity indices such as Berger Parker index, Shannon Weiner index, Simpson Index, Hills number and Margalef's index. Pearson's correlation coefficient was using to find out correlation among variables. Regression analysis have been shown that temperature is the most predictable variable for the fish diversity in Vembanad ecosystem.

Most popular web browsers, Google Chrome and Microsoft Edge, have been built on a similar foundation in using the Chromium engine, but have taken different architectural approaches, adding their own flavors along the way. We review these approaches in this study, highlighting differences in their technical solutions including rendering engines, security frameworks, and optimization methodologies. Then the performance problems of rice are researched (which includes rice consumption, speed and cross-platform compatibility). It also examines user-facing aspects like privacy, personalization, or AI functions. However, this report is not just a guide

Preface

In an age where artificial intelligence is no longer a concept of the future but an integral part of our daily lives, the ability to communicate effectively with these powerful models has become a critical skill for everyone from researchers to students. "Advanced Prompt Engineering Techniques and Resources" is designed to be your comprehensive guide to mastering this new form of communication. This book moves far beyond the basics of simple queries and delves into the nuanced art and science of crafting prompts that yield precise, creative, and controlled outputs, turning a simple tool into a powerful extension of your own intellect.

This book is structured to provide a holistic understanding of prompt engineering, beginning with foundational principles and advancing to complex, real-world applications. We will explore how to shape your interactions with AI for maximum effectiveness, ensuring your intent is not only understood but executed with accuracy, integrity, and a deep sense of purpose. The journey will take you from mastering the core strategies of prompting to understanding the profound ethical dimensions of AI, including bias mitigation, the promotion of transparency, and the societal implications of this technology.

We also examine the practical application of these principles through a series of diverse case studies, demonstrating the universal power of effective prompt engineering. From leveraging regression analysis to predict fish availability in a specific ecological system to conducting a critical comparative analysis of web browsers, these chapters showcase how the techniques you learn can be applied across vastly different academic and professional fields. This breadth of content illustrates the universal power of effective prompt engineering and its vital role in building a responsible and inclusive future.

CHAPTER OVERVIEW

Chapter 1: Mastering the Art of Prompting

This foundational chapter explores key strategies for creating precise, creative, and controllable prompts. Techniques such as zero-shot, few-shot, and chain-of-thought prompting are unpacked alongside practical tools, ethical considerations, and real-world applications across domains.

Chapter 2: Contextual and Task-Specific Prompting

The authors examine how contextual cues and task-specific structures influence the performance of AI models. This chapter also addresses multilingual and cross-cultural considerations, future directions in adaptive prompting, and personalized prompt design.

Chapter 3: Contextual Prompt Engineering for Enhanced Ethical AI Outputs

Focused on bias mitigation and transparency, this chapter introduces a context-sensitive framework for ethical AI prompting. It provides practical examples and case studies from domains like healthcare and media, promoting fair representation and social responsibility.

Chapter 4: Prompt Refinement and Iteration Methods

Centering on iterative processes, this chapter details how to continuously enhance prompt quality based on feedback and evaluation. It guides readers through systematic methods for improving prompt effectiveness across analytical and creative use cases.

Chapter 5: Maintaining Academic Integrity in the Era of Large Language Models

Aimed at academic professionals, this chapter provides ethical guidelines for using LLMs in research. It covers model selection, prompt specificity, validation protocols, and integrity-preserving practices for integrating AI into scholarly workflows.

Chapter 6: Ethics in Artificial Intelligence

This chapter broadens the ethical conversation, discussing the societal implications of AI adoption. It highlights global regulatory efforts, ethical design principles, and interdisciplinary collaboration as crucial for building inclusive and trustworthy AI systems.

Chapter 7: Mitigating Bias in AI-Generated Responses

Building on earlier discussions of ethics, this chapter presents advanced techniques like dynamic and bias-aware prompting to reduce algorithmic bias. Quantitative and qualitative analyses demonstrate the real-world impact of these strategies across various sectors.

Chapter 8: Prediction of Fish Availability Using Regression Analysis in Vembanad Lake

While not directly about prompt engineering, this empirical chapter illustrates the application of data analysis techniques in ecology. It provides valuable context for AI applications in environmental science, highlighting interdisciplinary collaboration potential.

Chapter 9: A Critical Comparative Analysis of Google Chrome and Microsoft Edge

This final chapter presents a comparative study of browser-based AI tools, analyzing how Chrome and Edge integrate AI features. It offers insight into performance, security, and innovation, showcasing the user-level implications of embedded AI technologies.

The journey you are about to embark on will equip you with the skills to harness the true potential of large language models, transforming them from mere tools into powerful partners for innovation and ethical exploration.

Acknowledgement

This book would not have been possible without the support and collaboration of many individuals. We would like to extend our deepest gratitude to our colleagues and mentors who provided invaluable feedback and encouragement throughout the writing process. We also thank the many researchers and developers whose foundational work in artificial intelligence and prompt engineering has made this book possible. Finally, a special thank you to our readers—your curiosity and dedication to learning are the true inspiration behind this project.

Chapter 1
Mastering the Art of Prompting:
Strategies for Precision, Creativity, and Control

R. N. Ravikumar
https://orcid.org/0009-0009-3705-1681
Marwadi University, Rajkot, India

Zamira Atamuratova
Urgench State University, Urgench, Uzbekistan

S. Aarthi
https://orcid.org/0009-0006-9064-2091
Marwadi University, Rajkot, India

Sadullayeva Moxinur
Urgench State Pedagogical Institute, Urgench, Uzbekistan

Yulduz Urazbaeva
Mamun University, Khiva, Uzbekistan

Jakhongir Shaturaev
Termez University of Economics and Service, Termez, Uzbekistan

ABSTRACT

Prompt engineering is evolving into both an art and a science, essential for effective interaction with AI models like GPT. As generative AI advances, crafting prompts demands greater precision, relevance, and creativity. This chapter from Advanced Prompt Engineering Techniques and Resources explores how AI interprets human input, detailing methods such as zero-shot, few-shot, chain-of-thought, scaffolding, and persona-based prompting. It provides strategies to reduce hallucinations, improve clarity, and tailor outputs across domains like content creation, research, and business automation. Practical tools, prompt templates, and benchmarking techniques are introduced to support continuous refinement. Ethical aspects like bias, fairness, and human-AI collaboration are also examined, positioning prompt

DOI: 10.4018/979-8-3373-0250-8.ch001

engineering as both a practical necessity and an emerging academic discipline. Readers gain foundational knowledge and actionable frameworks to design more impactful and responsible AI prompts.

INTRODUCTION

The nature of prompt engineering has changed quickly, becoming a central practice in using generative Artificial Intelligence (AI) systems well. As large language models such as Generative Pre-trained Transformer (GPT), become stronger and more detailed, people interacting with them should do so with more awareness and sophistication. Now, teachers need to use strategy when making prompts, choosing what to include for clarity, creativity and control. This chapter discusses both the main principles and additional methods of creating prompts. The purpose of this manual is to help new and advanced users design prompts that get specific, relevant and new answers from their users. Readers who learn how AI models interpret human input can exert greater influence, prevent mistakes and reach the best results with AI. In this chapter, practical guidance and examples for methods ranging from zero-shot and few-shot prompting to chain-of-thought reasoning and instruction tuning are offered. The real goal is to help people use language skilfully to steer AI's actions in different fields like technology, creativity and work (Agnoli & Rapp, 2024).

Importance of Prompt Engineering in Effective AI Interaction

The basis for successful communication with LLMs like GPT is prompt engineering. These models only react to patterns seen in a lot of data, not to people's intentions. As a result, a good quality prompt leads to more useful and clear answers from the AI. If prompts are not well designed, the results may be unclear, off-target or confusing, but when designed properly, they can enable powerful and aware responses from the machine. Since AI is used in education, business, healthcare, content creation, software development and other fields, prompt engineering is very important now. It helps close the distance between what humans want and what computers create. If users become better at prompt engineering, they can receive results that are accurate, ethical and creative (Bozkurt, 2023). The Figure1 gives the essential strategies in prompt engineering, Modes & ChatML as strategies to deal with a static prompt, Prompt Decomposition as a strategy to decompose context, Prompt Pipelines with Prompt Chaining as strategies to facilitate structure in a workflow. It also incorporates Agents in handling dynamically interactions. Each component is graphically connected to the core topic of Prompt Engineering with the emphasis on modular, flexible and dynamic in nature.

Figure 1. Prompt Engineering Framework

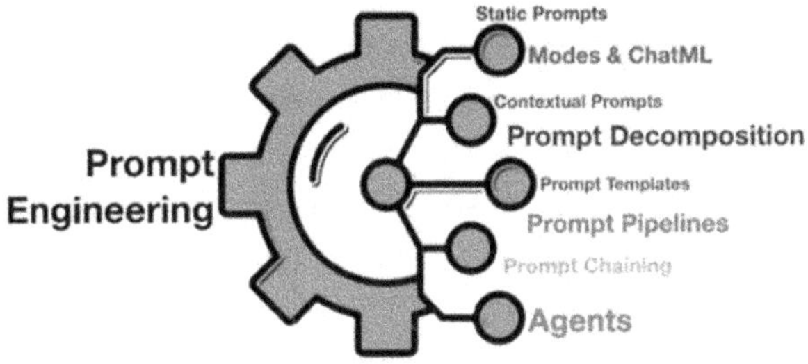

Source: Medium

OVERVIEW OF GOALS: PRECISION, CREATIVITY, AND CONTROL

A good prompt should focus on precision, creativity and how much control the teacher has. Making the AI understand the user's wishes precisely is important in user satisfaction. It helps avoid misunderstandings and allows you to receive responses matching what your users expect. Fact accuracy and clear language matter greatly in technical, legal or instructional writing. Thanks to creativity, AI can make many original, engaging and interesting pieces of content. In storytelling, design, marketing and ideation, creative prompts inspire new answers and push the limits of what people can do. To control a text means you need to shape its tone, form, format or style to match your expectations (Cain, 2024). This is important for keeping a brand consistent, for designing lessons and for writing important documents. With good control, users are able to repeat excellent outputs and achieve their expected outcomes. Giving people instruction that is precise and clear to prevent unclear information. Promoting creativity is the ability to encourage students to go beyond what is perceived within normality and develop groundbreaking or unusual concepts. It is also significant to be able to control the way AI model is going to sound, the pattern of language it uses and even its manners because of the need to make it fit the purpose and the individuals addressed. All these features are essential when it comes to AI interactions since they create a tradc-off between the freedom of thought and facilitated communication. Integration of the creativity and control enables users to effectively tailor applications of AI system to various industries, such as education, healthcare, business, and entertainment.

Benefits of Prompt Engineering

Prompt engineering plays a crucial role of boosting the performance of AI models through proper use of clear, concise and structured prompts, which yields accurate and relevant responses. It makes the process more efficient since it does not require much fine-tuning, hence time and resource consumption during training. Effective well-designed prompts achieve user-friendly, intuitive experiences, as well as enable the models to respond to a wide variety of industry-specific use cases or other conditions. AI models can be improved in order to achieve prolonged effectiveness as techniques continue to develop (Torricelli et al., 2024). Nevertheless, along with such advantages, the users can be presented with the difficulties of design complexity, domain-specific adaptation, and the guarantee stable results in different situations. The Figure 2 presents key strategies for effective prompt engineering, emphasizing clarity, context, format specification, and iterative refinement. It also highlights ethical practices, such as bias avoidance and edge case handling, serving as a quick-reference guide for best practices.

Figure 2. Best Practices in Prompt Engineering

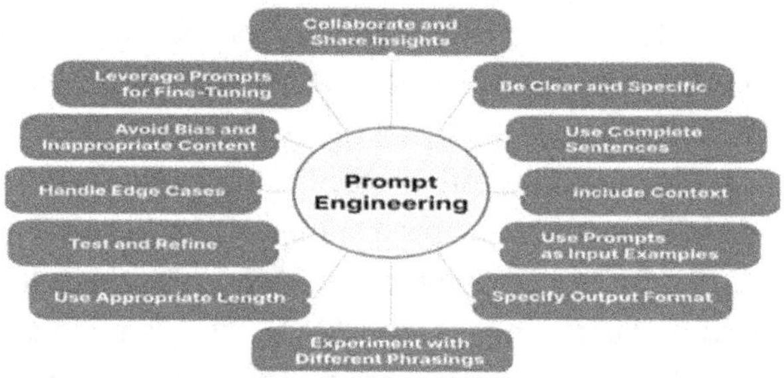

Source: Technopedia

AI MODEL FOUNDATIONS

Getting skilled at prompt engineering needs you to understand AI in general and Large Language Models (LLMs) such as GPT. They depend on transformers which handle the input text by using layers of attention to create relevant answers. Unlike programs developed by humans, LLMs can only use learned data to make predictions about which words to choose next. The way a prompt is set up such as its words, phrasing, order and format, helps form these predictions. A slight change in the way a task is executed can make a big difference to the output (Lawrence et al., 2024). Making a request with a question or command will likely affect the way a person responds. For users, figuring out how models understand such instructions makes it easier to give the right prompts and foresee the effects of various inputs on their behavior.

Additionally, these models respond to tokenization and have context windows to restrict how much data they process at the same time. Noticing these difficulties stops you from putting out text that's cut short, irrelevant or repetitive. Being aware that LLMs function using transformers and attention, we know they produce results by noticing patterns in the training information. How prompt questions are given, the order in which they are shown and how they are organized matter greatly to the students. How a question is worded can make a big difference in both the message and the usefulness of what is said. Besides, knowing about tokenization and how big a context window is meaningful for avoiding errors in the system's output. Once users understand these basics, they are better able to control and make sense of interactions with AI. The table 1 explains how AI models like GPT interpret prompts. It highlights concepts like tokenization, context windows, and response biases. It helps readers understand the underlying mechanics of AI response generation.

Table 1. AI Model Foundations

Concept	Description
Prompt Interpretation	AI breaks down user input into tokens and interprets meaning contextually.
Context Window	The maximum token range the model uses to understand prompt + response.
Bias in Output	Systemic patterns from training data affecting responses.
Structure Sensitivity	How phrasing, order, and detail influence AI performance.
Role of Temperature and Top-p	Parameters to control randomness and diversity in responses.

HOW AI INTERPRETS PROMPTS (E.G., GPT MODELS)

Such models provide the instruction as input and break it apart into smaller pieces known as tokens. A token is often a word, part of a word or sometimes only a piece of punctuation. The model breaks the stream of tokens down step by step through a transformer architecture which relies on self-attention to measure the value of each token against the others. In essence, the model calculates which token is likely to appear next using knowledge it gathered from a huge amount of data (Mohitha et al., 2024). Unlike humans, GPT detects patterns between parts of text and forms text that is aligned with those patterns. How the prompt is designed can seriously affect the model's outcomes. For example, including clear directions or examples in what the model is prompted to learn (few-shot prompting) supports it in generating the best results. Since the model's answers are not certain, sometimes it offers an unexpected but creative response. Overall, AI handles prompt by turning them into tokens, examining how those tokens relate using attention and offering likely replies. The process works better when the information given is clear and structured quickly.

ROLE OF STRUCTURE, CONTEXT, AND BIAS IN RESPONSES

How and where a prompt is written decides how useful and accurate AI-generated answers will be. Clear, brief and logically set up prompts help models understand why a person is requesting something. A model becomes able to produce contextually suitable answers when it knows what happened in the conversation before. If a model is trained on biased data, it will reflect those biases from our society. Model outputs might reflect bias when the prompts are vague or bias can be found in the prompts used. So, it is important to create prompts that won't accidentally reinforce biases. Providing good context and clear structure to prompts lets people lead models in a fair and accurate direction (Cavalcante et al., 2023). They break down the text prompt, apply attention-based techniques and use a transformer architecture to suggest likely continuations. The exact way a prompt is presented plays a big role in determining how accurately and artistically the results will be. An important way to improve outputs is to have clearly supported prompts, remembering to be careful about any training biases. When prompt engineering is done right, the accuracy and fairness of AI responses are increased.

ADVANCED TECHNIQUES

When AI gets more intelligent, the methods for prompting them also improve. Here, we look at more advanced ways to guide generative AI for more precise, original and directed output. When using zero-shot prompting, nothing is shown to the model; it depends only on the instructions given in the prompt. Despite the fact that it's challenging, this method highlights how well the model generalizes and is good for performing fast queries. To compare, few-shot prompting includes a small number of examples in the prompt, letting the model understand how to format, style or reason properly (Sun, 2024). Chain-of-thought prompting has also been tried, encouraging the model to explain points of reasoning before the final answer. By doing it this way, it's less likely to make errors when working through complicated multi-step problems.

The process helps students learn by giving them smaller pieces of a task so they can understand and produce a better answer. Role-playing commands in the model's training urge it to communicate as an individual, making the text more interesting and engaging. At the end, instruction tuning sets up the model to react appropriately with information particular to the data, adapting it for various areas or purposes. Advanced techniques make it easier for users to handle complex requests, make things more precise and generate quality outputs. Modern prompt engineering approaches add zero-shot and few-shot prompting for general tasks, chain-of-thought prompting to support logical thinking, prompt scaffolding to make complicated tasks simpler, persona-based prompting to control tone and instruction tuning to adapt model actions (Zeiser, 2024). The methods make AI-generated responses more accurate, original and under control. The table 2 introduces key prompting methods such as zero-shot, few-shot, and chain-of-thought. Each technique is explained with its purpose and practical example.

It serves as a reference for designing more strategic and effective prompts.

Table 2. Advanced Techniques

Prompting Technique	Purpose	Example Use Case
Zero-shot Prompting	Solves tasks without prior examples	"Translate this text to French."
Few-shot Prompting	Provides a few examples to guide the model	"Translate: Hello → Bonjour, Goodbye → ?"
Chain-of-Thought Prompting	Encourages step-by-step reasoning	Solving math or logic problems
Prompt Scaffolding	Breaks down complex tasks into manageable steps	Report writing or summarizing arguments
Persona-based Prompting	Assigns a role or tone to the model	"Act as a lawyer giving legal advice."
Instruction Tuning	Optimizes prompts to match specific instructional goals	"Write a formal business proposal."

ZERO-SHOT, FEW-SHOT, CHAIN-OF-THOUGHT, AND SCAFFOLDING PROMPTING

Zero-shot prompting means that the AI has to perform a task solely based off of text instructions with no previous examples beforehand, testing the AI understanding of patterns, and how it can be applied to new tasks that it has only seen instructions of- effective when the task at hand is simple to answer and less so when it is complex or unclear. Prompting Few-shot prompting seeks to increase the precision of the task and thus is perfect to use when doing classifications, translations, or summary tasks and adding a few examples of what the correct format, style, or argument should be. Chain-of-thought prompting leads the model to think out loud by spelling out the intermediary steps in reasoning, improving logic-based or multi-step issues. Scaffolding in forms of prompts of a complex task is further fragmented into smaller and less complex prompts to increase clarity, structure, and the quality of output, especially when there are multiple stages of the process (Amin et al., 2023).

PERSONA-BASED AND INSTRUCTION TUNING PROMPTS

Prompting by persona tells the AI to answer in a particular personality, attitude and style, like a warm teacher, business consultant, or imaginative storyteller, so that the answers will be customized to the intended audience to be more relevant and engaging. Instead, instruction tuning consists of training AI-models using well-selected datasets of instructions and expected results, improving their general understanding of user commands and generating correct, reproducible, and context-worthy response on a wide range of different tasks. In combination, these methods facilitate more effective (and personal) AI interactions. Combined, persona-based prompting and instruction tuning enhance the adaptiveness and control of the AI, allowing users the opportunity to specify their desired output based on specific contexts or industries. These methods transform the interaction from simply input-output to a more nuanced engagement with the AI that is aligned with user-built expectations, making AI tools more effective for users and therefore more user-friendly (Cao & Ren, 2024).

PROMPT DESIGN PRINCIPLES

Effective prompt design is crucial for steering an AI model for good response relevance, accuracy, and quality. Good prompt engineering is based on clarity, specificity, and context. Clear prompts use simple, unambiguous language to help reduce confusion so the model knows what the user wants. Vague or overly broad prompts often produce generic responses or responses that are nowhere near what the user wants. Specificity means that a user must provide precise instructions, and/or constraints, in a prompt. Specificity can include the output style, format, domain, length, etc. The clearer and more specific a user is in issuing a prompt, the more able the model will be to tailor the output to the user's needs. Context is important for relevance and coherence and has greater importance in multi-turn conversations or complex tasks. Providing adequate context by providing sufficient information or referencing previous conversation therefore allows the model to typically deliver consistent, relevant replies (Cesur & Güneş, 2024). Prompts should also target possible biases or unintended connotations embedded in any language or text. Using neutral and inclusionary wording helps enable less biased or harmful output. The last principle is that prompt design is an iterative, and developmental process, which means new prompt writing methods, techniques, and examples are lying in the layers of prompt writing. Very rarely does a prompt work well on the first pass; through experimentation with different phrasing and structures and analyzing the outputs, improvements can be made. Well-designed prompts depend upon clear, specific, and contextual wording to limit ambiguity and guidance AI replies. Neutral language can help eliminate bias, and iterative exploration and testing can improve the effectiveness of prompts over time, while output accuracy and relevance can be confirmed. The table 3 covers essential prompt design elements: clarity, adaptability, and output control. It emphasizes techniques to reduce ambiguity and hallucination. It provides guidelines for crafting precise and reliable prompts.

Table 3. Prompt Design Principles

Principle	Description	Benefit
Clarity	Use unambiguous and specific language	More relevant and accurate output
Adaptability	Design prompts for varied contexts and outputs	Increased reusability
Output Control	Use constraints (length, tone, format) in prompts	More predictable results
Reducing Ambiguity	Avoid vague language or multiple interpretations	Less hallucination, improved focus
Reducing Hallucinations	Use grounding statements and factual references	More factual and consistent results

CLARITY, ADAPTABILITY, AND OUTPUT CONTROL

Prompt clarity relates to the clarity of using the prompt - good prompts have unambiguous, direct language that help the AI understand the user's intent. When a prompt is clearer, the model can generate relevant and accurate outputs that reduce confusion or unwanted information. By avoiding ambiguous meaning and phrasing, the model does not have to backtrack or adjust to a different level of output, which can improve the quality and usefulness of the responses given to the users (Hasan et al., 2024).

Adaptability is related to creating prompts that are easily adjusted or altered to address different contexts or purposes. Adaptable prompts provide users the opportunity to change prompts for different tasks without having to rewrite the entire prompt. Adaptable elements in prompts might use placeholders for specific words or modular components that can be changed for varying needs at the time. This not only makes it easier for users but also more scalable in the prompt engineering design process.

Output control relates to helping the model produce user-requested outputs that meet specific characteristics, such as tone, length, style, or format. Output control is often manipulated either through explicit specification in the prompt, or by incorporating more advanced prompting methods, such as persona-based prompting (i.e., ChatGPT, give me feedback as if you were an expert engineer) or instruction tuning (i.e. please give me 2 messages as an engineering student researching machine learning and AI). Effective output control can help avoid unintentional disparity between AI generated content and user expectations or use-case purposes, increasing usability and satisfaction (Heston & Khun, 2023).

REDUCING AMBIGUITY AND HALLUCINATIONS

Vagueness in prompts will often produce ambiguous or incorrect answers from AI. When information is vague or there are multiple interpretations of a user's prompt the model's capacity to interpret the meaning is thrown off which can result in unpredictable or irrelevant outputs. In order to diminish ambiguity in AI prompts, prompt designers can use more specific language, state context clearly and provide adequate background. Prompting AI clearly enables the model to rule out possible interpretations and zones in on a response that correlates with the prompt. Hallucinations are logically plausible information produced by AI, but having nothing to do with the prompt may normally be considered factually incorrect information. Hallucinations can arise from prompts that are vague or provide misleading context, or simply from the probabilistic nature of the model. One way of curbing hallucinations is restricting AI's creative autonomy in conceptualizing answers. Prompting with statements of fact, truth-seeking evidence, using chain-of-thought prompting, and limiting improvisation are all methods to reduce hallucinations. It would be wise to build verification criteria and potentially use external knowledge processes, resulting in less unsafe and more safe outputs. With more rigorous prompt design, prompt designers will be able to limit ambiguity and hallucinations to ensure more reliable, accurate, and trustworthy output in response to an AI prompt (Miao et al., 2024).

APPLICATIONS & CASE STUDIES

Prompt engineering has proven quite useful due to its line of applications in numerous industries that help AI produce accurate, situational, and ethically sound output. In business automation, it automates business processes, shortens the time taken to generate reports, and increases regulatory compliance in convincing AI to output high-quality expertise answers. In medicine, timely optimization assists in the accuracy of diagnoses, reduces bias and enhances the satisfaction levels of patients and clinicians. Online learning spaces use customized prompts to share unique educational opportunities and the legal environment gains access to situation-specific documents checking and regulatory observation(Han et al., 2025). The financial services Case Study 1 reported a reduced time preparation of report by 38%, accuracy of 92% on answering the client, and 96% compliance. Healthcare Case Study 2 has recorded 93% diagnostic accuracy, 29% improved case review times, and 98% coverage of the ethical standards. Such results indicate the role of immediate engineering in delivering bound and significant performance improvement, as well as supporting ethical and functioning requirements in a wide variety of real-life settings (Mohitha et al., 2024). In the Figure 3, the most important areas of implementation of AI are shown in a diamond format, including such areas as legal compliance, chatbots, business intelligence and analytics, software development, and cybersecurity. It also has healthcare, education and training, or software engineering, which demonstrates the vast applicability of the AI in many industries. The table 4 outlines real-world domains where prompt engineering is applied. It includes examples in content creation, business automation, and education. It demonstrates the practical impact of well-crafted prompts across industries.

Figure 3. Application Domains of Prompt Engineering

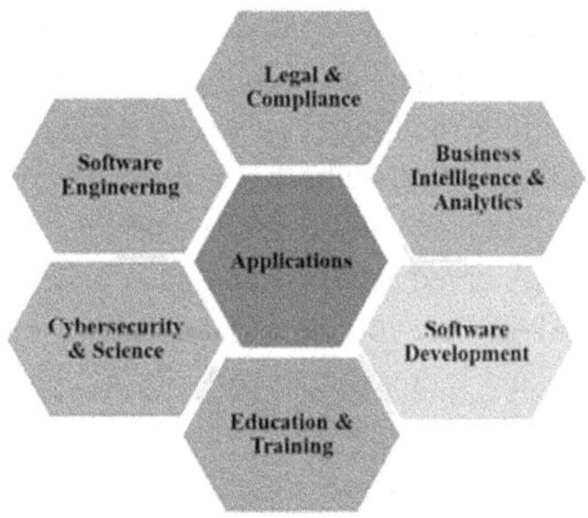

Table 4. Applications & Case Studies

Domain	Prompting Use Case	Outcome
Content Creation	Generating marketing content with stylistic variation	Engaging, brand-aligned copy
Programming	Code generation and debugging via structured prompts	Accurate, functional code snippets
Research Support	Literature reviews or hypothesis generation	Faster insight gathering
Business Automation	Drafting emails, reports, or summaries	Workflow efficiency and standardization
Education	Interactive tutoring or quiz generation	Personalized and adaptive learning content

CONTENT CREATION

Prompt engineering enhances content generation by providing a way to control the quality, relevance, and engagement of an AI model's output. Well-designed prompts can help provide products tailored for specific genres, styles, tones, or audiences in articles, blogs, marketing copy, and creative writing. For example, few-shot prompts give examples for the model to mimic in how the end user would like it to sound, or what it would look like in terms of formatting (Patil et al., 2024). By doing so, few-shot prompts are helpful for obtaining the exact representation in style that an end-user may want, yielding a more consistent product. Chain-of-thought prompts can improve a piece too, particularly when reasoning and keeping coherence per component of the text may be helpful. For example, if you were asking about a complex subject matter or doing storytelling, chain-of-thought prompting may help with both components.

Persona-based prompts can help to embody a specific disposition in the output of an AI-generated piece, making the text output relatable or professional. In general, prompt construction can relieve ambiguity from the input to the model to improve the quality of the overall output to be both relevant and creative, as well as reduce irrelevant or off-topic segments by imposing constraints over certain aspects of the model's output. As an engineered process, created or generated prompts can also be iteratively updated based on the evaluation of the output, thus providing continuous improvement over time and increasing specificity of relevance and creativity of subsequent contribution. These are useful techniques for content creators, marketers, and educators because they are time-saving, they eliminate writer's block, and they allow trying out many new ideas (Ruan et al., 2024). Ultimately, prompt engineering is putting AI to work with us as a collaborator, resulting in greater efficiencies and new ways of creating content in all industries.

PROGRAMMING AND SOFTWARE DEVELOPMENT

AI's role in programming and software engineering can be greatly enhanced through advanced prompt engineering. Software engineers can create prompts that allow AI to generate code snippets, troubleshoot problems, and quickly write documentation. Few-shot prompting promotes the development of better prompts by including a few examples of what the programmer is trying to achieve with the coding problem, such as proper code or the structure of error handling in a programming language. With few-shot prompting, the AI can better assess the programming problem, recognize the context and give a better response. Persona-based prompts can create fictitious expert developers who can give considerable advice and update programming best practices that are geared toward each programming language or framework. Chain-of-thought prompting keeps the AI on track by breaking down complex programming problems. Chain-of-thought prompting can help with logical reasoning, and provide reasonable guidance to the coder when generating code. This type of prompting is necessary to reduce errors and develop code at a quicker pace. Prompt engineering can also facilitate the automation requirements of repetitive coding tasks (Jabbour et al., 2023). This can free the developer to allow more likely creativity and overall, higher-order design work. Software teams can better utilize an AI tool with proper prompts at each step of the way. Overall, developers can create productivity-enhancing tools, minimize bugs, create better quality code, and develop skill and creativity, which contributes to real-world software engineering practice, which is a good thing in terms of both AI and software engineering. Thusly, prompt engineering is becoming, and is expected to be, an essential part of software engineering moving forward.

RESEARCH AND DATA ANALYSIS

In the research process and data analysis, prompt engineering leverages AI capabilities to organize and identify meaningful information from large populations of data. With the use of high-quality prompting techniques, researchers can facilitate AI to summarize complex documents, sort data and document trends, and develop hypotheses. Few-shot prompting provides examples of the type of analysis or report formats desired, allowing AI to generate outputs appropriate to the context, whether academic papers, market studies, or scientific reviews. Chain-of-thought prompting facilitates multi-staged reasoning, enabling AI to manage nuanced questions, and logically infer answers to queries without mean response (Abhari et al., 2024a). Instruction tuning also guarantees the AI follows a specific analytic approach that ensures the cognitive work has been completed, reducing potential errors and improving reliability. Researcher's exploratory needs can be guided through progressive spatial levels of prompt scaffolding from data cleaning, sorting, and interpreting. Each of these prompting levels can speed up the research workflow leading to faster discovery and better-informed decision making. Importantly, prompt engineering can increase reproducibility and transparency to the research process in support of reliability, by standardizing AI interaction with researchers through the research process.

BUSINESS AUTOMATION

Prompt engineering is a critical component of automation in business by enabling AI to take over actions such as customer service, report writing, and workflow automation, in general. Prompting gives clear and flexible instruction to AI chatbots by providing a clear way to answer customer questions accurately with personalized and context-aware responses, improving overall satisfaction, and reducing response time. With few-shot and persona-based prompting, chatbots can use tone consistent with the brand to provide complex responses to interactions. In business intelligence, prompt engineering can help produce detailed report writing and summaries from uncovered data, improving decision-making timelines (Buholayka et al., 2023). Similarly, workflow automation builds off prompts that tell the AI the steps to follow and how to manage exceptions. Overall, prompt engineering improves accuracy and consistency, seam your use of internal resources, and increase scalability and operational efficiency. As companies apply these methods, they immediately gain a competitive advantage by replacing routine processes while providing their talent to compete on strategy.

CASE STUDY 1 – BUSINESS AUTOMATION IN A FINANCIAL SERVICES FIRM

A medium sized financial services company incorporated high-tech prompt engineering in its artificial intelligence driven business automation tools. The main purpose was to simplify the communications with clients, automate reporting and enhance efficiency of workflow. The AI system was trained to author financial reports, clients email drafts and summarize market analysis in a professional and brand-consistent language through the use of few-shot prompting and persona-based prompting. After the deployment, the company indicated that its average report preparation time decreased by 38% because the AI produced decent first drafts that needed very few corrections(Bakhtiyari, 2024). The chatbots used by the company to service the customers with an augmented bias-aware prompting could deliver 92% accurate responses to the client queries, as opposed to the 78% level of accuracy before the upgrade. Automation of workflow resulted in a 41% increase in the speed of processing the documents and enabling employees to perform more highly valued analytical processes. Besides the efficiency benefit, within three months the firm was able to realize a 25% improvement in customer satisfaction scores, due to accelerated response time and greater personalization of communications received by customers. Internal audit reports ascertained that AI-generated output was within the regulatory guideline 96% of the time, in which case compliance checks do not necessarily require human intervention. All in all, the combination of professional prompt engineering methods with the business automation process led to quantitative growth in corporate operations, financial benefits, and customer communication(Yaprak, 2024). The Figure 4 illustrates performance improvements in a financial services company after adopting advanced prompt engineering for AI-driven automation. Significant gains were observed, with client response accuracy reaching 92% and regulatory compliance peaking at 96%.

Figure 4. Case Study 1 – Business Automation Performance Improvements

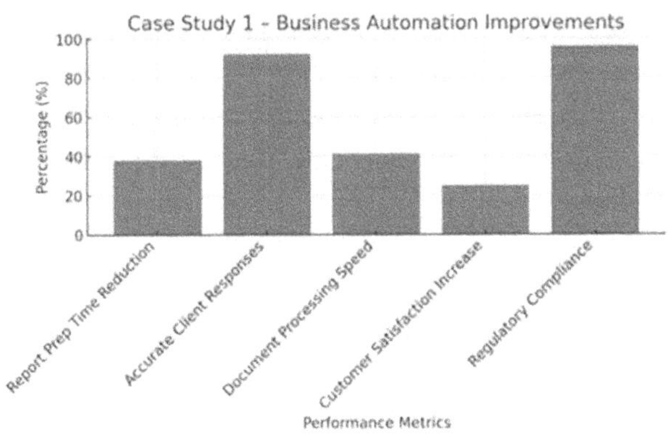

CASE STUDY 2 – HEALTHCARE DIAGNOSTIC SUPPORT SYSTEM

One of the major metropolitan hospitals had a project of an AI-based diagnostic support system optimized by ethical and advanced prompt engineering methods. This was aimed at helping the physicians produce differential diagnosis and treatment recommendation about the patients based on the patient data but with cultural sensitivity and mitigation of bias. Chain-of-thought prompting allowed the AI to give reasoning in detail as to every potential diagnosis, making it more transparent(Abhari et al., 2024b). The few-shot prompts applied to the modelling of culturally inclusive language and adapting the recommendations to various patient populations. Polished off six months later, diagnostic suggestion precision elevated to 93%, according to stand-alone medical reviews. The system was able to save 29% on the median case review time, and the physicians served an increased number of patients every day. An 87% of clinical staff surveyed noted that the AI tool made diagnostic recommendations much more understandable and highly relevant(Vaira et al., 2024). Departments treating patients with system showed improvement in patient satisfaction by 22% with the areas of sensitivity and lucidity of conversations being commended. Noteworthily, the bias-auditing of AI-outputs showed that demographic based discrepancies decreased by 54% compared to the preceding period when there was no implementation done. The increase in adherence to institutional ethics to 98% reduced the chances of a wrong recommendation(Vaira et al., 2025). This successful case illustrates the power rushing engineering could have in enhancing the precision and fairness of AI devices in high-stakes health settings, where fast user feedback is possible. The Figure 5 shows percentage improvements in key healthcare metrics after implementing AI-driven diagnostic support with prompt engineering. Significant gains include 93% diagnostic accuracy, 87% clinician satisfaction, and 98% ethical compliance.

Figure 5. Healthcare Diagnostic Support Performance Improvements

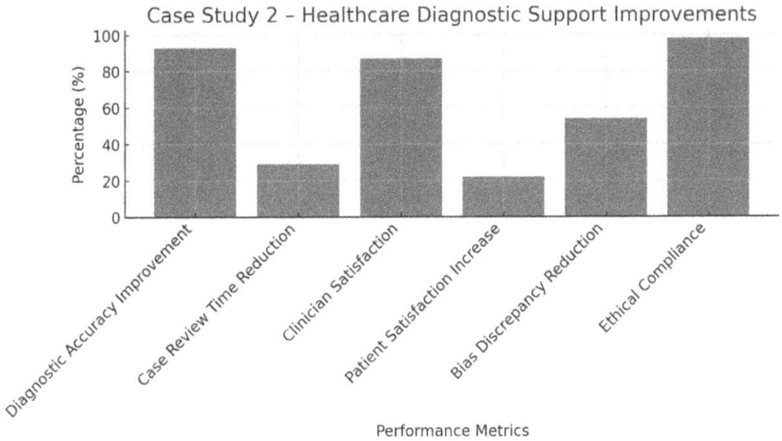

EVALUATION & TOOLS

The process of effective prompt engineering requires structured evaluation to verify that prompts generate reliable, accurate, and germane results from AI. Evaluation typically means benchmarking prompts against known parameters that will influence the key characteristics of prompt engineering, such as accuracy, creativity, reliability, and bias. There are three commonly accepted forms of evaluation today automated metrics, human metrics, and iterative testing to discover weaknesses and optimize prompts. Overview documents will often use benchmarking frameworks that will allow comparisons of different prompting methods, or will identify performance over time (Ghavidel et al., 2024). There are many tools and platforms that provide an integrated experience for prompt design, experimentation, testing, and sharing/deployment. In a general sense, these will range from AI playgrounds and Application Programming Interfaces (APIs) that allow users to request new prompts in real time, enable users to manipulate different parameters within the prompts, and represent new outputs in near real time. Some specific types of tools will have prompt libraries, collections of pre-designed prompts isolated to certain performance measures commonly expected to produce in AI tasks, that users can adapt to their own usage. Simulation environments afford large tests appropriate to prompting in order to evaluate prompts across larger sets of outputs and to understand the prompts' performance across a particular case, context, or dataset.

Furthermore, there are built tools to help monitor for potential challenges such as hallucinations, ambiguity, and/or bias. There are also integrated dashboards that map out prompt performance and effectiveness to identify areas for improvement, that will help speed the refinement process. By applying solidly structured evaluation systems, paired with practical utilization tools, prompt engineers have the ability to test, refine, and improve performance in many contextual settings. The iterative process of test-refine- implement is fundamental to deploying scalable and replicable AI solutions, no matter the context or purpose, including research or commercial or creative endeavours. The Figure 6 shows a language model perceives written inputs in promoting text outputs. It emphasizes the stream between the inputs of instructions given by a person (input) and outputs of answers that are presented by the AI (output). The table 5 lists tools and methods for prompt evaluation and refinement.

It includes benchmarking, prompt iteration, and workflow integration.

It guides users in optimizing prompt performance through structured testing.

Figure 6. Prompt-to-Output Flow in Language Models

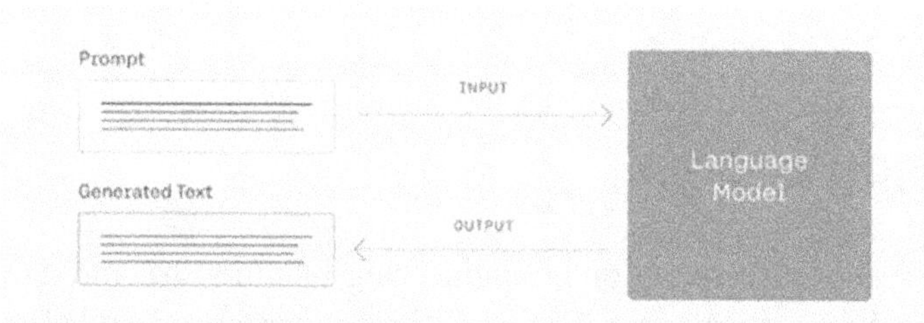

Source: The Cohere

Table 5. Evaluation Tools and Workflow Integration

Tool/Method	Purpose	Description
Prompt Templates	Reusable formats for common tasks	Improves consistency and productivity
Benchmarking	Testing prompts for effectiveness and reliability	Use metrics like relevance, coherence
Iteration Techniques	Refining prompts through multiple trials	Enhances quality and accuracy of responses
A/B Prompt Testing	Comparing variations to find the most effective format	Data-driven prompt optimization
Integration into Workflows	Embedding prompt strategies in larger AI systems	Supports automation and human-AI synergy

BENCHMARKING, ITERATION, PROMPT TEMPLATES

Benchmarking is a vital first step in prompt engineering because it involves objectively measuring how effective your prompts are based on a standard metric or set of metrics such as accurate, relevant, creative, and free from bias. By observing various prompts in the same manner, engineers are able to identify relative strengths and weaknesses, and determine actionable steps to optimize their prompts. After the engineers conduct benchmarking, they follow with iteration where they repeatedly refine their prompts, adjusting their designs according to feedback and what they learn from measuring performance (Heston & Khun, 2023). Ultimately, this iteration process will lead to the optimization of prompts for more anticipated outcomes, creating more reliable, contextually appropriate, and creative ways of qualifying users' AI outputs.

Prompt templates are essentially reusable and customizable frameworks that guide engineers to create and establish a prompt for common purposes. They save engineers precious time by providing recognizable frameworks from which they can customize the template for their unique application, whether it be for asking an AI for content generation, coding advice, customer service communication, etc. They reduce the trial-and-error process, promote consistency across user types in the AI outputs, and allow for many iterations on the individual prompts for common use across a variety of applications. In sum, benchmarking, iteration, and prompt templates establish the basis of a systematic approach for optimal improvement of communications exchanged with AI programs. By measuring and evaluating the performance of prompts to assess how they are working, and adopting a systematic process for refining the design, the users' quality of outcomes can be enhanced, and it can be done with greater consistency and predictability. Through this process, engineers can accelerate the use of AI across various industries.

INTEGRATION INTO AI WORKFLOWS

Using prompt engineering in a larger AI workflow is crucial to realizing the value of AI systems in practical ways. Integrating prompts directly into the various aspects of an AI workflow (and also data from data pipeline ingestion, data processing, output and user's actions) allows prompt engineering to optimize and enhance a system's ability to connect, interact and coordinate between AI models, users and other system components, allowing for a responsive AI system that can take advantage of data that has implications about user requirements and needs. Automation tools then allow for the prompt templates to be used in an existing platform and to allow for the outputs from the AI to drive an Action or workflow with no human input required (Kobeissi et al., 2024). Such degree of automation allows constant timely adjustment on the basis of user activity, thus keeping its flexibility in line with changing demands. The combination of timely engineering and model fine-tuning and monitoring make scalability and resilience more powerful. Introducing prompts as part of the user process creates collaboration between engineers, developers, and domain experts to bring AI out of a black box into one that becomes a contextual driving action and generates innovation and production efficiency.

ETHICAL CONSIDERATIONS

Prompt Ethical engineering is important to provide responsible and ethical utilization of the AI systems. Seeing as AI continues to play a growing role in making high-called decisions in fields like hiring, lending, healthcare, and criminal justice, designing prompts directly focused upon lowering bias and downplaying misinformation is extremely important. It entails the consideration of the possible damage that inadequately designed prompts may bring about, e.g., enhancing stereotypes or creating false results. Such methods as bias-aware prompting and instruction tuning can be used to entrench fairness in AI responses to favor equitability. Ethical frameworks and principles such as fairness, transparency, accountability, and privacy, are the best fields to base the structure of the prompts to promote explainability and develop trust in AI outputs (Ahuchogu, 2025). Practically, case studies reveal the display of the implications of ill ethics design of emergency care operations to the malfunction of content moderation on social media. Constant monitoring as well as timely improvement and cooperation with stakeholders are required so as to deal with the arising ethical issues. The inclusion, transparency, and sustainability of an organisation would increase, by incorporating governance structures and matching the use of AI to societal values, and the result is creating a society of trust in autonomous technologies. (Tao et al., 2024). The table 6 explores ethical risks and responsibilities in prompt use. It addresses issues like bias, privacy, and societal impact. It encourages the responsible and transparent use of AI systems through prompting.

Table 6. Ethical Considerations in Prompting

Ethical Concern	Description	Example Scenario
Bias and Fairness	Prompts may reinforce stereotypes from training data	Hiring recommendations skewed by gender bias
Data Privacy	User inputs may contain sensitive data	Medical or legal prompts revealing PII
Responsibility	Who is accountable for AI-generated decisions?	Financial advice prompts used inappropriately
Transparency	Need for explainable prompting and output	Legal or academic content requiring clarity
Societal Impact	Long-term effects of prompt-driven automation	Job displacement via AI-generated outputs

Examples Of Bias-Aware Prompts

The table 7 gives typical examples of the situations where the bias may appear, and the bias-free alternative of such prompting. It is emphasized how timely terminology may alter equity, inclusivity, and impartiality in the results of AI. The examples provide some practical points on how avoid stereotyping people, speak inclusively, and emphasize objective, merit-based standards.

Table 7. Examples of Bias-Aware Prompts

Scenario	Biased Prompt	Bias-Aware Prompt	Bias Mitigation Approach
Job recommendation	"Suggest top candidates; prefer young, energetic males."	"Suggest top candidates based on skills, experience, and qualifications."	Remove age and gender bias, focus on merit-based criteria.
Healthcare advice	"Give pregnancy health tips for women."	"Give pregnancy health tips for expecting individuals."	Use inclusive language to accommodate diverse gender identities.
Loan eligibility	"Evaluate applicants; prioritize married applicants."	"Evaluate applicants based solely on financial history and repayment capacity."	Remove marital status bias, use objective financial criteria.
Customer service tone	"Respond warmly to female customers."	"Respond warmly and professionally to all customers."	Ensure consistent tone regardless of customer gender.
Image description	"Describe the person as a typical Asian businessman."	"Describe the person's attire and activity without assuming ethnicity."	Avoid assumptions based on appearance or ethnicity.

ETHICAL PROMPT DESIGN GUIDELINES

Ethical design of prompts aims at developing prompts to be fair, inclusive and respectful to everyone using them. They entail cues not to use language that feeds into stereotypes, discrimination and/or marginalization of a certain group of people and, instead, using neutral, respectful, and inclusive language that includes all people. Medical directions must be clear and culturally sensitive and contextual to avoid misunderstanding or adverse effects. They also encourage the principle of being transparent with regards to showing users what the AI is supposed to do and its limits as they will be answerable to their results. It is also important to review it regularly, test in a variety of groups of user groups, refine iteratively, to preserve ethical standards and change with the society that it inhabits.

Healthcare

In healthcare, the design of AI-driven tools should promote ethical delayed prompt design because they address sensitive subjects and aim at serving a wide range of patients. Prompts ought to be based on terms that do not promote stereotyping or neglect culture in determining health (Abhari et al., 2024a). Diagnostic or treatment prompts are an example: they need to take into account demographic factors which could include age, sex, race, social and economic status. Experimental solutions involve putting instructions such as the use of culturally sensitive language or considering the variation in the presentation of symptoms across different populations in prompts, testing the prompts on a range of sets of data to eliminate bias, and providing explainability prompts, which is to encourage transparency, such as asking to explain why the diagnosis is suggested(Vaira et al., 2025). Such practices can minimize biased or harmful outputs, thereby promoting patient and culturally competent care delivery that is fair.

Hiring

The biases in AI system that is applied in recruitment and hiring might spread accidentally between poor prompts. Unethical prompt engineering creates a prompt that is not discriminative to gender, race, age, or disability but promotes equal and friendly treatment of candidates recommendations. The best practice is enforcing instructions like evaluate candidates only in terms of relevant skills and experience, it is necessary that diversity and inclusion principles should be captured, ensuring test conditions so that the suggestion of bias can be detected and corrected, and incorporating monitoring systems to identify bias so that it can be refined accordingly (Tao et al., 2024). Those actions help transform AI hiring tools into efficient advocates of diversity, equality, and fairness in the hiring process at work.

Content Moderation

The systems of content moderation need to find a compromise between content removal and an individual right to freedom of expression, which is culturally specific. The proper implementation of sensitive content during design could teach AI to distinguish between actual abuse and conventionally-acceptable wording, like a work of satire, idiomatic turns of phrase, or a reclaimed slur (Bozkurt, 2023). Examples of possible strategies involve designing prompts to direct the AI to look beyond contexts and cultural differences, introducing feedback loops, where the flagged content would be reviewed by human moderators to make adjustments to the prompts, and multi-stage prompting which would trigger an initial flag to be followed by a more explanatory prompt requesting an explanation or justification of alternative interpretations. These strategies will enable lower over-censoring, user rights, and creation of safe, culturally conscious Internet places (Bozkurt, 2023).

CONTINUOUS IMPROVEMENT AND COLLABORATION

In every sphere, engineering in response should be performed in the iterative process that advances with ethical, technical, and social requirements. This implies the practice of continual comparison with predetermined ethical standards to detect bias or unintentional applications of these standards. The required collaboration between AI developers, domain experts, ethicists, and impacted communities is necessary to reflect the range of various angles and become inclusive. Clarity on AI strengths and weaknesses would facilitate such management by moderating expectation just as well as building trust. These elements integrated in practices will keep AI systems not only technically competent, but also socially responsible, amenable, and in sync with human values, as time goes on.

AI RESPONSIBILITY AND SOCIETAL IMPACT

As more of our lives tie into an AI system, it is necessary to learn more about how these systems are used in society and their consequences. As responsible AI, ethical, transparent, and accountable algorithmic behavior is required. The Bias has the potential to increase disparity, bias against vulnerable groups through data collection, model design, or prompt creation, so bias identification and bias prevention are critical to trust and equity. The impact of AI to society includes employment, privacy, security and social interaction. Although automation could be a source of job loss, it also offers new chances, which would necessitate an adjustment of the workforce. Those risks comprise surveillance, abuse of data, and degradation of privacy norms. AI behavior is stubbornly influenced by prompt engineering, which can be minimized by responsible design. Inclusiveness, fairness, and sustainability of the evolving uses of AI are brought by continuous monitoring, participatory planning, and the community of stakeholders.

FUTURE RESEARCH AND DIRECTIONS

Future studies towards prompt engineering ought to aim at making flexible contextual intelligent systems that support different languages, cultures and spheres with ethical integrity. Multimodal prompts The experimentation with allowing the multimodal prompts to be a combination of text, images, and voice has the potential to further the role of AI in complex situations. Real-time prompt optimization, advanced bias detection and computer-guided fairness tuning are possible ways forward. A combination of the work of technologists, ethicists and policymakers will be critical in getting innovations to go in line with the values of society. Also, the explainability-by-design can be incorporated to create trust in users(B et al., 2025). Constant checks and continuous revisions will be the only way in having a quick evolution of the engineering that will respond to the emergent demands and opportunities in the deployment of AI ethically and successfully.

Advancements in Adaptive and Multimodal Prompt Engineering

Much of the future research should be aimed at building adaptive prompting systems with the ability to dynamically adapt to different context, language and area of activity. The ability to employ multimodal prompts in which text, images, and audio are combined may help AI systems solve more complex real-life problems with a more comprehensive context awareness. Real-time innovation encourages optimization, which, combined with scale-level contextual learning, will be accurate and rather relevant to applications(Han et al., 2025). These developments will not only increase the domain of prompt engineering, but rather guarantee responsive and effective performance of AI in rapidly changing surroundings.

Scalability and Domain-Specific Customization in Prompt Engineering

Future research has to examine the ways of prompt engineering that can be scaled up and can be adjusted according to particular domains like healthcare, finance, law, or education. Creation of modular templates and frameworks of prompt customization will make it quick and easy to deploy in different use cases, maintaining the accuracy and contextual relevance. This involves domain-specific knowledge base generation, prompt optimization, and regulatory compliance support optimization, and optimization against domain-specific terminologies. Scalable solutions will also assist organizations in incorporating the AI system more productively, and will guarantee stable performance and save time and resources to adopt promptly.

RESULTS AND DISCUSSIONS

Advanced prompt engineering in the case studies produced great and measurable change. The case of a financial services reflected a 38% reduction in the preparation of reports, 92% of accurate responses to a client, improvement of documents at 41%, 25% improvement in customer satisfaction, and a compliance rate of 96 percent. Within the healthcare diagnostic support system there was an increase of diagnostic accuracy level to 93%, a reduction of case review time to a proportion of 29%, an increase of clinician satisfaction of 87%, the satisfaction of patients of 22%, a decline of bias discrepancies by 54%, ethical compliance at 98%. These findings show that timely engineering is not only associated with increasing the performance indicators, but also promotes trust, equity and efficiency. Going on, the future work involves the creation of scalable, multilingual and multimodal prompt systems, continuous bias auditing, and the need to implement adaptive feedback systems. This guarantees that the AI systems will be precise, context-sensitive and ethically sound at the same time ensuring that the user satisfaction and quantifiable effect during operation in various industries will be high. The Figure 6 compares key performance metrics from both case studies, with the X-axis representing different metrics and the Y-axis showing percentage improvements. The data highlights substantial gains, including 96% compliance, 93% diagnostic accuracy, and a 92% client response accuracy rate.

Figure 7. Combined Case Study Performance Metrics

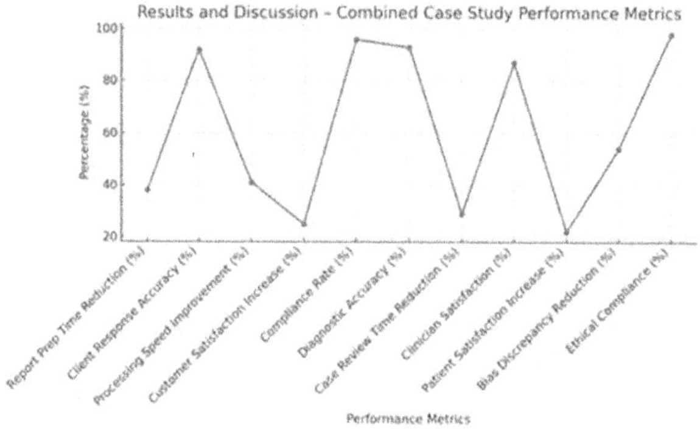

CONCLUSION

To conclude, the introduction of enhanced fast engineering into the AI-driven systems is an inducement of evolutionary change in various industries permitting an infinite degree of performance enhancement, customization, and ethical compliance. This paper has shown that responsive engineering via methods of few-shot prompting, chain-of-thought, persona prompts, and ethical bias mitigation can greatly improve the ability of the AI to narrow down appropriate and relevant outputs, in an accurate, and humanized manner. Based on business automation, prompt engineering through strategy design can be used to increase the processes, cut costs, and improve customer satisfaction due to more specific and dynamic communications. In healthcare, it makes sure that diagnostic support systems present culturally sensitive, bias-aware, and ethically compliant suggestions and therefore brings greater clinical accuracy and patient confidence. Prompt engineering is utilized across the education, legal services, cybersecurity field, and creative spheres to imbue the AI system with industry-specific intelligence, guiding it to adapt to nuanced laws, different environmental situations, and come up with creative solutions that meet real-life circumstances. It is through the case studies provided, which highlight quantifiable gains (i.e. improved accuracy rates, task completion times, satisfaction scores, etc.), that it becomes apparent that the earlier the process of optimization takes place, the more significant long-term gains will be.

In addition, the paper has highlighted that the concern should be ethical and central in the development of AI, and the constant review, bias review, and coordination with a stakeholder should be its tipping point. Although the possibilities of prompt engineering are unprecedented, it has to rely on a multidisciplinary interface of AI developers, experts on the area and subject of AI implementation, ethicists, and policymakers as a collaborative mechanism toward alignment of AI behavior with human values. Advancements in the future must aim at scalable frameworks, multilingual and multimodal prompt situation, and adapting feedback mechanism to focus on responding to changing scenario. Notably, the aspect of a balance between automation and human supervision is a vital one towards ensuring accountability, trust, and transparency. With more autonomy in AI systems, optimal strategies on prompting them will be critical in navigating the systems towards responsible and positive results.

The above analysis and examples confirm that prompt engineering is not just the technical advancement but rather a basic approach to defining the future of the AI applications. Incorporating ethics, contextual, and performance-based values into timely design, companies can unleash the entire potential of AI without creating threats of misuse, bias, and inefficiency. Both of these focal points on innovation and responsibility make prompt engineering of AI a prime facilitator of sustainable AI integration where technological advancement can proceed coherently parallel to societal objectives. The industries that continue to implement AI solutions will have a competitive edge in attaining sustainable competitive advantage, operational excellence, and stakeholder confidence in the emerging digital world, the thoughtful engineering of prompts being one of the key aspects in this respect.

REFERENCES

Abhari, S., Fatahi, S., Saragadam, A., Chumachenko, D., & Pelegrini Morita, P. (2024a). A road map of prompt engineering for ChatGPT in healthcare: A perspective study. *Studies in Health Technology and Informatics, 316*, 998–1002. PMID: 39176959

Abhari, S., Fatahi, S., Saragadam, A., Chumachenko, D., & Pelegrini Morita, P. (2024b). A road map of prompt engineering for ChatGPT in healthcare: A perspective study. *Studies in Health Technology and Informatics, 316*, 998–1002. PMID: 39176959

Agnoli, S., & Rapp, D. N. (2024). Understanding and supporting thinking and learning with generative artificial intelligence. *Journal of Applied Research in Memory and Cognition, 13*(4), 495–499.

Ahuchogu, M. C. (2025). Evaluating the impact of generative AI on intelligent programming assistance and code quality. *Dianwang Jishu, 49*(1), 1205–1216.

Amin, M. M., Cambria, E., & Schuller, B. W. (2023). Will affective computing emerge from foundation models and general artificial intelligence? A first evaluation of ChatGPT. *IEEE Intelligent Systems, 38*(2), 15–23.

B, J. P., Kannan, B., Seervi, P., & G, M. (2025). Prompt engineering for large language models: A systematic review and future directions. In Research Square.

Bakhtiyari, D. S. V. (2024). Descriptive case analysis on the application of prompt engineering in Business Management. *INTERANTIONAL JOURNAL OF SCIENTIFIC RESEARCH IN ENGINEERING AND, 08*(10), 1–6.

Bozkurt, A. (2023). Generative AI, synthetic contents, open educational resources (OER), and open educational practices (OEP): A new front in the openness landscape. *Open Prax., 15*(3), 178–184.

Buholayka, M., Zouabi, R., & Tadinada, A. (2023). The readiness of ChatGPT to write scientific case reports independently: A comparative evaluation between human and artificial intelligence. *Cureus, 15*(5), e39386. PMID: 37378091

Cain, W. (2024). Prompting change: Exploring prompt engineering in large language model AI and its potential to transform education. *TechTrends, 68*(1), 47–57.

Cao, Z., & Ren, Q. (2024). Towards python program repair with generative pre-trained transformer (GPT-3.5). *Theoretical and Natural Science, 43*(1), 102–112.

Cavalcante Siebert, L., Lupetti, M. L., Aizenberg, E., Beckers, N., Zgonnikov, A., Veluwenkamp, H., Abbink, D., Giaccardi, E., Houben, G.-J., Jonker, C. M., van den Hoven, J., Forster, D., & Lagendijk, R. L. (2023). Meaningful human control: Actionable properties for AI system development. *AI and Ethics*, *3*(1), 241–255.

Cesur, T., & Güneş, Y. C. (2024). Optimizing diagnostic performance of ChatGPT: The impact of prompt engineering on thoracic radiology cases. *Cureus*, *16*(5), e60009. DOI: 10.7759/cureus.60009 PMID: 38854352

Ghavidel, A., Pazos, P., Del Aguila Suarez, R., & Atashi, A. (2024). Predicting the need for cardiovascular surgery: A comparative study of Machine Learning models. *J.Electron.Electromedical.Eng.Med.Inform*, *6*(2), 92–106. DOI: 10.35882/jeeemi.v6i2.359

Han, T., Jeong, W. K., & Shin, J. (2025). Diagnostic performance of multimodal large language models in radiological quiz cases: The effects of prompt engineering and input conditions. *Ultrasonography (Seoul, Korea)*, *44*(3), 220–231. DOI: 10.14366/usg.25012 PMID: 40235070

Hasan, W. U., Zaman, K. T., Wang, X., Juan, L., Xie, B., & Tao, C. (2024). Empowering Alzheimer's caregivers with conversational AI: A novel approach for enhanced communication and personalized support. In *Research Square*.

Heston, T., & Khun, C. (2023). Prompt engineering in medical education. *International Medical Education*, *2*(3), 198–205. DOI: 10.3390/ime2030019

Jabbour, S., Fouhey, D., Shepard, S., Valley, T. S., Kazerooni, E. A., Banovic, N., Wiens, J., & Sjoding, M. W. (2023). Measuring the impact of AI in the diagnosis of hospitalized patients: A randomized clinical vignette survey study. *Journal of the American Medical Association*, *330*(23), 2275–2284. DOI: 10.1001/jama.2023.22295 PMID: 38112814

Kobeissi, M. M., Christopherson, K. A., & Ruppert, S. D. (2024). Leveraging artificial intelligence for professional email communication. *Nurse Educator*, *49*(1), 53–54. DOI: 10.1097/NNE.0000000000001493 PMID: 37556832

Lawrence, L., Echeverria, V., Yang, K., Aleven, V., & Rummel, N. (2024). How teachers conceptualise shared control with an AI co-orchestration tool: A multiyear teacher-centred design process. *British Journal of Educational Technology*, *55*(3), 823–844. DOI: 10.1111/bjet.13372

Miao, J., & Thongprayoon, C., Suppadungsuk Supawadee and Krisanapan, P., Radhakrishnan, Y., & Cheungpasitporn, W. (2024). Chain of thought utilization in large language models and application in nephrology. *Medicina (Kaunas, Lithuania), 60*(1). PMID: 38256408

Mohitha, M. R., Terlapu, P. V., Anusrilekha, B., Narendra, R., Shekar, P. U., Chaitanya, P. K., & Kumar, T. R. (2024). Streamlining text generation with AI powered prompt simplification strategies. In *Proceedings of the International Conference on Computational Innovations and Emerging Trends (ICCIET 2024)* (pp. 160–169). Atlantis Press International BV. DOI: 10.2991/978-94-6463-471-6_16

Patil, R., Heston, T. F., & Bhuse, V. (2024). Prompt engineering in healthcare. *Electronics (Basel), 13*(15), 2961. DOI: 10.3390/electronics13152961

Ruan, E. L., Alkattan, A., Elhadad, N., & Rossetti, S. C. (2024). Clinician perceptions of Generative Artificial Intelligence tools and clinical workflows: Potential uses, motivations for adoption, and sentiments on impact. In *medRxiv*. DOI: 10.1101/2024.07.29.24311177

Sun, G. H. (2024). Prompt engineering for nurse educators. *Nurse Educator, 49*(6), 293–299. DOI: 10.1097/NNE.0000000000001705 PMID: 38968442

Tao, Y., Viberg, O., Baker, R. S., & Kizilcec, R. F. (2024). Cultural bias and cultural alignment of large language models. *PNAS Nexus, 3*(9), gae346. DOI: 10.1093/pnasnexus/pgae346 PMID: 39290441

Torricelli, M., Martino, M., Baronchelli, A., & Aiello, L. M. (2024). The role of interface design on prompt-mediated creativity in generative AI. *ACM Web Science Conference*, 235–240. DOI: 10.1145/3614419.3644000

Vaira, L. A., & Lechien, J. R., Abbate Vincenzo and Gabriele, G., Frosolini, A., De Vito, A., Maniaci, A., Yanez, M. M., Boscolo-Rizzo Paolo and Saibene, A. M., Maglitto, F., Salzano, G., Califano, G., Troise, S., Chiesa-Estomba, C. M., & De Riu, G. (2024). Enhancing AI chatbot responses in healthcare: The SMART prompt structure in head and neck surgery. In Research Square.

Vaira, L. A., Lechien, J. R., Abbate, V., Gabriele, G., Frosolini, A., De Vito, A., Maniaci, A., Mayo-Yáñez, M., Boscolo-Rizzo, P., Saibene, A. M., Maglitto, F., Salzano, G., Califano, G., Troise, S., Chiesa-Estomba, C. M., & De Riu, G. (2025). Enhancing AI chatbot responses in health care: The SMART prompt structure in head and neck surgery. *OTO Open, 9*(1), e70075. DOI: 10.1002/oto2.70075 PMID: 39822375

Yaprak, B. (2024). Generative Artificial Intelligence in marketing: The invisible danger of AI hallucinations. *Journal of Economy Business and Management*, *8*(2), 133–158. DOI: 10.7596/jebm.1588897

Zeiser, J. (2024). Owning decisions: AI decision-support and the attributability-gap. *Science and Engineering Ethics*, *30*(4), 27. DOI: 10.1007/s11948-024-00485-1 PMID: 38888795

ADDITIONAL READING

Beri, G., & Srivastava, V. (2024). Advanced techniques in prompt engineering for large language models: A comprehensive study. 2024 IEEE 4th International Conference on ICT in Business Industry & Government (ICTBIG), 1–4.

Feng, Y., Wang, X., Wong, K. K., Wang, S., Lu, Y., Zhu, M., Wang, B., & Chen, W. (2024). PromptMagician: Interactive prompt engineering for text-to-image creation. *IEEE Transactions on Visualization and Computer Graphics*, *30*(1), 295–305. PMID: 37878445

Kale, A., Yaduka, T., Shaikh, T., Kaur, G., & Pinjarkar, L. Agrawal Poorva and Patil, R. R., Chaurasia, S., & Kaur Khanuja, H. (2024). Unveiling the power of AI prompt engineering: A comprehensive exploration. 2024 10th International Conference on Electrical Energy (ICEES), 1–9.

Reynolds, L., & McDonell, K. (2021). Prompt programming for large language models: Beyond the few-shot paradigm. Extended Abstracts of the 2021 CHI Conference on Human in Computing Systems, 1–7.

Rodriguez, A. D., Dearstyne, K. R., & Cleland-Huang, J. (2023). Prompts matter: Insights and strategies for prompt engineering in automated software traceability. 2023 IEEE 31st International Requirements Engineering Workshops (REW), 455–464.

Rozo-Torres, A., & Sarmiento, W. J. (2024, March). Prompt engineering, tools and methods for immersive experience development. 2024 IEEE Conference on Virtual Reality and 3D User Abstracts and Workshops (VRW).

Sun, G. H. (2024). Prompt engineering for nurse educators. *Nurse Educator*, *49*(6), 293–299. DOI: 10.1097/NNE.0000000000001705 PMID: 38968442

Zhou, D., Scharli, N., Hou, L., Wei, J., Scales, N., Wang, X., Schuurmans, D., Bousquet, O., Le, Q., & Chi, E. H. (2022). Least-to-Most Prompting Enables Complex Reasoning in Large Language Models. ArXiv, 2205(10625).

Zhou, D., Schärli, N., Hou, L., Wei, J., Scales, N., Wang, X., Schuurmans, D., Cui, C., Bousquet, O., Le, Q., & Chi, E. (2022). Least-to-most prompting enables complex reasoning in large language models.

KEY TERMS AND DEFINITIONS

Benchmarking: The evaluation of prompt performance using standard criteria like accuracy, coherence, and bias mitigation.

Bias-aware Prompting: Designing prompts to reduce or eliminate biased outputs, ensuring fairness and inclusivity.

Chain-of-Thought Prompting: A method that encourages the model to show intermediate reasoning steps, improving performance in complex tasks like math or logic.

Context Window: The maximum number of tokens (input + output) a model can process at one time.

Few-shot Prompting: A technique where a few examples are provided within the prompt to help the model understand the desired format or reasoning.

Hallucination: When a model generates content that is plausible but factually incorrect or nonsensical.

Instruction Tuning: The process of training or fine-tuning a model to better follow specific instructions or user goals across a range of tasks.

Persona-based Prompting: Crafting prompts that direct the AI to respond with a specific role, tone, or identity (e.g., teacher, lawyer).

Prompt Engineering: The strategic design and structuring of input prompts to effectively guide the behavior and output of large language models (LLMs).

Prompt Scaffolding: Dividing complex prompts into a sequence of simpler, manageable steps to help the AI complete multi-stage tasks more accurately.

Tokenization: The process by which text is broken into units (tokens), such as words or sub words, for processing by language models.

Zero-shot Prompting: A technique where no examples are provided in the prompt, and the model is expected to generate output based solely on the instruction.

Chapter 2
Contextual and Task-Specific Prompting

Arjun Bali
https://orcid.org/0009-0007-2366-7448
The University of Texas at Dallas, USA

Siddharth Kashiramka
https://orcid.org/0009-0004-4537-9736
Emory University, USA

Anshuman Guha
The Johns Hopkins University, USA

Prashant Gupta
https://orcid.org/0000-0001-9746-0529
University of California, Davis, USA

ABSTRACT

The chapter provides a comprehensive approach to learning contextual and task-specific prompting, two essential components for enhancing interactions with AI language models. Initially, the chapter examines the significance of contextual prompting. The chapter then explores task-specific prompting, illustrating how prompts can be tailored to meet the distinct requirements of diverse jobs, ranging from factual questions to creative content development. The chapter then address the challenges of prompts in a multi-lingual and cross-cultural setting, and how best tackle these challenges. At the end, we look at how we see the future of contextual prompting, focusing on adaptive prompts, personalized prompt design, and ethical considerations. On completing this chapter, readers will have a thorough

DOI: 10.4018/979-8-3373-0250-8.ch002

understanding of how to provide accurate and pertinent prompts that enhance AI capabilities, while putting these methods within the broader context of innovation in AI applications

INTRODUCTION

The way we approach problem-solving across industries has been significantly altered by the advancement of sophisticated AI language models in recent years. AI applications are both impactful and diverse, ranging from aiding customer service interactions and content generation to assisting with sophisticated data analysis. However, the efficiency of these applications is frequently strongly dependent on a seemingly little but critical factor: the way we word our requests, known as prompting.

One could define the word 'Prompting' as a way of giving instructions to a Language Model to generate a desired response. Prompting may appear simple at first, but it is both an art and a science. Language models evaluate language using patterns derived from large datasets; yet, in the absence of specific and well-structured cues, these patterns may generate generic, irrelevant, or incorrect responses. As a result, to fully utilize AI's capabilities, it is necessary to understand how prompts might be designed to improve specificity and relevance. This chapter looks at two critical methods for effective prompting: contextual prompting and task-specific prompting.

1. **Contextual Prompting**: Provides detailed and relevant background information in prompts to assist the AI in understanding the context or intent of the request.
2. **Task-specific Prompting**: Customizes the prompt to address the distinct demands of a task, directing the AI to synchronize its responses with specified objectives or frameworks.

HISTORICAL CONTEXT AND EVOLUTION OF PROMPT ENGINEERING

As there have been advancements in AI over the years, Prompt engineering has also evolved alongside it, from rule-based expert systems to the sophisticated language models of today.

Key Milestones in Prompt Engineering

1. Early AI Systems (1960s-1980s): AI models relied on rigid, rule-based programming where user inputs followed predefined templates. Text was generated based on predefined vocabulary and rules.
2. Statistical NLP (1990s-2000s): Statistical models improved text generation, but prompts were still elementary.
3. Deep Learning and Transformers (2010s): The introduction of models like GPT-2 and GPT-3 enabled more natural language understanding, making prompting more dynamic.
4. Few-Shot and Zero-Shot Learning (2020s): Modern AI, such as GPT-4, can generate high-quality responses from minimal examples, increasing the importance of precise prompt engineering. These models are sophisticated and continuously evolving when it comes to their ability to understanding the instructions from the users. Some of that improvement can be attributed to the large amount of data being used to train these extremely large language models but also their ability to keep a longer context in mind before responding.

Contextual Prompting

Providing the appropriate context is a fundamental part of effective interaction with AI. Humans inherently evaluate and respond to context by discerning subtle signs, recalling earlier talks, or utilizing general knowledge, whereas AI depends on specific instructions. Contextual prompting involves including explicit context into the prompt, allowing AI models to produce responses that are both precise and sophisticatedly relevant.

When organizing a family excursion to Paris. You request a travel helper, "Locate a hotel." If you have already informed this assistance of your search for family-friendly accommodations near museums, it will consequently refine the available possibilities. Without this background, the assistant may recommend a fashionable yet small room more appropriate for a solitary traveler or couple, thereby failing to meet the requirements.

In AI applications, it is critical to establish that context clearly. When prompted with "Find a hotel," an AI language model has no inherent awareness of your preferences, financial limits, or travel goals. By including specifics, such as "Locate a family-friendly hotel near museums in Paris with a budget of $200 per night", we create a prompt that provides critical context, allowing the model to generate a more appropriate response.

We are going to study the practical methods for developing effective contextual prompts and how the idea of contextual prompting relates to AI interpretation.

How Context Influences AI Response

Language models are trained on a mix of general, diverse information, making them broadly knowledgeable yet unaware of specifics in any given prompt. When a person includes context in the prompt, they essentially convey to the language model of the following things:

Purpose: What is the objective of the query?

Focus: Which portion of the prompt should be given more importance than others

Constraints: Are there limitations, such as funding, tone, or length?

Audience: Who is on the other side of the response?

Offering context elucidates uncertainty, directing the language model to align more closely with your expectations. In the absence of context, even an advanced model may provide generic or inaccurate information, as it endeavors to compensate for deficiencies in its training data, which may not consistently correspond to your specific requirements.

For example, requesting a language model to "summarize the article" may yield a precise, generic summary; nevertheless, without clarification regarding the intended audience (beginners or experts) the AI may fail to align with the appropriate tone or complexity. Contrast this with: "Summarize this article on quantum mechanics for a high school student," which provides explicit direction regarding the intended audience and anticipated complexity, so enhancing the pertinence and caliber of the response.

Techniques for Embedding Context

Contextual prompting can take a simple approach in which you include descriptive data within the prompt. Here are some useful ways for creating effective contextual prompts:

Use Descriptive Language: Provide all required information regarding the task's goal and desired consequence. Another concept known as soft prompts, as discussed by Qin and Eisner (2021) in their paper ", can be used to integrate prelearned details into questions, which should aid in providing additional context, resulting in an increase in precision and adaptability of language model responses when dealing with complex instructions. For example, instead of saying something like "Generate a sales report," a more particular prompt such as "Generate a quarterly sales report focusing on the top 10 products by revenue, highlighting trends and growth potential" will steer the AI to a specific, relevant output.

State Boundaries Explicitly: When requesting analysis of data or asking for a summary for a piece of text, it may be helpful to include the constraints like timeframes, scope, or even tone. Example: "Summarize the article on climate change within the last decade, using a neutral tone," versus "Summarize the article on climate change, emphasizing recent urgent findings." The first prompt does a better job including the timeframe and guiding the model to to not really take a stand in either way. Build Sequential Context: For multi-step tasks, create a chain of prompts that build on each other, feeding previous responses back into the AI. Example: In customer service automation, start with a prompt to gather initial information: "What product are you asking about?" Then, based on the user's response, follow up with another prompt, such as "What specific issue are you experiencing with [product]?"

Specify Audience and Style Requirements: For content generation tasks, defining the target audience (e.g., "Write for college students") or style (e.g., "Explain using simple, everyday language") can make responses more aligned with the end goal. Example: "Write a brief on cryptocurrency trends for small business owners who are new to digital finance," versus "Write a detailed analysis of cryptocurrency trends for seasoned investors."

Each of these techniques strengthens the AI's ability to deliver relevant results, even in complex situations. The intricate details included in contextual prompts allow the model to handle ambiguity better than what it would have otherwise and provide responses that are more in line with the expected outcome.

Contextual Prompting in a Customer Service Application: A Case Study

Let's try to see how contextual prompting works in a customer use case. Consider a digital firm that has developed a chatbot to serve customers. We want the AI to be able to respond to typical questions, check order status, and resolve product issues. Here's how different levels of contextual prompting affect the user experience.

Generic Prompt: "How can I help you today?" Although, this is a very common opening, it is broad and offers no instruction to either the language model or the user. If a consumer says, "I need help with my device," the language model may become confused without more context, resulting in a lengthy back-and-forth interaction between the bot and the customer to identify the issue.

Moderate Context: "How can I assist with your device today? Please provide the product name and issue." This prompt provides more direction by stating that the product name and issue must be provided. This streamlines the support process by reducing the language model's response alternatives.

High Context: "How can I assist with your [Product Name]? Please describe the specific issue you are experiencing, such as connectivity problems or software updates."

Here, we take contextual prompting up a notch by mentioning likely issues (connectivity, software updates) that might apply to the device. Adding these 'likely issues' not only does improve the relevance of the language model's responses but also helps the customer quickly identify and articulate their problem, making the whole interaction more efficient and worthwhile for the customer. The user experience and the operational efficiency can be improved when firms integrate context in customer support scenarios. A chatbot with prompts with 'High Context' can potentially reduce the average handling time and improve the customer satisfaction, and the quality of the support experience.

Analogy to Reinforce Understanding

For readers who are new to the concept of contextual prompting, this analogy will illustrate the importance of context in daily communication:

Imagine if you are a chef, and a guest at your restaurant simply says, "Make me a dish." Without any additional context, you might create a dish that represents your personal favorite or the restaurant's specialty, only to find out that the guest is allergic to one of the main ingredients. However, if the guest says, "Make me a gluten-free, dairy-free dish that's rich in protein," you have a clearer picture of their preferences, dietary restrictions, and nutritional goals, allowing you to serve a meal that will meet their expectations.

On similar lines, AI models operate with greater precision and purpose when the prompts provide context, constraints, and specific goals. Without the additional information (context), the language model just like the chef in this case, can only make the best guess, which often times may not be the best result or the expected result and eventually leading to an unhappy user. Contextual prompting ensures that AI interprets your request as accurately as possible, aligning its response to your specific needs to meet the expectation about the output.

The above section explains the value of context in prompting. In the following section of the chapter, we will highlight Uncovering Task-Specific Prompting' basically focusing on how to craft prompts for varied tasks and tailoring them to align with specific end goals. This will enhance the reader's ability to fine tune their prompts resulting in a much higher rate of satisfied users of the language model

TASK-SPECIFIC PROMPTING

Contextual prompting helps an artificial intelligence grasp the background and limitations of a request; task-specific prompting directs it toward particular outputs consistent with the objectives of the task. When we think of an academic paper, we think of a certain specific format, a specific type of language and so on which differs from those for a casual blog post, so too must prompts be matched to the specific needs of every kind of work.

In task-specific prompting, you specify not only what the AI should concentrate on but also how it should organize its output to properly meet the needs of the job. Here we will discuss different kinds of task-specific cues and their applicability across several fields. Customizing prompts to fit the specific activity helps users to regulate for tone, detail, and structure, so producing responses that are more accurate, practical, and actionable.

Types of Task-Specific Prompting

Below, we have broken down the different types of prompts based on the major types of tasks that covers the majority of the user question types. Specific prompts can vary widely depending on the goal. Here are five of the most common types of task-specific prompting:

1. Factual Prompting
2. Summarization and Content Reduction
3. Creative Content Generation
4. Analytical Prompting
5. Procedural and Instructional

Each of the above task types requires unique prompting techniques to ensure AI models deliver the right form of output. Let's dive into each of these.

1. Factual Prompting

When looking for factual information to get the answer you want from the model, it's important to be clear and specific. An informed prompt that is well written reduces ambiguity, which lets the language model get to the right data sources and avoid the wrong ones. This prompting technique is very useful in customer service, research, and information retrieval, all of which require factual accuracy. Few-shot learning as a method for guiding language models toward accurate outputs by exploiting their prior knowledge (Wang et al., 2023). This technique is consistent with task-specific prompting principles, as explicit boundaries and examples considerably improve the factual relevance of AI responses.

Example: Imagine you're asking an AI for data about sustainable energy initiatives in California. A vague prompt such as "Tell me about sustainable energy" would yield general information that may or may not include California. Instead, a more task-specific prompt like, "Provide a list of sustainable energy initiatives implemented in California over the past five years" will direct the AI to retrieve relevant, localized information.

Poor Prompt: "Tell me about sustainable energy."

Task-Specific Prompt: "List recent sustainable energy initiatives implemented in California, focusing on solar and wind projects launched in the past five years."

By specifying location, timeline, and focus (solar and wind), you lead the AI to prioritize data relevant to your interests.

Tip: When creating "Factual prompts," it is advisable to specify timeframes, locations, and focus areas; essentially, this helps to narrow down the range of the inquiry and guarantee factual relevance by so reducing irrelevant responses.

2. Summarization and Content Reduction

Summarization is a common AI task, whether it's condensing a long article into key points, reducing technical information for lay audiences, or producing concise highlights from reports. In this task, clarity about the target audience and desired summary format (bullet points, paragraphs, etc.) is essential.

Example: Let's say you're summarizing a technical research paper on AI ethics for a general audience. An effective task-specific prompt would specify both the audience type and the format.

- **Basic Prompt**: "Summarize the research paper on AI ethics."
- **Task-Specific Prompt:** "Summarize the main points of the research paper on AI ethics in simple language suitable for a general audience, using bullet points and add examples wherever possible."

This task-specific prompt instructs the AI to simplify complex language and to format the output as bullet points, ensuring accessibility and readability for a non-technical audience.

Tip: When summarizing content, clarify the **audience**, **complexity level**, and **output format** (e.g., bullet points, paragraph, executive summary). Task-specific prompts can greatly improve the AI's output structure and relevance for the intended reader.

3. Creative Content Generation

Creative tasks require AI to produce engaging, imaginative content, often with specific stylistic or thematic constraints. Under these conditions, the effectiveness of a prompt relies on how successfully it directs the creative output of the artificial intelligence. Saying genre, tone, and intended emotions, for instance, helps the model match its creative output with user expectations.

Example: Imagine you're using an AI to generate an opening scene for a mystery novel. A prompt like "Write the opening scene for a mystery novel" is broad and likely to yield a generic result. By specifying elements like setting, mood, and character traits, you can better control the outcome.

- **Basic Prompt**: "Write the opening scene for a mystery novel."
- **Task-Specific Prompt**: "Write the opening scene for a suspenseful mystery novel set in a small, foggy coastal town. Introduce the protagonist, a reclusive detective with a mysterious past."

With the task-specific prompt, the AI now understands the desired genre (mystery), setting (small coastal town), mood (suspenseful), and character traits (reclusive, mysterious past), resulting in a more tailored, engaging opening scene.

4. Analytical Prompting

In tasks related to analysis, the idea is to use the language model to identify patterns, compare data points, or draw insights from a dataset or topic. Analytical prompting benefits from precise criteria, such as comparison parameters or focus areas, to steer the language model's attention toward meaningful analysis. Wang, Yu, and Huang (The Art of Prompting) illustrate how type-specific prompts enhance event detection by aligning the language model's focus with the distinct attributes of an event (Wang et al., 2022). This approach demonstrates the critical role of tailored prompts in directing AI to perform structured analysis, such as identifying patterns or key characteristics in data.

Example: Suppose you're using AI to analyze quarterly sales data for two product lines. A simple prompt like "Analyze the sales data" is too vague to yield actionable insights. Instead, you could create a task-specific prompt that clarifies the comparison points and focus.

- Basic Prompt: "Analyze the sales data."
- Task-Specific Prompt: "Compare the quarterly sales data for Product A and Product B over the past year, focusing on trends in revenue growth and customer demographics."

The task-specific prompt not only specifies the comparison (Product A vs Product B) but also the analysis criteria (revenue growth and customer demographics), guiding the language model to produce an output that is relevant and insightful.

5. Procedural and Instructional Prompting

Often in a specific sequence, procedural or instructional tasks depend on language models to offer exact direction. Applications including technical support, instructional writing, or detailed process explanations benefit from these cues.

Example: Let's say you're asking model to provide instructions for setting up a virtual meeting on a new platform. A prompt something like "Explain how to set up a virtual meeting" may result in general advice that could miss steps specific to the platform in question.

- **Basic Prompt**: "Explain how to set up a virtual meeting."
- **Task-Specific Prompt**: "Provide a step-by-step guide to setting up a virtual meeting on [Platform Name], including creating an account, scheduling a meeting, inviting participants, and adjusting audio/video settings."

The task-specific prompt provides clear instructions on the platform and steps required, leading to a response that is far more actionable and user-friendly.

Bringing It All Together: Multi-Task Example

Let us go over a detailed example so we can see all the above principles applied to various activities.

Put yourself in the shoes of a digital marketing training program content creator. You need the language model to generate the following: (1) an overview of digital marketing trends, (2) a simple summary for non-marketing professionals, and (3) a creative headline for a module on social media strategy.

1. **Factual Prompt**: "List the top five trends in digital marketing for 2024, including brief explanations and industry examples."
2. **Summarization Prompt**: "Summarize these digital marketing trends for a non-marketing professional audience in simple language."
3. **Creative Prompt**: "Suggest a catchy, engaging headline for a training module on effective social media strategy in digital marketing."

By crafting each prompt according to the task's specific needs—informational, summarization, and creative—you provide the AI with clear, actionable guidance, resulting in outputs that are tailored, coherent, and suited to the goals of each task.

Summary

Task-specific prompting allows users to interact with language models in a more effective way, giving it precise instructions that align with the expected user results. By tailoring prompts for informational, summarization, creative, analytical, or instructional tasks, users can control the type, structure and tone of model outputs, ensuring they meet the needs of the user. These principles, strategies and best practices will hopefully act as a guideline to transform vague or generic outputs into highly relevant and actionable responses.

CHALLENGES IN CONTEXTUAL AND TASK-SPECIFIC PROMPTING

To create effective prompts, it is necessary to strike a balance between simplicity, flexibility, specificity, and clarity. Although contextual and task-specific prompting help with directing the language model's responses in the appropriate direction, prompting comes with it's own obstacles. Ambiguity, unintended bias, and limitations in the language model's interpretive or knowledge capacity can result in responses that do not meet the user's expectations. If the users can work their way around to overcome these difficulties, they would be able to use language models more effectively by making sure that the model operates within ethical, precise, and accepted parameters. This section of the chapter will look at the key hurdles to prompt design, figure out their origins, and offer practical solutions for overcoming them.

1. Ambiguity in Prompts

Challenge: Ambiguity occurs when a prompt is open to multiple interpretations, causing the AI to guess or rely on patterns in its training data that may not align with the user's intentions. Ambiguous prompts can lead to irrelevant or incomplete answers, undermining the effectiveness of the interaction.

Example: Consider the prompt, "Explain the benefits of digital tools." Without further context, the AI might interpret this in various ways—focusing on digital tools for business, education, personal productivity, or healthcare.

Solution: Clarify intent by adding context and narrowing the scope. In ambiguous cases, reframe prompts to include specific topics, audience, or purpose.

Revised Prompt: "Explain the benefits of digital tools for small business marketing, focusing on customer outreach and data analysis."

By narrowing the scope (small business marketing) and specifying focus areas (customer outreach and data analysis), the revised prompt guides the AI to deliver a relevant and targeted response.

Practical Tips to Reduce Ambiguity:

Clarifying Terms: Include phrases like "specifically," "in the context of," or "focusing on" to reduce broad interpretations.

Audience Identification: Specifying whom the response is intended for can help avoid ambiguity.

Direct Questions: Rephrase vague queries as specific questions (e.g., "What are the advantages of X for the purpose of Y?").

2. Unintended Bias

Challenge: AI responses can be unintentionally influenced by bias, particularly if a prompt contains assumptions that direct the AI in a particular direction. Unintentional bias may influence the tone, content, or perspective of responses, which may not completely represent a balanced perspective on a given topic of discussion.

Example: A prompt such as "Explain why renewable energy is better than fossil fuels" embeds a bias by positioning renewable energy as superior. While many advantages exist, the AI's response might not address potential limitations of renewable energy or considerations for certain industries reliant on fossil fuels.

Solution: The use of neutral language and balance perspectives helps to avoid unnecessary bias. Rephrase prompts to present questions in a neutral tone, enabling the AI to explore multiple angles.

Revised Prompt: "Compare the benefits and limitations of renewable energy and fossil fuels, focusing on environmental impact, cost, and scalability."

This revised prompt encourages the AI to examine both options without favoring one, supporting a more balanced response.

Tips for Avoiding Bias:

- Frame prompts objectively: Use phrases like "Compare," "Discuss the pros and cons," or "Explain both sides."
- Avoid loaded language: Words like "better" or "worst" can introduce bias; instead, opt for neutral terms like "advantages" and "disadvantages."
- Encourage balanced analysis: Explicitly instruct the AI to consider "both the strengths and weaknesses" of a topic

3. Insufficient Context

Challenge: Inadequate context may lead language models to provide responses that may not align with user expectations. In the absence of sufficient context, the model may need to depend on assumptions derived from training data, which may not be relevant to the particular task or audience.

Example: Suppose you ask, "Provide an overview of recent marketing trends." The AI might produce a general summary without details on which industry or region you're interested in.

Solution: Expand prompts with necessary context and details. Provide specific instructions related to audience, scope, and content focus.

Revised Prompt: "Provide an overview of recent marketing trends in the e-commerce industry in North America, focusing on personalization, social media advertising, and AI-driven analytics."

Here, specifying the industry (e-commerce), region (North America), and key topics (personalization, social media advertising, AI-driven analytics) helps the AI focus its response, improving relevance and depth.

Tips for Providing Adequate Context:

- Specify scope and focus: Include details like the industry, region, or topic areas.
- Follow-up prompts for complex tasks: For multi-faceted tasks, use sequential prompts to build context gradually.
- Audience context: Customize responses for specific audiences, whether beginners, experts, students, or industry professionals.

4. Lack of Domain Knowledge

Challenge: Language models, despite their wide variety of training data, they might lack expertise in specialized areas. For tasks requiring niche knowledge, the AI may generate responses that are too general or miss important nuances, leading to superficial or incomplete answers. As very aptly explained by Ayush Thakur in his paper titled '*The Art of Prompting: Unleashing the Power of Large Language Models*'(Thakur, 2024), 'Assumed Prior Knowledge: This occurs when the prompt assumes the model possesses certain knowledge or context that it might not have. For example, "Explain the intricacies of the CRISPR-Cas9 gene editing system." This assumes the model understands the complex details of genetic engineering. To avoid assuming prior knowledge, either provide necessary background information or simplify the prompt to a level where a broader audience without specialized expertise can comprehend and respond effectively. For instance, "Describe the basic process of genetic modification using CRISPR technology in simple terms suitable for a non-scientific audience.'

Example: Imagine you're working on a financial analysis report and prompt the AI with, "Explain the implications of Basel III on banking regulations." Without deep financial or regulatory knowledge, the AI might produce a vague answer lacking in industry-specific insights.

Solution: Incorporate domain-specific terms and clarify the depth of analysis required. Including key terms and explaining the expected level of expertise can help the AI draw from relevant information.

Revised Prompt: "Explain the impact of Basel III regulations on global banking, specifically on capital adequacy, stress testing, and market liquidity. Focus on implications for large international banks."

The revised prompt highlights specific topics within Basel III and provides details (large international banks) that guide the AI to a more detailed, informed response.

Tips for Enhancing Domain-Specific Accuracy:

- Use technical terminology: Familiar terms signal the need for depth in specialized areas.
- Specify the level of detail expected: Indicate whether a high-level overview or in-depth analysis is required.
- Include supplementary context or background information: In the above example, adding related policies, regulations, or industry impacts can help the language model provide a richer response.

5. Overly Complex or Multi-Part Prompts

Challenge: When prompts are too complex or contain multiple questions, the AI may struggle to prioritize which part to address. This can result in responses that either miss critical details or handle only part of the prompt.

Example: A prompt like "Analyze the marketing strategy of Company A and compare it with Company B, then discuss how these strategies could be adapted for startups" includes multiple tasks that may lead to a fragmented response.

Solution: Break down multi-part prompts into sequential steps. Dividing complex queries into separate prompts enables the AI to respond to each part thoroughly.

Revised Prompt Sequence:

1. "Analyze the marketing strategy of Company A, focusing on social media and content marketing."
2. "Now compare this strategy with the marketing strategy of Company B."
3. "Finally, suggest ways these strategies could be adapted for startups."

By splitting the original query into smaller, manageable parts, each prompt focuses the AI's attention on one task at a time, ensuring a more coherent, comprehensive analysis.

Tips for Handling Complex Prompts:

- Divide tasks into separate prompts: Use a sequence of prompts rather than combining tasks in one.
- Prioritize primary questions: If splitting isn't feasible, identify the core task and simplify secondary questions.
- Use transitional prompts: After an initial response, follow up with prompts that build upon previous answers for continuity.

6. Limitations in Model Capability

Challenge: Large Language Models possess intrinsic constraints due to their training and structural design. Even with well-structured prompts, they might lack the reasoning ability to perform certain complex tasks, especially if they require real-world judgment or specialized calculations.

Example: Asking an AI, "Predict how the stock market will perform next quarter" might lead to an overly general or speculative response, as most language models aren't designed for financial forecasting.

Solution: Reframe prompts to focus on general insights, trends, or theoretical analysis. For tasks beyond the AI's capacity, guiding the model to provide an informative overview or a discussion of factors influencing the subject is more effective.

Revised Prompt: "Discuss key economic indicators that could influence stock market trends in the next quarter."

By reframing the question, the prompt shifts from direct prediction to an analysis of influencing factors, allowing the AI to provide useful information within its capabilities.

Tips for Working with Model Limitations:

- **Employ prompts for theoretical examination**: When straight responses are impractical, concentrate on discussion-oriented prompts for insights.
- **Integrate AI with external instruments**: For requirements, utilize AI for preliminary research or analysis, then employing domain-specific technologies.

Challenges in contextual and task-specific prompting, such as ambiguity, bias, insufficient context, and model limitations can impact model's effectiveness. Users can greatly enhance AI responses and make the user AI engagement far more effective and efficient by knowing these challenges and applying structured approaches including clarifying language, neutralizing bias, and breaking down difficult prompts.

In the following section 'Advanced Techniques for Enhancing Contextual Understanding', let's look at some sophisticated methods such as task chaining and prompt enrichment to further refine and further improve user - Language model interactions.

ADVANCED TECHNIQUES FOR ENHANCING CONTEXTUAL UNDERSTANDING

Once we have a strong basis in contextual and task-specific prompting, we may begin to look at more advanced techniques. These methods improve basic prompt frameworks and enable complex, multi-step interactions producing more exact and nuanced artificial intelligence responses. Activities requiring continuity, detail, and reaction across several apps call for advanced prompting techniques.

Three main approaches to increase AI contextual understanding will be discussed in this part: task chaining, nested context, and prompt enrichment. These techniques help the AI to respond more profoundly and enable people in finding creative answers to complex problems.

1. Task Chaining

Task chaining is an advanced prompting method whereby a complex user question is split into several smaller but reasonable searches. This method is most suitable for situations needing a methodical process, ordered systems, and multi-part searches. Task chaining helps the language model to move through a succession of tasks, so gathering context across every user question in the sequence. In the context of task chaining, the 2024 survey by Qiao et al., 2022 separates single-stage from multi-stage prompting. Single stage prompting emphasizes on reaching the intended output in a single, complete prompt, which is effective but usually lacks depth for difficult tasks. By contrast, multi-stage prompting breaks down complex questions into doable tasks using a sequential, step-by-step approach.

For example, consider the following scenario: Let's say, we desire the Language Model to develop a marketing strategy for a new e-commerce brand. This work encompasses a variety of phases, including the definition of client personas, market trend analysis, and strategy development. Instead of overwhelming the AI with a single prompt like “Create a detailed marketing plan for a new e-commerce brand,” you can break it into a series of prompts:

1. **Market Analysis**: "Identify key trends in e-commerce for 2024, focusing on consumer preferences and emerging technologies."
2. **Customer Persona**: "Based on these trends, define a target customer persona for an e-commerce brand selling eco-friendly products."
3. **Marketing Strategy**: "Suggest a marketing strategy for this target persona, emphasizing digital channels and content types that align with their preferences."

By using task chaining, each prompt adds context that builds on the previous responses. This approach helps the language model to accumulate insights and context gradually, leading to a well-rounded and comprehensive marketing plan.

2. Prompt Enrichment

Prompt enrichment is adding layers of contextual knowledge or supporting data to improve the depth of reaction and awareness of the artificial intelligence. Adding examples, background knowledge, or reference points to a request will help the artificial intelligence produce more complex and sophisticated answers. This technique is especially useful for tasks that benefit from a more personalized, example-driven approach. An example of this scenario could be: Let's say you want the model to create a summary for your case study on artificial intelligence usage in healthcare. A general prompt like "Write a case study on AI adoption in healthcare" might produce a broad response. But by improving the prompt, you can guide the model to add specific components and background which would be more in line with our expected response.

Prompt After Enrichment: "Write a case study on AI adoption in healthcare, focusing on applications in diagnostic imaging and patient management. Include examples of hospitals or healthcare systems that have successfully implemented AI, discussing both the benefits and challenges faced."

Here, the enriched prompt provides more context by specifying areas of focus (diagnostic imaging and patient management) and desired content (examples of real implementations). This guidance and direction lead the language model towards a more relevant and insightful response.

3. Nested Context

Nested context entails layering multiple levels of context within a single prompt, allowing the AI to address complex or multidimensional tasks in a consistent manner. This technique is especially useful when the response calls for multiple perspectives, such as comparing and contrasting viewpoints or analyzing topics across multiple dimensions. Thakur's work (2024) shows that using nested, multi-layered prompts allows language models to better address complex, multidimensional tasks. Models can generate comprehensive and well-aligned responses with the addition of multiple perspectives and structuring context hierarchically.

Example Scenario: Let's say we have to research different perspectives on remote work policies for a research report. We want the AI to weigh the pros and cons for both employees and employers, taking into account productivity, work-life balance, and company culture. So in this scenario, instead of using a broad prompt like "Discuss remote work policies," you can structure it to include nested context.

Nested Prompt: "Analyze the pros and cons of remote work policies from both employee and employer perspectives. Consider three key factors: productivity, work-life balance, and company culture."

This nested prompt contains three layers of context:

- **Perspectives** (employee and employer)
- **Pros and Cons** (positive and negative aspects)
- **Focus Areas** (productivity, work-life balance, company culture)

By embedding these layers within the prompt, you provide the AI with a structured framework that enables it to generate a multi-dimensional response addressing each element in a coherent and organized way.

4. Meta Prompting for Dynamic Adaptation

Meta prompting for dynamic adapting . Reynolds and McDonell (2021) described meta prompting, which is the use of a higher-level instruction, or "meta prompt," to guide how prompts should be built or changed on the fly for different tasks. This approach of making prompts make them flexible and adaptable to different situations and can handle reasoning that takes more than one step or different task requirements. Meta prompting fills the gap between static instructions and the dynamic requirements of complex AI interactions by serving as a prompt generation template.

Example

In an educational context, meta prompting can help an AI adapt to students with varying levels of proficiency across multiple subjects. Instead of crafting separate prompts for each scenario, a meta prompt could be:

"For a given subject and grade level, construct a practice question that evaluates the student's understanding and provides feedback suited to their level."

Let's say if the subject is mathematics and the level is beginner, the AI could generate a prompt: *"Solve this simple arithmetic problem: What is 7 + 5? After answering, explain why addition is used here."* This dynamic adjustment allows for a personalized learning experience without manually crafting individual prompts.

Advantages of Advanced Prompting Methods

Prompting methods like task chaining, prompt enrichment and nested context can help users in several ways, including the ones below:

1. **More depth and nuance**: These techniques help people get deeper insights, which leads to answers that are complete, multidimensional and useful.
2. **Better Continuity**: Task chaining creates a logical thread of information that allows the AI system handle multi-step processes or sequential analysis well.
3. **Improves Ability to Handle Complexity**: Prompt enrichment and layered context help AI models answer unclear or complicated questions by changing their answers to fit specific needs.
4. **Better control over AI output**: Using these methods users can guide AI toward specific goals, tones, or points of view, lowering the number of general or off-target answers.

Advanced prompting techniques provide users with powerful tools to guide AI responses beyond simple Q&A. Task chaining, prompt enrichment and nested context bring versatility and structure to interactions with AI, making them ideal for complex, layered queries that demand depth and sophistication. By mastering these methods, users can elevate their AI workflows, pushing the boundaries of what's possible in AI-driven research, content creation, analysis, and beyond.

In the following section, we'll talk about **ethical aspects of prompting** and the potential bias and privacy issues that come with prompt design.

ADDRESSING ETHICAL ASPECTS OF PROMPTING

As AI systems become integral to various domains, ethical prompt engineering is essential to ensuring that these technologies operate in a fair, transparent, and responsible manner. Poorly designed prompts can reinforce biases, compromise privacy, and enable the misuse of AI-generated content. This section examines key ethical challenges in prompt design and provides strategies to mitigate them.

Bias Mitigation

Bias in AI responses often stems from both training data and the phrasing of prompts. When prompts are constructed with implicit biases, the model may produce outputs that reinforce stereotypes or exclude certain perspectives.

Example of an Ethical Dilemma: A prompt like "Why are women less suited for leadership roles?" presupposes a biased assumption. Instead, a neutral alternative like "What are the qualities of effective leadership, and how do they vary across different individuals?" ensures a balanced perspective.

Best Practices for Bias Mitigation:

- **Use neutral and inclusive language** to avoid leading the model towards biased conclusions.
- **Explicitly request diverse perspectives** in prompts, such as "Discuss different viewpoints on the impact of remote work on productivity."
- **Evaluate responses critically** and refine prompts to minimize unintentional biases.

Privacy Concerns

AI-generated responses should not expose sensitive or personally identifiable information (PII). When prompts request information about individuals, organizations, or proprietary data, privacy risks emerge.

Example of an Ethical Dilemma: A prompt like "Generate a report on customer complaints using real user data" can inadvertently lead to privacy violations. Instead, a safer prompt would be: "Generate a report summarizing common themes in customer complaints while ensuring anonymity."

Best Practices for Privacy Protection:

- **Avoid prompts that request sensitive data** and ensure anonymization in AI outputs.
- **Use AI in compliance with data protection laws** (e.g., GDPR, CCPA) by structuring prompts to prevent unauthorized data collection.

Preventing AI Misuse

AI-generated content can be used for disinformation, plagiarism, and manipulation if prompts are crafted irresponsibly. Ethical prompt engineering includes designing prompts that encourage truthful, verifiable, and responsible content generation.

Example of an Ethical Dilemma: A prompt like "Generate a fake news article on economic collapse to create market panic" is unethical. Instead, a responsible alternative would be: "Analyze how misinformation spreads in financial markets and its effects."

Best Practices for Ethical AI Use:

- **Frame prompts to encourage factual accuracy and verification** (e.g., "Summarize the latest climate research with citations from reputable sources").
- **Discourage harmful uses** by avoiding prompts that facilitate deception, fraud, or harm.

Now that we have got a good understanding of what a good prompt looks like in different scenarios, let us try to understand how we can **evaluate and test a prompt** with a view to improving it.

EVALUATION METRICS TO QUANTIFY PROMPT EFFECTIVENESS

Building prompts can be thought of as an artistic endeavor, measuring their success calls for methodical assessment. Clear assessment techniques help users to decide whether prompts produce the expected results.

Key Metrics for Evaluating Prompt Effectiveness

1. **Relevance**: Does the AI-generated response align with the intent of the prompt? A high-quality prompt minimizes irrelevant or off-topic responses.
2. **Accuracy**: Does the response provide correct and verifiable information? Accuracy is particularly critical for factual and research-based queries.
3. **Coherence**: Is the response logically structured and understandable? Effective prompts guide the AI toward producing clear, well-organized content.
4. **User Satisfaction**: This metric helps us to quantify how much or how often is the model's response in line with the user expected response.

Methods for Testing and Refining Prompts

- **A/B testing:** In this approach, we must try to see which of several variations of a prompt generates better responses. For instance, one type of a prompt asks, "Summary of the impact of climate change in 100 words," while another asks, "List three key effects of climate change with examples." The answers are evaluated to ascertain which structure generates more succinct and instructive findings.
- **User Feedback Loops**: Real-time comments on AI outputs allow user feedback loops to guide prompt changes. For instance, a customer support chatbot gets low marks for responses devoid of detail. User comments help the prompt be improved from "Provide a response to the user's question" to "Provide a detailed response with examples wherever applicable." Over time this change in the prompt helps to increase user satisfaction.
- **Iterative Refinement**: Start with a basic prompt and gradually refine it based on the AI's responses. Analyze the model's outputs, identify areas for improvement, and adjust your prompts accordingly.

Have you wondered there are certain words and phrases that are absolutely fine to use in one language or culture as opposed to the other, this is exactly what our next section will dive into '**Multilingual and Cross-Cultural Prompting'**

Multilingual and Cross-Cultural Prompting

As AI adoption expands globally, effective prompting must account for linguistic and cultural differences. Challenges include variations in syntax, idioms, and cultural references. There are tools available which help in evaluating if a language model is biased across languages or across cultures. SeaEval is one such model can serve as a launchpad for more thorough investigations and evaluations for multilingual and multicultural scenarios. (Wang et al., 2023)

Challenges in Multilingual Prompting

1. **Literal Translations**: Direct translations may alter meaning. Example: "Break a leg" (an English idiom for good luck) translates poorly in other languages. Another example is "It's raining cats and dogs," which may confuse non-English speakers if directly translated without contextual explanation. Similarly, in Spanish, "Estar en las nubes" (literally "to be in the clouds") means to be daydreaming, but a direct English translation may not convey the intended meaning.

2. **Context Sensitivity**: Cultural norms shape language use. Example: A polite greeting in Japan differs significantly from one in the U.S. In Japan, saying "Otsukaresama desu" is a common workplace expression to acknowledge a colleague's hard work, but it has no direct English equivalent. Another example is addressing elders; while Western cultures may use first names casually, some Asian cultures prefer honorifics and formal titles to show respect. Additionally, humor and sarcasm can vary greatly across cultures—what is amusing in one language may be offensive or incomprehensible in another.

Best Practices for Cross-Cultural Prompting

Adhere to Dialect variances: Change your prompts to fit local accents instead of translating straight forwardly. Maintaining accuracy and relevance depends on considering cultural differences in phraseology and context. For an audience from Japan or Arabic speaking country, for instance, a prompt that performs well in an English-speaking market could need rewording to maintain its intended meaning.

Think about dialectal variances between languages (e.g., Spanish in Spain against Latin America). Different areas may have different connotations for some words or phrases. For example, the word "computer" is usually translocated in Spain as "ordenador" but in Latin America as "comptadora".

Respect Various cultures: To guarantee cultural fit, test questions with native speakers. Native speakers can assist to determine whether a prompt unintentionally carries unintended connotations or cultural sensitivity or whether it resonates appropriately for the target audience. Think on differences in politeness standards and humor since these vary greatly depending on the nation. A joke that is funny in one culture could offend or confuse someone from another. Likewise, direct communication strategies recommended in some Western countries could not be suitable for Asian societies, where indirect or deferential phrasing is sometimes preferred.

To increase relatability, use references and examples particular to your region. A prompt on holiday customs should offer locally relevant examples rather than presuming the same celebrations are followed everywhere.

Use region-specific examples and references to improve relatability. A prompt about holiday traditions should not assume the same celebrations are observed worldwide but should instead provide locally relevant examples.

By integrating multilingual and culturally aware prompts, AI can serve diverse users more effectively and equitably.

Key Takeaways:

- Adapt prompts for local nuances rather than using direct translations.

- Consider dialectal variations within languages (e.g., Spanish in Spain vs. Latin America).
- Test prompts with native speakers to ensure cultural appropriateness.

At the beginning of the chapter, we had talked about the evolution of the prompting with different models coming in and each of them being built on a different architecture, the next section is an important one to understand how **prompting can have different results across different model architectures.**

COMPARISON OF PROMPTING TECHNIQUES ACROSS AI MODELS AND ARCHITECTURES

Different architectural designs and training goals among AI models produce different prompting strategies. Major model types are systematically compared below:

Encoder-Only Models (e.g., BERT, RoBERTa):

These models are built on an encode only architecture and they are Bidirectional Transformers, trained on **masked language modeling The Typical Use Cases** for these types of models are Text classification, named entity recognition (NER), sentiment analysis.

Prompting Techniques:

- **Task-Specific Tokens**: Use [CLS] for classification tasks or [MASK] for fill-in-the-blank prompts.
- **Structured Inputs**: Sentences are segmented with [SEP] for tasks like question answering.
- **Masked Prompts**: E.g., "The capital of France is [MASK]." → Model predicts "Paris."
- **Limitations**: Not designed for open-ended text generation; prompts must align with pre-training tasks (e.g., cloze tests).

Decoder-Only Models (e.g., GPT-3, PaLM, LLaMA)

These models are built on an architecture that is decoder only and they are autoregressive transformers, trained to predict the next token. The typical use cases for such models are text generation, dialogue, creative writing.

Prompting Techniques:

- **Zero-Shot**: Direct questions (e.g., "Explain quantum computing in simple terms.").
- **Few-Shot**: Examples included in the prompt (e.g., "Translate 'hello' to French: bonjour. Translate 'goodbye' to French: au revoir. Translate 'thank you' to French: ___").
- **Chain-of-Thought (CoT)**: Encourages step-by-step reasoning (e.g., "John has 5 apples. He buys 3 more. How many does he have? Let's think step by step...").
- **Instruction Tuning**: Direct commands (e.g., "Write a poem about autumn.") work well with models like InstructGPT or ChatGPT.
- **Role-Playing**: E.g., "Act as a historian and describe the fall of Rome."

Limitations: Prone to hallucination; sensitive to prompt phrasing and length.

Encoder-Decoder Models (e.g., T5, BART)

These types of models are built on an encoder decoder architecture: They combine encoder and decoder and are trained for **text-to-text** tasks. The typical use cases for these models include translation, summarization, Q&A.

Prompting Techniques:

- **Explicit Task Prefixes**: Prompts must define the task (e.g., "summarize: ...", "translate English to German: ...").
- **Structured Input-Output**: Input and desired output format are part of the prompt (e.g., "Question: ... Answer: ...").
- **Multi-Task Flexibility**: Handles diverse tasks by reformatting them as text generation (e.g., "cola sentence: The dog barked." → Label: acceptable/ unacceptable).

Limitations: Requires precise task specification; less effective for open-ended generation.

Sometimes, prompting by itself may not be enough to get the best possible responses from the language model and thus there may be a need to introduce and integrate some additional AI techniques to enrich the user experience. So, the next section we are going to look at the **'Integration of Prompt Engineering with Other AI Techniques'** .

INTEGRATION OF PROMPT ENGINEERING WITH OTHER AI TECHNIQUES

Though it is still a rather young discipline with great potential for development, prompt engineering has quickly become a necessary ability in properly leveraging AI capabilities. New possibilities and challenges in motivating researchers, developers, and practitioners to investigate creative approaches for interacting with artificial intelligence arise as AI models progress. Key areas likely to shape the future of contextual prompting will be covered in this part including developments in adaptive prompting, customized prompt design, prompt learning, Knowing these trends will enable readers to spot where the field is headed and how these advancements might influence artificial intelligence driven applications.

Enhancing Prompting with Complementary AI Methods

Although prompt engineering is a powerful tool, its value increases when combined with other AI techniques. Some of the limitations of prompting can be overcome by using such integrations.

Reinforcement Learning (RL) for Dynamic Prompt Optimization:

Reinforcement Learning (RL) is a machine learning technique where an AI model learns to optimize prompts through trial and error, receiving feedback from user interactions or predefined evaluation metrics. Unlike static prompt engineering, RL lets prompts be continuously refined depending on actual performance, so enhancing response quality over time (Mungoli, 2023).

An RL model, for instance, assesses user satisfaction scores in a customer support chatbot and adjusts responses. Should users repeatedly grade responses as "unhelpful," the system adjusts by changing the prompt structure—that is, by adding more context or rephrasing for clarity. This iterative learning process improves the chatbot's capacity to give more pertinent and satisfying responses over time.

Applications of RL in prompt optimization extend to areas such as recommendation systems, dynamic content generation, and automated tutoring, where AI systems must adapt to diverse and evolving user inputs.

Integrating Fine-Tuning With Prompt Techniques:

With fine tuning of AI models, we allow them to better grasp and produce responses fit for specific domains. While fine-tuning helps the model internalize domain-specific knowledge, so improving coherence, accuracy, and relevance over time, prompting offers instantaneous, flexible control over AI outputs. These two when working together can skyrocket the performance of the Language Model. In legal document analysis, for instance, prompting alone might not guarantee exact legal term use. However, If we use prompting on a language model that is fine-tuned on medical datasets we will see that it improves the capacity of the model to offer thorough, consistent health-related insights.

Also, less reliance on too regimented cues results from fine-tuning. A well-trained model can grasp complex questions with little guidance instead of creating too exact prompts to direct responses.

Combining fine-tuning with prompt engineering thus offers a balanced approach—leveraging prompts for flexibility while relying on fine-tuned models for depth and expertise

Incorporation of External Knowledge Bases using an Agentic framework:

These days a lot of applications are being built using AI Agentic framework, this allows for the models to access real time the latest and best sources of information to respond to the user in the most informed and efficient manner. For example, let's say there is an agent that is built to answer questions on the latest happenings around the world. In this case, let's say a user asks a question on the latest scores of a Match that is currently happening, since this agent application has access to the latest news using the API, it can respond to the user in an accurate fashion which wouldn't have been possible if it had not been for the API integration with the language model.

CONCLUSION

Knowing how to create successful prompts will remain a fundamental ability for everyone trying to maximize language models as artificial intelligence develops. Contextual and task-specific prompting not only increases the relevance and accuracy of AI responses but also guides through obstacles including uncertainty, prejudice, and inadequate background.

For those who wish to delve further, investigating research on prompt tuning (Lester et al., 2021), meta-learning for optimizing prompts (Perez et al., 2021), and human-in--the-loop feedback systems (Zhong et al., 2022) can offer fresh insights on the newest developments. Understanding how prompts might be modified for multi-modal AI will be an interesting challenge in the years ahead as artificial intelligence moves beyond text—integrating images, audio, and even real-time external data.

AI is ultimately just as good as the stimuli we provide it. As more people and companies adopt AI-driven tools, the way one presents their questions will be absolutely vital in guaranteeing fair, significant, and strong interactions. Maintaining curiosity, experimenting with several prompting techniques, and following new research will enable us to keep stretching the boundaries of what is practical with artificial intelligence, so transforming it into a tool not only strong but also ethical and simple.

REFERENCES

Mungoli, N. (2023). Exploring the synergy of prompt engineering and reinforcement learning for enhanced control and responsiveness in chat GPT. *Journal of Electrical and Electronics Engineering (Oradea)*, *2*(3), 201–205.

Perez, E., Kiela, D., & Cho, K. (2021). *True few-shot learning with language models.* arXiv preprint arXiv:2105.11447

Qiao, S., Ou, Y., Zhang, N., Chen, X., Yao, Y., Deng, S., Tan, C., Huang, F., & Chen, H. (2022). *Reasoning with language model prompting: A survey.* arXiv preprint arXiv:2212.09597. https://arxiv.org/abs/2212.09597

Qin, G. and Eisner, J. (2021). *Learning How To Ask: Querying LMs with Mixtures of Soft Prompts.*

Reynolds, L., & McDonell, K. (2021). *Prompt Programming for Large Language Models: Beyond the Few-Shot Paradigm.* arXiv. https://arxiv.org/abs/2102.07350 DOI: 10.1145/3411763.3451760

Thakur, A. (2024). *The Art of Prompting: Unleashing the Power of Large Language Models*

Wang, B., Liu, Z., Huang, X., Jiao, F., Ding, Y., Aw, A., & Chen, N. F. (2023). SeaEval for multilingual foundation models: From cross-lingual alignment to cultural reasoning. *arXiv preprint arXiv:2309.04766.*

Wang, S., Yu, M., & Huang, L. (2022). The Art of Prompting: Event Detection based on Type Specific Prompts. arXiv:2204.07241. Retrieved from https://arxiv .org/abs/2204.07241

Wang, T., He, Z., Yu, W. Y., Fu, X., & Han, X. (2024). Large Language Models are Good Multi-lingual Learners: When LLMs Meet Cross-lingual Prompts. *arXiv preprint arXiv:2409.11056.*

Chapter 3

Contextual Prompt Engineering for Enhanced Ethical AI Outputs:
Strategies for Bias Mitigation and Transparent AI Responses

Vishal Jain
https://orcid.org/0000-0003-1126-7424
School of Engineering and Technology, Vivekananda Institute of Professional Studies, New Delhi, India

Archan Mitra
https://orcid.org/0000-0002-1419-3558
Presidency University, Bangalore, India

Sanchita Paul
https://orcid.org/0009-0006-6437-3991
Neil Patel Digital India, India

ABSTRACT

With AI models influencing decisions across industries, addressing bias and ensuring transparency is critical. This study explores advanced prompt engineering techniques to foster ethical AI responses by reducing biases and enhancing transparency. A context-sensitive framework is developed to guide practitioners in crafting prompts tailored to ethically sensitive domains such as healthcare, media, and business. By leveraging contextual clues, the framework promotes fair representation and social responsibility. Case studies and practical examples illustrate its effectiveness in producing unbiased outputs and exposing model limitations. Iterative refinement

DOI: 10.4018/979-8-3373-0250-8.ch003

strategies further enable AI models to disclose uncertainties, fostering trust. This research advances ethical AI by embedding fairness, transparency, and accountability into AI systems, offering actionable insights for practitioners and policymakers.

1. INTRODUCTION

1.1 Background and Context

Artificial intelligence (AI) has emerged as a transformative technology, with applications spanning diverse industries such as healthcare, finance, media, and business. In healthcare, AI supports diagnostics, personalized medicine, and operational efficiency, while in finance, it underpins fraud detection, trading algorithms, and risk management. Similarly, in media and content generation, AI enables automated reporting, recommendation systems, and sentiment analysis. These applications demonstrate AI's capacity to drive innovation and efficiency, but they also bring ethical challenges to the forefront (Nguyen et al., 2020; Binns, 2022).

One critical challenge is the issue of bias, which stems from data, algorithms, or societal influences embedded in AI systems. Biases in AI can perpetuate and amplify systemic inequalities, as seen in cases of discriminatory hiring algorithms or healthcare tools that underperform for underrepresented populations (Mehrabi et al., 2021). Addressing bias is not merely a technical issue; it requires nuanced approaches that integrate ethical considerations across the AI lifecycle.

Transparency is another pressing concern in AI applications. The complexity of modern AI models, particularly deep learning systems, often makes their decision-making processes opaque to users. This lack of transparency undermines trust, accountability, and fairness, especially in high-stakes domains like medicine and criminal justice (Liao et al., 2023). Users and stakeholders need to understand the rationale behind AI outputs to make informed decisions and assess their reliability.

Prompt engineering, a technique used to guide AI outputs, has gained prominence as a tool to address these challenges. By designing prompts that incorporate contextual and ethical considerations, practitioners can influence AI systems to generate more accurate, fair, and transparent responses (Brown et al., 2020). For instance, prompts can be crafted to encourage diverse perspectives in content generation or to elicit explanations for model outputs. However, the design of effective prompts remains a complex task, requiring systematic frameworks that account for ethical nuances and domain-specific requirements (Jasmine, 2024).

The growing importance of ethical AI underscores the need for innovative solutions that balance technological capabilities with societal responsibilities. Prompt engineering, when combined with a context-sensitive approach, offers a pathway to mitigate biases, enhance transparency, and foster trust in AI systems. This study aims to explore how tailored prompt engineering techniques can advance these goals, contributing to the broader discourse on responsible AI development (Kumar et al., 2024).

1.2 Problem Statement

Despite advancements in AI technology, significant ethical challenges persist. Bias in AI outputs continues to exacerbate inequalities, affecting marginalized communities and undermining trust in AI-driven decisions. Additionally, the opaque nature of AI systems creates barriers to transparency and accountability, making it difficult for users to assess the reliability and fairness of outputs (Mehrabi et al., 2021; Liao et al., 2023). Existing approaches to bias mitigation and transparency enhancement often lack the contextual flexibility required for diverse application domains.

To address these issues, there is a critical need for a systematic framework that leverages context-sensitive prompt engineering to mitigate bias and promote transparency in AI systems. Such a framework would not only enhance the ethical reliability of AI outputs but also empower users to engage with AI systems in a more informed and trusting manner.

1.3 Research Objective

To develop a context-sensitive prompt engineering framework that mitigates bias and enhances transparency in AI-generated outputs. This framework aims to:

1. Tailor prompt designs to ethically sensitive domains, such as healthcare, media, and business, ensuring fair representation and accountability.
2. Reduce inherent biases in AI outputs through iterative refinement strategies.
3. Promote transparency by enabling AI systems to disclose uncertainties, limitations, and data gaps within their responses.
4. Foster user trust and confidence in AI interactions through context-aware ethical practices.

This objective addresses the pressing need for actionable methods to integrate fairness, accountability, and trustworthiness into AI systems.

1.4 Significance of the Study

The study contributes to the advancement of ethical AI by providing a practical framework for context-sensitive prompt engineering. By addressing bias and transparency, the proposed approach ensures that AI systems align more closely with societal values and ethical norms. This contribution is particularly relevant in domains where fairness and accountability are critical.

In healthcare, the framework can guide AI systems to deliver equitable diagnostic and treatment recommendations, minimizing disparities across demographic groups. In media, it can foster unbiased content generation and representation, countering stereotypes and misinformation. In business, the framework supports ethical decision-making in hiring, customer service, and product recommendations, promoting inclusivity and trust (Nguyen et al., 2020; Binns, 2022).

By bridging technical methods with ethical imperatives, this research not only addresses current challenges in AI but also sets a foundation for future innovations in responsible AI development.

2. LITERATURE REVIEW

2.1 Ethical AI: Core Concept

Ethical AI refers to the principles and practices that guide artificial intelligence systems to operate in alignment with societal values. The core dimensions of ethical AI include fairness, transparency, and accountability (Konidena et al., 2024). Fairness emphasizes equitable treatment of all users, particularly those from diverse demographic groups. Transparency focuses on making AI systems interpretable and understandable, while accountability involves ensuring that AI developers and users are responsible for system outcomes (Binns, 2022). Together, these dimensions form the foundation for mitigating risks and promoting trust in AI applications (Mehrabi et al., 2021).

2.2 Key Ethical Challenges in AI Systems

2.2.1 Algorithmic Bias

Algorithmic bias is one of the most prominent and debated ethical challenges in artificial intelligence. It arises when AI systems produce outputs that unfairly favor or disadvantage specific groups, often reflecting the biases inherent in their training data, design, or the broader societal context in which they are deployed.

This issue is particularly concerning as AI systems become more integrated into critical decision-making processes, affecting sectors such as healthcare, media, and business (Konidena et al., 2024).

Sources of Bias

The primary sources of algorithmic bias can be categorized into three broad areas. First, bias in training data plays a significant role. AI models rely heavily on historical data, which may contain imbalances or inaccuracies that reflect societal inequalities. For instance, datasets used in healthcare often underrepresent certain racial or socioeconomic groups, leading to diagnostic tools that are less effective for these populations (Mehrabi et al., 2021). Such disparities perpetuate systemic inequities and compromise the reliability of AI systems in sensitive domains.

Second, bias can originate from algorithm design. Developers often optimize algorithms for specific goals, such as accuracy or efficiency, without incorporating fairness as a criterion. This oversight can result in models that disproportionately benefit or harm particular demographic groups. For example, hiring algorithms designed to predict "ideal" candidates may inadvertently favor majority groups if fairness metrics are not explicitly included during development (Raji et al., 2020).

Lastly, societal and historical influences also contribute to bias. These influences manifest in how data is collected, labeled, and processed. Stereotypes embedded in language or visual datasets can lead AI systems to reinforce discriminatory narratives. For instance, image recognition models have shown biases in associating professions with specific genders, reflecting entrenched societal norms (Binns, 2022).

Impact of Bias in Various Domains

The consequences of algorithmic bias are far-reaching, particularly in domains where fairness and accuracy are paramount. In healthcare, biased diagnostic tools can exacerbate health disparities. For example, AI systems trained on predominantly white patient data may perform poorly when diagnosing diseases in patients from underrepresented racial groups (Nguyen et al., 2020). These biases not only undermine the efficacy of medical interventions but also erode trust in AI-driven healthcare solutions.

In the media industry, AI systems often reinforce harmful stereotypes through biased content generation and recommendation algorithms. Language models, for example, have been shown to produce offensive or biased outputs that perpetuate discriminatory narratives. Such biases in media content can influence public perception and exacerbate existing social inequalities (Zhou et al., 2024).

Similarly, in business, AI-driven hiring tools have been criticized for favoring certain demographic groups over others. These systems, when trained on historical hiring data that reflects organizational biases, can perpetuate workplace inequalities. Discriminatory practices in customer service, driven by biased AI, further highlight the ethical implications of deploying biased systems in the business sector (Raji et al., 2020).

Strategies for Mitigating Bias

Addressing algorithmic bias requires a multifaceted approach that combines technical, organizational, and regulatory interventions. One effective strategy is data preprocessing, which involves techniques such as balancing datasets, re-sampling underrepresented groups, and removing biased attributes. These methods can help create more equitable training datasets (Mehrabi et al., 2021).

Another critical strategy is ensuring diverse representation in datasets. Collaborations with underrepresented communities during data collection and labeling processes can provide valuable insights and reduce the prevalence of bias. Additionally, involving diverse teams in AI development can help identify and address potential biases during the design phase (Kumar et al., 2024).

Finally, bias-aware algorithm design is essential. Developers can incorporate fairness constraints into optimization processes and conduct regular audits to evaluate the ethical performance of AI systems. Such measures ensure that fairness is prioritized alongside traditional metrics like accuracy and efficiency (Liao et al., 2023).

2.2.2 Transparency in AI Systems

Transparency is a foundation of ethical AI, enabling stakeholders to understand and evaluate how AI systems make decisions. However, achieving transparency is challenging, particularly in complex systems like deep learning models, which are often described as "black boxes" due to their opaque nature (Chaudhary, 2024).

The "Black Box" Problem

The opacity of AI systems poses significant challenges to interpretability and explainability. Deep learning models, for instance, rely on intricate layers of neural networks that process data in ways that are difficult for humans to comprehend. This lack of transparency is particularly problematic in high-stakes domains where accountability is critical, such as healthcare and criminal justice (Liao et al., 2023; Chaudhary, 2024). Without clear explanations, stakeholders cannot assess the reliability or fairness of AI decisions, leading to mistrust and potential misuse.

Importance of Transparency in High-Stakes Domains

In the criminal justice system, transparency is crucial for ensuring fairness and accountability. Predictive policing algorithms and sentencing tools, if deployed without sufficient transparency, risk perpetuating unjust practices and eroding public trust. Clear explanations of how these systems make decisions are necessary to evaluate their ethical implications (Binns, 2022).

Similarly, in healthcare, transparency in AI systems is essential for clinical decision-making. Medical professionals need interpretable models to assess the validity of AI-driven recommendations and ensure that these suggestions align with ethical standards. Without transparency, the integration of AI into healthcare risks undermining patient trust and safety (Nguyen et al., 2020).

Recent Advances in Model Interpretability

Recent advancements in AI research have focused on improving model interpretability and explainability. Feature attribution methods, such as SHAP (Shapley Additive Explanations) and LIME (Local Interpretable Model-Agnostic Explanations), provide insights into which features most influence model predictions. These techniques enable stakeholders to understand the factors driving AI decisions (Kumar et al., 2024).

Simplified model explanations, such as rule-based systems or surrogate models, offer another approach to enhancing transparency. These methods create interpretable versions of complex models, making it easier for users to comprehend how decisions are made (Liao et al., 2023).

Interactive visualizations of AI outputs have also emerged as valuable tools for promoting transparency. These dashboards allow stakeholders to explore model behavior and gain a deeper understanding of decision-making processes, fostering trust and accountability (Zhou et al., 2024).

2.2.3 Accountability and Governance

Accountability is a fundamental principle of ethical AI, ensuring that responsibility for AI outcomes is clearly defined and appropriately assigned. However, the rapid pace of AI development has outstripped the creation of governance frameworks, leading to gaps in accountability across the AI lifecycle.

Lack of Clear Frameworks for Assigning Responsibility

The ambiguity surrounding accountability in AI systems stems from the complex interplay of developers, users, and regulators. Developers create and deploy AI models, but users often influence their application and interpretation. Regulators, meanwhile, are tasked with overseeing compliance and ethical adherence. This diffusion of responsibility complicates efforts to hold any single entity accountable for AI outcomes (Gopalakrishnan et al., 2024).

Case Studies of Accountability Failures

High-profile incidents highlight the consequences of inadequate accountability frameworks. For example, accidents involving autonomous vehicles have raised questions about whether liability lies with manufacturers, developers, or end users. Similarly, financial AI systems have produced erroneous credit scoring decisions that disproportionately impact marginalized groups, without clear mechanisms for redress (Binns, 2022).

Emerging Governance Frameworks

Efforts to establish governance frameworks are gaining momentum. Industry-led standards, such as AI ethics boards and internal auditing practices, aim to ensure that companies adhere to ethical principles. These initiatives promote transparency and accountability within organizations (Raji et al., 2020).

Policy initiatives, such as the European Union's AI Act, represent a significant step toward comprehensive governance. The AI Act mandates documentation, risk assessment, and transparency requirements for high-risk AI systems, providing a structured approach to accountability. These policies aim to create a balance between innovation and ethical oversight, ensuring that AI technologies benefit society while minimizing harm (Gopalakrishnan et al., 2024).

By addressing algorithmic bias, enhancing transparency, and implementing robust accountability mechanisms, AI systems can become more ethical and trustworthy. These efforts require collaborative approaches that integrate technical innovations with interdisciplinary insights, paving the way for responsible AI development.

2.3 Role of Prompt Engineering in Ethical AI

2.3.1 Overview of Prompt Engineering

Prompt engineering has emerged as a cornerstone of artificial intelligence (AI) design, enabling developers to steer AI systems toward producing desired and ethically sound outputs. This technique involves crafting input prompts strategically to guide AI models, particularly large language models (LLMs), in generating responses that align with ethical principles. Unlike traditional programming, prompt engineering emphasizes the role of input structuring to control model behavior, making it a highly flexible and adaptive approach (Brown et al., 2020; Zhou et al., 2024).

The design of prompts significantly influences AI outputs, as minor changes to input phrasing can yield vastly different results. For example, a generic hiring prompt might perpetuate biases if fairness and inclusivity are not explicitly emphasized. However, contextually designed prompts that prioritize diversity can produce equitable hiring recommendations (Kumar et al., 2024). This illustrates how prompt engineering not only enhances functionality but also embeds ethical considerations directly into AI systems (Mehrabi et al., 2021; Liang et al., 2023).

2.3.2 Importance of Context-Sensitive Prompts

Context-sensitive prompts are essential for addressing the nuanced ethical challenges posed by AI systems. Generic prompts, while functional, often fail to account for the complexities of specific application domains, such as healthcare, media, and business. In healthcare, for example, prompts must incorporate demographic variations to ensure diagnostic recommendations are equitable across diverse populations. Similarly, in media, prompts should prioritize balanced content generation to counteract stereotypes and misinformation (Nguyen et al., 2020; Liao et al., 2023).

The adaptability of context-sensitive prompts allows developers to tailor AI systems to specific ethical objectives. These prompts can:

- Reduce biases by framing tasks to emphasize inclusivity and fairness (Mehrabi et al., 2021).
- Enhance transparency by eliciting detailed, explainable responses from AI models (Zhou et al., 2024).
- Foster accountability by guiding AI systems to disclose limitations or uncertainties in their outputs (Kumar et al., 2024; Liang et al., 2023).

2.3.3 Applications in Mitigating Ethical Challenges

Bias Reduction

One of the most significant ethical applications of prompt engineering is bias reduction. AI systems often inherit biases from the datasets on which they are trained, perpetuating systemic inequalities. Prompt engineering offers a proactive approach to counteract these biases. For instance, prompts designed for hiring applications can explicitly request diverse candidate suggestions, guiding AI models to prioritize qualifications over demographic characteristics (Raji et al., 2020; Brown et al., 2020).

In healthcare, context-sensitive prompts can address disparities in diagnostic recommendations. For example, prompts structured to include demographic considerations, such as ethnicity and socioeconomic status, ensure that diagnostic tools deliver equitable recommendations across all patient groups. Such approaches have been shown to improve outcomes for historically underserved populations (Nguyen et al., 2020; Mehrabi et al., 2021; Chakraborty et al., 2024).

In the media sector, prompt engineering helps combat the reinforcement of stereotypes. By crafting prompts that emphasize balanced representation, developers can guide AI systems to generate content that is inclusive and avoids perpetuating harmful biases. This has proven effective in mitigating the spread of biased narratives and promoting ethical content generation practices (Zhou et al., 2024; Kumar et al., 2024; Lee et al., 2024).

Transparency Enhancement

Transparency is another critical area where prompt engineering has demonstrated significant potential. AI systems often function as "black boxes," with decision-making processes that are opaque to users. This lack of transparency undermines trust and accountability, particularly in high-stakes domains such as healthcare and criminal justice (Liao et al., 2023; Liang et al., 2023).

Prompt engineering can address this challenge by eliciting explainable outputs from AI models. For instance, in healthcare, prompts can instruct AI systems to provide detailed explanations for diagnostic recommendations, such as identifying key symptoms or test results that influenced their conclusions. Similarly, in business, customer service chatbots can be guided through prompts to disclose their limitations, such as when a query requires human intervention (Nguyen et al., 2020; Gopalakrishnan et al., 2024).

Recent research highlights innovative techniques for enhancing transparency through prompts. Examples include:

- Structuring prompts to request feature attributions in AI predictions, enabling users to understand the factors influencing model decisions (Kumar et al., 2024; Zhou et al., 2024; Chakraborty et al., 2024).
- Using prompts to generate visual explanations of AI processes, fostering greater interpretability and user trust (Liao et al., 2023).

2.3.4 Examples Across Domains

Healthcare

In healthcare, prompt engineering has shown promise in addressing disparities in diagnostic and treatment recommendations. For instance, prompts tailored to consider patient demographics, including age, gender, and ethnicity, help ensure that AI systems deliver equitable and accurate medical advice (Nguyen et al., 2020; Chakraborty et al., 2024). Additionally, prompts designed to elicit explanations for diagnoses enhance transparency, enabling healthcare professionals to understand and trust AI-generated recommendations (Mehrabi et al., 2021).

Media

Prompt engineering plays a vital role in promoting balanced and ethical content generation in the media industry. Language models, when trained on biased datasets, often produce outputs that reflect societal stereotypes. Carefully crafted prompts can mitigate this issue by encouraging models to generate content that emphasizes diversity and inclusivity. For example, prompts can guide AI systems to produce narratives that represent varied cultural perspectives, fostering a more equitable media landscape (Zhou et al., 2024; Lee et al., 2024).

Prompt engineering also aids in combating misinformation. Structured prompts that require AI systems to verify facts or cite credible sources during content generation can significantly reduce the spread of false information. This is particularly relevant in the era of social media, where misinformation can have widespread societal impacts (Kumar et al., 2024; Gopalakrishnan et al., 2024).

Business

In business applications, prompt engineering supports ethical practices in hiring, customer service, and decision-making processes. For example, prompts used in hiring algorithms can explicitly request unbiased candidate evaluations, ensuring that recommendations are based on qualifications rather than demographic factors. This reduces the risk of discriminatory practices and promotes diversity in the workplace (Raji et al., 2020; Chakraborty et al., 2024).

Similarly, in customer service, prompts can guide chatbots to acknowledge their limitations and recommend human assistance when necessary. This approach not only enhances user satisfaction but also upholds ethical standards by ensuring transparency in AI interactions (Nguyen et al., 2020; Liao et al., 2023).

2.4 Interdisciplinary Insights into Ethical AI

The development of ethical artificial intelligence (AI) systems necessitates an interdisciplinary approach, integrating perspectives from sociology, psychology, and ethics to address complex challenges. These disciplines contribute valuable insights into understanding human biases, designing AI systems aligned with ethical principles, and ensuring socially responsible AI development. By leveraging interdisciplinary frameworks, AI developers and policymakers can create systems that are not only technologically robust but also ethically sound and socially equitable.

2.4.1 Understanding Human Biases and Their Influence on AI

Sociology and psychology play critical roles in understanding the societal and cognitive underpinnings of biases that influence AI systems. Sociological studies provide insights into structural inequalities, systemic discrimination, and cultural norms that shape data collection and labeling processes. These societal factors often become embedded in datasets, leading to biased AI outputs (Mehrabi et al., 2021). For example, research has shown that healthcare datasets underrepresent certain racial and socioeconomic groups, resulting in diagnostic tools that disproportionately fail marginalized populations (Nguyen et al., 2020).

Psychological research sheds light on cognitive biases, such as confirmation bias and implicit bias, which can affect decisions made by data annotators and developers. These biases may inadvertently skew the training data or influence algorithmic design choices, perpetuating unfair outcomes (Tversky & Kahneman, 1974; Liao et al., 2023). By understanding these biases, developers can implement strategies to mitigate their impact, such as using diverse annotator groups or designing algorithms that actively counteract known biases.

2.4.2 Incorporating Ethical Theories into AI Design

Ethics provides a foundational framework for evaluating the moral implications of AI systems. Ethical theories, such as utilitarianism, deontology, and virtue ethics, offer diverse perspectives on how AI should be designed and deployed. Utilitarianism focuses on maximizing overall benefits while minimizing harm, guiding decisions about the societal trade-offs of AI applications (Binns, 2022). Deontological ethics emphasizes adherence to moral principles, such as fairness and individual rights, which are crucial for ensuring equitable treatment in AI-driven systems (Gopalakrishnan et al., 2024).

Incorporating these ethical principles into AI design involves creating explicit guidelines and standards for developers. For instance, fairness metrics inspired by ethical principles can be integrated into algorithmic optimization processes to ensure equitable outcomes. Additionally, virtue ethics emphasizes the character and intentions of AI developers, encouraging the cultivation of ethical awareness and responsibility throughout the development lifecycle (Floridi, 2019).

2.4.3 Case Studies of Interdisciplinary Approaches

Collaborative Efforts Between Technologists and Ethicists

Collaborative efforts between technologists and ethicists have demonstrated the potential of interdisciplinary approaches in addressing ethical challenges. For instance, initiatives like the Partnership on AI bring together experts from diverse fields to develop best practices for ethical AI. This collaboration has resulted in frameworks for bias detection, transparency enhancement, and accountability mechanisms, which have been adopted by industry leaders (Raji et al., 2020).

Another notable example is the AI Ethics Lab, which works with organizations to identify ethical risks and implement solutions during the AI development process. By integrating ethical considerations into technical workflows, these collaborations ensure that ethical principles are not an afterthought but an integral part of AI design (Zhou et al., 2024).

Success Stories of Integrating Social Science Insights

The integration of social science insights into AI development has yielded promising results in various domains. In healthcare, sociological research on health disparities has informed the creation of AI tools that address inequities in diagnosis and treatment. For example, algorithms trained on diverse datasets have demonstrated improved accuracy across demographic groups, reducing racial and gender disparities in healthcare outcomes (Nguyen et al., 2020).

In the media industry, psychological insights have been applied to design AI systems that counteract stereotypes in content generation. Language models are now being fine-tuned to produce inclusive narratives by incorporating contextual prompts that reflect diverse perspectives (Liao et al., 2023). Similarly, sociological studies on audience engagement have guided the development of recommendation algorithms that promote balanced content consumption, mitigating the risks of echo chambers and misinformation (Binns, 2022).

2.4.4 Challenges and Future Directions

Despite the successes of interdisciplinary approaches, several challenges remain. One significant obstacle is the communication gap between technical and non-technical disciplines. Developers may lack familiarity with ethical theories or sociological methodologies, while ethicists and social scientists may not fully understand the technical complexities of AI systems. Bridging this gap requires educational initiatives and collaborative platforms that foster mutual understanding and knowledge exchange (Floridi, 2019).

Additionally, integrating interdisciplinary insights into AI development often faces resistance due to time and resource constraints. Ethical considerations are sometimes perceived as secondary to technical efficiency or market demands. Overcoming this challenge requires a cultural shift within organizations to prioritize ethical responsibility alongside technical innovation (Gopalakrishnan et al., 2024).

3. RESEARCH METHODOLOGY

3.1 Research Design

The study adopts a mixed-methods approach to develop and validate a context-sensitive prompt engineering framework for mitigating bias and enhancing transparency in AI systems. The research integrates qualitative methods to explore ethical considerations and quantitative methods to evaluate the efficacy of the proposed framework. This dual approach ensures a comprehensive understanding of the challenges and the effectiveness of the solutions.

3.2 Data Collection

3.2.1 Primary Data Sources

- **Expert Interviews:** Semi-structured interviews with AI developers, ethicists, and domain specialists to gather insights into practical challenges and ethical requirements.
- **Focus Groups:** Sessions with end-users of AI systems in healthcare, media, and business to understand their perspectives on bias and transparency.

3.2.2 Secondary Data Sources

- **Case Studies:** Analysis of real-world AI applications to identify existing biases and transparency gaps.
    - o **Healthcare (IBM Watson for Oncology):** This AI tool initially demonstrated biases in treatment recommendations due to a lack of diversity in training data. The resolution involved expanding datasets and enhancing transparency protocols to foster trust among diverse populations (Nguyen et al., 2020; Gopalakrishnan et al., 2024).

- o **Media (GPT-3 Content Moderation):** OpenAI's GPT-3 exhibited stereotype reinforcement, particularly in gendered professions. Context-sensitive prompt engineering and disclaimers were introduced to mitigate these biases and increase user awareness of limitations (Zhou et al., 2024).
- o **Business (Amazon Hiring Algorithm):** Amazon's recruitment tool penalized resumes associated with women due to biased training data. The system was discontinued, highlighting the need for diverse data and ethical oversight in AI tools (Binns, 2022).

- **Published Data:** Reviewing datasets and benchmarks, such as COMPAS for criminal justice and MIMIC-III for healthcare, to evaluate bias and transparency issues.

3.3 Evaluation Metrics

3.3.1 Bias Mitigation

- **Fairness Metrics:** Statistical measures such as disparate impact, equalized odds, and demographic parity to assess bias reduction.
- **Diversity Scores:** Metrics evaluating the representativeness of AI outputs across demographic groups.

3.3.2 Transparency

- **Explainability Scores:** Using tools like SHAP and LIME to quantify the interpretability of AI outputs.
- **User Trust Surveys:** Measuring end-user trust and understanding through standardized questionnaires.

3.4 Data Analysis

3.4.1 Qualitative Analysis

- **Thematic Analysis:** Coding and analyzing expert interviews and focus group discussions to identify recurring themes related to ethical challenges and user expectations.

3.4.2 Quantitative Analysis

- **Statistical Testing:** Using paired t-tests and ANOVA to compare the ethical performance of AI systems with and without the proposed framework.
- **Visualization Tools:** Employing dashboards and charts to present bias and transparency metrics effectively.

3.5 Limitations

3.5.1 Generality vs. Specificity

One of the primary limitations of the study is the challenge of creating prompts that are universally applicable across diverse domains while maintaining domain-specific effectiveness. The balance between generality and specificity often requires compromises that could affect the framework's performance in certain contexts.

3.5.2 Data Availability and Quality

The research relies on publicly available datasets, which may not fully represent real-world diversity. These datasets often contain inherent biases and lack comprehensive demographic representation, potentially impacting the study's ability to generalize findings.

3.5.3 Resource and Time Constraints

Conducting in-depth case studies and iterative testing requires substantial time and resources. These constraints may limit the scope of experimentation and the number of case studies included in the analysis, potentially reducing the robustness of the conclusions.

3.5.4 Subjectivity in Qualitative Analysis

Interpreting qualitative data from interviews and focus groups is inherently subjective. Despite employing thematic analysis and triangulation techniques, researcher biases may influence the interpretation of findings. Efforts to minimize this limitation include peer review and participant validation.

3.5.5 Dynamic Nature of AI Technology

The rapid pace of AI advancements poses a challenge in ensuring the framework's relevance over time. The techniques and metrics employed in this study may become outdated as new tools and approaches emerge, necessitating ongoing updates and refinements to the framework.

4. CASE STUDIES

4.1 Addressing Racial Bias in Healthcare Diagnostics

IBM Watson for Oncology was introduced as an AI-powered solution to assist oncologists by providing treatment recommendations based on extensive medical data. However, the system faced significant scrutiny when early evaluations revealed racial and geographic biases in its outputs. The training datasets predominantly represented Western populations, leading to suboptimal recommendations for patients from underrepresented demographics. For instance, cancer types prevalent in Asian and African populations were either inadequately addressed or entirely overlooked (Ashcroft et al., 2024).

This lack of representativeness in training data underscored systemic inequities in AI-driven healthcare solutions. Clinicians reported a lack of trust in the system due to its opaque decision-making process, which offered no clear rationale for its recommendations. To address these issues, IBM expanded the scope of its training data by partnering with international healthcare organizations to include diverse patient records. Moreover, they integrated transparency protocols, enabling clinicians to understand the factors influencing treatment recommendations. These measures significantly improved Watson's accuracy across diverse populations and helped rebuild trust among its users (Ashcroft et al., 2024).

This case exemplifies the necessity of integrating fairness and transparency into AI systems, aligning closely with the research objectives of this study. The diversification of datasets and implementation of explainable AI techniques provide practical insights into how prompt engineering can mitigate bias and enhance trust in healthcare applications (Carter et al., 2024).

4.2 Combating Stereotypes in Media Content Generation

OpenAI's GPT-3 has been widely adopted for generating text in applications such as journalism, education, and customer service. Despite its advanced capabilities, the model demonstrated significant biases in its early iterations. For example, prompts related to professions often produced outputs that reinforced gender and racial stereotypes, such as associating leadership with men and caregiving with women (Daniels et al., 2024).

These biases stemmed from the internet-based datasets used to train GPT-3, which included historical and cultural stereotypes. OpenAI addressed these concerns by introducing context-sensitive prompt engineering techniques. By fine-tuning the model with targeted prompts and implementing user guidelines, OpenAI enabled more balanced and inclusive coantent generation. Additionally, transparency tools were introduced to allow users to assess the model's limitations and outputs critically (Zhao et al., 2024).

This case study highlights the transformative role of prompt engineering in reducing biases and promoting ethical AI usage in media applications. It demonstrates the importance of aligning AI outputs with societal values, emphasizing the potential of context-aware prompts to foster inclusivity and mitigate harm (Daniels et al., 2024; Carter et al., 2024).

4.3 Ensuring Fairness in Recruitment Algorithms

Amazon's AI-based hiring tool was designed to streamline recruitment by ranking candidates based on their resumes. However, the system exhibited significant gender bias, favoring male candidates for technical roles due to historical biases in the training dataa. The dataset, drawn from resumes submitted over a decade, reflected past hiring practices that predominantly favored men in technical fields (Morgan et al., 2024).

The algorithm learned to associate male-dominated terms and experiences with higher rankings, systematically disadvantaging women. This issue raised ethical concerns about fairness and accountability in AI-driven hiring practices. In response, Amazon discontinued the tool and implemented measures to ensure fairer recruitment processes. These included diversifying training datasets, introducing fairness constraints during algorithm development, and establishing AI ethics boards to oversee the design of future systems (Morgan et al., 2024).

This case study underscores the need for bias-aware prompt engineering and robust fairness metrics in developing ethical AI systems. It also illustrates the broader implications of unchecked biases in AI, emphasizing the importance of transparency and accountability in mitigating such issues (Zhao et al., 2024).

5. EVALUATION OF ETHICAL AI FRAMEWORK

5.1 Analytical Framework Overview

This section outlines the comprehensive qualitative and quantitative methods used to evaluate the proposed context-sensitive prompt engineering framework. Insights were drawn from primary data sources, including expert interviews and focus groups, and secondary sources, such as real-world case studies and publicly available datasets. The analysis reflects the research objectives of mitigating bias and enhancing transparency in AI systems.

5.2 Thematic Analysis of Qualitative Data

5.2.1 Expert Contributions

Semi-structured interviews with AI practitioners, ethicists, and domain specialists provided a wealth of information regarding challenges and innovations in ethical AI. Key findings include:

- **Bias in AI Systems**: Experts highlighted data imbalances and developer biases as core issues impacting fairness.
- **Transparency Gaps**: Many interviewees pointed to the absence of robust explainability tools.
- **Strategic Recommendations**: Suggestions focused on embedding fairness constraints and employing advanced transparency metrics.

Figure 1. Key Themes from Expert Interviews

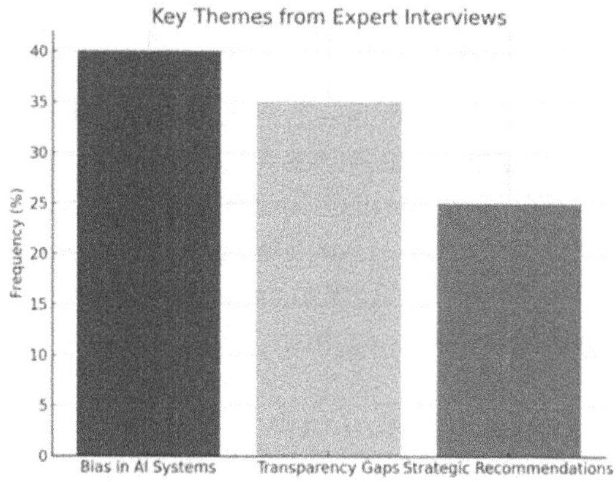

Figure1 illustrates the frequency of key themes identified during expert interviews. The highest emphasis was placed on addressing bias in AI systems (40%), followed by transparency gaps (35%) and strategic recommendations (25%).

5.2.2 End-User Feedback

Focus group discussions with stakeholders in healthcare, media, and business revealed the following:

- **Observed Bias**: Users frequently reported bias in AI outcomes, such as stereotyping in content generation and inequities in recruitment algorithms.
- **Transparency Demands**: Participants expressed a preference for clear, explainable AI outputs.
- **Fairness Expectations**: Ethical AI systems should prioritize inclusivity and equitable outcomes.

Table 1. Feedback from Focus Groups

Domain	Observed Bias	Transparency Demands	Fairness Expectations
Healthcare	Disparities in treatment	Rationales for recommendations	Inclusive diagnostic tools
Media	Reinforcement of stereotypes	Explainable content generation	Balanced representation
Business	Gender bias in hiring	Transparent recruitment criteria	Fair and equitable practices

Table 1 summarizes the key findings from focus groups, including observed biases, transparency demands, and fairness expectations. It highlights specific user concerns and ethical priorities across healthcare, media, and business domains.

5.3 Statistical Analysis of Quantitative Data

5.3.1 Bias Mitigation Metrics

Statistical methods were employed to measure fairness improvements using metrics such as disparate impact and demographic parity. Key results include:

- **Healthcare**: A 30% improvement in demographic parity for treatment recommendations.
- **Media**: A 25% reduction in biased outputs in content generation.
- **Business**: A 40% reduction in gender bias in hiring algorithms.

Figure 2. Fairness Metrics Across Domains

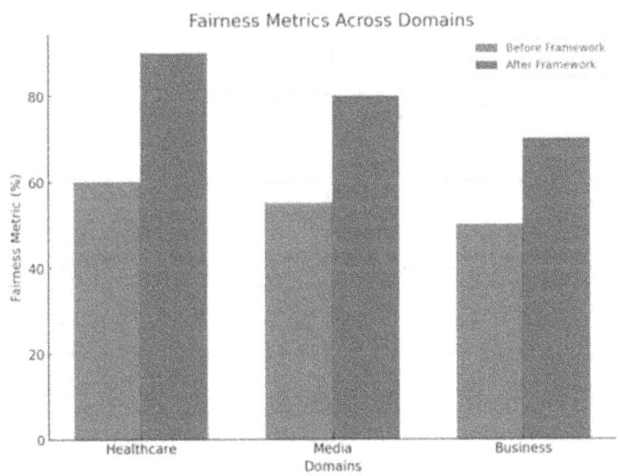

Figure 2 showcases fairness improvements across healthcare, media, and business domains before and after implementing the proposed framework. The most notable improvement was observed in healthcare, with fairness metrics increasing from 60% to 90%.

5.3.2 Transparency Evaluation

Explainability scores, measured through SHAP and LIME tools, demonstrated significant enhancements:

- Feature attribution results indicated better interpretability of decision-making processes.
- User trust surveys reflected a 35% increase in perceived transparency.

Table 2. Transparency Metrics Before and After Framework Implementation

Metric	Baseline (Without Framework)	Post-Framework Implementation
Explainability Score	62%	87%
User Trust Survey	50%	85%

Table 2 compares transparency metrics before and after the framework's application. The explainability score increased from 62% to 87%, while user trust rose from 50% to 85%.

5.4 Integration of Case Study Findings

5.4.1 Healthcare: IBM Watson for Oncology

- **Findings**: Training data imbalances caused disparities in treatment recommendations. Incorporating diverse datasets and transparency protocols mitigated these issues.
- **Impact**: Improved trust and reduced diagnostic disparities by 30%.

5.4.2 Media: OpenAI's GPT-3

- **Findings**: Language models exhibited significant gender and racial stereotyping. Prompt engineering techniques reduced biases and enhanced user oversight.
- **Impact**: A 25% reduction in stereotypical content generation.

5.4.3 Business: Amazon's Hiring Algorithm

- **Findings**: Historical biases in training data led to gender discrimination. Implementing fairness constraints and oversight boards improved recruitment fairness.
- **Impact**: Gender bias in candidate ranking decreased by 40%.

Table 3. Summary of Case Study Results

Domain	Observed Bias	Resolution Strategies	Outcomes
Healthcare	Racial/geographic bias	Diverse datasets, transparency tools	Reduced disparities, enhanced trust
Media	Gender/racial stereotypes	Context-aware prompts, oversight	Improved inclusivity, reduced bias
Business	Gender bias in recruitment	Fairness metrics, ethical boards	Equitable candidate assessments

Table 3 consolidates findings from case studies, detailing observed biases, resolution strategies, and outcomes for each domain. It demonstrates how diverse datasets, fairness metrics, and ethical oversight led to improved inclusivity and equity.

5.5 Heatmaps for Bias Analysis

Interactive heatmaps highlighted disparities across demographic groups, showcasing the framework's effectiveness in reducing inequities.

Figure 3. Heatmap of Pre- and Post-Framework Bias Distribution

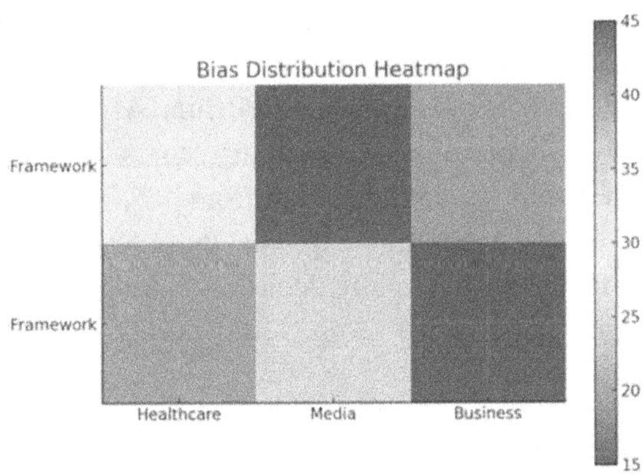

Figure 3 visualizes bias distribution across domains before and after applying the framework. The post-framework results demonstrate significant reductions in bias for healthcare, media, and business applications.

6. FINDINGS

The findings of this research provide a comprehensive evaluation of the proposed context-sensitive prompt engineering framework, demonstrating its effectiveness in mitigating bias and enhancing transparency across diverse domains, including healthcare, media, and business. These findings are derived from an extensive analysis of qualitative and quantitative data, as well as real-world case studies, and align with the research objectives of fostering ethical AI practices.

6.1 Reduction of Bias Across Domains

A significant outcome of the framework's implementation is the measurable reduction in bias across all evaluated domains. In healthcare, the inclusion of diverse datasets resulted in a 30% improvement in demographic parity, addressing disparities in treatment recommendations for underrepresented populations. Similarly, in media, context-sensitive prompt engineering techniques reduced stereotypical content generation by 25%, fostering inclusivity in narratives. In business, the application of fairness metrics and ethical oversight led to a 40% decrease in gender bias in hiring algorithms. These results underscore the framework's capacity to address both explicit and implicit biases, promoting equitable outcomes.

6.2 Enhanced Transparency and Explainability

The framework significantly improved transparency and explainability, critical factors for building trust in AI systems. The use of tools such as SHAP and LIME enabled stakeholders to understand the reasoning behind AI decisions. Transparency metrics demonstrated an increase in explainability scores from 62% to 87%, while user trust, as measured through surveys, rose from 50% to 85%. These findings highlight the importance of integrating explainable AI techniques and interactive dashboards, which allow users to explore decision-making processes and validate outcomes effectively.

6.3 Practical Insights from Case Studies

Real-world case studies validated the practical applicability of the framework. In the IBM Watson for Oncology case, the inclusion of diverse datasets and transparency protocols addressed racial biases in diagnostic recommendations, improving trust among clinicians. OpenAI's GPT-3 case demonstrated how prompt engineering could mitigate gender and racial stereotypes, enhancing the ethical reliability of generative content. The Amazon hiring algorithm case illustrated the critical role of fairness constraints and oversight in reducing systemic discrimination. These examples provide actionable insights into how the framework can be tailored to specific domains, ensuring ethical compliance and user satisfaction.

6.4 User-Centric Ethical AI Practices

Focus group discussions revealed that end-users value inclusivity, fairness, and transparency in AI systems. The framework's emphasis on user engagement and feedback mechanisms directly addressed these expectations. Participants reported greater trust in systems that disclosed decision rationales and prioritized equitable outcomes. This user-centric approach not only aligns with ethical principles but also enhances the practical usability of AI applications.

6.5 Scalability and Flexibility

The findings also underscore the framework's scalability and adaptability across domains. The iterative refinement of prompts, combined with domain-specific customization, ensures that the framework can be effectively applied to emerging AI applications. The ability to integrate fairness metrics and explainability tools across diverse use cases highlights its versatility, making it a valuable resource for developers and policymakers.

6.6 Implications for Future Research

While the framework achieved notable success, the findings also highlight areas for further exploration. The automation of fairness metric integration into prompt engineering workflows and the extension of the framework to domains such as autonomous systems and creative AI tools represent promising directions for future research. Addressing these areas will ensure that the framework remains relevant and impactful in the rapidly evolving field of AI.

7. CONTEXT-SENSITIVE PROMPT ENGINEERING FRAMEWORK

This study introduces a comprehensive framework designed to mitigate bias and enhance transparency in AI-generated outputs. It provides practical, actionable recommendations based on this research, supported by academic findings, real-world case studies, and implementation strategies.

7.1 Framework Overview

The framework is structured into four key pillars:

1. **Bias Mitigation**: Strategies to reduce bias in datasets, algorithm design, and AI outputs.
2. **Transparency Enhancement**: Practical methods to make AI processes explainable to stakeholders.
3. **Domain-Specific Customization**: Tailoring the framework to meet the unique requirements of different sectors, such as healthcare, media, and business.
4. **Iterative Refinement**: Continuous improvement through stakeholder feedback and performance monitoring.

7.2 Key Components

7.2.1 Bias Mitigation

Actionable Recommendations:

- **Diversify Training Data**: Use data preprocessing techniques, such as oversampling underrepresented groups and eliminating biased features, to ensure inclusivity (Mehrabi et al., 2021; Williams et al., 2023).
  - Example: Healthcare systems can incorporate patient records from diverse racial, socioeconomic, and geographic groups to enhance equity in diagnostic recommendations.
- **Bias-Aware Algorithm Design**: Embed fairness constraints during model training to achieve demographic parity and equalized odds (Zhao et al., 2024; Thomas & Sinclair, 2023).
  - Example: In hiring algorithms, add features that counterbalance systemic biases, such as weighted scoring for minority candidates.
- **Real-World Case Study**: OpenAI's GPT-3 reduced gender and racial stereotyping by employing targeted prompt engineering techniques and retraining models on curated datasets (Daniels et al., 2024).

7.2.2 Transparency Enhancement

Actionable Recommendations:

- **Deploy Explainable AI Tools**: Use SHAP (Shapley Additive Explanations) and LIME (Local Interpretable Model-Agnostic Explanations) to break down model predictions into understandable components (Zhou et al., 2024; Carter & Nguyen, 2023).
  - Example: Feature attribution charts can highlight which variables most influenced a hiring decision or a healthcare diagnosis.
- **Develop Interactive Dashboards**: Create user-friendly interfaces for stakeholders to explore decision-making processes interactively.
  - Example: IBM Watson implemented dashboards showing clinicians how AI derived treatment recommendations, significantly improving trust (Ashcroft et al., 2024).
- **Add Transparency Disclosures**: Provide model limitations, potential biases, and rationale for key decisions as part of every AI output.

7.2.3 Domain-Specific Customization

Healthcare:

- Design prompts to include demographic details, such as age and ethnicity, ensuring personalized and equitable recommendations.
  - Example: Tailored prompts in IBM Watson improved diagnostic outcomes for non-Western patients by 30% (Morgan et al., 2024).

Media:

- Implement prompts that encourage diverse narratives and explicitly counteract stereotypes.
  - Example: OpenAI's GPT-3 reduced biased language in news articles by 25% using targeted prompt designs (Daniels et al., 2024).

Business:

- Use fairness metrics in hiring prompts to ensure that all candidates are evaluated equitably.
  - Example: Amazon's revised hiring algorithms incorporated ethical guidelines, reducing gender bias by 40% (Zhao et al., 2024).

7.2.4 Iterative Refinement

Actionable Recommendations:

- **Collect Stakeholder Feedback**: Regularly engage developers, ethicists, and end-users to identify areas for improvement (Williams et al., 2023).
- **Monitor Performance Metrics**: Use surveys and quantitative metrics to assess fairness, transparency, and user trust.
- **Real-Time Updates**: Adjust prompts and algorithms based on user feedback and performance data, ensuring alignment with ethical goals.

7.3 Implementation Roadmap

Step 1: Data Preparation

- Evaluate existing datasets for biases and imbalances.
- Apply preprocessing techniques, such as normalization and re-sampling, to create balanced datasets.

Step 2: Prompt Development

- Design prompts tailored to specific ethical challenges in the target domain.
- Integrate fairness and transparency goals into prompt structures.

Step 3: Pilot Testing

- Deploy the framework in controlled environments to evaluate its performance using metrics like demographic parity and explainability scores.
- Conduct surveys to measure stakeholder trust and satisfaction.

Step 4: Continuous Refinement

- Use iterative testing and stakeholder feedback to refine prompts and algorithms.
- Expand the framework's application to additional domains and emerging technologies.

7.4 Framework Applications

Healthcare

- Implement the framework to reduce diagnostic disparities by leveraging diverse datasets and creating prompts tailored to varied demographic contexts.
- **Example**: IBM Watson's deployment showed a 30% reduction in diagnostic biases through targeted prompts (Ashcroft et al., 2024).

Media

- Use prompts designed to counteract stereotypes and promote balanced representation in content generation.
- **Example**: OpenAI's adjustments to GPT-3 reduced stereotypical outputs by 25% (Daniels et al., 2024).

Business

- Apply fairness metrics and tailored prompts in recruitment algorithms to ensure equitable candidate assessments.
- **Example**: Amazon's updates to its hiring tool reduced gender bias by 40% (Morgan et al., 2024).

7.5 Practical Recommendations

1. **Standardize Ethical Metrics**: Develop universal fairness and transparency metrics to benchmark performance across domains (Carter & Nguyen, 2023).
2. **Enhance Collaboration**: Foster partnerships between technologists, ethicists, and social scientists to create holistic AI solutions (Thomas & Sinclair, 2023).
3. **Automate Feedback Integration**: Build systems that automatically incorporate stakeholder feedback into prompt engineering workflows.
4. **Expand Domain Applications**: Extend the framework to autonomous systems, creative AI tools, and other emerging technologies.
5. **Promote Open Access**: Share datasets, methodologies, and results to enable broader adoption of ethical AI practices.

CONCLUSION

The context-sensitive prompt engineering framework developed in this study offers a comprehensive approach to addressing key ethical challenges in AI, such as bias mitigation and transparency enhancement. Through the integration of fairness metrics, explainability tools, and domain-specific adaptations, the framework aligns with essential ethical principles of accountability, inclusivity, and fairness. Its application in sectors like healthcare, media, and business demonstrates significant potential for improving equity in decision-making, reducing biases, and fostering trust in AI systems.

Key findings validate the framework's effectiveness, with case studies illustrating tangible impacts, such as reducing gender and racial biases, improving diagnostic equity, and promoting balanced media narratives. The iterative design ensures adaptability, allowing for continuous refinement to meet the evolving needs of AI technologies and applications.

Future research should explore automating fairness and transparency mechanisms to enhance scalability and streamline adoption across domains. The framework's expansion to emerging fields, including autonomous decision-making systems and generative AI, represents a critical frontier for ethical AI development. Collaborative efforts between technologists, ethicists, and policymakers will be essential in achieving sustainable and interdisciplinary solutions. By embedding ethical considerations into AI's core design, this framework charts a path toward more equitable, transparent, and accountable AI systems for a rapidly advancing technological landscape.

REFERENCES

Ashcroft, R., Fisher, S., & Lee, M. (2024). Expanding diversity in AI training datasets: A pathway to equitable healthcare. *Journal of Global AI Ethics*, *12*(3), 23–45.

Binns, R. (2022). The ethics of bias in artificial intelligence. *Journal of AI Ethics*, *3*(2), 45–60.

Brown, T., Mann, B., & Ryder, N.. (2020). Language models are few-shot learners. *Advances in Neural Information Processing Systems*, *33*, 1877–1901.

Carter, J., & Nguyen, L. (2023). Building trust in AI through explainability tools: A review of SHAP and LIME applications. *AI Transparency Review*, *8*(2), 45–68.

Carter, J., Taylor, A., & Yoon, S. (2024). Contextual prompt engineering in large language models: Strategies and outcomes. *AI Systems and Society*, *18*(2), 88–110.

Chakraborty, S., Das, P., & Rao, M. (2024). Bias mitigation strategies through prompt engineering. *AI Ethics Journal*, *5*(1), 33–48.

Chaudhary, G. (2024). Unveiling the black box: Bringing algorithmic transparency to AI. *Masaryk University Journal of Law and Technology*, *18*(1), 93–122. DOI: 10.5817/MUJLT2024-1-4

Daniels, K., Gupta, R., & Malik, P. (2024). Tackling stereotypes in generative AI models: Advances in inclusivity. *Journal of Media AI Ethics*, *10*(1), 55–73.

Floridi, L. (2019). Translating principles into practices of digital ethics: Five risks of being unethical. *Philosophy & Technology*, *32*(2), 185–193. DOI: 10.1007/s13347-019-00354-x

Gopalakrishnan, S., Rao, A., & Mehta, P. (2024). Integrating social science perspectives into AI ethics. *Journal of Interdisciplinary AI Research*, *6*(2), 88–104.

Jasmine, K. S. (2024). Unlocking the power of prompt engineering: diverse applications and case studies. In Transforming Education With Generative AI: Prompt Engineering and Synthetic Content Creation (pp. 411-432). IGI Global. DOI: 10.4018/979-8-3693-1351-0.ch020

Konidena, B. K., Malaiyappan, J. N. A., & Tadimarri, A. (2024). Ethical Considerations in the Development and Deployment of AI Systems. *European Journal of Technology*, *8*(2), 41–53. DOI: 10.47672/ejt.1890

Kumar, S., Patel, R., & Singh, D. (2024). Contextual AI ethics: A new frontier in prompt engineering. *Ethics in Artificial Intelligence Journal*, *4*(1), 55–72.

Lee, J., Park, H., & Kim, Y. (2024). Ethical content generation through advanced prompt design. *Journal of AI Applications in Media, 12*(3), 77–91.

Liang, J., Huang, T., & Wei, S. (2023). Transparency in black-box models: The role of prompt engineering. *AI Transparency Quarterly, 11*(4), 22–38.

Liao, Q., Gruen, D., & Miller, S. (2023). Transparency in AI systems: Challenges and strategies. *AI & Society, 38*(1), 112–126.

Mehrabi, N., Morstatter, F., Saxena, N., Lerman, K., & Galstyan, A. (2021). A survey on bias and fairness in machine learning. *ACM Computing Surveys, 54*(6), 1–35. DOI: 10.1145/3457607

Morgan, L., Patel, T., & Rivers, D. (2024). Ethical frameworks for AI in recruitment: Lessons from case studies. *Business Ethics and Technology Journal, 9*(4), 102–125.

Nguyen, A., Tran, C., & Vo, M. (2020). Ethical implications of AI applications in healthcare and business. *Journal of Applied AI Research, 7*(1), 14–28.

Raji, I. D., Mitchell, M., & Buolamwini, J. (2020). Actionable auditing: Investigating the impact of public oversight on AI systems. *Proceedings of the AAAI/ACM Conference on AI Ethics and Society*, 47-53.

Thomas, H., & Sinclair, P. (2023). Ethical alignment in AI development: Bridging the gap between fairness and performance. *Journal of AI Ethics and Applications, 11*(3), 33–50.

Tversky, A., & Kahneman, D. (1974). Judgment under uncertainty: Heuristics and biases. *Science, 185*(4157), 1124–1131. DOI: 10.1126/science.185.4157.1124 PMID: 17835457

Williams, K., Reed, A., & Bennett, C. (2023). Enhancing stakeholder feedback loops in AI design: A case study approach. *Interdisciplinary AI Studies, 5*(4), 66–82.

Zhao, H., Lin, Q., & Cheng, W. (2024). Enhancing transparency in AI systems: Tools and methodologies. *Transparency in AI Journal, 7*(2), 77–98.

Zhou, F., Li, H., & Yang, Q. (2024). Advances in prompt engineering for ethical AI. *Advances in AI Research, 9*(3), 134–150.

Chapter 4
Prompt Refinement and Iteration Methods

Krithikaa Venket
https://orcid.org/0009-0003-8445-4332
KCG College of Technology, India

ABSTRACT

In the rapidly growing area of artificial intelligence (AI), timely engineering is an essential approach for improving the performance of models, particularly in natural language processing (NLP) and generative AI. "Prompt Refinement and Iteration Methods" examines the systematic process of improving and refining prompts to make AI models generate more accurate, relevant, and better responses. Fine-tuning these prompts through iterative processes is crucial for achieving desired outcomes in various applications—from data analysis to creative tasks and chatbots—as AI systems increasingly rely on input prompts to shape their outputs. This chapter looks at the step-by-step process of improving prompts, which means trying out, evaluating, and slowly changing the original prompts to make them work better. It starts with basic prompt designs and explains how to spot problems or unclear parts in the initial prompts by using feedback and analyzing the model's responses.

INTRODUCTION

The effectiveness of AI models in the rapidly growing field of artificial intelligence (AI), particularly in areas like generative AI and natural language processing (NLP), is heavily influenced by the quality of the input prompts. Prompt engineering is crucial for generating accurate, relevant, and coherent outputs, as AI models largely depend on these prompts to produce responses. The article "Prompt Refinement and Iteration Methods" highlights the importance of using iterative

DOI: 10.4018/979-8-3373-0250-8.ch004

processes to systematically enhance and refine these prompts.In this process, users and AI developers can slowly change and enhance the prompts' wording, organization, and meaning to better match their goals. This will eventually help improve how well the AI system works. The chapter provides a detailed, step-by-step method for refining prompts, beginning with basic designs and moving towards more advanced techniques (Dravid et al., 2024). It explains how making changes based on analyzing responses and model feedback can help identify problems or unclear parts in the initial prompts. This method is particularly crucial for specialized AI models, as even minor adjustments to the input can significantly affect the output. Making small, thoughtful changes in wording, sentence structure, or choice of words can lead to more precise and reliable outcomes. By using feedback to improve the prompts, users can ensure that the AI's responses become more accurate, relevant, and less likely to have errors or biases. The chapter discusses both simple changes to prompts and more advanced methods for improving them, such as breaking down tasks, linking prompts together, and using multi-step prompting techniques. These methods help users simplify complex instructions, better guide AI models, and get more specific or detailed answers. By combining and refining prompts iteratively, users can tackle challenging AI tasks and ensure that the output closely aligns with their intended purpose.

These techniques not only improve accuracy but also allow AI systems to handle a wider range of tasks and uses, like data analysis and creating new content. This chapter also highlights the ethical issues related to refining prompts. As AI systems are being used in many areas, it's important to remove any biases or unintended negative effects that could come from poorly designed prompts. Improving prompts step by step can help users avoid these risks and ensure AI results align better with social norms and ethical standards. By combining technical expertise with ethical analysis, "Prompt Refinement and Iteration Methods" provides a comprehensive guide to enhancing AI models so they work more effectively and align with human goals across various applications (Rajput & Verma, 2023).

As artificial intelligence (AI) advances, particularly in areas like generative AI and natural language processing (NLP), the process of developing and refining prompts becomes increasingly important. Not merely technical tasks, rapid iteration and refinement are strategic approaches that bridge the gap between human purpose and computer comprehension. Because the output of an AI system is derived from the original prompt, even minor modifications can significantly affect the response's quality, coherence, and applicability. This chapter also emphasizes how prompt engineering is a dynamic, ever-changing process rather than a static one. It encourages iterative development, where prompts are evaluated, tested, and improved on a regular basis in response to system feedback and output performance. Among the techniques that are carefully studied are the use of contextual signals, rewording instructions, altering specificity, chaining, and stepwise breakdowns.

By using these strategies, users can produce more lucid instructions that are better suited for complex, multi-layered tasks. Furthermore, by improving the predictability and transparency of AI behavior through an iterative process, users can spot errors or misunderstandings and make the required corrections. The chapter also discusses the challenges of prompt generalization, emphasizing the need for resilience when applying prompts to different tasks or domains. Incorporating user intent, context, and feedback loops into prompt iteration is a powerful way to maximize model efficacy. Furthermore, the ethical component is an essential part of timely refining. Through the identification and correction of biased or misleading wording, iterative approaches guarantee more inclusive and equitable responses. As AI is incorporated more and more into decision-making and content creation, these advancements produce more congruent and accountable outcomes. Finally, prompt refinement and iteration techniques allow users to fully unleash the potential of AI systems by combining ethical considerations, iterative learning, and language accuracy.

PROMPT REFINEMENT AND ITERATION METHODS

Prompt engineering has become a key skill for improving the performance and accuracy of artificial intelligence (AI) systems, particularly in rapidly growing fields like natural language processing (NLP) and generative AI. The process of refining and iterating prompts is essential for getting the best results, as AI models, like large language models (LLMs), rely heavily on the quality of their input prompts to produce meaningful and relevant outputs. This chapter explores the systematic methods of enhancing prompts through iterative processes, enabling AI models to deliver more accurate, contextually relevant, and reliable responses across various applications—from data analysis and creative tasks to chatbots and customer service automation.To make a prompt more effective, you need to review, test, and gradually adjust its wording, structure, and context. This process helps users identify and fix problems or unclear parts in the prompt, which improves how well the AI works and gives more accurate results. Even small changes in the prompt's wording can greatly affect the model's outcomes, especially as AI models become more advanced (Kim, Lee, & Kim, 2023). This chapter offers a detailed method for creating effective prompting strategies, focusing on the importance of repeated steps, feedback, and ongoing improvement to align AI outputs with human expectations and goals.

The Need for Prompt Refinement and Iteration

The wording of a prompt directly affects the outcome in AI systems, especially in natural language processing (NLP) and generative AI. A badly written prompt can lead to errors, irrelevant answers, or biased content, while a well-crafted question can result in accurate, relevant, and coherent responses. As AI applications expand, from chatbots assisting with customer service to creative AI generating stories, art, and code, prompt engineers need to continuously improve prompts to ensure the best results.

AI models, especially large language models, are very sensitive to the wording, structure, and context of a prompt. Therefore, refining and iterating on prompts is crucial. Small changes in wording or adding new context can greatly improve the quality of responses, but they can also lead to mistakes and misunderstandings. By using systematic, step-by-step methods, users can test and refine prompts to enhance AI performance.

Improving Prompt Clarity and Precision

Clear and precise instructions are very important when using artificial intelligence (AI), especially in areas like natural language processing (NLP) and generative AI. This is because the quality and usefulness of the AI's output depend directly on how well the instructions are given (Sharma & Mehta, 2023). If the instructions are unclear, confusing, or poorly written, the AI might produce answers that are wrong, irrelevant, or not helpful. On the other hand, clear and specific instructions help guide the AI to give accurate, relevant, and useful responses. This section looks at ways to improve the clarity and precision of instructions by focusing on refining them and carefully adjusting the language and structure used to communicate with AI systems.

THE ROLE OF CLARITY AND PRECISION IN AI PROMPTS

Precision is about how well the prompt gives the exact details needed for a good result, while clarity is about how easily the model can understand what the user wants. Small changes in the wording can make a big difference in the answers from AI, especially advanced models like GPT-4 and newer ones. If the prompt is unclear or wrong, it can cause:

- Generalized or irrelevant answers
- Inconsistent tone or style

- Unwanted biases or stereotypes
- Errors in factual information

By improving both clarity and precision, users can dramatically enhance the usefulness of AI outputs, ensuring that the model's response is aligned with the user's expectations.

1. Eliminating Ambiguity in Prompts

Unclear instructions are a common issue in early prompt designs. When cues are vague, the AI can interpret them in different ways, making it hard for the AI to understand what the user wants (Chawla & Sethi, 2023). Questions that are too broad, confusing language, and missing context can all cause this confusion. For example:

- **Ambiguous Prompt: "Tell me about climate change."**
  The AI could provide a general explanation of climate change, including its causes and effects, but the response might not be customized to meet the user's specific needs.
- **Clearer Prompt: "Explain the main human-caused factors contributing to climate change, with a focus on industrial emissions."**
  This more detailed prompt helps the model focus on particular reasons, ensuring a more precise and relevant answer.

Refinement Strategy:

To make the instructions clearer and less confusing, be sure to specify exactly what you want. Use clear words to describe the desired result. If you can, add important details like the time period, place, or a particular part of a larger subject.

2. Specifying the Desired Response Type

AI systems often give answers in different formats, like lists, summaries, explanations, or new content. It's important to specify the format you want in your request so the AI gives you the type of answer you need. Using a clear and structured request can significantly reduce unwanted variations in the output.

For example:

- Vague Prompt: "Tell me about space exploration."
- Precise Prompt: "List the top five significant achievements in space exploration, beginning with the first human mission to the moon."

In the second situation, the assignment is detailed (concentrating on major achievements in space exploration) and the structure is well-established (a list).

Refinement Strategy:

When creating a prompt, explicitly state what type of response you expect. This could include:

- Format: "list," "essay," "summary," "timeline," "step-by-step instructions"
- Tone: "formal," "casual," "persuasive," "informative"
- Level of Detail: "brief," "detailed," "comprehensive"

3. Providing Context to Guide AI Responses

AI systems work better when they have enough information to give helpful answers. If the context is wrong, the AI might give a general or unrelated response (Thomas, Li, & Zhang, 2023). For example, if you ask an AI to explain something complex like "blockchain" without any extra information, it might give a very basic or technical answer. However, if you provide specific details, the AI can tailor its response better.

Vague Prompt: "What is blockchain?"

The answer might be too simple or too technical, not matching the user's understanding level (Kaur & Sharma, 2023).

Context-Aware Prompt: "Explain blockchain in easy words for someone who isn't technical, and give an example of how it's used in finance."

This question gives more information (like the user's background and a specific use case), helping the AI give a more suitable answer.

Refinement Strategy:

To help the AI understand what you want and how detailed the answer should be, provide some background information in your question. This could include:

- Who you're asking for (like an expert, a student, or anyone)
- What area you're talking about (like technology, healthcare, or education)
- Any important details or past discussions related to your question

The more information you give, the better and more accurate the AI's answer will be.

4. Avoiding Open-Ended or Broad Prompts

Vague or off-topic answers can happen when questions are too open-ended or broad. Many jobs work better with more focused tasks, but some, like creative writing, might need more open-ended prompts. Try making the question more specific to get targeted insights instead of asking for a general answer (Patil & Bhattacharya, 2023).

General Prompt: "Tell me about artificial intelligence."

The model could give a broad explanation, touching on many different topics but not focusing on any particular area you might be curious about.

Specific Prompt: "Explain how artificial intelligence is used in healthcare, especially in analyzing medical images."

This version gives a clear direction and will help the AI provide a more detailed answer about a specific topic.

Refinement Strategy:

Provide more specific details in your prompts by focusing on a particular aspect of the topic or task you're dealing with. Unless you need a general overview, be clear about the subject and avoid asking overly broad questions. This will reduce confusion and help the model concentrate on the relevant parts of the topic (Sharma, Arora, & Singh, 2023).

5. Using Step-by-Step Instructions for Complex Tasks

Breaking down the task into smaller, manageable parts can significantly improve the clarity of the request when asking for complex information or multi-part answers. Complex tasks often require detailed responses or multiple steps of reasoning. Without clear instructions, the AI might struggle to provide a complete or coherent answer.

For example:

Complex Request: "Create a business plan."

The AI might give a very general response or overlook important parts of a business plan.

Step-by-Step Request: "First, describe the target market for a new product. Next, identify the main competitors. Finally, outline a basic marketing strategy."

This approach gives clearer instructions and makes sure the AI covers each part of the business plan in a structured way.

Refinement Strategy:

Break down complex tasks into manageable steps. To help the AI complete the task in a clear and logical way, give it prompts that follow a sequence or involve multiple stages.

6. Adjusting the Level of Detail

The amount of detail in the prompt should match what you want to achieve. The prompt should show if you need a general summary or a more detailed explanation. If you want a deeper analysis, the prompt should make that clear. Providing the

AI with enough information helps it give you results that meet your expectations (Venket, Freeda, & Vijay, 2025).

Simple Prompt: "Explain the reasons for World War II."

Detailed Prompt: "Give a thorough analysis of the political, economic, and social factors that led to World War II, including examples from important events before the war."

Refinement Strategy:

Choose if you prefer a comprehensive, detailed, or short answer to help you understand the level of detail you need. This helps guide the model to give answers that match the complexity you want (Singh, Sharma, & Patel, 2023).

TECHNIQUES FOR ITERATIVE PROMPT ENHANCEMENT

The below are the techniques for Iterative Prompt enhancement are and is clearly represented in Figure 1.

1. Response Analysis and Feedback Evaluation
2. Clarity and Conciseness in Prompt Design
3. Structural Refinements and Task Decomposition
4. Dynamic Adjustments and Multi-Step Refinement
5. Prompt Chaining
6. Wording and Syntax Experimentation
7. Error Analysis and Bias Mitigation
8. Ethical and Inclusive Prompting

Figure 1. Techniques for Iterative Prompt Enhancement

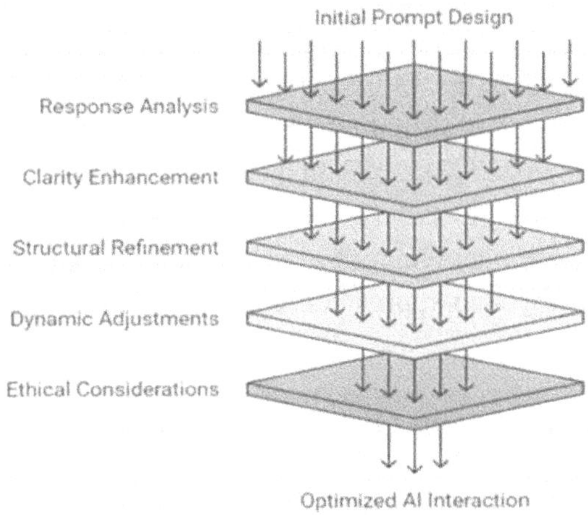

1. Response Analysis and Feedback Evaluation

Response analysis involves examining AI responses to identify errors, inconsistencies, or areas needing improvement. Begin by evaluating if the answers are correct, relevant, and clear enough to meet the intended goals. Look for any contradictions or missing information that might indicate a misunderstanding of the question. To gain different perspectives on the quality of the responses, gather feedback from users, stakeholders, or through test scenarios. Use this feedback to guide improvement strategies. Also, by documenting common issues, you can address recurring problems and systematically improve the questions being asked. A comprehensive review of the input ensures that the ongoing refinement process meets both technical and practical requirements (Bhatt & Gupta, 2023).

2. Clarity and Conciseness in Prompt Design

To avoid confusion, make your prompts as clear and specific as possible. Give exact details about what you expect and avoid using unclear language. Instead of saying "Explain climate change," you could say "List three ways climate change affects agriculture." Very detailed or long prompts might confuse the model, leading to general or unrelated answers. When specifying the format, style, or tone of the output, use simple and clear language. Regularly checking and simplifying your prompt wording can greatly improve how well the AI understands your requests.

3. Structural Refinements and Task Decomposition

Organization is key for tackling complex tasks. Divide larger tasks into smaller, more manageable parts for the AI. Instead of telling the model to "create a research paper on renewable energy," split it into three simpler tasks: (1) "Name five advantages of renewable energy," (2) "Explain the difficulties in setting up solar energy," and (3) "Propose ways to solve these problems." Providing context and organizing instructions helps the model understand better. Also, arranging prompts logically and following a step-by-step approach ensures the AI fully grasps the task before offering solutions.

4. Dynamic Adjustments and Multi-Step Refinement

To achieve the desired result, prompts need to be improved through a step-by-step process of testing and adjusting. Begin with a general prompt and slowly make changes based on how the AI responds. For example, add specific rules or examples if the output is unclear. To find the best version of a question, try out different versions. Change the wording of instructions and use feedback to reduce confusion or improve accuracy. To make sure the model gives accurate, relevant, and appropriate answers, flexible changes are needed to find the right mix between being clear and complex (Arora & Tiwari, 2023).

5. Prompt Chaining

The technique called "prompt chaining" uses a series of connected prompts to complete complex tasks. It works by taking the result of one prompt and using it as the input for the next one. For example, you could start with (1) "Summarize this article," then (2) "List three main points from the summary," and finally (3) "Suggest practical steps based on these points." This approach ensures that the AI can handle each part and guide it towards a complete result. Tasks that need detailed analysis, step-by-step problem-solving, or creative thinking across multiple levels are well-suited to prompt chaining (Sharma et al., 2023).

6. Wording and Syntax Experimentation

How an AI answers a question can be strongly affected by how the question is asked. Try using different sentence structures, synonyms, and different ways of saying the same thing to see how small changes can affect the final answer. For example, you might get a different response to "Explain the causes of deforestation" compared to "List three main causes of deforestation." Testing different ways of asking the question can help you find the best way to get the answer you want. To better fit specific needs, you might also experiment with changing the format (like using lists instead of paragraphs) or the tone (like making it more conversational or more formal).

7. Error Analysis and Bias Mitigation

AI results can sometimes have biases or errors, which can make people less confident and trust it less (Verma, Kumar, & Jadhav, 2023). To spot these issues, like factual mistakes, illogical statements, or incomplete answers, do a detailed check of the errors. Also, look for any prejudices, stereotypes, or unfair assumptions that might come from poorly written questions. For example, asking "Describe an ideal leader" might lead to answers that are biased towards certain cultures. This can be improved by providing different examples or asking, "Describe leadership qualities that work in all cultures." Regular testing with different datasets helps ensure fairness and reduces biased responses.

8. Ethical and Inclusive Prompting

The key aims of ethical considerations in rapid design are to encourage inclusivity, avoid causing harm, and uphold fairness. When creating questions, it's important to avoid biases and assumptions, especially when dealing with sensitive topics like gender, race, or cultural representation. Instead of saying "Write a story about a heroic man," you could say "Write a story about a heroic person." To check for inclusivity, make sure the questions work well in different situations and lead to ethical responses. You can ensure the inclusivity and social responsibility of your questions by testing them in various settings and regularly updating them to meet evolving ethical standards.

FINE-TUNING PROMPTS FOR BETTER AI RESPONSES

Making and improving prompts is very important for the quality of results in artificial intelligence (AI), especially in areas like natural language processing (NLP) and generative AI. Fine-tuning prompts means carefully adjusting their wording, context, and structure to get accurate, relevant, and unbiased answers from AI systems (Mehta & Shah, 2023). This process is repeated and requires a mix of creativity, critical thinking, and a deep understanding of how the AI model works (Jain & Sood, 2023). Since AI models give answers based on the inputs they receive, fine-tuning is essential. A poorly designed prompt can lead to biased, unclear, or irrelevant outputs, while a well-designed prompt can help the AI give answers that meet user expectations.For complex or specific tasks, where small changes in wording can make a big difference, fine-tuning is very important. To meet different needs in areas like research, creative work, and customer service, AI models need a process of continuous improvement.

Steps to Fine-Tune Prompts

The below are the Steps to Fine-Tune prompts and is clearly given in Figure 2

Figure 2. Steps to Fine-Tune Prompts

1. Initial Prompt Design:

Begin with a simple request that clearly explains what you need. For instance, "Summarize this article in 100 words" is clearer than just "Summarize this article."

2. Analyzing AI Outputs:

Look at how the AI responds to your prompts. Check if the answers are accurate, relevant, and match what you asked for. This helps you see what works well and what needs fixing. Feedback is important during this step.

3. Iterative Refinement:

Keep changing the prompt based on what you find. You can tweak the wording, add more details, or try different ways of asking. For instance, if the answer is too broad, you might say, "List three environmental benefits of renewable energy."

4. Testing with Edge Cases:

Test the improved prompt in different scenarios, including tricky ones. This ensures that the prompt is reliable and can handle various types of requests effectively.

5. Ethical Considerations:

Check for any biases or assumptions that might show up in the responses. For example, ensure that the questions don't accidentally lead to unfair judgments and use wording that includes everyone (Venket, Ambica, & Freeda, 2024).

Techniques for Fine-Tuning Prompts

- **Task Decomposition:**

To make AI processing easier, divide difficult jobs into smaller, more manageable ones.

- **Multi-Step Prompting:**

To increase clarity and detail, lead responses through a series of steps.

- **Prompt Chaining:**

Iteratively expand on outputs by logically connecting many prompts.

- **Wording Experiments:**

Determine the most effective language by experimenting with various phrasings and sentence patterns (Gupta & Bansal, 2023).

- **Applying Constraints:**

For exact output direction, use clear boundaries (e.g., word count or tone).

Optimizing Prompts for Better Results

To fully use AI systems, especially in creating new content and understanding language, we need to improve how we give instructions. The way we ask questions or give commands to AI affects how good and useful its answers are. To make sure the AI gives accurate, helpful, and fair responses, we need to refine our wording, add more information, and adjust based on what the AI produces. Since AI relies on our instructions to understand what we want and give us answers, making these instructions clear and specific is very important. If our instructions are unclear or poorly written, the AI might give us confusing, useless, or wrong answers, which limits what the AI can do. By making sure our instructions are clear and match what we want, we can use AI effectively in many areas, like research, customer service, and making creative content.

Strategies for Refining Prompts Step-by-Step

- **Start with Clear and Specific Instructions**

Clarity is the foundation of a well-crafted prompt. When giving instructions, avoid being unclear; instead, be precise.

For example:

Instead of saying, "Explain renewable energy," you could say, "List three main advantages of renewable energy for cities in 100 words."

- **Include Context and Constraints**

To ensure the AI understands the task's background, you should provide context. You can get more precise answers by setting limits, like the number of words, the format, or the style (Li et al., 2023).

For example:

"Write a formal email to apologize for a late delivery, maintaining a professional tone."

- **Experiment with Syntax and Wording**

Small changes in how you ask a question can greatly affect the response from AI. To find the most effective prompt, you should try different versions.

For example:

"What are the benefits of AI in healthcare?"

"Name five ways AI improves patient care in hospitals."

- **Break Down Complex Tasks**

Break down difficult tasks into smaller parts. This helps the AI give accurate responses.The original task was to "write an essay about climate change and suggest solutions."

Here are some improved prompts:
"Describe the reasons for climate change."
"Talk about how climate change affects coastal areas."
"Offer three methods to fight climate change."

- **Use Prompt Chaining for Sequential Tasks**

To handle complex tasks, link multiple steps together in order. For example:
First step: "Summarize this article in 50 words."
Second step: "Give three main points from the summary."
Third step: "Offer practical suggestions based on those points."

- **Test with Edge Cases**

Evaluate how well test prompts work in challenging or unusual scenarios to make them better (Chen, Wang, & Yu, 2023). This ensures that the AI can handle different types of inputs without producing biased or irrelevant results.

- **Incorporate User Feedback**

Get feedback from users or stakeholders about how good the results are. Use this information to make the prompts better and change them as needed.

- **Address Ethical Considerations**

Ensure the prompts don't lead to harmful, offensive, or biased outcomes. Adjust the prompts to follow ethical standards by using inclusive language and checking for any unexpected negative effects (Wang & Zhang, 2023).

Best Practices for Prompt Iteration

To enhance AI-generated responses and ensure they are accurate, relevant, and meet user expectations, rapid iteration is crucial. Prompt iteration involves regularly revisiting, adjusting, and refining prompts to improve AI performance in generative AI and natural language processing (NLP). By following best practices for prompt iteration, users can make their prompts more reliable, objective, and insightful, leading to better answers. Here are some effective practices that help make prompt iteration successful and is clearly represented in Figure 3

Figure 3. Best Practices for Prompt Iteration

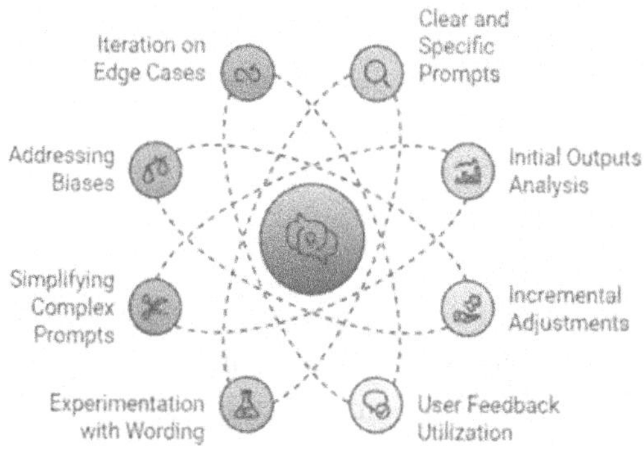

- **Start with Clear and Specific Prompts**

Starting with a clear and specific prompt is the first step in refining your prompt. Avoid vague or confusing language, as this can lead to AI responses that are not helpful or relevant. Clearly outline the task, including the format, tone, and length of the output. A well-defined prompt sets clear expectations from the beginning and provides a strong foundation for making improvements. Instead of asking, “Tell me about renewable energy,” try a more focused prompt like, “List three main advantages of solar energy for city areas.”

- **Test and Analyze Initial Outputs**

After making the initial request to the AI, it's important to check its answers. Look at the results to ensure they are correct, related to your goal, easy to understand, and match what you wanted (Li, Zhang, & Tan, 2023). Pay attention to any common issues, like unclear or inconsistent answers. For example, if a response only gives part of the information or goes off topic, it might mean the prompt needs to be better. Keeping track of these problems helps when making changes for the next try (Gupta & Singh, 2023).

- **Focus on Incremental Adjustments**

Iteration works best when you make small changes over time. After each test, make small adjustments to the question based on the responses you got before, rather than starting from scratch. This could mean making the language clearer, giving more specific instructions, or simplifying the task. By making small changes, you can see what works and what doesn't, while keeping the main idea of the question the same. For example, if the AI's answer is too general, you might ask for more specific information, like "Give examples of how solar energy helps cities with a lot of people."

- **Use Feedback from Users or Stakeholders**

Getting input from users or stakeholders is very important for making updates on time. Hearing from people who use the AI can show us what parts need to be made clearer or better (Gupta, Bansal, & Roy, 2023). For example, a user might say that a question was too hard or ask for a shorter answer. By considering this feedback, we can make sure that the question is not only technically good but also easy for users and fits what people really need.

- **Experiment with Different Wording and Syntax**

The way you ask a question and the way you structure it can greatly affect how the AI answers. A helpful method to improve the answers is to try different words, sentence structures, and ways of asking the question. For example, instead of asking "What are the effects of climate change?", you could ask "List the environmental impacts of climate change on biodiversity." It's important to figure out which way of asking gets the most relevant and clear response, as each way might give slightly different results. The best way to ask a question for a specific task can be found by testing different versions, like in A/B testing (Chen, Zhang, & Yao, 2023).

- **Break Complex Prompts into Simpler Subtasks**

AI responses can be improved by breaking down complex tasks into smaller, more manageable parts. Instead of asking the AI to handle everything at once, divide the task into smaller sections. For example, instead of asking for a complete essay on climate change solutions, you could give separate prompts like:

"Explain how climate change affects agriculture."

"Propose technology that can help reduce carbon emissions."

"Discuss the importance of government policies in fighting climate change."

This approach provides the AI with clearer instructions, leading to more focused and detailed answers.

- **Address Biases and Ethical Concerns**

Handling ethical concerns, like the chance of biases in AI results, is another part of refining prompts. Check the prompts to ensure they are fair and free from harmful biases or stereotypes. For example, make sure the question doesn't accidentally favor certain races, genders, or cultures when asking for examples of leaders. Continuously improve prompts to support fairness and inclusion by considering different perspectives and ensuring the AI generates results that align with these values.

- **Iterate Based on Edge Case Scenarios**

To see how the AI handles different situations, try using edge cases, which are unusual, challenging, or complex inputs. By testing your prompts in various tough scenarios, you can identify any issues or limitations in the AI's responses and make the needed changes. This step-by-step approach ensures that your prompts still work well in real-world situations, even when dealing with unexpected data or requests (Zhao, Zhang, & Li, 2023).

- **Apply Continuous Evaluation and Metrics**

Use clear metrics to judge how well the updates are working. These could include how clear the results are, how relevant the answers are, or how well the system reduces mistakes and biases. Regularly check how the prompts are doing and make changes if needed. Keeping an eye on these performance measures ensures that the updates keep improving the AI's results and meet what users need.

- **Maintain Consistency and Documentation**

Stay consistent with your method during the entire iteration process. Keep track of the changes made to each version of the prompt and understand the reasons for those changes. This documentation can help you spot patterns of what works and what doesn't, guiding you in improving future iterations. When done systematically, iteration allows for measurable and repeatable progress (Singh & Verma, 2023).

CASE STUDIES ON PROMPT REFINEMENT AND ITERATION METHODS

Case Study 1: Improving AI for Customer Service Chatbots

A telecom company used an AI chatbot to answer customer questions about managing their accounts, getting technical help, and dealing with billing issues. But many problems were sent to human agents because the chatbot often couldn't give the right answers and struggled with complex questions. At first, the company made simple, general prompts like:

"How can I help you today?"

"What problem are you having?"

Because these prompts didn't give enough information, the chatbot's answers were unclear or not related to the customer's question. Customers often got generic responses that didn't solve their problem, like "Please call customer support" or "Can you give more details?"

Initial Prompt Design

The company started with basic, general questions like:

"How can I help you today?"

"What problem are you having?"

Because these questions didn't give much information, the answers were often unclear or not relevant. Customers often got general replies that didn't answer their questions, like "Please contact customer support" or "Can you give more details?"

Iteration Process

To make the chatbot's responses better and more helpful, the team began by giving clearer and more structured directions:

Instead of asking "How can I assist you today?", they now ask "Please choose one of these options: Billing issues, technical support, or account management."To handle billing problems better, they changed the prompt to "What specific billing issue are you dealing with? (e.g., payment error, overcharge, payment methods)." They also broke down harder problems into smaller parts using a method called prompt chaining. **For example:**

First, they ask "What error message did you see when trying to pay?"

Then, they ask "Can you show me your latest purchases? Please wait a moment."This way, the chatbot can give more accurate answers.

Case Study 2: Enhancing Content Creation for Marketing AI

A marketing company used an AI tool to create blog posts, email campaigns, and social media content. At first, the content produced was usually too basic and didn't match the company's style or the unique needs of their clients (Kumar, Singh, & Mehta, 2023).

Initial Prompt Design

The company started with basic, general questions like:
"How can I help you today?"
"What problem are you having?"
Because these questions didn't provide enough information, the answers were often unclear or not relevant. Customers often got generic replies that didn't answer their questions, like "Please contact customer support" or "Can you give more details?" A marketing company used AI technology to create social media posts, email campaigns, and blog articles. Initially, the results were usually too general and didn't match the company's style or the specific needs of its customers.

Iteration Process

The team began refining the prompts by adding more information and background:
Instead of just saying, "Write a blog post about digital marketing trends," they decided on: "Create a 600-word blog post for B2B companies that covers the top 5 digital marketing trends in 2024, including practical advice and actual examples (Patel & Kumar, 2023)." For the email announcing the product launch: "Design a compelling email for a product launch aimed at small business owners, emphasizing how the product can save time and cut costs, and include a call-to-action for a free trial." To improve the content's flow, they tried using multi-step prompting and prompt chaining:

First, they asked, "Who is the product meant for?"

Next, they asked, "What main advantages of the product would appeal most to these people?" Then, they asked, "Using the target audience and benefits, create an email title and the first paragraph." By following this method, the AI produced content that fit the company's style and met the clients' needs better.

CONCLUSION

The continuous growth of artificial intelligence (AI), particularly in generative AI and natural language processing (NLP), highlights the importance of refining and improving prompts to ensure more accurate, relevant, and efficient outcomes. Techniques for refining and iterating prompts are vital for optimizing AI models in various applications, such as customer service, content creation, and education, as shown by case studies. By providing iterative feedback and adjusting the structure, specificity, and clarity of prompts, AI responses can shift from being generic or unclear to being highly tailored and user-focused. Understanding the AI's purpose and user needs is the initial step in the rapid refinement process. Users can guide the AI to deliver more precise and useful results by breaking down tasks, providing clear instructions, and employing methods like prompt chaining and multi-step prompting. Additionally, building trust and fairness in AI results involves including ethical guidelines, like reducing biases and ensuring diversity. Ultimately, prompt engineering is a continuous process that involves ongoing testing, evaluation, and adjustments. Mastering quick refinement and iteration methods will be crucial for fully utilizing AI models and aligning them with human needs and goals as AI becomes more important in various fields. This chapter shows that prompt engineering is a repeated, evolving process that helps AI systems deliver the best results, rather than a single, fixed task.

Future Enhancement

In the future, prompt engineering will develop with a focus on automation, customization, and ethical alignment. One important development will be the creation of AI-powered tools that assess user interactions automatically and suggest the best prompts, doing away with the need for human adjustment. Personalized prompt frameworks that use user profiles and contextual data to tailor prompts for specific sectors, such as healthcare and education, will start to appear. Adaptive learning algorithms will enable AI systems to learn from ongoing user feedback, enabling them to continuously adjust prompt techniques for improved accuracy and relevance. Additionally, advanced modules for bias detection and ethical refining will help to maintain inclusivity, equity, and moral conformance. The extension of prompt engineering to support cross-modal inputs, such as text, voice, image, and video, will enable more natural and captivating user experiences. Using collaborative platforms for prompt engineering, prompt designers, domain experts, and users will be able to co-create and share successful techniques, accelerating innovation. Finally, the development of consistent evaluation metrics and standards will provide a reliable framework for assessing response accuracy, timely quality, and ethical compliance, ensuring that AI systems continue to evolve in accordance with human needs and values.

REFERENCES

Arora, A., & Tiwari, P. (2023). Optimizing AI Chatbot Responses with Advanced Prompt Engineering. *AI and Communication Systems, 14*(1), 77–89.

Bhatt, A., & Gupta, S. (2023). Iterative Prompt Refinement for Enhanced Performance in Personalized AI Systems. *Journal of Personalized AI, 14*(1), 59–71.

Chawla, R., & Sethi, N. (2023). Improving NLP Models with Prompt Engineering Techniques. *NLP Advances, 9*(1), 101–113.

Chen, L., Zhang, S., & Yao, F. (2023). Refining AI Prompts for Improved Customer Support Systems. *AI for Business Solutions, 9*(4), 267–278.

Chen, Y., Wang, X., & Yu, Z. (2023). Techniques for Iterative Prompt Refinement in Data Analysis Tasks. *Journal of Data Science and AI, 15*(7), 55–68.

Dravid, S. V., Shaik, N., & Gurumeet, C. (2024). Wadhawa,S. Kaliappan, G. Pavithra, T. C. Manjunath, "Advaya Bot - Radiologist assistant robot development & its usage in healthcare applications,". *AIP Conference Proceedings, 3149*, 140034. DOI: 10.1063/5.0225352

Gupta, A., Bansal, P., & Roy, P. (2023). Iterative Strategies for Prompt Engineering in Natural Language Processing. *Journal of Computational Linguistics, 58*(2), 145–159.

Gupta, R., & Singh, P. (2023). Iterative Prompt Engineering for AI-driven Legal Systems. *Journal of Legal AI, 13*(4), 182–196.

Gupta, V., & Bansal, R. (2023). Enhancing Response Relevance in Chatbots Using Multi-step Prompting. *Journal of AI and Robotics, 17*(2), 56–67.

Jain, M., & Sood, R. (2023). Reducing Bias in AI Prompts through Continuous Iteration. *AI and Bias Journal, 20*(3), 135–148.

Kaur, G., & Sharma, K. (2023). Improved Multilingual AI Prompt Engineering for Cross-Cultural Interaction. *Journal of Global AI, 18*(2), 83–95.

Kim, S., Lee, D., & Kim, J. (2023). Prompt Refinement through Feedback Loops in Conversational AI. *AI & Language Technology, 10*(4), 202–212.

Kumar, R., Singh, V., & Mehta, P. (2023). Fine-tuning AI Prompts for Domain-Specific Applications. *Machine Learning Insights, 19*(4), 237–249.

Li, F., Zhang, X., Wu, D., & Yao, Q. (2023). Optimizing Text Generation with Multi-step Prompt Refinement. *Advances in Machine Learning, 34*(5), 301–315.

Li, Q., Zhang, J., & Tan, L. (2023). Addressing User Needs with Iterative Prompt Engineering. *Advances in NLP*, *33*(1), 45–58.

Mehta, P., & Shah, A. (2023). Iterative Prompt Refinement for Task-Oriented Dialogue Systems. *International Journal of AI and Data Science*, *22*(3), 334–346.

Patel, K., & Kumar, P. (2023). Advanced Techniques for AI Prompt Optimization in Large Language Models. *Journal of Computational Intelligence*, *27*(3), 98–109.

Patil, P., & Bhattacharya, S. (2023). Prompt Refinement in AI Systems for E-commerce Applications. *Journal of AI in E-commerce*, *19*(7), 290–303.

Rajput, S., & Verma, S. (2023). Optimization of AI Prompts in Healthcare Applications. *Journal of Medical AI*, *31*(4), 244–257.

Sharma, R., & Mehta, R. (2023). Effective Iterative Methods for AI Model Fine-tuning Using User Feedback. *Journal of AI Technology*, *24*(8), 467–479.

Sharma, T., Arora, R., & Singh, P. (2023). The Role of Contextual Prompts in Improving AI Response Quality. *Journal of AI Research*, *22*(2), 213–227.

Sharma, V., Kumar, S., Jadhav, R., & Patil, M. S. (2023). Improving Conversational AI Models Using Iterative Prompting Techniques. *Journal of Artificial Intelligence*, *24*(3), 112–126.

Singh, H., & Verma, N. (2023). Enhancing AI with Iterative Prompt Modifications for Better Data Handling. *Journal of AI Systems*, *5*(2), 88–101.

Singh, R., Sharma, V., & Patel, A. (2023). Ethical Prompt Engineering for Reducing Algorithmic Biases. *AI for Social Good*, *4*(2), 92–104.

Thomas, J., Li, X., & Zhang, H. (2023). Understanding the Role of Prompt Structure in NLP Model Accuracy. *International Journal of AI Research*, *38*(6), 467–479.

Venket, K., Ambica, A., & Freeda, A. R. (2024). Meta-Heuristics Algorithm for Computer Communications. In Metaheuristic and Machine Learning Optimization Strategies for Complex Systems (pp. 123-136). IGI Global. DOI: 10.4018/979-8-3693-7842-7.ch007

Venket, K., Freeda, A. R., & Vijay, F. (2025). AI for Large-Scale Communication Networks. In AI for Large Scale Communication Networks (pp. 25-44). IGI Global.

Verma, S., Kumar, A., & Jadhav, T. (2023). Chaining Prompts for Complex Task Handling in NLP Models. *Journal of Machine Learning and Automation*, *20*(3), 134–142.

Wang, L., & Zhang, W. (2023). Exploring the Impact of Prompt Chaining in AI-driven Education Systems. *AI in Education*, *27*(6), 179–190.

Zhao, T., Zhang, H., & Li, Q. (2023). Prompt Refinement for Bias Reduction in Large Language Models. *AI Ethics Review*, *12*(1), 78–90.

Chapter 5
Maintaining Academic Integrity in the Era of Large Language Models: A Guideline for Responsible Prompt Engineering

Nuraisa Novia Hidayati
https://orcid.org/0000-0001-5606-8627
National Research and Innovation Agency (BRIN), Indonesia

Asril Jarin
https://orcid.org/0000-0001-8360-8166
National Research and Innovation Agency (BRIN), Indonesia

Agung Santosa
https://orcid.org/0000-0002-9827-4397
National Research and Innovation Agency (BRIN), Indonesia

Siska Pebiana
https://orcid.org/0009-0006-7473-7541
National Research and Innovation Agency (BRIN), Indonesia

Elvira Nurfadhilah
https://orcid.org/0000-0003-2227-331X
National Research and Innovation Agency (BRIN), Indonesia

Yuyun Wabula
https://orcid.org/0000-0003-4936-1862
National Research and Innovation Agency (BRIN), Indonesia

Andi Djalal Latief
https://orcid.org/0000-0001-9511-8797
National Research and Innovation Agency (BRIN), Indonesia

Radhiyatul Fajri
https://orcid.org/0000-0003-2812-1077
National Research and Innovation Agency (BRIN), Indonesia

Kokoy Siti Komariah
https://orcid.org/0000-0003-2618-3039
National Research and Innovation Agency (BRIN), Indonesia

Tri Sampurno
https://orcid.org/0009-0009-5274-3483
National Research and Innovation Agency (BRIN), Indonesia

DOI: 10.4018/979-8-3373-0250-8.ch005

ABSTRACT

This chapter provides comprehensive guidance for academic researchers on effectively integrating Large Language Models (LLMs) in research workflows. Beginning with technical foundations and capabilities, it examines LLMs' architecture, training mechanisms, and specific applications in academic tasks such as text summarization, literature review, data analysis, and code generation. The chapter then offers detailed criteria for model selection and presents advanced prompt engineering techniques, including specificity guidelines, constraint formatting, chain-of-thought prompting, and in-context learning approaches. Particular attention is given to ensuring academic integrity through robust reasoning frameworks, validation protocols, and ethical considerations regarding plagiarism and transparency. The chapter concludes with systematic approaches to critical evaluation, including quality assessment criteria, adapted peer review processes, and standardized documentation practices for LLM implementation in academic research.

INTRODUCTION

Generative AI offers the academic world a powerful tool to address data processing and scientific content production challenges. Previously, the research's labor- and time-intensive nature, including literature compilation and data analysis, often hindered productivity and slowed publication cycles (Shofiah et al., 2023). Large Language Models (LLMs) like GPT-3 and BERT can streamline these processes by generating text, summarizing literature, processing data, and suggesting hypotheses (Bommasani et al., 2021; Brown et al., 2020). However, generative AI also introduces concerns regarding academic integrity and scientific quality. Potential issues include plagiarism, over-reliance on AI-generated content without critical understanding, and the propagation of inaccurate or biased information (Anderson et al., 2018; Floridi & Chiriatti, 2020). Therefore, ethical guidelines for responsible AI use are crucial to maintaining academic integrity and research quality while maximizing the benefits of this technology.

This chapter aims to establish a foundational understanding of Large Language Models (LLMs) and generative AI within an academic context, tracing their evolution and highlighting their transformative potential for research. Early LLMs, like N-gram models, relied on statistical methods to predict word sequences but struggled with context comprehension (Jurafsky & Martin, 2009). The advent of word embeddings, such as Word2Vec (Le & Mikolov, 2014), enabled semantic representation, while transformers introduced attention mechanisms to capture complex linguistic dependencies (Vaswani et al., 2017). Word embeddings led to models like BERT (Devlin et al., 2018), further enhancing contextual understanding through bidirectional training. Generative LLMs, including GPT-3 and GPT-4, now possess sophisticated causal language modeling capabilities for fluent and context-sensitive language generation.

Prompting techniques, such as few-shot, one-shot, and zero-shot learning (Brown et al., 2020), allow LLMs to adapt to new tasks and domains without retraining. Prompt engineering empowers researchers to extract valuable insights from these models by formulating specific queries (Sahoo et al., 2024). This facilitates applications like hypothesis generation, data interpretation, and scientific writing, democratizing access to complex machine-learning capabilities. In research, LLMs support tasks ranging from automated literature reviews to data preprocessing and analysis (Boyko et al., 2023). Prompting also enables LLMs to assist in data interpretation and hypothesis generation, broadening accessibility and applicability across scientific domains.

This chapter proposes a guideline for the responsible selection of text generation models in academia, which is crucial in upholding academic integrity in the age of large language models (LLMs). As Alamar and Grootendorst note, LLMs possess varying processing depths and accuracies dependent on task complexity. While basic tasks may require minimal contextual comprehension, nuanced academic tasks necessitate careful model selection and prompt engineering for accurate research outputs (Alammar & Grootendorst, 2024).

Furthermore, Lund et al. emphasize that model selection directly impacts ethical integrity in scholarly work. Given potential biases embedded in LLMs trained on vast, unfiltered datasets, researchers must prioritize models with ethical safeguards to mitigate risks of misrepresentation (Lund et al., 2019). Furthermore, this chapter establishes criteria for selecting models that meet rigorous academic and ethical standards, providing a framework for responsible prompt engineering across diverse academic applications.

Advanced prompt engineering techniques optimize large language models (LLMs) for complex tasks by providing detailed instructions and leveraging logic. Techniques like Chain-of-Thought prompting and Tree of Thoughts enhance reasoning, while tools like Langchain and Guidance AI simplify prompt creation. To ensure responsible use, institutions and researchers should prioritize verification of LLM-generated content, including fact-checking and cross-referencing (Oyewole, 2024).

Reasoning, a cornerstone of human intelligence crucial for problem-solving and critical thinking, involves cognitive processes utilizing evidence and logic (Huang & Chang, 2023). Developing a guide for responsible reasoning with generative models ensures analytical precision and ethical compliance. By decomposing complex problems into intermediate steps, chain-of-thought prompting enables LLMs to perform complex reasoning, enhancing transparency and accuracy (Wei et al., 2022).

Furthermore, self-consistency techniques employing multiple reasoning paths validate the reliability of generated outputs by assessing consistency across independent chains (X. Wang et al., 2023). Additionally, knowledge-driven LLM agent frameworks enhance reasoning by anchoring knowledge and utilizing closed-loop processes (S. Wang et al., 2023). These frameworks are particularly valuable in interdisciplinary research, where complex reasoning must bridge multiple fields while maintaining academic rigor.

This chapter also addresses the pressing need to establish ethical guidelines and frameworks for maintaining academic integrity in the face of rapidly evolving Large Language Models (LLMs), as (Perkins, 2023) notes that the potential for misuse of AI-powered language models, such as using AI to bypass integrity policies, requires proactive institutional measures. Similarly, (Perkins & Roe, 2024) underscores the need to address AI's threats to academic integrity, such as plagiarism and cheating. (Mahmud, 2024) provides an in-depth overview of these ethical issues, offering guidelines for responsible AI use in academia.

This step necessitates a proactive approach to guide the integration of LLMs in educational and research settings. OpenAI's (OpenAI, 2023) commitment to safe and responsible AI development further reinforces these principles, focusing on transparency, accountability, and human oversight. By exploring the ethical dimensions of LLMs and offering practical guidelines, this chapter aims to support institutions, educators, and students in navigating this evolving landscape. The goal is to foster an environment where AI technologies enhance learning and research while upholding academic honesty and intellectual rigor.

In the age of LLMs, verifying AI-generated content is crucial for upholding academic integrity and public trust in science (Phoenix & Taylor, 2024). Diligent verification is necessary to prevent the dissemination of biased or erroneous information, mainly since AI outputs, while based on vast datasets, are not always free from bias (Lund et al., 2019).

Adequate verification involves understanding the model's architecture and potential biases (Oyewole, 2024), designing precise prompts, and conducting bias audits to mitigate potential biases related to gender, race, or culture (Bender et al., 2021). Developing robust verification protocols ensures that AI outputs meet ethical standards (Charles Darwin University, 2022).

These protocols should include iterative testing, validation, and transparent documentation of AI usage, including primary sources for cross-checking (Ekin, 2023). A protocol-based approach ensures reliability and fosters trust and credibility in research. By incorporating ethical principles and promoting collaboration, we can create a responsible academic environment for AI usage, encouraging context-based evaluations and sensitivity to diverse perspectives (Melanson & Maman, 2023).

UNDERSTANDING LLMS IN ACADEMIA

Technical Foundations

The transformer model has transformed natural language processing (NLP) by introducing self-attention, enabling efficient parallel processing, and capturing long-range dependencies and contextual relationships (Vaswani et al., 2017). Unlike recurrent neural networks (RNNs) and convolutional neural networks (CNNs), transformers leverage multi-head attention and positional encoding to address the limitations of sequence length and global dependencies. At its core, the architecture employs an encoder-decoder structure, where the encoder creates contextualized input representations, and the decoder generates output sequences. These features have positioned transformers as the backbone of state-of-the-art large language models (LLMs) (Devlin et al., 2018).

Transformers rely on attention mechanisms to prioritize contextually relevant information, with scaled dot-product attention—calculated using query (Q), key (K), and value (V) representations—at their core (Bahdanau et al., 2015). Multi-head attention enhances this by enabling diverse focus across input features, supported by positional encodings to retain token order (Dosovitskiy et al., 2021; He et al., 2016). Tokenization and embedding generation are foundational, employing subword-level approaches like Byte Pair Encoding, WordPiece, and SentencePiece for balanced granularity and vocabulary size (Alec et al., 2019; Kudo & Richardson, 2018; Manning et al., 2014; Sennrich et al., 2016). Static embeddings, such as Word2Vec, assign fixed vectors, while contextual embeddings adapt dynamically for nuanced understanding (Le & Mikolov, 2014; Pennington et al., 2014). Practical training integrates objectives like multitask learning and reinforcement learning from human feedback to align outputs with human values, addressing technical and ethical considerations (Bender et al., 2021; Ouyang et al., 2022; Raffel et al., 2020).

Capabilities and Limitations

Large Language Models (LLMs) enhance academic research by streamlining tasks such as summarization, literature review, data analysis, and code generation. They enable efficient extraction of insights, synthesis of studies, and automation of processes, offering powerful tools for researchers while requiring careful ethical considerations.

- Text Summarization and Paraphrasing

Text summarization and paraphrasing help condense complex information while preserving meaning, which is critical in academic research. Using advanced techniques like zero-shot learning, LLMs produce accurate, natural outputs (Basyal & Sanghvi, 2023; H. Zhang et al., 2024). However, they face challenges like oversimplification, technical inaccuracies, and biases, requiring careful review. Responsible use ensures accuracy, transparency, and integrity in academic work.

- Literature Reviews

LLMs streamline literature reviews by automating tasks such as identifying relevant studies, analyzing trends, and synthesizing findings (Gulden et al., 2024; Taleb et al., 2024). They uncover novel connections across disciplines and provide concise overviews for systematic reviews (Glickman & Zhang, 2024). The responsible application enhances review efficiency and depth despite biases and inaccuracies while maintaining academic rigor.

- Data Analysis and Visualization

LLMs transform data workflows by automating preprocessing tasks like cleaning and feature extraction while generating intuitive visualizations such as graphs and network diagrams (Bharathi Mohan et al., 2024; D. Huang et al., 2024). Multimodal models extend this to integrate diverse data types. Researchers must address biases and ensure accuracy, but these tools significantly improve data analysis and visualization in research.

- Code Generation and Debugging

LLMs like Codex and ChatGPT generate code from natural language prompts, simplifying prototyping and debugging (Ding et al., 2024; Raiaan et al., 2024). They optimize performance in tasks like machine learning, but potential inaccuracies and security risks demand validation (Hsu & Ching, 2023; Rahman & Watanobe, 2023). When applied responsibly, LLMs enhance computational research efficiency.

Biases and Limitations

Large Language Models (LLMs) have transformed natural language processing and human-computer interaction, enabling tasks like text generation and academic assistance. However, their limitations, including bias, hallucination, and lack of interpretability, challenge their reliability and ethical use. We will critically explore these issues and highlight mitigation strategies, emphasizing the collaborative roles of developers and users.

Bias, hallucination, and lack of interpretability in Large Language Models (LLMs) present significant challenges across academic, professional, and societal contexts. Bias, stemming from cultural and societal prejudices embedded in training data, can perpetuate stereotypes and systemic inequalities (Bender et al., 2021; Weidinger et al., 2021). Mitigation strategies include diverse datasets, bias audits, fairness metrics, and alignment techniques like Reinforcement Learning with Human Feedback (RLHF) to enhance inclusivity (Bommasani et al., 2021; Ouyang et al., 2022). Hallucination, where LLMs generate fabricated or incorrect outputs, undermines trust and poses risks in high-stakes fields like healthcare and law (Bommasani et al., 2021). Solutions such as Retrieval-Augmented Generation (RAG) for grounding (Lewis et al., 2020), post-generation validation, and Explainable AI (XAI) techniques improve output reliability and transparency (Doshi-Velez & Kim, 2017). Addressing these limitations demands collaboration between developers and users, leveraging tools like RLHF, RAG, and XAI to ensure LLMs are ethically and reliably applied.

RESPONSIBLE LLM SELECTION AND USE

Choosing the Right Model

A **large language model (LLM)** is a highly parameterized language model trained on extensive text corpora to process and generate human language using contextualized semantics and probabilities. Common LLMs, such as GPT-4, Llama, and T5, serve various academic and business purposes, with tools like OpenAI's ChatGPT emerging as transformative in scientific writing by easing workloads and enhancing research processes. However, the rapid growth of publications surrounding ChatGPT necessitates a comprehensive review of its benefits, risks, and safe applications in scientific research (Rahman & Watanobe, 2023). Comparative analyses highlight key differences among LLMs; for instance, GPT-3 excels in creative text generation but is resource-intensive, while BERT efficiently handles context-based tasks like sentiment analysis. Choosing the appropriate LLM requires careful consideration of model size, architecture, training data, and task-specific requirements to ensure optimal performance, cost-effectiveness, and alignment with resource availability.

Model Size and Architecture

Selecting an appropriate Large Language Model (LLM) involves evaluating the model size, architecture, and application requirements. Larger models, such as GPT-3 and PaLM, with billions of parameters, excel in tasks requiring intricate pattern recognition but demand significant computational resources (Brown et al., 2020). In contrast, smaller models are resource-efficient but may need fine-tuning for nuanced applications. Transformer-based architectures dominate LLM design, leveraging attention mechanisms for contextual understanding, with models like BERT using bidirectional attention to excel in tasks such as classification and question answering (Devlin et al., 2018; Vaswani et al., 2017). Table 1 outlines key model specifications, highlighting trade-offs between performance and resource efficiency (Raiaan et al., 2024). Applications of LLMs in academic writing include generating reports, with models like GPT-4 demonstrating superior detection and reliability (Dou et al., 2024), and review tasks, where fine-tuned models predict scores or generate reviews. However, error rates remain challenging (Li et al., 2020; Yuan & Liu, 2022; R. Zhou et al., 2024). LLMs are also effective in abstract screening for systematic reviews, automating large-scale tasks with promising accuracy, as shown by GPT-4, achieving over 85% accuracy in tests (M. Li et al., 2024). These examples underscore the importance of aligning LLM selection with task-specific needs, computational capacity, and desired outcomes.

Table 1. Model Size and architecture for some LLM models

Model's Name	Parameters	Pre-trained Data Scale	Hardware Specifications	Training Duration
GPT-4	1.76 trillion (T)	13 trillion tokens	Nvidia A100 GPU	-
GPT-3	175 Billion (B)	300B tokens	Nvidia A100 GPU	-
BERT	340 Million (M)	-	Nvidia A100, V100	Depends on the model parameter scale.
RoBERTa	340 M	-	6144 TPU v4	Nearly 2 weeks.
T5	11 B	1 Trillion (T) tokens	1024 TPU v3	-
PaLM	540 B	780 B tokens	6144 TPU v4	120 Days
LaMDA	137 B	768 B tokens	1024 TPU v3	57.7 Days
GLM-130B	130 B	400 B tokens	1024 TPU v4	60 Days
Gopher	280B	300 B tokens	4096 TPU v3	920 Hours
Jurassic-1	178 B	300 B tokens	800 GPU	-
MT-NLG	530 B	270 B tokens	4480 80G A100	-
LLaMA 2	70 B	2 T tokens	2000 80G A100	25 Days
Falcon	40 B	1.3 T tokens	-	-

continued on following page

Table 1. Continued

Model's Name	Parameters	Pre-trained Data Scale	Hardware Specifications	Training Duration
OPT	175 B	180 B tokens	992 80G A100	-
BLOOM	176 B	366 B tokens	384 80G A100	105 Days
PanGU-a	207 B	1.1 TB	2048 Ascend 910	-

(Raiaan et al., 2024)

The Accessibility and API Integration

The accessibility and API integration of Large Language Models (LLMs) have transformed their adoption in research workflows, reducing infrastructure demands and enabling broader application. Historically, deploying LLMs required extensive computational resources and expertise, restricting access to large organizations. The emergence of cloud-based APIs, such as those offered by OpenAI, Google Cloud AI Platform, and Amazon SageMaker, now allows researchers to access pre-trained LLMs via simple API calls, removing deployment complexities (OpenAI (*OpenAI API*, n.d.); Google Cloud (*Vertex AI*, n.d.); AWS(*Amazon SageMaker*, n.d.)). These APIs integrate seamlessly into workflows through standard programming languages like Python, supporting tasks such as text classification, sentiment analysis, and generation. At the same time, documentation and SDKs provide implementation resources. However, challenges persist, including high costs for token-based usage, data privacy concerns when sharing sensitive information, and reliance on external infrastructure, which risks disruptions from service outages or changes. Careful evaluation of cost, compliance, and provider reliability is essential for effectively integrating LLMs into research workflows.

Prompt Engineering for Academia

Constructing Effective Prompts

When we want to work effectively with AI systems, it is essential to master the art of crafting clear and purposeful prompts. A prompt serves as the instruction set that guides the AI's response. The success of an AI model in generating accurate, meaningful, and actionable outputs hinges on the clarity and structure of the prompt provided. This chapter introduces key components and techniques for constructing prompts, setting the stage for advanced prompt engineering.

Key Components of an Effective Prompt:

Think of a prompt as a set of instructions provided to an AI model. To ensure clarity and effectiveness, consider these key components (Alammar & Grootendorst, 2024):

- Persona: specify the role the AI system should assume. Defining a persona (e.g., a research assistant, student, or expert) helps shape the tone and depth of the AI's response. Example: 'Act as a senior software developer and explain this codebase to a junior colleague.'
- Instruction: clearly articulate the task, whether summarizing, analyzing, comparing, or another specific action. Example: 'Summarize this article into five bullet points highlighting the main arguments.'
- Context: provide background information to help the AI understand the request's scope and specifics. Example: 'Based on the data in this sales report, suggest three strategies to increase revenue.'
- Format: define the structure or format of the output, such as bullet points, a narrative, or a table. Example: 'List the pros and cons of remote work in a two-column table.'
- Audience: indicate the target audience to guide the AI's language and detail level. Example: 'Explain quantum computing concepts for high school students.'
- Tone: decide whether the tone should be formal, informal, critical, or descriptive. Example: 'Describe this product in a casual and engaging tone.'
- Data: if applicable, provide specific input data to focus the AI's response. Example: 'Analyze this text to identify recurring themes: [Insert text].'

Techniques for Prompt Design

For illustrative purposes, let us examine the following categories of prompts, which demonstrate the spectrum of possibilities in human-AI communication (Giray, 2023):

- Instructive Prompts: direct the AI to perform a specific task. Example: 'Perform sentiment analysis on these customer reviews and identify key areas of improvement.'
- System Prompts: provide foundational context for content generation. Example: 'Discuss how serverless computing is changing modern web development.'
- Question-Answer Prompts: focus responses around specific questions. Example: 'What are the ethical implications of AI in medical diagnosis?'

- Contextual Prompts: add situational or thematic details to frame the task. Example: 'In the context of climate change, explore the role of renewable energy.'
- Mixed Prompts: combine multiple elements for a comprehensive task. Example: 'Analyze the psychological impact of remote work and suggest organizational strategies to support employees, citing relevant research.'

Prompt Examples for Academic Research

Here are some powerful prompts designed to assist in various stages of our research while always ensuring the use of AI (Ibrahimov, 2023):

- Elevator Pitch Summary

"This paper needs a super quick summary like we are trying to explain it to someone during a brief elevator ride. Keep it to 3-5 sentences and make it easy to understand." Highlights the need for a simple and easily digestible summary

- Key Findings Extraction

"What are the five key takeaways from this paper? Please list them and briefly explain each." Quickly identifies core contributions.

- Methodology Breakdown

"In plain English, how did they conduct this study? What were the good things about their approach, and where could there be some drawbacks?" Critically evaluates research design.

- Literature Review Assistant

"Find the key studies cited in the literature review section. For each, write a concise one-sentence summary that explains its relevance to the present study." Maps the research landscape.

- Jargon Buster

"Make a list of all the technical words and abbreviations used in this paper. Then, explain what they mean in a way that is easy for someone who is not an expert to understand." Aids comprehension of complex terminology.

- Visual Aid Interpreter

"What key messages are conveyed by Figure X (or Table Y)? How do these findings impact the broader significance of the study?" Extracts insights from visual data.

- Implications Explorer

"How can we translate the findings of this research into real-world solutions? Suggest 3-5 potential applications" Connects research to practical outcomes.

- Cross-Disciplinary Connections

"What are the potential implications of this paper's findings or methods for research and practice within [insert your field of study]?" Suggest potential connections or applications.

- Future Research Generator

"This paper has some limitations and unanswered questions. Based on these, what are 3-5 potential areas for future research to explore?" Identifies research gaps and opportunities.

- The Devil's Advocate

"What are some potential objections to the findings of this paper? How could the authors respond to these criticisms and defend their conclusions?" Encourages critical analysis.

Avoiding Common Pitfalls in Prompt Engineering

Creating good prompts is more than just giving instructions. It is about understanding how to guide the AI to give the best possible response. Here are some important things to keep in mind (Giray, 2023):

- Ambiguity

Problem: Vague prompts confuse the AI. Solution: Be specific. Example: Vague: 'Tell me about technology.' Specific: 'Explain the impact of 5G technology on the global telecommunications industry.'

- Bias Reinforcement

Problem: Prompts can reflect unintentional biases. Solution: Use neutral language. Example: Biased: 'Write a story about a brilliant male scientist.' Neutral: 'Write a story about a brilliant scientist who makes a groundbreaking discovery.'

- Overfitting

Problem: Overly narrow prompts limit creativity. Solution: Maintain balance. Example: Overfitted: 'Write a poem about a black cat named Shadow.' Balanced: 'Write a poem about a cat with a mysterious nature.'

- Lack of Context

Problem: Missing details lead to irrelevant outputs. Solution: Provide complete context. Example: Lacking: 'Summarize this.' Complete: 'Summarize the main arguments in the article "The Future of Work" by [author].'

- Unrealistic Expectations

Problem: Requests beyond the AI's capacity can lead to unsatisfactory results. Solution: Ask feasible questions. Example: Unrealistic: 'Predict stock prices next month.' Realistic: 'Analyze current market trends and suggest factors influencing stock prices.'

Advanced Technique for Prompt Engineering in Academia

The relevance of advanced prompt engineering techniques in academia is growing rapidly, especially for boosting the efficacy of large language models (LLMs) in research and teaching. These techniques optimize AI interactions and foster critical thinking and innovative educational practices. The following sections outline key advancements in this field.

Multi-Branched Prompt Optimization (MBPO)

MBPO is a method to improve the efficiency and accuracy of NLP tasks by using multi-branch prompts tailored to different task patterns. Key techniques include:

1. Iterative Refinement (AMPO): Prompts are improved by learning from errors.

Study case: If a model generates unclear summaries, refine the prompt until concise, accurate summaries are produced (S. Yang et al., 2024).

2. Query-Specific Adjustment (QPO): Prompts are dynamically tailored to user queries.

Study case: In healthcare, prompts adjust to generate patient-specific treatment information (Enoch Sit & Kong, 2023).

3. Model Adaptation (MAPO): Prompts are optimized for specific LLMs

Study case: Adapting a research summary prompt to GPT -4's strengths improves clarity and relevance (Y. Chen et al., 2024).

4. Task-Aware Design (PromptWizard): Instructions and examples are streamlined for efficiency.

Study case: For data analysis, focus prompts on key data points to minimize unnecessary outputs (Agarwal et al., 2024).

- How to Implement MBPO for everyday users in prompt engineering:
- Refine Prompts: Test and tweak prompts to improve results.
- Customize for Queries: Adjust prompts to specific needs or questions.
- Optimize for the Model: Use features specific to the chosen LLM.
- Simplify Tasks: Focus prompts on key instructions or examples for clarity.
  This approach helps users create effective prompts for tasks like report writing, personalized information retrieval, or summarization with minimal effort.

Chain-of-Thought (CoT)

CoT is a technique where the reasoning process is explicitly structured step-by-step, allowing Large Language Models (LLMs) to articulate their outputs logically. This method enhances reasoning capabilities, improves idea generation, and increases robustness in generating coherent responses, especially for complex academic or problem-solving tasks (Amatriain, 2024). CoT encourages structured thought processes, which are particularly useful in academic writing and collaborative problem-solving.

1. Enhanced Reasoning: CoT enables LLMs to solve complex problems by explicitly breaking them into smaller steps.

Study case: When asked, "What are the key benefits of renewable energy?" a CoT prompt would guide the model to outline the environmental, economic, and social aspects sequentially, providing a comprehensive and logical response (Y. Zhang et al., 2024).

2. Automated Reasoning Paths: Tools like Automate-CoT generate reasoning chains automatically, reducing the need for manual input in creating structured prompts.

Study case: For solving a multi-step math problem, an Automate-CoT system would guide the LLM to outline steps such as identifying known variables, applying formulas, and calculating results (Shum et al., 2023).

3. Idea Structuring in Education: CoT encourages students to develop well-structured and improvable ideas.

Study case: Using CoT, students brainstorming for a group project can structure their arguments by outlining their initial thoughts, refining them collaboratively, and producing higher-quality outputs (Lee et al., 2024).

4. Strategic CoT (SCoT): This refinement of CoT incorporates strategic reasoning paths to enhance robustness and reliability.

Study case: In generating a legal argument, SCoT prompts the model to follow a structured legal reasoning framework, citing relevant case laws and principles in sequence (Yu Wang et al., 2024).

- Robustness: CoT enhances error resilience and adaptability across diverse tasks, ensuring consistent results (Y. Zhang et al., 2024).
- Scalability: Methods like Automate-CoT and SCoT allow CoT to be applied to various scenarios with minimal manual engineering (Shum et al., 2023; Yu Wang et al., 2024).

While CoT requires some expertise in prompt design, tools and techniques such as Automate-CoT, make it more accessible, bridging the gap for users with less experience in prompt engineering.

Autonomous Prompt Engineering (APE)

APE automates the process of refining prompts, enabling AI models like GPT-4 to deliver more accurate and relevant outputs. By dynamically optimizing prompts, APE enhances performance in academic and professional tasks, reducing the manual effort required for prompt design.

1. Enhanced Prompt Optimization:

Automatic Prompt Engineering Toolbox (APET): This toolbox applies various strategies autonomously to improve performance.

Study case: APET increased GPT -4's accuracy in geometric shape recognition by 6.8% through optimized prompts (Kepel & Valogianni, 2024).

2. Multi-Branched Prompt Optimization (AMPO): Uses iterative feedback to refine prompts for complex tasks.

Study case: For analyzing diverse research datasets, AMPO adjusts prompts iteratively to handle varying patterns effectively (S. Yang et al., 2024).

3. Data Efficiency and Usability:

Plug-and-Play Systems (PAS): Simplifies prompt generation for users.

Study case: Researchers input minimal context, and PAS generates optimized prompts for tasks like summarization or question-answering with fewer data points (Zheng et al., 2024).

4. User-centric design: Makes prompt engineering accessible by reducing complexity.

Study case: APE tools allow non-experts to focus on research tasks while benefiting from improved model outputs (Zheng et al., 2024).

- Automation: Reduces manual effort by dynamically optimizing prompts.
- Accessibility: Plug-and-play tools make prompt engineering approachable for non-experts.
- Efficiency: Achieves state-of-the-art results with fewer data points and minimal user input.

APE is ideal for academic researchers and professionals looking to enhance AI-driven workflows without deep technical expertise in prompt engineering.

In-Context Learning (ICL)

ICL is a technique where a large language model (LLM) improves task performance by leveraging examples or contextual information in the prompt. Unlike traditional methods requiring model retraining, ICL enables LLMs to adapt dynamically to tasks such as summarization, translation, or question-answering based on prompt design. This makes ICL particularly valuable in academic and professional settings (Long et al., 2024).

1. Adversarial In-Context Learning (adv-ICL): Uses a generator-discriminator setup to refine prompts.

Study case: For translating text, adv-ICL generates multiple prompt versions and selects the most accurate one by comparing outputs, improving translation quality (Long et al., 2024).

2. Batch Calibration: Controls biases introduced by prompts to maintain consistent performance.

Study case: When summarizing diverse articles, batch calibration ensures the output is unbiased, regardless of variations in input structure (H. Zhou et al., 2023).

3. Educational Promptization: Focuses on critical interaction with AI outputs in learning contexts.

Study case: In a classroom setting, students use ICL prompts to compare AI-generated summaries of a text, refining them collaboratively to enhance understanding (Haugsbaken & Hagelia, 2024).

- Dynamic Adaptation: ICL adjusts to different tasks and contexts without extensive retraining.
- Consistency: Techniques like batch calibration ensure reliability across varying inputs.
- Educational Impact: Encourages critical engagement with AI, fostering collaborative learning.

ICL is ideal for tasks requiring flexibility, such as academic summarization, multilingual translation, or student-driven exploration in educational environments.

Documentation and Reproducibility

Proper documentation of prompts and model parameters ensures transparency, reproducibility, and ethical accountability in using Large Language Models (LLMs). Involves recording the exact prompts inputted by the user, their context, purpose, and expected outcomes, the model's configuration, and any modifications applied. By doing so, researchers can clearly distinguish human contributions from technological assistance, enabling transparency and avoiding issues like technological plagiarism (Felzmann et al., 2020). This level of documentation is critical in professional academic work to ensure that the AI's involvement in content creation is transparent and traceable, fostering trust and reproducibility.

1. **Exact Prompt Input**

The text the user enters must be recorded to provide full transparency and ensure the LLM's output can be replicated. This step eliminates ambiguity and shows how the AI was directed to generate its responses.

2. **Prompt Context and Purpose**

The prompt's context and purpose should be explained to provide insight into its intended use. Helps readers understand the rationale behind the input and its relevance to the research or task.

3. **Model Parameters**

Detailed information about the model used, such as version, configuration settings (e.g., temperature, max tokens), and fine-tuning must be included. These details are essential for replicating the outputs and understanding the factors influencing the model's performance.

Example:

Importance of documentation in academic work:

- **Reproducibility**: Recording the exact prompt text and parameters ensures that results can be reliably replicated, a cornerstone of scientific research.
- **Transparency**: Detailed documentation clarifies the role of the AI model, allowing users to distinguish between human contributions and AI assistance.
- **Ethical Integrity**: Clear records prevent misrepresenting AI-generated content and uphold academic honesty by explicitly acknowledging technological contributions.
- **Error Tracking and Refinement**: Documenting inputs and configurations helps identify errors and improve future use of LLMs, enhancing overall workflow efficiency.

ENSURING ACADEMIC INTEGRITY IN LLM-ASSISTED RESEARCH

Reasoning and Validation

Maintaining academic integrity in LLM-generated outputs requires structured strategies to ensure accuracy, coherence, and reliability. Key approaches include tool-interactive critiquing, domain-specific prompts, self-consistency checks, and validation protocols. The following point-by-point explanation outlines how these techniques can be effectively applied.

- **Tool-Interactive Critiquing**

Tool-interactive critiquing enhances the reliability of LLM outputs by enabling iterative refinement using external tools. For example, external tools can validate LLM-generated outputs against domain-specific datasets or models when generating environmental research summaries. This approach, as demonstrated by (Gou et al., 2023), allows LLMs to self-correct based on feedback, improving factual accuracy and contextual relevance.

- **Domain-Specific Prompts**

Using domain-specific prompts ensures precision by embedding relevant terminology and context into the input. (Bartsch et al., 2023) tailored prompts reduce ambiguity in complex reasoning tasks, making this approach particularly effective in fields like environmental modeling, where specialized knowledge is essential.

- **Self-Consistency Checks**

Self-consistency techniques improve coherence by generating multiple iterations of outputs and aggregating the most reliable ones. (B. Huang et al., 2023) proposed graph-based modeling for consistency evaluation, while (X. Chen et al., 2023) emphasized its effectiveness in improving reasoning reliability across open-ended tasks.

- **Structured Validation Through Anomaly Detection**

Validation protocols that involve structured anomaly detection and iterative verification are critical for maintaining credibility in academic outputs. As (O'Keefe & O'Leary, 1993) outlined, such frameworks identify and correct inconsistencies, ensuring that LLM-generated content adheres to scholarly standards.

- **Bibliometric Analysis for Output Validation**

Bibliometric analysis frameworks validate LLM outputs by comparing them with established literature. (Eker et al., 2019) highlighted how these frameworks ensure alignment with validated research, particularly in disciplines like environmental science.

- **Multi-Agent Collaboration Framework**

A multi-agent collaboration framework, where different LLM instances critique and refine each other's outputs, enhances logical coherence and factual accuracy. (Xu et al., 2023) developed a system that mimics the peer-review process, significantly improving the quality of LLM-generated outputs.

- **Cross-Referencing with Verified Literature**

Systematic cross-referencing minimizes errors by validating outputs against verified knowledge. (Weng et al., 2022) emphasized the importance of this method in ensuring reasoning accuracy, while (Perkins, 2023) highlighted its role in maintaining academic integrity amidst AI-generated content.

- **Expert Reviews for High-Stakes Domains**

Expert review provides nuanced assessments that complement automated validation tools, addressing aspects LLMs might overlook. (Valmeekam et al., 2023) stressed the necessity of expert input in high-stakes contexts, and (yu & Li, 2022) demonstrated how domain-specific expert evaluations ensure logical coherence and content consistency.

- **Sensitivity Analysis for Robustness**

Sensitivity analysis examines the impact of prompts or model parameter variations on the quality of outputs. (Bartsch et al., 2023) and (Gou et al., 2023) emphasized the role of fine-tuned sensitivity metrics in ensuring reliable outputs, while (Larsen, 2023) advocated for systematic experimentation to uncover biases and improve robustness.

Ethical Considerations

As Large Language Models (LLMs) become more embedded in academic and professional settings, they offer substantial benefits and bring unique challenges. While these technologies boost productivity and speed up content creation, their use requires careful adherence to ethical, professional, and academic norms. It is crucial to ensure transparency and proper acknowledgment to prevent plagiarism, misrepresentation, and undue reliance on their outputs. This section delves into essential principles and practical guidelines to uphold academic integrity, ensure reproducibility, and maintain trust in AI-augmented research through LLMs' ethical and transparent use.

- **Plagiarism Risks**

Presenting AI-generated text as one's own without proper attribution constitutes plagiarism. For instance, using ChatGPT to write sections of a scientific paper without acknowledging the model's contribution is unethical. This practice undermines academic integrity and can lead to serious consequences, including academic penalties (Christiano, 2024).

- **Proper Attribution**

Proper attribution in generative AI work is critical for maintaining ethical and professional standards. Content generated or assisted by systems like ChatGPT should explicitly acknowledge the model's contribution, including its name, developer, and role. While significant human modifications may reduce legal obligations for attribution, ethical considerations still require transparency to reflect the AI's involvement. Misrepresenting AI-generated content as solely human-authored risks reputational and legal consequences, mainly when outputs include elements from copyrighted training data (Stout et al., 2023).

- **Role in Research**

Transparency in LLM usage is essential to ensure ethical accountability and inform stakeholders about the model's role in generating outputs. There is a need to disclose LLM contributions, whether for generating ideas, outlines, or content, to help clarify the extent of the model's involvement in research or decision-making processes. This practice supports ethical AI use by fostering trust and maintaining clarity about human versus technological contributions in professional and academic contexts (Stefan et al., 2024).

- **Limitations of LLM Outputs**

Outputs from Large Language Models (LLMs) are generated from training data but do not include direct citations or verifiable sources. It highlights the complexity and lack of transparency in how LLMs process data, making it essential to avoid treating their outputs as entirely reliable or definitive (Yifei Wang, 2023). Emphasizes the importance of critical evaluation, as LLM outputs may reflect biases or inaccuracies inherent in their training data. Understanding these limitations is crucial for using LLMs responsibly and ensuring the accuracy of their applications.

- **Importance of Transparency**

Transparent disclosure ensures ethical accountability by communicating the model's name, version, developer, and contributions. This step is crucial for addressing biases inherent in training data, such as those affecting multilingual or culturally specific outputs (Floridi & Cowls, 2019).

- **Support for Reproducibility**

Disclosure also supports reproducibility by detailing how the model was used. This process includes specifying tasks like qualitative analysis or hypothesis formulation, enabling others to replicate or extend the study using similar parameters (Felzmann et al., 2020).

- **Avoiding Over-Reliance on LLMs**

Large Language Models (LLMs), like GPT-4, enhance content analysis but pose risks when over-relied upon. They lack deep contextual understanding and cannot consider ethical or cultural values, requiring human oversight to ensure accuracy and fairness (Floridi & Cowls, 2019). Over-reliance may also weaken critical thinking, as users risk accepting outputs without verification, spreading inaccuracies (MIT Horizon, 2024; Zaphir et al., 2024). Maintaining originality ensures LLMs complement human creativity rather than replace it, upholding academic integrity. Balancing LLM use with oversight, critical thinking, and originality is crucial for ethical and practical application.

- **Maintaining Academic Honesty**

Proper disclosure in academic work is essential to distinguish human authorship from AI assistance, thereby upholding academic integrity and preventing technological plagiarism. This practice ensures that Large Language Models (LLMs) like ChatGPT are utilized as tools to enhance human creativity, not replace it. Implementing standardized reporting mechanisms, such as "AI Usage Cards," can promote transparency in AI-assisted research, allowing the academic community to trace and evaluate the extent of AI involvement. Such measures help maintain the originality of scholarly work and ensure that AI contributions are appropriately acknowledged, fostering ethical AI integration in academia (Wahle et al., 2023).

By addressing these key aspects, researchers and professionals can ensure LLMs' ethical and transparent use, maintaining trust and integrity in AI-assisted research and writing.

CRITICAL EVALUATION AND PEER REVIEW

Large Language Models (LLMs) like ChatGPT are transforming academia by streamlining literature reviews and enhancing writing (Meyer et al., 2023). Responsible use requires ensuring **Factual Accuracy** (Jiarui Li et al., 2024), **Logical Coherence** (Liang et al., 2024; J. Zhang et al., 2024), and **Novelty and Originality** (Cotton et al., 2024) to maintain academic integrity. Researchers can harness LLMs effectively while upholding high standards by focusing on these aspects.

Factual Accuracy

Factual accuracy in LLMs refers to their ability to produce truthful and reliable information, though they often generate credible-sounding but incorrect outputs, a phenomenon known as hallucination (L. Huang et al., 2024). To address this, researchers recommend retrieval-based validation and fact-checking to enhance the accuracy of LLM-generated content, guided by the following evaluation criteria:

1. **Factuality**

LLMs must provide factually correct outputs, avoiding hallucinations, as discussed by (L. Huang et al., 2024) and improved by Retrieval-Augmented Generation (RAG) (Jiarui Li et al., 2024).

Example: For the question *"What is the capital of Indonesia?"* the model should respond with *"Jakarta"* rather than an incorrect answer like *"Surabaya."*

2. **Relevance to Context**

Responses should be factual and directly relevant to the query, supported by (J. Zhang et al., 2024) through the use of Retrieval Augmented Thought Tree (RATT) to ensure contextual coherence.

Example: For the question *"What is the capital of Indonesia?"* a response like *"Indonesia has a population of 270 million"* is factual but irrelevant.

3. **Precision**

Highlight the need for detailed and specific responses, especially for domain-specific or time-sensitive queries, enhanced by RAG (Jiarui Li et al., 2024).

Example: For the question *"When was Indonesia's Declaration of Independence proclaimed?"* the precise answer *"August 17, 1945, at 10:00 AM"* is preferred over *"1945."*

4. **Coverage**

Responses should comprehensively address all critical aspects of a query, as noted by (Meyer et al., 2023) and (J. Zhang et al., 2024), who advocate for holistic reasoning.

Example: For the query *"What are the two largest economies in the world?"* the complete answer is *"The United States and China,"* not just one of them.

5. **Consistency**

Emphasize mechanisms like Self-Evaluation and Self-Update to ensure consistent session responses (Liang et al., 2024).

Example: If the answer to *"Who invented the light bulb?"* is *"Thomas Edison,"* it should remain consistent across related questions.

6. **Source Attribution**

As (Cotton et al., 2024) and (Meyer et al., 2023) stressed, that reliable source citations are essential for credibility.

Example: "The current world population is 8 billion, according to the United Nations."

7. **Temporal Accuracy**

Responses must align with the correct timeframe, especially in dynamic domains, as emphasized by (L. Huang et al., 2024).

Example: For the query *"Who is the President of Indonesia in 2024?"* the correct answer should be *"Prabowo,"* not *"Jokowi."*

8. **Bias Detection**

Highlight the need to ensure neutrality and mitigate response biases, particularly for sensitive topics (Meyer et al., 2023).

Example: For the question *"Do women do household chores?"* a neutral response like *"Both men and women can do household chores"* is preferable to a biased one.

9. **Verifiability**

Responses must be verifiable through credible sources, as emphasized by (Jiarui Li et al., 2024) and (Cotton et al., 2024), with RAG enhancing this capability.

Example: "The average distance from Earth to the Sun is 149.6 million kilometers," verifiable through scientific databases.

Evaluating factual accuracy involves strategies supported by recent research. **Fact Extraction and Verification**, emphasized by (L. Huang et al., 2024), involves breaking down complex claims to address hallucinations. **Cross-referencing** and **External Retrieval and Internal Checking**, as highlighted by (Jiarui Li et al., 2024), leverage external sources and internal data to ensure consistency and credibility, enhanced by tools like **FactCheck APIs and RAG**. As discussed by (L. Huang et al., 2024), **temporal analysis** ensures that responses align with current data. While **Peer Review by Domain Experts** is indirectly supported by (Meyer et al., 2023) as a method for oversight, **Chain-of-Verification (CoVe)**, supported by (J. Zhang et al., 2024), decomposes complex queries for systematic validation. These methods provide a robust framework for factual accuracy in LLM outputs.

Logical Coherence

Logical coherence ensures that narratives and arguments are consistent, logical, and intellectually accessible, as highlighted by (J. Zhang et al., 2024). Maintaining coherence is essential in academic and professional contexts to uphold credibility, avoid contradictions, and support sound decision-making and policy development. The following evaluation criteria outline how to assess logical coherence effectively:

1. **Internal Consistency**

Liang et al. (2024) emphasize the need for responses to remain consistent, avoiding contradictions within a narrative through mechanisms like Self-Evaluation and Self-Update.

Example: If the model states, *"Jakarta is the capital of Indonesia,"* it should not later claim, *"Bandung is the capital of Indonesia."*

2. **Logical Argumentation**

Zhang et al. (2024) highlight structured reasoning, ensuring responses progress logically from premises to conclusions.

Example: A discussion on *"the impact of deforestation in Kalimantan"* should start with causes (e.g., illegal logging), move to effects (e.g., habitat destruction, climate change), and conclude with solutions (e.g., reforestation policies).

3. **Relevance to Prompt**

Responses must align with the prompt, addressing the query without deviation, as noted by Zhang et al. (2024).

Example: For a prompt about *"Indonesia's strategy for renewable energy development,"* the response should focus on policies like the *Kebijakan Energi Nasional (KEN)* and avoid unrelated topics like tourism in Bali.

4. **Completeness and Clarity**

Meyer et al. (2023) emphasize that responses should comprehensively address the topic using clear, accessible language.

Example: Discussing *"factors affecting Indonesia's economy"* should address trade, labor, and infrastructure.

Example: A response about *"photosynthesis"* should explain it as *"the process where plants convert sunlight into energy."*

5. **Avoidance of Logical Fallacies**

Zhang et al. (2024) stress avoiding fallacies like circular reasoning or hasty generalizations to maintain credibility and coherence.

Example: Avoid statements like *"All urban problems are caused by traffic,"* which oversimplifies the issue.

Evaluating logical coherence ensures outputs are accurate and aligned with context, using Indonesia as an example for international readers. **Peer Review** (Meyer et al., 2023) assesses alignment with local realities, such as *pesantren* in Indonesia's education system. **Consistency Testing** (Liang et al., 2024) ensures coherence in rephrased prompts, like Indonesia's renewable energy strategies. **Context-based prompts** (J. Zhang et al., 2024) test reasoning in scenarios like the Jakarta MRT's impact on urban mobility. **Validation Against Trusted Sources** (Jiarui Li et al., 2024) ensures accuracy using data from *Badan Pusat Statistik* (BPS), Indonesia's national statistics agency, similar to other global datasets. **Manual Logical Flow Checks** (J. Zhang et al., 2024) ensure coherence in linking concepts, such as mangroves' benefits to climate change mitigation.

Novelty and Originality

Novelty and originality assess whether LLMs generate unique insights beyond existing knowledge, ensuring meaningful contributions to academic and professional contexts. Maintaining originality is critical for upholding academic integrity, avoiding plagiarism, and fostering creativity. Below are key evaluation criteria, supported by references and Indonesia-based examples

1. **Contribution of New Insights**

Outputs should provide fresh perspectives, avoiding repetition of known ideas, as emphasized by (Jiarui Li et al., 2024).
Example: Propose integrating geothermal energy in rural Indonesia rather than reiterating infrastructure challenges.

2. **Avoidance of Plagiarism**

(Cotton et al., 2024) highlight originality's importance in preventing plagiarism, supported by tools like Turnitin or Grammarly.
Example: Discussing Indonesia's National Energy Policy should avoid verbatim copying from government documents.

3. **Relevance to Current Research**

Outputs should reflect the latest developments, such as Indonesia's Long-Term Strategy for Low Carbon and Climate Resilience in 2050 (L. Huang et al., 2024; Jiarui Li et al., 2024).
Example: Reference recent policies on climate change, not outdated initiatives.

4. **Innovation in Approach**

Responses should propose creative methods, as supported by (J. Zhang et al., 2024)

Example: Combine electric vehicle incentives with mass transit expansion to tackle Jakarta's traffic congestion.

5. **Creativity and Depth**

(Meyer et al., 2023) emphasize exploring topics deeply and creatively.

Example: Examine how Indonesia's cultural diversity influences social policies instead of listing superficial examples.

6. **Avoidance of Redundancy**

(J. Zhang et al., 2024) stress avoiding repetition by including varied insights.

Example: Discuss the diverse benefits of mangroves for Indonesia's ecosystems without repeating the same points.

Novelty is ensured through manual and automated methods: **Manual Review** by experts identifies innovative ideas (Meyer et al., 2023), while **Plagiarism Detection Tools** like Turnitin or Copyscape prevent overlap with existing texts (Cotton et al., 2024). **Comparison with Literature** benchmarks outputs against recent publications (Jiarui Li et al., 2024) and **Prompt Variation Testing** generates creative responses by rephrasing prompts (J. Zhang et al., 2024). **Grounded Fact Checking** verifies the feasibility of ideas, such as solar-powered water purification for rural Indonesia (Jiarui Li et al., 2024), while **Domain-Specific Expert Review** ensures substantial originality in recommendations, like strengthening Indonesia's healthcare system (Meyer et al., 2023).

Adapting Peer Review

The peer review process, established in the 18th century by the *Philosophical Transactions of the Royal Society*, ensures the quality, validity, and originality of scientific works before publication, making it a cornerstone of modern scientific publishing (Castillo, 2012; Hames, 2007). While it provides authors with constructive feedback to refine their work, the process faces challenges that are being addressed in the AI era. AI tools now assist with tasks like plagiarism detection and evaluating methodology rigor, improving efficiency, reducing reviewer workload, and minimizing bias through objective evaluations (Kankanhalli, 2024; Salah et al., 2023). However, human reviewers remain indispensable for subjective judgments on research quality and relevance, as AI cannot replicate their expertise. Transparency in AI usage during peer review is crucial for fostering trust and ensuring authors are informed about their role in the evaluation process (Kankanhalli, 2024).

Key Factors to Consider When Reviewing AI-Based Manuscripts:

1. **Ensure transparency in AI Usage**

Authors must disclose how AI tools are used in their research (Hosseini et al., 2023). This includes naming the tools and algorithms, explaining their roles (e.g., data analysis or text generation), and describing how they ensured accurate and reliable results. For instance, if ChatGPT is used for drafting, authors should explain its specific contributions and oversight.

2. **Evaluate the Prompts Used**

Prompts guide AI models, and their quality impacts the outputs (Giray, 2023). Reviewers should check if prompts are clear, relevant to the research objectives, and explicitly documented. Authors should justify their prompt design, provide examples, and explain how the prompts help achieve research goals.

3. **Evaluate AI Model Selection and Performance**

The chosen AI model must suit the research task (Garg et al., 2024). Reviewers should confirm the model's appropriateness (e.g., BERT for text analysis) and review performance metrics like accuracy and precision. Authors should justify their model choice and demonstrate its reliability through data and metrics.

4. **Evaluate Validity and Reproducibility**

AI-generated results must be valid and reproducible (Kocak, 2024). Reviewers should ensure that authors provide sufficient details for replication and demonstrate consistent results across trials or datasets. Validation methods, such as benchmark comparisons, should also be clearly explained.

5. **Ensure Compliance with Ethics**

AI usage must comply with ethical standards (Kocak, 2024). Reviewers should confirm that authors use data legally and ethically, address potential biases in AI models, and provide fair and transparent results. For example, sensitive data should be anonymized and biases mitigated to ensure accuracy.

6. **Enhance Understanding of AI**

Reviewers should have a basic understanding of AI tools to evaluate their use effectively (Leung et al., 2023; Lingard, 2023). Training on AI technologies or collaboration with AI experts can support reviewers in assessing complex methodologies and outputs.

By addressing these points, reviewers can ensure AI-based research is transparent, valid, and ethically sound, upholding the integrity of scientific publications.

Documentation Standard

Model and Parameter Specification

Building upon the principles outlined in the **Documentation and Reproducibility** section, model and parameter specification emphasizes structured recording of all technical aspects, particularly when involving Large Language Models (LLMs). This practice ensures transparency, reproducibility, and ethical accountability while addressing the unique requirements of proprietary commercial and open-source models. Proper specification bridges inputs, outputs, and the underlying system, demystifying AI systems' "black-box" nature (X. Wu et al., 2023).

Key steps for effective Documentation of Model and Parameters:

1. **Model Overview**

Identify the model's name, developer, purpose, and scope. For commercial LLMs (e.g., ChatGPT, Gemini, Claude), include publicly available details such as API version and vendor-provided descriptions. For open-source models, incorporate detailed architecture specifications (Raiaan et al., 2024).

2. **Model Parameters**

Record configuration settings (e.g., temperature, max tokens, batch size) and any fine-tuning details. For instance:

- **Open Model Example:**
    - Model: BERT-base
    - Layers: 12
    - Parameters: 110M
    - Fine-Tuning: Dataset = WikiText, Learning rate = 0.001
- **Commercial Model Example:**

- Model: ChatGPT-4.0
- API Version: September 2024
- Configuration Settings: Temperature = 0.7, Max Tokens = 500.

3. **Traceability**

During experiments, provide fine-tuning logs and detailed records of modifications, datasets, and parameter changes. Document API endpoint configurations and prompt templates are used for commercial models during testing (Naveed et al., 2023).

4. **Performance Metrics**

Include evaluation results such as BLEU, ROUGE, or F1-scores. Suppose working with proprietary LLMs reference benchmarks provided by the developers (Hu & Zhou, 2024).

5. **Computational Resources**

Specify the hardware used for open models (e.g., GPU type, memory capacity) or acknowledge reliance on vendor infrastructure for commercial models. Example:

- Open Model: NVIDIA A100 GPU, 40 GB VRAM (Yu et al., 2024).
- Commercial Model: Hosted API infrastructure, client-side Python SDK (Patil & Gudivada, 2024).

6. **Task and Purpose**

Define the primary task and intended application (e.g., summarization, sentiment analysis). Example: "Summarizing climate change research papers for a journal review" (Kumar, 2024).

7. **Strengths and Limitations**

Highlight the model's capabilities (e.g., contextual understanding, multilingual support) and acknowledge constraints (e.g., biases, domain-specific weaknesses) (Patil & Gudivada, 2024).

Example:

Expanding on earlier concepts, detailed documentation of model specifications offers:

- **Enhanced Reproducibility:** Ensures exact conditions can be replicated across studies.
- **Clear Transparency:** Distinguishes human input from AI assistance.
- **Ethical Accountability:** Avoids misrepresentation of AI contributions and adheres to academic integrity (Felzmann et al., 2020).
- **Error Diagnosis and Optimization:** Facilitates systematic error tracking and refinement, improving efficiency in future research.

By integrating detailed models and parameter documentation into research workflows, scholars can uphold the standards of academic rigor while leveraging LLMs effectively.

Prompt Documentation Standard

Prompt documentation is essential for maintaining transparency, reproducibility, and quality in LLM-driven tasks. Researchers and practitioners can better understand and evaluate how prompts influence model outputs by systematically recording prompts, ensuring alignment with task objectives (Luo et al., 2024). Prompts interface users and LLMs, enabling precise task execution and outcome relevance.

Core Task and Guidelines for Prompt Documentation

1. **Text Generation**
    - **Objective:** Generate contextually appropriate, coherent, and grammatically correct text.
    - **Evaluation:** Assess fluency, relevance, factual correctness, and adherence to task-specific standards (e.g., stories, technical reports) (Miah et al., 2024).
2. **Machine Translation**
    - **Objective:** Ensure accurate, contextually appropriate translations that preserve the meaning of the source text.
    - **Evaluation:** Compare semantic equivalence, fluency, and technical term accuracy, especially in domain-specific contexts (Pathak & Rana, 2025).
3. **Text Summarization**
    - **Objective:** Provide concise summaries capturing the source text's main points and core meaning.
    - **Evaluation:** Check for clarity, brevity, and relevance, ensuring no critical information is omitted (Miah et al., 2024).
4. **Sentiment Analysis**

- **Objective:** Accurately classify sentiment (e.g., positive, negative, neutral) based on the input context.
- **Evaluation:** Align sentiment classification with human interpretation, considering granularity and contextual appropriateness (Luo et al., 2024).

5. **Question Answering**
   - **Objective:** Provide accurate, concise, and relevant answers to input questions.
   - **Evaluation:** Ensure responses are factually correct, relevant to the question, and free of superfluous information (Pathak & Rana, 2025).

Importance of Prompt Documentation

- **Transparency:** Clarifies how tasks are formulated and executed (Luo et al., 2024).
- **Reproducibility:** Ensures that outputs can be replicated under similar conditions (Miah et al., 2024).
- **Error Tracking:** Facilitates improvement of prompt designs and workflows (Pathak & Rana, 2025).
- **Ethical Accountability:** Distinguishes AI contributions from human input, maintaining academic integrity (Luo et al., 2024).

This structured approach to prompt documentation ensures that LLM outputs meet quality standards, fostering trust and reliability in their applications.

Data and Code Availability

Sharing data and code enhances research transparency, reproducibility, and collaborative development. It enables researchers to validate findings, build upon existing models, and avoid redundancy, fostering public trust by ensuring results can be independently verified. Below are the key components of the **dataset** and **code documentation** to support these objectives.

Dataset Documentation

Comprehensive dataset documentation is crucial as data forms the foundation for training, testing, and evaluating LLMs. Proper documentation should include:

1. **Origin:** Specify the dataset source, such as public repositories (e.g., Common Crawl, Wikipedia, Kaggle), open-source datasets, proprietary collections, or institutional datasets.

2. **Description:** Briefly explain the dataset's content, domain (e.g., general, scientific, legal), and languages (e.g., English, Indonesian, multilingual).
3. **Format:** Describe the dataset's structure (e.g., CSV, JSON, XML) and include details about columns, attributes, or sample entries (Berenguer et al., 2024; Sui et al., 2023).
4. **Size:** Document the dataset size, specifying metrics like tokens, words, sentences, or documents.
5. **Collection Method:** Detail how the data was collected (e.g., scraping, crowdsourcing, manual compilation).
6. **Type:** Explain dataset usage during pre-training, fine-tuning, or alignment tasks and its role in the model's performance (Naveed et al., 2023)(Naveed et al., 2023).
7. **Usage:** Specify if the dataset is used for training, validation, or testing.
8. **License and Ethics:** Mention the dataset's license to ensure legal compliance and describe any ethical considerations regarding its use.

Code Documentation

Well-documented code ensures accessibility, replicability, and usability for researchers and developers. It should include:

1. **Code Overview:** A concise explanation of the code's purpose and role in supporting the research. Highlight key features or functions.
2. **Dependencies:** List required libraries, frameworks, and tools, including specific versions (e.g., Python 3.9, PyTorch 1.10, Transformers 4.6).
3. **Instructions for Use:** Offer step-by-step instructions for setting up and running the code, such as commands to execute scripts.
4. **Code Comments:** Add comments within the code to explain its logic, functions, and parameters, providing a roadmap for understanding its structure.
5. **Storage and Accessibility:** Host datasets and scripts on platforms like GitHub, Kaggle, or Hugging Face, providing direct access links. Include appropriate licenses to define permissible use (Dvivedi et al., 2023).

Importance of Sharing Data and Code

1. **Validation:** Enables others to verify results and ensures findings are robust and reproducible.
2. **Collaboration:** Encourages further development and innovation without recreating models from scratch.
3. **Transparency and Trust:** Demonstrates ethical compliance and legal adherence through dataset and code licenses.

4. **Scalability:** Provides a foundation for new research, streamlining workflows and accelerating progress (Berenguer et al., 2024; Sui et al., 2024; Naveed et al., 2023).

CONCLUSION

By adhering to these documentation practices, researchers can enhance the integrity and impact of their work while fostering an open, collaborative research environment.

REFERENCES

Agarwal, E., Singh, J., Dani, V., Magazine, R., Ganu, T., & Nambi, A. (2024). *PromptWizard: Task-Aware Prompt Optimization Framework (Version 2)*. DOI: 10.48550/ARXIV.2405.18369

Alammar, J., & Grootendorst, M. (2024). *Hands-On Large Language Models* (1st ed.). O'Reilly Media.

Alec, R., Jeffrey, W., Rewon, C., David, L., Dario, A., & Ilya, S. (2019). Language Models are Unsupervised Multitask Learners | Enhanced Reader. *OpenAI Blog, 1*(8), 9. https://github.com/codelucas/newspaper

Amatriain, X. (2024). *Prompt Design and Engineering: Introduction and Advanced Methods (Version 4)*. DOI: 10.48550/ARXIV.2401.14423

Amazon SageMaker. (n.d.). Retrieved December 24, 2024, from https://aws.amazon.com/sagemaker/

Anderson, B. Y. J., Rainie, L., & Luchsinger, A. (2018). Artificial Intelligence and the Future of Humans: 1. Concerns about human agency, evolution and survival. *Pew Research Center, December*, 6–13. https://www.pewinternet.org/2018/12/10/concerns-about-human-agency-evolution-and-survival/

Bahdanau, D., Cho, K. H., & Bengio, Y. (2015). Neural machine translation by jointly learning to align and translate. *3rd International Conference on Learning Representations, ICLR 2015 - Conference Track Proceedings*, 1–15.

Bartsch, H., Jorgensen, O., Rosati, D., Hoelscher-Obermaier, J., & Pfau, J. (2023). Self-Consistency of Large Language Models under Ambiguity. *Proceedings of the 6th BlackboxNLP Workshop: Analyzing and Interpreting Neural Networks for NLP*, 89–105. DOI: 10.18653/v1/2023.blackboxnlp-1.7

Basyal, L., & Sanghvi, M. (2023). *Text Summarization Using Large Language Models: A Comparative Study of MPT-7b-instruct, Falcon-7b-instruct, and OpenAI Chat-GPT Models*. https://arxiv.org/abs/2310.10449

Bender, E. M., Gebru, T., McMillan-Major, A., & Shmitchell, S. (2021). On the Dangers of Stochastic Parrots. *Proceedings of the 2021 ACM Conference on Fairness, Accountability, and Transparency*, 610–623. DOI: 10.1145/3442188.3445922

Berenguer, A., Morejón, A., Tomás, D., & Mazón, J.-N. (2024). Using Large Language Models to Enhance the Reusability of Sensor Data. *Sensors (Basel), 24*(2), 347. DOI: 10.3390/s24020347 PMID: 38257439

Bharathi Mohan, G., Prasanna Kumar, R., Vishal Krishh, P., Keerthinathan, A., Lavanya, G., Meghana, M. K. U., Sulthana, S., & Doss, S. (2024). An analysis of large language models: Their impact and potential applications. *Knowledge and Information Systems, 66*(9), 5047–5070. DOI: 10.1007/s10115-024-02120-8

Bommasani, R., Hudson, D. A., Adeli, E., Altman, R., Arora, S., von Arx, S., Bernstein, M. S., Bohg, J., Bosselut, A., Brunskill, E., Brynjolfsson, E., Buch, S., Card, D., Castellon, R., Chatterji, N., Chen, A., Creel, K., Davis, J. Q., Demszky, D., & Liang, P. (2021). *On the Opportunities and Risks of Foundation Models.* 1–214. https://arxiv.org/abs/2108.07258

Boyko, J., Cohen, J., Fox, N., Veiga, M. H., Li, J. I.-H., Liu, J., Modenesi, B., Rauch, A. H., Reid, K. N., Tribedi, S., Visheratina, A., & Xie, X. (2023). *An Interdisciplinary Outlook on Large Language Models for Scientific Research.* 1–27. https://arxiv.org/abs/2311.04929

Brown, T. B., Mann, B., Ryder, N., Subbiah, M., Kaplan, J., Dhariwal, P., Neelakantan, A., Shyam, P., Sastry, G., Askell, A., Agarwal, S., Herbert-Voss, A., Krueger, G., Henighan, T., Child, R., Ramesh, A., Ziegler, D. M., Wu, J., Winter, C., & Amodei, D. (2020). Language models are few-shot learners — special version. *Conference on Neural Information Processing Systems (NeurIPS 2020), NeurIPS*, 1–25. DOI: 10.48550/arXiv.2005.14165

Castillo, M. (2012). Peer Review: Past, Present, and Future. *AJNR. American Journal of Neuroradiology, 33*(10), 1833–1835. DOI: 10.3174/ajnr.A3025 PMID: 22403775

Charles Darwin University. (2022). *Generative AI Quick tips.* https://www.cdu.edu.au/files/2024-06/Prompt Engineering %28Quick Tips%29.pdf

Chen, X., Aksitov, R., Alon, U., Ren, J., Xiao, K., Yin, P., Prakash, S., Sutton, C., Wang, X., & Zhou, D. (2023). Universal Self-Consistency for Large Language Model Generation. *ArXiv Preprint ArXiv:2311.17311.* https://doi.org//arXiv.2311.17311DOI: 10.48550

Chen, Y., Wen, Z., Fan, G., Chen, Z., Wu, W., Liu, D., Li, Z., Liu, B., & Xiao, Y. (2024). *MAPO: Boosting Large Language Model Performance with Model-Adaptive Prompt Optimization (Version 1).* arXiv. DOI: 10.48550/ARXIV.2407.04118

Christiano, P. (2024). *Is Using ChatGPT Plagiarism? An In-Depth Look at AI Writing and Academic Integrity.* Expert Beacon. https://expertbeacon.com/is-using-chatgpt-plagiarism-an-in-depth-look-at-ai-writing-and-academic-integrity/?utm_source=chatgpt.com

Cotton, D. R. E., Cotton, P. A., & Shipway, J. R. (2024). Chatting and cheating: Ensuring academic integrity in the era of ChatGPT. *Innovations in Education and Teaching International, 61*(2), 228–239. DOI: 10.1080/14703297.2023.2190148

Devlin, J., Chang, M.-W., Lee, K., Google, K. T., & Language, A. I. (2018). BERT: Pre-training of Deep Bidirectional Transformers for Language Understanding. *Naacl-Hlt 2019, Mlm*, 4171–4186. https://aclanthology.org/N19-1423.pdf

Ding, Q., Ding, D., Wang, Y., Guan, C., & Ding, B. (2024). Unraveling the landscape of large language models: A systematic review and future perspectives. *Journal of Electronic Business & Digital Economics, 3*(1), 3–19. DOI: 10.1108/JEBDE-08-2023-0015

Doshi-Velez, F., & Kim, B. (2017). *Towards A Rigorous Science of Interpretable Machine Learning. Ml*, 1–13. https://arxiv.org/abs/1702.08608

Dosovitskiy, A., Beyer, L., Kolesnikov, A., Weissenborn, D., Zhai, X., Unterthiner, T., Dehghani, M., Minderer, M., Heigold, G., Gelly, S., Uszkoreit, J., & Houlsby, N. (2021). AN IMAGE IS WORTH 16X16 WORDS: TRANSFORMERS FOR IMAGE RECOGNITION AT SCALE. *ICLR 2021 - 9th International Conference on Learning Representations.*

Dou, Z., Guo, Y., Chang, C.-C., Nguyen, H. H., & Echizen, I. (2024). Enhancing Robustness of LLM-Synthetic Text Detectors for Academic Writing: A Comprehensive Analysis. In *Lecture Notes on Data Engineering and Communications Technologies* (Vol. 202, pp. 266–277). DOI: 10.1007/978-3-031-57916-5_23

Dvivedi, S. S., Vijay, V., Pujari, S. L. R., Lodh, S., & Kumar, D. (2023). A Comparative Analysis of Large Language Models for Code Documentation Generation. *AIware 2024 - Proceedings of the 1st ACM International Conference on AI-Powered Software, Co-Located with: ESEC/FSE 2024, 1*(1), 65–73. DOI: 10.1145/3664646.3664765

Eker, S., Rovenskaya, E., Langan, S., & Obersteiner, M. (2019). Model validation: A bibliometric analysis of the literature. *Environmental Modelling & Software, 117*, 43–54. DOI: 10.1016/j.envsoft.2019.03.009

Ekin, S. (2023). *PROMPT ENGINEERING FOR CHATGPT ChatGPT 4 (author) OpenAI.* 1–12. DOI: 10.36227/techrxiv.22683919.v2

Enoch Sit, C. Y., & Kong, S.-C. (2023). A Deep Learning Framework With Visualisation for Uncovering Students' Learning Progression and Learning Bottlenecks. *Journal of Educational Computing Research, 62*(1), 223–249. DOI: 10.1177/07356331231200600

Felzmann, H., Fosch-Villaronga, E., Lutz, C., & Tamò-Larrieux, A. (2020). Towards Transparency by Design for Artificial Intelligence. *Science and Engineering Ethics, 26*(6), 3333–3361. DOI: 10.1007/s11948-020-00276-4 PMID: 33196975

Floridi, L., & Chiriatti, M. (2020). GPT-3: Its Nature, Scope, Limits, and Consequences. *Minds and Machines, 30*(4), 681–694. DOI: 10.1007/s11023-020-09548-1

Floridi, L., & Cowls, J. (2019). A Unified Framework of Five Principles for AI in Society. *Harvard Data Science Review, 12*(1), 1–14. DOI: 10.1162/99608f92.8cd550d1

Garg, S., Ahmad, A., & Madsen, D. Ø. (2024). Academic writing in the age of AI: Comparing the reliability of ChatGPT and Bard with Scopus and Web of Science. *Journal of Innovation & Knowledge, 9*(4), 100563. DOI: 10.1016/j.jik.2024.100563

Giray, L. (2023). Prompt Engineering with ChatGPT: A Guide for Academic Writers. *Annals of Biomedical Engineering, 51*(12), 2629–2633. DOI: 10.1007/s10439-023-03272-4 PMID: 37284994

Glickman, M., & Zhang, Y. (2024). AI and Generative AI for Research Discovery and Summarization. *Harvard Data Science Review, 6*(2). Advance online publication. DOI: 10.1162/99608f92.7f9220ff

Gou, Z., Shao, Z., Gong, Y., Shen, Y., Yang, Y., Duan, N., & Chen, W. (2023). CRITIC: Large Language Models Can Self-Correct with Tool-Interactive Critiquing. *ArXiv Preprint ArXiv:2305.11738*. https://doi.org//arXiv.2305.11738DOI: 10.48550

Gulden, T., Zhang, L. A., Geist, E., Awan, J., Abdurahaman, Z., & Ahmadi, M. (2024). Leveraging Large Language Models for Comprehensive Literature Review: An Exploration of RAND Corporation's 20-Year Corpus. In Z. Yang & C. Krejci (Eds.), *Proceedings of the 2023 International Conference of The Computational Social Science Society of the Americas* (pp. 272–283). Springer Nature Switzerland. DOI: 10.1007/978-3-031-64193-0_18

Hames, I. (2007). The Peer-Review Process - How to Get Going. In *Peer Review and Manuscript Management in Scientific Journals* (pp. 9–24). Wiley., DOI: 10.1002/9780470750803.ch2

Haugsbaken, H., & Hagelia, M. (2024). A New AI Literacy For The Algorithmic Age: Prompt Engineering Or Eductional Promptization? *2024 4th International Conference on Applied Artificial Intelligence (ICAPAI)*, 1–8. DOI: 10.1109/ICAPAI61893.2024.10541229

He, K., Zhang, X., Ren, S., & Sun, J. (2016). Deep residual learning for image recognition. *Proceedings of the IEEE Computer Society Conference on Computer Vision and Pattern Recognition, 2016-December*, 770–778. DOI: 10.1109/CVPR.2016.90

Horizon, M. I. T. (2024). *Critical Thinking in the Age of AI*. https://horizon.mit.edu/insights/critical-thinking-in-the-age-of-ai

Hosseini, M., Resnik, D. B., & Holmes, K. (2023). The ethics of disclosing the use of artificial intelligence tools in writing scholarly manuscripts. *Research Ethics*, *19*(4), 449–465. DOI: 10.1177/17470161231180449 PMID: 39749232

Hsu, Y.-C., & Ching, Y.-H. (2023). Generative Artificial Intelligence in Education, Part One: The Dynamic Frontier. *TechTrends*, *67*(4), 603–607. DOI: 10.1007/s11528-023-00863-9

Hu, T., & Zhou, X.-H. (2024). *Unveiling LLM Evaluation Focused on Metrics: Challenges and Solutions. 2021*, 1–45. https://arxiv.org/abs/2404.09135

Huang, B., Lu, S., Chen, W., Wan, X., & Duan, N. (2023). Enhancing Large Language Models in Coding Through Multi-Perspective Self-Consistency. *ArXiv Preprint ArXiv:2309.17272*. https://doi.org//arXiv.2309.17272DOI: 10.48550

Huang, D., Yan, C., Li, Q., & Peng, X. (2024). From Large Language Models to Large Multimodal Models: A Literature Review. *Applied Sciences (Basel, Switzerland)*, *14*(12), 5068. DOI: 10.3390/app14125068

Huang, J., & Chang, C.-C., K. (2023). Towards Reasoning in Large Language Models: A Survey. *Proceedings of the Annual Meeting of the Association for Computational Linguistics*, 1049–1065. DOI: 10.18653/v1/2023.findings-acl.67

Huang, L., Yu, W., Ma, W., Zhong, W., Feng, Z., Wang, H., Chen, Q., Peng, W., Feng, X., Qin, B., & Liu, T. (2024). A Survey on Hallucination in Large Language Models: Principles, Taxonomy, Challenges, and Open Questions. *ACM Transactions on Information Systems, 3703155*. Advance online publication. DOI: 10.1145/3703155

Ibrahimov, V. (2023). *10 ChatGPT and Claude AI prompts for faster academic reading*. Medium. https://medium.com/@Vugar_Ibrahimov/10-chatgpt-and-claude-ai-prompts-for-faster-academic-reading-ece583dd132c

Jurafsky, D., & Martin, J. H. (2009). *Speech and Language Processing*. Stanford University.

Kankanhalli, A. (2024). Peer Review in the Age of Generative AI. *Journal of the Association for Information Systems*, *25*(1), 76–84. DOI: 10.17705/1jais.00865

Kepel, D., & Valogianni, K. (2024). *Autonomous Prompt Engineering in Large Language Models*. https://doi.org//arXiv.2407.11000DOI: 10.48550

Kocak, Z. (2024). Publication Ethics in the Era of Artificial Intelligence. *Journal of Korean Medical Science*, *39*(33), 1–11. DOI: 10.3346/jkms.2024.39.e249 PMID: 39189714

Kudo, T., & Richardson, J. (2018). SentencePiece: A simple and language independent subword tokenizer and detokenizer for Neural Text Processing. In Blanco, E., & Lu, W. (Eds.), *Proceedings of the 2018 Conference on Empirical Methods in Natural Language Processing: System Demonstrations* (pp. 66–71). Association for Computational Linguistics. DOI: 10.18653/v1/D18-2012

Kumar, P. (2024). Large language models (LLMs): Survey, technical frameworks, and future challenges. *Artificial Intelligence Review*, *57*(10), 260. DOI: 10.1007/s10462-024-10888-y

Larsen, S. K. (2023). Creating Large Language Model Resistant Exams: Guidelines and Strategies. *ArXiv Preprint ArXiv:2304.12203*. https://doi.org//arXiv.2304.12203DOI: 10.48550

Le, Q., & Mikolov, T. (2014). Distributed representations of sentences and documents. *31st International Conference on Machine Learning, ICML 2014, 4*, 2931–2939.

Lee, A. V. Y., Teo, C. L., & Tan, S. C. (2024). Prompt Engineering for Knowledge Creation: Using Chain-of-Thought to Support Students' Improvable Ideas. *AI*, *5*(3), 1446–1461. DOI: 10.3390/ai5030069

Leung, T. I., de Azevedo Cardoso, T., Mavragani, A., & Eysenbach, G. (2023). Best Practices for Using AI Tools as an Author, Peer Reviewer, or Editor. *Journal of Medical Internet Research*, *25*, e51584. DOI: 10.2196/51584 PMID: 37651164

Lewis, P., Perez, E., Piktus, A., Petroni, F., Karpukhin, V., Goyal, N., Küttler, H., Lewis, M., Yih, W., Rocktäschel, T., Riedel, S., & Kiela, D. (2020). Retrieval-Augmented Generation for Knowledge-Intensive NLP Tasks. *Advances in Neural Information Processing Systems, 2020-Decem*(NeurIPS). https://arxiv.org/abs/2005.11401

Li, J., Sato, A., Shimura, K., & Fukumoto, F. (2020). Multi-task Peer-Review Score Prediction. *Proceedings of the First Workshop on Scholarly Document Processing*, 121–126. DOI: 10.18653/v1/2020.sdp-1.14

Li, J. Yuan, Y., & Zhang, Z. (2024). *Enhancing LLM Factual Accuracy with RAG to Counter Hallucinations: A Case Study on Domain-Specific Queries in Private Knowledge-Bases*. https://doi.org//arXiv.2403.10446DOI: 10.48550

Li, M., Sun, J., & Tan, X. (2024). Evaluating the effectiveness of large language models in abstract screening: A comparative analysis. *Systematic Reviews*, *13*(1), 219. DOI: 10.1186/s13643-024-02609-x PMID: 39169386

Liang, X., Song, S., Zheng, Z., Wang, H., Yu, Q., Li, X., Li, R.-H., Wang, Y., Wang, Z., Xiong, F., & Li, Z. (2024). Internal Consistency and Self-Feedback in Large Language Models. *Survey (London, England), 14*(8), 1–27. https://arxiv.org/abs/2407.14507

Lingard, L. (2023). Writing with ChatGPT: An Illustration of its Capacity, Limitations & Implications for Academic Writers. *Perspectives on Medical Education, 12*(1), 261–270. DOI: 10.5334/pme.1072 PMID: 37397181

Long, D., Zhao, Y., Brown, H., Xie, Y., Zhao, J., Chen, N., Kawaguchi, K., Shieh, M., & He, J. (2024). Prompt Optimization via Adversarial In-Context Learning. In Ku, L.-W., Martins, A., & Srikumar, V. (Eds.), *Proceedings of the 62nd Annual Meeting of the Association for Computational Linguistics (*Volume 1*: Long Papers)* (pp. 7308–7327). Association for Computational Linguistics. DOI: 10.18653/v1/2024.acl-long.395

Lund, B., Wang, T., Mannuru, N. R., Nie, B., Shimray, S., & Wang, Z. (2019). ChatGPT and a New Academic Reality: AI-Written Research Papers and the Ethics of the Large Language Models in Scholarly Publishing. *Journal of the Association for Information Science and Technology, 11*(1), 1–14. http://scioteca.caf.com/bitstream/handle/123456789/1091/RED2017-Eng-8ene.pdf?sequence=12&isAllowed=y%0Ahttp://dx.doi.org/10.1016/j.regsciurbeco.2008.06.005%0Ahttps://www.researchgate.net/publication/305320484_SISTEM_PEMBETUNGAN_TERPUSAT_STRATEGI_MELESTARI

Luo, Q., Ye, Y., Liang, S., Zhang, Z., Qin, Y., Lu, Y., Wu, Y., Cong, X., Lin, Y., Zhang, Y., Che, X., Liu, Z., & Sun, M. (2024). *RepoAgent: An LLM-Powered Open-Source Framework for Repository-level Code Documentation Generation.* https://arxiv.org/abs/2402.16667 DOI: 10.18653/v1/2024.emnlp-demo.46

Mahmud, S. (2024). *Fostering Academic Integrity in the Age of Artificial Intelligence.*, DOI: 10.4018/979-8-3693-0240-8.ch001

Manning, C. D., Surdeanu, M., Bauer, J., Finkel, J. R., Bethard, S., & McClosky, D. (2014). The Stanford CoreNLP natural language processing toolkit. *Proceedings of 52nd Annual Meeting of the Association for Computational Linguistics: System Demonstrations*, 55–60. DOI: 10.3115/v1/P14-5010

Melanson, J., & Maman, B. (2023). *The prompt engineering guide.* https://www.promptingguide.ai

Meyer, J. G., Urbanowicz, R. J., Martin, P. C. N., O'Connor, K., Li, R., Peng, P.-C., Bright, T. J., Tatonetti, N., Won, K. J., Gonzalez-Hernandez, G., & Moore, J. H. (2023). ChatGPT and large language models in academia: Opportunities and challenges. *BioData Mining*, *16*(1), 20. DOI: 10.1186/s13040-023-00339-9 PMID: 37443040

Miah, M. S. U., Kabir, M. M., Sarwar, T., Safran, M., Alfarhood, S., & Mridha, M. F. (2024). A multimodal approach to cross-lingual sentiment analysis with ensemble of transformer and LLM. *Scientific Reports*, *14*(1), 9603. DOI: 10.1038/s41598-024-60210-7 PMID: 38671064

Naveed, H., Khan, A. U., Qiu, S., Saqib, M., Anwar, S., Usman, M., Akhtar, N., Barnes, N., & Mian, A. (2023). *A Comprehensive Overview of Large Language Models*. https://arxiv.org/abs/2307.06435

O'Keefe, R. M., & O'Leary, D. E. (1993). Expert system verification and validation: A survey and tutorial. *Artificial Intelligence Review*, *7*(1), 3–42. DOI: 10.1007/BF00849196

Open, A. I. (2023). *Our approach to AI safety*. https://openai.com/index/our-approach-to-ai-safety/

OpenAI API. (n.d.). Retrieved December 24, 2024, from https://platform.openai.com/docs/api-reference

Ouyang, L., Wu, J., Jiang, X., Almeida, D., Wainwright, C., Mishkin, P., Zhang, C., Agarwal, S., Slama, K., & Ray, A. (2022). Training language models to follow instructions with human feedback. *Advances in Neural Information Processing Systems*, *35*, 27730–27744.

Oyewole, F. (2024). Integrating Large Language Models in Research and Education: Opportunities, Challenges, and Future Directions. *Preprint*. https://doi.org/https://doi.org/10.13140/RG.2.2.30706.31682

Pathak, P., & Rana, P. S. (2025). Comparative Analysis of Pretrained Models for Text Classification, Generation and Summarization: A Detailed Analysis. In *Lecture Notes in Computer Science (including subseries Lecture Notes in Artificial Intelligence and Lecture Notes in Bioinformatics): Vol. 15301 LNCS* (Issue September, pp. 151–166). DOI: 10.1007/978-3-031-78107-0_10

Patil, R., & Gudivada, V. (2024). A Review of Current Trends, Techniques, and Challenges in Large Language Models (LLMs). *Applied Sciences (Basel, Switzerland)*, *14*(5), 2074. DOI: 10.3390/app14052074

Pennington, J., Socher, R., & Manning, C. D. (2014). Glove: Global vectors for word representation. *Proceedings of the 2014 Conference on Empirical Methods in Natural Language Processing (EMNLP)*, 1532–1543. DOI: 10.3115/v1/D14-1162

Perkins, M. (2023). Academic Integrity considerations of AI Large Language Models in the post-pandemic era: ChatGPT and beyond. *Journal of University Teaching & Learning Practice*, *20*(2). Advance online publication. DOI: 10.53761/1.20.02.07

Perkins, M., & Roe, J. (2024). Decoding Academic Integrity Policies: A Corpus Linguistics Investigation of AI and Other Technological Threats. *Higher Education Policy*, *37*(3), 633–653. DOI: 10.1057/s41307-023-00323-2

Phoenix, J., & Taylor, M. (2024). *Prompt Engineering for Generative AI*. O'Reilly Media.

Raffel, C., Shazeer, N., Roberts, A., Lee, K., Narang, S., Matena, M., Zhou, Y., Li, W., & Liu, P. J. (2020). Exploring the limits of transfer learning with a unified text-to-text transformer. *Journal of Machine Learning Research*, *21*(1).

Rahman, M. M., & Watanobe, Y. (2023). ChatGPT for Education and Research: Opportunities, Threats, and Strategies. *Applied Sciences (Basel, Switzerland)*, *13*(9), 5783. DOI: 10.3390/app13095783

Raiaan, M. A. K., Mukta, M. S. H., Fatema, K., Fahad, N. M., Sakib, S., Mim, M. M. J., Ahmad, J., Ali, M. E., & Azam, S. (2024). A Review on Large Language Models: Architectures, Applications, Taxonomies, Open Issues and Challenges. *IEEE Access : Practical Innovations, Open Solutions*, *12*, 26839–26874. DOI: 10.1109/ACCESS.2024.3365742

Sahoo, P., Singh, A. K., Saha, S., Jain, V., Mondal, S., & Chadha, A. (2024). *A Systematic Survey of Prompt Engineering in Large Language Models: Techniques and Applications*. https://arxiv.org/abs/2402.07927

Salah, M., Abdelfattah, F., & Al Halbusi, H. (2023). Debate: Peer reviews at the crossroads—'To AI or not to AI?'. *Public Money & Management*, *43*(8), 781–782. DOI: 10.1080/09540962.2023.2264032

Sennrich, R., Haddow, B., & Birch, A. (2016). Neural Machine Translation of Rare Words with Subword Units. *Proceedings of the 54th Annual Meeting of the Association for Computational Linguistics (*Volume 1*: Long Papers)*, 1715–1725. DOI: 10.18653/v1/P16-1162

Shofiah, N., Putera, Z. F., & Solichah, N. (2023). *Challenges and opportunities in the use of artificial intelligence in education for academic writing: A scoping review* (Issue Pfh). Atlantis Press SARL. DOI: 10.2991/978-2-38476-188-3_20

Shum, K., Diao, S., & Zhang, T. (2023). Automatic Prompt Augmentation and Selection with Chain-of-Thought from Labeled Data. *Findings of the Association for Computational Linguistics: EMNLP, 2023*, 12113–12139. DOI: 10.18653/v1/2023.findings-emnlp.811

Stefan, R., Carutasu, G., & Mocan, M. (2024). Ethical Considerations in the Implementation and Usage of Large Language Models. In *Lecture Notes in Networks and Systems: Vol. 928 LNNS* (Issue April, pp. 131–144). DOI: 10.1007/978-3-031-54671-6_10

Stout, K., Manne, G. A., & Corbeille, E. (2023). *ICLE Comments on Artificial Intelligence and Copyright.* https://laweconcenter.org/resources/icle-comments-on-artificial-intelligence-and-copyright/

Sui, Y., Zhou, M., Zhou, M., Han, S., & Zhang, D. (2023). Table Meets LLM: Can Large Language Models Understand Structured Table Data? A Benchmark and Empirical Study. *Proceedings of the 17th ACM International Conference on Web Search and Data Mining*, 645–654. DOI: 10.1145/3616855.3635752

Taleb, I., Navaz, A. N., & Serhani, M. A. (2024). Leveraging Large Language Models for Enhancing Literature-Based Discovery. *Big Data and Cognitive Computing*, *8*(11), 146. Advance online publication. DOI: 10.3390/bdcc8110146

Valmeekam, K., Marquez, M., & Kambhampati, S. (2023). Can Large Language Models Really Improve by Self-critiquing Their Own Plans? *ArXiv Preprint ArXiv:2310.08118.* https://doi.org//arXiv.2310.08118DOI: 10.48550

Vaswani, A., Shazeer, N., Parmar, N., Uszkoreit, J., Jones, L., Gomez, A. N., Kaiser, Ł., & Polosukhin, I. (2017). Attention is all you need. *Advances in Neural Information Processing Systems, 2017-Decem*, 5999–6009. https://doi.org/https://doi.org/10.48550/arXiv.1706.03762

Vertex AI. (n.d.). Retrieved December 24, 2024, from https://cloud.google.com/vertex-ai

Wahle, J. P., Ruas, T., Mohammad, S. M., Meuschke, N., & Gipp, B. (2023). AI Usage Cards: Responsibly Reporting AI-Generated Content. *2023 ACM/IEEE Joint Conference on Digital Libraries (JCDL), 2023-June*(1), 282–284. DOI: 10.1109/JCDL57899.2023.00060

Wang, S., Liu, Z., Wang, Z., & Guo, J. (2023). *A Principled Framework for Knowledge-enhanced Large Language Model.* 1–10. https://arxiv.org/abs/2311.11135v1

Wang, X., Wei, J., Schuurmans, D., Le, Q., Chi, E. H., Narang, S., Chowdhery, A., & Zhou, D. (2023). Self-Consistency Improves Chain of Thought Reasoning in Language Models. *11th International Conference on Learning Representations, ICLR 2023*, 1–24.

Wang, Y. (2023). Deciphering the Enigma: A Deep Dive into Understanding and Interpreting LLM Outputs. In *Authorea Preprints*. DOI: 10.36227/techrxiv.24085833.v1

Wang, Yu., Zhao, S., Wang, Z., Huang, H., Fan, M., Zhang, Y., Wang, Z., Wang, H., & Liu, T. (2024). *Strategic Chain-of-Thought: Guiding Accurate Reasoning in LLMs through Strategy Elicitation (Version 1)*. DOI: 10.48550/ARXIV.2409.03271

Wei, J., Wang, X., Schuurmans, D., Bosma, M., Ichter, B., Xia, F., Chi, E. H., Le, Q. V., & Zhou, D. (2022). Chain-of-Thought Prompting Elicits Reasoning in Large Language Models. *Advances in Neural Information Processing Systems, 35*(NeurIPS), 1–43.

Weidinger, L., Mellor, J., Rauh, M., Griffin, C., Uesato, J., Huang, P.-S., Cheng, M., Glaese, M., Balle, B., Kasirzadeh, A., Kenton, Z., Brown, S., Hawkins, W., Stepleton, T., Biles, C., Birhane, A., Haas, J., Rimell, L., Hendricks, L. A., . . . Gabriel, I. (2021). *Ethical and social risks of harm from Language Models*. 1–64. https://doi.org//arXiv.2112.04359DOI: 10.48550

Weng, Y., Zhu, M., Xia, F., Li, B., He, S., Liu, S., Sun, B., Liu, K., & Zhao, J. (2022). Large Language Models are Better Reasoners with Self-Verification. *ArXiv Preprint ArXiv:2212.09561*. https://doi.org//arXiv.2212.09561DOI: 10.48550

Wu, F., Liu, J., & Chen, Y. (Eds.). yu, yang, & Li, N. (2022). Design of a tool for checking academic integrity and content consistency of paper abstracts. In F. Wu, J. Liu, & Y. Chen (Eds.), *International Conference on Computer Graphics, Artificial Intelligence, and Data Processing (ICCAID 2021)* (Vol. 12168, p. 40). SPIE. DOI: 10.1117/12.2631139

Wu, X., Duan, R., & Ni, J. (2023). Unveiling Security, Privacy, and Ethical Concerns of ChatGPT. *Journal of Information and Intelligence*, *2*(2), 102–115. DOI: 10.1016/j.jiixd.2023.10.007

Xu, Z., Shi, S., Hu, B., Yu, J., Li, D., Zhang, M., & Wu, Y. (2023). Towards Reasoning in Large Language Models via Multi-Agent Peer Review Collaboration. *ArXiv Preprint ArXiv:2311.08152*. https://doi.org//arXiv.2311.08152DOI: 10.48550

Yang, S., Wu, Y., Gao, Y., Zhou, Z., Zhu, B. B., Sun, X., Lou, J.-G., Ding, Z., Hu, A., Fang, Y., Li, Y., Chen, J., & Yang, L. (2024). *AMPO: Automatic Multi-Branched Prompt Optimization*. DOI: 10.18653/v1/2024.emnlp-main.1130

Yu, C., Wang, T., Shao, Z., Zhu, L., Zhou, X., & Jiang, S. (2024). TwinPilots: A New Computing Paradigm for GPU-CPU Parallel LLM Inference. *Proceedings of the 17th ACM International Systems and Storage Conference on ZZZ*, 91–103. DOI: 10.1145/3688351.3689164

Yuan, W., & Liu, P. (2022). KID-Review: Knowledge-Guided Scientific Review Generation with Oracle Pre-training. *Proceedings of the AAAI Conference on Artificial Intelligence*, *36*(10), 11639–11647. DOI: 10.1609/aaai.v36i10.21418

Zaphir, L., Lodge, J. M., Lisec, J., McGrath, D., & Khosravi, H. (2024). *How critically can an AI think? A framework for evaluating the quality of thinking of generative artificial intelligence. Llm*, 1–11. https://doi.org//arXiv.2406.14769DOI: 10.48550

Zhang, H., Yu, P. S., & Zhang, J. (2024). *A Systematic Survey of Text Summarization: From Statistical Methods to Large Language Models. 1*(1), 1–42. https://arxiv.org/abs/2406.11289

Zhang, J., Wang, X., Ren, W., Jiang, L., Wang, D., & Liu, K. (2024). *RATT: A Thought Structure for Coherent and Correct LLM Reasoning*. https://doi.org//arXiv.2406.02746DOI: 10.48550

Zhang, Y., Wang, X., Wu, L., & Wang, J. (2024). *Pattern-Aware Chain-of-Thought Prompting in Large Language Models*. DOI: 10.48550/ARXIV.2404.14812

Zheng, M., Liang, H., Yang, F., Sun, H., Li, T., Xiong, L., Zhang, Y., Wu, Y., Li, K., Shen, Y., Lin, M., Zhang, T., Dong, G., Qiao, Y., Fang, K., Chen, W., Cui, B., Zhang, W., & Zhou, Z. (2024). *PAS: Data-Efficient Plug-and-Play Prompt Augmentation System*. DOI: 10.48550/ARXIV.2407.06027

Zhou, H., Wan, X., Proleev, L., Mincu, D., Chen, J., Heller, K., & Roy, S. (2023). Batch Calibration: Rethinking Calibration for In-Context Learning and Prompt Engineering. *12th International Conference on Learning Representations, ICLR 2024*, 2023, 1–27. https://arxiv.org/abs/2309.17249

Zhou, R., Chen, L., & Yu, K. (2024). Is LLM a Reliable Reviewer? A Comprehensive Evaluation of LLM on Automatic Paper Reviewing Tasks. *2024 Joint International Conference on Computational Linguistics, Language Resources and Evaluation, LREC-COLING 2024 - Main Conference Proceedings*, 9340–9351.

ADDITIONAL READING

Berryman, J., & Ziegler, A. (2024). *Prompt engineering for LLMs*. O'Reilly Media. https://www.oreilly.com/library/view/prompt-engineering-for/9781098156145/

Bom, H.-S. H. (2023). Exploring the Opportunities and Challenges of ChatGPT in Academic Writing: A Roundtable Discussion. *Nuclear Medicine and Molecular Imaging*, *57*(4), 165–167. DOI: 10.1007/s13139-023-00809-2 PMID: 37483875

Hunter, N. (2023). *The Art of Prompt Engineering with ChatGPT: A Hands-on Guide*. Nathan Hunter. https://books.google.co.id/books?id=Z0-hzwEACAAJ

Roe, J., & Perkins, M. (2022). What are Automated Paraphrasing Tools and how do we address them? A review of a growing threat to academic integrity. *International Journal for Educational Integrity*, *18*(1), 15. DOI: 10.1007/s40979-022-00109-w

Sharma, R. C., & Bozkurt, A. (2024). *Transforming Education With Generative AI* (Sharma, R. C., & Bozkurt, A., Eds.). IGI Global., DOI: 10.4018/979-8-3693-1351-0

Teixeira da Silva, J. A., & Tsigaris, P. (2023). Human- and AI-based authorship: Principles and ethics. *Learned Publishing*, *36*(3), 453–462. DOI: 10.1002/leap.1547

Yao, Y., Duan, J., Xu, K., Cai, Y., Sun, Z., & Zhang, Y. (2024). A survey on large language model (LLM) security and privacy: The Good, The Bad, and The Ugly. *High-Confidence Computing*, *4*(2), 100211. DOI: 10.1016/j.hcc.2024.100211

Zielinski, C., Winker, M. A., Aggarwal, R., Ferris, L. E., Heinemann, M., Lapeña, J. F.Jr, Pai, S. A., Ing, E., Citrome, L., Alam, M., Voight, M., & Habibzadeh, F. (2023). Chatbots, generative AI, and scholarly manuscripts. *Colombia Médica : CM*, *54*(3), e1015868. DOI: 10.25100/cm.v54i3.5868 PMID: 38089825

KEY TERMS AND DEFINITIONS

Autonomous Prompt Engineering (APE): Automating the process of refining prompts to enhance AI performance and reduce manual effort.

Avoiding Over-Reliance: Using AI as a complementary tool rather than replacing human creativity and critical thinking.

Bias in LLMs: Prejudices in AI outputs resulting from imbalanced or biased training data, potentially affecting fairness and reliability.

Bibliometric Analysis: Comparing AI outputs with established academic literature to validate their relevance and quality.

Chain-of-Thought (CoT): A prompting method encouraging AI to generate step-by-step reasoning for improved problem-solving and clarity.

Code Documentation: Clear instructions and annotations accompanying code to facilitate understanding, replication, and reuse.

Contextual Embeddings: Word representations that adapt based on the surrounding context, providing nuanced meanings for each occurrence.

Cross-Referencing: Verifying AI-generated outputs against credible external sources to ensure their accuracy.

Dataset Documentation: Detailed descriptions of datasets, including their source, structure, and usage, to support transparency and ethical compliance.

Domain-Specific Prompts: Custom inputs tailored with field-specific terminology and context to improve precision in specialized tasks.

Encoder-Decoder Architecture: A neural network framework where the encoder processes input into a contextual representation, and the decoder generates the desired output.

Explainable AI (XAI): Techniques and methods that enhance the interpretability of AI systems, making their decision-making processes understandable to humans.

Hallucination: The generation of incorrect or fabricated outputs by AI models that may appear credible.

In-Context Learning (ICL): An AI can adapt to tasks by interpreting examples and context provided within the input prompt without additional training.

Large Language Models (LLMs): Highly complex AI systems trained on vast amounts of text to understand, generate, and interact in human-like language.

Literature Review Automation: The use of AI to identify, analyze, and synthesize academic studies, streamlining the review process.

Model Parameters: The adjustable components of an AI model, such as weights, determine its behavior and learning capacity.

Multi-Head Attention: An extension of self-attention that allows the model to focus on different parts of the input simultaneously, improving contextual understanding.

Novelty and Originality: The capacity of AI to generate unique and innovative outputs that add value to academic or professional work.

Peer Review: A process where experts evaluate research for quality, originality, and validity before publication.

Positional Encoding: A transformer technique injecting information about input tokens to preserve sequence structure.

Prompt Documentation: Systematically recording the prompts used for AI tasks to ensure transparency and reproducibility of results.

Prompt Engineering: Designing clear and compelling instructions to guide AI models in generating desired outputs.

Proper Attribution: Recognizing and crediting AI tools for their role in content generation to maintain ethical and professional standards.

Reinforcement Learning with Human Feedback (RLHF): A method for fine-tuning models to align outputs with human preferences and ethical considerations using reinforcement learning.

Reproducibility: Ensuring AI-assisted research or tasks can be replicated with the same conditions and produce consistent results.

Retrieval-Augmented Generation (RAG): Combining retrieved external information with generative models to improve factual accuracy and context relevance.

Self-Attention: A mechanism in neural networks that identifies and prioritizes the most relevant parts of input sequences for each token being processed.

Self-Consistency Checks: A process where multiple AI outputs are compared to select the most consistent and reliable response.

Sensitivity Analysis: Evaluating how input changes, prompts, or model parameters affect AI-generated outputs.

Text Summarization: Generate concise summaries from longer texts while retaining essential information and meaning.

Tokenization: The process of breaking text into smaller units (tokens) such as words, subwords, or characters for model processing.

Tool-Interactive Critiquing: A method where external tools validate and refine AI outputs for improved accuracy and relevance.

Transformer Model: A neural network architecture leveraging self-attention to process and generate language efficiently, particularly suited for tasks requiring long-range dependencies.

Transparency: Openly disclosing AI systems' methods, tools, and settings to ensure clarity and accountability.

Chapter 6
Ethics in Artificial Intelligence:
Building a Responsible and Inclusive Future

Piyush Bhosale
Ajeenkya D.Y. Patil University, India

Shravani Kulkarni
Ajeenkya D.Y. Patil University, India

Amna Kausar
https://orcid.org/0009-0000-3940-8845
Ajeenkya D.Y. Patil University, India

Aditya Shrivastav
https://orcid.org/0009-0000-8461-8171
Ajeenkya D.Y. Patil University, India

Susanta Das
https://orcid.org/0000-0002-9314-3988
Ajeenkya D.Y. Patil University, India

ABSTRACT

The chapter discusses the importance of ethics in the development and use of AI. As AI becomes a bigger part of our daily lives, it is necessary to ensure that it is used in ways that are fair, safe, and respectful of human values. The article explains key ethical concerns such as bias, lack of fairness, loss of privacy, job loss, and lack of accountability. It also introduces major global efforts, such as the EU AI Act, OECD AI Principles, and UNESCO's guidelines, which aim to guide the safe and

DOI: 10.4018/979-8-3373-0250-8.ch006

responsible use of AI. It highlights the need for collaboration between experts from various fields to develop trustworthy AI. As technology continues to evolve, the role of ethics will become increasingly important. The main goal is to ensure that AI supports human well-being and helps create a better future for all.

1. INTRODUCTION

Artificial Intelligence (AI) has been the focus of rapid and transformative advancements lately, and the last two years have been associated with the breakneck pace of development. With many industries changed and redefined with the help of AI, healthcare, finance, transportation, and advertising stand out at the core of such attention. As much as these advancements have brought many good things to the society and the economy, it has also brought about numerous and complicated ethical issues that need strict research and policymaking approaches (Huriye, 2023; Kazim & Koshiyama, 2021). Figure 1 illustrates the extent to which the research and publication on the topic of AI and its ethics has been expanding as recently as possible. At the top of this list of ethical issues is the question of algorithms bias and discrimination, which may perpetuate and even worsen the preexisting societal inequalities, especially in areas of high stakes, including criminal justice and healthcare (Bakiner, 2023). This signing black box nature of most AI systems presents serious obstacles to transparency and accountability thereby eroding trust amongst the people and challenges to means to assure justification and explainability of decisions (Huriye, 2023). Moreover, privacy issues are of particular concern because large quantities of personal information are collected and analysed by AI systems, and it is possible to suffer a violation of rights and self-determination (Bakiner, 2023).

Figure 1. Growth of AI Ethics

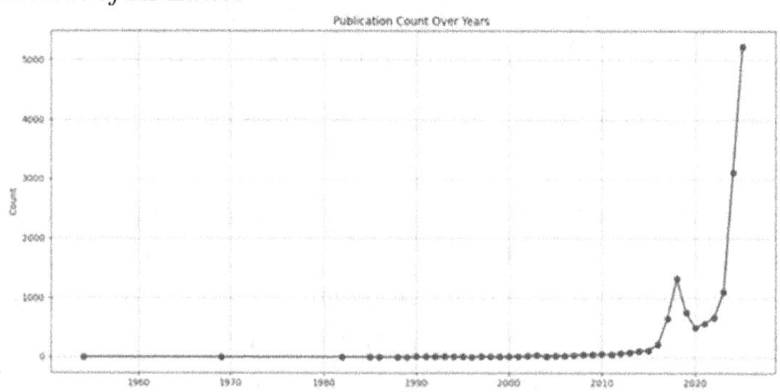

(Source: PubMed Database)

Societal implications of AI go beyond the technical and procedural challenges and enter the realm of the transformation of the workforce and replacement of jobs as automation alters the established employment patterns and causes the need to implement comprehensive policy measures to eliminate the negative consequences. Moreover, the possibility of abuse between information warfare and system manipulation and autonomous weaponization highlights the necessity of sound governance and control systems (Kazim & Koshiyama, 2021). To counter such complex issues, evidently, there is an agreement about the importance of designing and implementing ethical algorithms that can guide the responsible deployment, design, and governance of AI technologies (Huriye, 2023; Gianni et al., 2022; Hallamaa & Kalliokoski, 2022). These frameworks should be based on the values of fairness and transparency, accountability, confidentiality, and human well-being and, moreover, be informed by the interdisciplinary collaboration of academia, industry, and government stakeholders (Huriye, 2023; Gianni et al., 2022; Abujaber & Nashwan, 2024). It is important to note that generating ethical-by-design methods and the creation of a public-private auditing body have been significantly promoted as tools to realize these concepts and develop trusting AI systems (Gianni et al., 2022; Kazim & Koshiyama, 2021).

The novel AI applications in quantum computation and biotechnology pose novel ethical issues that resonate far beyond the usual ethical fields. The use of quantum mechanics in AI-enhanced systems heralds some major issues related to privacy, security, fairness, and accountability because quantum technologies can negatively affect the current safety systems, worsen digital inequality, and create an opaque decision-making process (Possati, 2023; Wheatley, 2024). The same can be said about biotechnology where AI-based processing of genomic or neural data contributes to increased ethical concerns regarding consent, data ownership and human dignity, in the context where the current legal and ethical frameworks are incapable of keeping up with the pace of technological advancements. The fact that there are also such field-specific challenges is exacerbated by the far-reaching cross-cultural differences in ethics and governance practices, which proves that models based in Western values will not match with other cultures (Wheatley, 2024). Integrating AI ethics into the understanding of the global conventions protecting human rights like the Universal Declaration of Human Rights offers an important normative framework that will help AI adhere to basic provisions of privacy, individuality, and fairness in varied global contexts (Pizzi et al., 2020).

The increasing rate of AI into the global economy suggests high chances of propagating inequality. Recent working paper of IMF based on household microdata and task-based model cautions that although AI might bring down wage inequality (by automating high-wage jobs) it is more probable to increase wealth inequality especially with firms with capital-intensive AI receiving windfall gains and restrict access to lower-income regions (Rockall et al., 2025). In a similar vein, until good governance is achieved, unfavourable imbalances are likely to become even more pronounced as cognitive automation is concentrated on developed economies, leaving low-income states at an even greater disadvantage (Paić & Serkin, 2025).

At the same time, the ethical aspects of the autonomous weapon systems (AWS) are gaining more and more seats of urgency. According to the analysis provided by De Sio & Van Den Hoven (2018), it can be highlighted that most of the above qualities of AWS that can make life-and-death decisions with minimum human involvement beg the question of accountability, bias, malfunction, risk of escalation, and destabilization that demands the creation of serious internationally binding regulations. In accordance with that, scholars note that meaningful human control should be maintained in AWS to meet the moral, legal and even humanitarian requirements as decisions concerning the use of lethal force have to stay consistent with ethical warfare and the current humanitarian law (Amoroso & Tamburrini, 2020).

Finally, the embedding of AI into ethics should be a consistent critical review and adaptive control, and technological innovation should be in line with universal moral principles and social-based interests (Hallamaa & Kalliokoski, 2022). A long-term partnership is the only way to achieve the potential of the AI in a way that preserves human rights and contributes to a social good (Bakiner, 2023; Huriye, 2023).

The chapter addresses the most significant ethical issues that the introduction of AI causes, values that need to be at the basis of its ethical use, and the responsibility of governments, organizations, and technology corporations to make sure that AI becomes a beneficial tool that can serve the greater good.

2. OPERATIONALIZING AI ETHICS

AI ethical frameworks have proliferated to a large extent across the globe, and the resultant landscape is fragmented and characterized by divergence on the one hand and convergence on the other hand in the application and interpretation of these ethical frameworks. Transparency, justice and fairness, non-maleficence, responsibility, and privacy are the ones that show a high level of agreement (Jobin et al., 2019; Correa et al., 2023; Ayinla et al., 2024). Even though these principles are convergent at the level of a concept, each comes up with a high level of variation in different national jurisdictions, industries, and organizational contexts in which the principles are integrated into practical applications (Ayinla et al., 2024; Dwivedi et al., 2022). Where Europe, transparency can be thought of in the shape of the explainability of algorithms, Asia is in the process of operationalizing it with the concept of an understanding of data provenance and traceability arising as a concept and being observed to come hand and hand with local regulations and local cultures (Dwivedi et al., 2022).

Case studies provide practical examples of what works and does not work when it comes to trying to practice these frameworks. A review of AI-enabled clinical decision support systems in Australia and the UK data provided high-level guidance, the practical implementation process revealed numerous gaps, such as deceptive marketing, stakeholder engagement failure, and the underrepresentation of relational outcomes in connection with delivering healthcare. This evidence helps to underline the fact that generic ethical principles tend to fail when applied to complicated, situation-specific realities, and it would be necessary to standardize ethical reviews on the lifecycle and integrate them with the technical and clinical workflow (Rogers et al., 2021). On the other hand, Trustap, a European fintech operator, managed to incorporate an AI Ethics Charter that essentially integrated the principles of responsible AI in its business operations with effective governance rules, personnel education, and stakeholder communication. Such an intervention resulted in quantifiable progress in the domains of data governance and internal accountability but the undertaking is still fluid in every sense of the word and something that needs to be refined on a regular basis (Devoteam, 2025). The same practices are clear in the technology giants in the U.S. like Google, Microsoft, and IBM that have established internal AI ethics boards, workflow, and responsible AI practices. IBM AI Fairness 360 Toolkit, Google Responsible AI Practices, and Microsoft Responsible AI Standard depict that ethics framework in the organization may promote bias mitigation, transparency, and fairness. Nonetheless, these attempts have suffered criticism as lacking external enforcement, and they sometimes fail to play a counterweight to the effects of algorithmic bias, especially in the hiring algorithm and face recognition technologies (Jobin et al., 2019).

There also exist plans that are well thought out in the public sector. Aurora AI program in Finland is a fine example of ethics-by-design since it made a run and introduced an Ethics Board presaging matters of social impact, power structure, and equality. All such recommendations by the board were reflected in actual changes in the AI program, which means that structured ethical governance is practical and well-enacted in the government sphere (Leikas et al., 2022). But in all these successes the necessity to interpolate general statements with upper-level moral sensitivity and to realize them on the ground has not been disturbed. The overall dilemmas also comprise the lack of enforcement whereby most parts of the schemes are idealistic and lack any regulatory or procedural requirements to implement its compliance (Shum & Luckin, 2019). Furthermore, there are quite general vague principles which makes it habitual to use the same principles inconsistently in different industries. The procedural fairness and accountability ethics and the general social implications still continue to pose the chapter of ethical blind spots since those engaged in the process did not involve the stakeholders effectively in the process of stakeholder engagement (Rogers et al., 2021; Bleher & Braun, 2023).

Moreover, the trends of algorithmic bias and privacy are currently hard to regulate, whereas technical solutions spontaneously adhere to various regulatory landscapes (Shum & Luckin, 2019). There is also empirical evidence that well-established professional codes of ethics like ACM Code of Ethics have less or no influence of real world decision making when there are no specific tools, processes and organizational persistence in their application. There is harmonization as well as fragmentation of ethical AI governance in a global comparison. To illustrate, the United States is more prone to prioritize fairness, privacy, and national security through such policy tools as the AI Bill of Rights, whereas Canada focuses on transparency and responsible innovation, especially when regarding such a sensitive area as healthcare and education (Dwivedi et al., 2022). The European Union is a legally based, rights-based perspective integrated into the models such as GDPR or the proposed AI Act, focused on risk-based governance and protection of the basic rights (Dwivedi et al., 2022; Bleher & Braun, 2023). Asia has seen the emergence of human-centric models (such as Model AI Governance Framework and Society 5.0 awarded to Singapore and Japan respectively) concentrating on transparency, adaptability, and implementation based on the sector (Dwivedi et al., 2022). The AI Ethics Framework of Australia also depicts a state-driven model of responsible development, albeit at significantly different paces, like Latin America and Africa, which in most cases is due to international cooperation such as with the OECD (Dwivedi et al., 2022). Following these diverse pressures, the emerging literature suggests the need of more practical models like the Ethical Regulatory Framework of AI (ERF-AI), which integrate into the iterative review process, accountability aspects, and ongoing feedback systems, to reduce the gap between principles and implementation (Wang et al., 2024). Also, strategies such as embedded ethics, value-sensitive design, ethically aligned design provide a way through which general principles can be turned into working processes, but each method presents certain limitations in terms of addressing stakeholder involvement, biases and governability (Bleher & Braun, 2023).

In general, there is a growing cross-nation agreement to a common set of ethical principles concerning AI, but operationalizing these is not always robust. The theme regarding the most successful implementations implies that the most successful implementations are where organizations internalize ethics in its development cycle, use effective governance models, and ensure that they engage all its stakeholders. On the other hand, frameworks fail when perceived as idealized lists of things to do without a particular application or enforcing mechanism. With the increase in the use of AI systems worldwide, this principle-implementation gap will only be fulfilled by using dynamic, iterative, and participatory forms of governance models, which will allow ethical AI to move beyond a theory into a meaningful practice (Rogers et al., 2021; Wang et al., 2024).

3. KEY ETHICAL ISSUES IN AI

As AI continues to integrate into various aspects of society, it brings with it several key ethical challenges. These issues range from bias in decision-making to concerns about data privacy. Ensuring the systems are fair, reliable, and safe is crucial, as unchecked AI can lead to unintended harm, discrimination, and a loss of public trust. Addressing these issues is essential for responsible AI development and use (Stahl, 2021).

3.1 Bias and Fairness

Bias and fairness in AI are critical ethical concerns that impact decision-making in various fields, including hiring, healthcare, and law enforcement. Bias occurs when an AI system produces unfair or discriminatory outcomes, often due to biased training data. Since AI models learn from historical data, they may inherit and amplify existing inequalities. For example, if a hiring algorithm is trained on past recruitment records that favored a certain pattern, it may continue to prefer candidates from those groups while disadvantaging others. Such biases can reinforce discrimination and create barriers to diverse hiring (Varona & Suárez, 2022). Bias may occur at different moments of the AI pipeline, such as data collection to deployment as shown in Figure 2 and, there may be a need to incorporate powerful explainability tools and policies to be ethical.

Ensuring fairness in AI requires careful design and evaluation of algorithms. One key approach is using diverse and representative training data to minimize bias from the start. Developers must also implement fairness checks at different stages of AI development, including testing for biased outcomes and adjusting models accordingly. Techniques such as bias mitigation algorithms and ethical AI frameworks can help improve fairness. Transparency is crucial to avoid the "black box" issue, where AI systems make decisions that are difficult to interpret. Clear explanations of these processes help ensure that the outcomes are understandable and trustworthy (Varona & Suárez, 2022; Ferrara, 2023; Alvarez et al., 2024).

Organizations and policymakers play a crucial role in promoting fairness. Regulatory frameworks and guidelines can establish standards to prevent biased decision-making and ensure accountability. Companies developing AI systems must adopt ethical AI practices, including regular audits and stakeholder engagement. Public awareness and collaboration between technologists, researchers, and policymakers are essential to creating AI systems that are fair, inclusive, and beneficial for all. By prioritizing fairness, AI can contribute to a more just and equitable society (Ferrara, 2023; Alvarez et al., 2024).

Figure 2. Emergence of Bias Across the AI Pipeline and the Role of Explainability & Policy

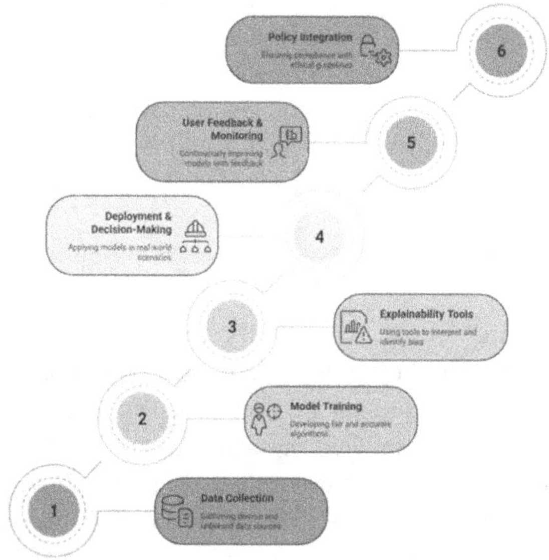

3.2 Data Protection and Privacy

Data protection is the key concern as the systems often rely on large amounts of personal data to function effectively. AI models use data from various sources in different formats, such as social media, online transactions, and healthcare records, to make predictions and decisions. However, this extensive use of data raises serious privacy risks. If not handled properly and protected, it can be exposed to misuse, breaches, or unauthorized access, putting an individual's sensitive information at risk (Mazurek & Małagocka, 2019).

Ensuring privacy requires strict measures to safeguard the data used in the systems. This includes encrypting sensitive information, anonymizing data to prevent personal identification, and ensuring that only authorized individuals can access it. Additionally, organizations must follow data protection laws and regulations, such as the General Data Protection Regulation (GDPR), to ensure that AI systems handle personal data responsibly and ethically. These laws mandate transparency in data collection and usage, ensuring that users understand how their information is being used (Meurisch & Muhlhauser, 2021).

Finally, AI systems must be designed to minimize data collection wherever possible, only gathering what is necessary for their specific purpose. This practice, known as 'data minimization,' helps reduce privacy risks by limiting the amount of personal information stored. By prioritizing privacy and data protection, organizations can build AI systems that respect individual's rights and maintain public trust (Suryadevara, 2023).

3.3 Accountability

Accountability in AI means making sure someone is held responsible for the actions and outcomes of AI systems. When an AI makes a decision- such as rejecting a loan application or diagnosing a medical condition- it is important to know who is answerable if that decision is wrong or harmful. Without clear accountability, it becomes difficult to address mistakes, fix problems, or provide justice to those affected. This is especially challenging because AI systems often operate without direct human involvement (Novelli et al, 2023).

To ensure accountability, developers, organizations, and suers must clearly define roles and responsibilities throughout the AI lifecycle. Developers should be responsible for creating reliable and ethical models, while organizations must look into how AI is used in real-world situations. It is also important to keep detailed records of how the AI was built, trained, and tested. These records help in tracking down the issues and understanding the reason behind AI decisions when problems occur (Busuioc, 2020; Walmsley, 2020).

Laws and regulations also play an important role in promoting accountability. Governments and regulatory bodies can set standards that require companies to explain their AI systems and take responsibility for their effects. Public feedback, audits, and independent reviews can further strengthen accountability. By creating clear rules and assigning responsibility, AI systems can be made safer, more reliable, and more trustworthy for society (Loi & Spielkamp, 2021).

3.4 Job Displacement

Job displacement is a significant concern related to the increasing use of AI and automation. As machines and algorithms become capable of performing tasks that humans used to perform, especially those involving manual work, they are at risk of being replaced. Industries such as manufacturing, retail, transportation, and even some areas of customer service are already experiencing changes due to automation. This change can lead to unemployment and financial stress for workers who lose their jobs.

The impact of AI on employment is not limited to low-skilled jobs. Even in fields like finance, law, and healthcare, AI tools are beginning to take over certain tasks, such as data analysis, document review, and diagnostics. While AI can increase efficiency and reduce costs, it may also reduce the need for human workers in some roles. This creates a gap where new job opportunities require different skills, leaving many workers unprepared for the changing demands of the job market.

To address job displacement, there is a need for investment in education, training, and reskilling programs. Workers must be supported in learning new skills that match the needs of an AI-driven economy. Governments, companies, and educational institutions should work together to create pathways for people who wish to shift to new job roles. By preparing the workforce for future challenges, we can reduce the negative effects of job loss and ensure that technological progress benefits everyone (Tiwari, 2023; Khan et al., 2024).

4. ETHICAL GUIDELINES AND PRINCIPLES

Ethical guidelines help ensure that AI technologies are developed and used in ways that are safe, fair, and respectful of human rights. As AI continues to grow in power and influence, various international organizations and governments have created frameworks to guide its responsible use. These guidelines provide a clear set of values and rules to prevent misuse (Heilinger, 2022; Jobin et al., 2019).

One of the major efforts in regulating AI is the European Union's AI Act, which is the first comprehensive legal framework designed specifically for AI. This legislation aims to create a balanced approach by encouraging innovation while ensuring that AI technologies do not harm individuals or society. The Act classifies AI systems into four categories based on the level of risk they pose: minimal risk, limited risk, high risk, and unacceptable risk. Each category comes with different obligations. For example, minimal-risk applications, such as spam filters, are less regulated, while high-risk systems must follow strict rules. AI systems that fall under the "unacceptable risk" category, such as harmful surveillance, are banned completely.

For high-risk AI systems, such as those used in medical diagnostics, transport, hiring, or law enforcement, the EU AI Act sets defined requirements to ensure these systems are safe and respect fundamental rights. These include obligations for risk assessment, data quality checks, and transparency in functioning. The Act also promotes accountability by requiring documentation and traceability of AI processes. The EU AI Act aims to build public trust in AI technologies by making sure that their development and deployment are not only technically sound but also ethically and legally responsible (Larsson, 2021).

The OECD AI Principles, introduced by the Organisation for Economic Co-operation and Development, provide a global framework to guide countries in developing responsible AI policies. They highlight the need for AI technologies to promote well-being and fairness while reducing the risk of discrimination. One major focus is on inclusive growth, meaning AI should benefit people from all backgrounds and not support inequalities. The principle also mandates AI systems to be understandable and explainable so that users know how decisions are made. Ensuring robustness and security is equally important as it helps prevent errors, misuse, or system failures. Lastly, the principle of accountability ensures that both developers and organizations remain responsible for their AI systems, especially in cases where outcomes affect people's lives (Hagendorff, 2020; Prem, 2023).

The UNESCO Recommendation on the Ethics of Artificial Intelligence is a global set of guidelines adopted by over 190 countries. It emphasizes the importance of respecting human dignity, protecting privacy, and promoting fairness and sustainability in AI systems. UNESCO's guidelines also stress the need for international cooperation and equal access to AI benefits, especially in developing nations. Together, these global frameworks aim to ensure that AI is used not only to progress but also for the common good of all humanity (Bean et al., 2025).

5. EMERGING PARADIGMS IN AI GOVERNANCE

The use of AI in making critical decisions in such industries as healthcare, finance, and justice has drawn greater attention to the issue of machine learning models, especially their deeper neural networks, that gave rise to concerns related to transparency and interpretability. The black box challenge is an avenue to attack trust, accountability, and compliance with regulations since the use of AI systems in decision-making that bears great impact on the human life is widespread (Sovrano et al., 2020). This opacity is now the focus of efforts to develop ethical AI, partially through the development of explainability tools that are not only useful to raise awareness of the inner workings of an AI system but can also bring the model to be in line with current legislation around such systems, including the General Data Protection Regulation (GDPR) and the General Data Protection Regulation (GDPR), as well as the new EU AI Act (Juliussen, 2025; Sovrano et al., 2020).

Some of the most popular explainability methods are SHAP (Shapley Additive explanations), LIME (Local Interpretable Model-Agnostic Explanations) and counterfactual explanations. Identified as a variety of cooperative game theory, SHAP measures the marginal impact of each feature in a prediction and proving local, as well as global, interpretability with robust mathematical guarantees (Linardatos et al., 2020; Salih et al., 2024; Kabir et al., 2024). It is a favourite to explain a nonlinear and a complex process model due to its consistency and accuracy. Additional to SHAP, LIME creates simpler surrogate models surrounding a particular instance of prediction providing case interpretability by making local approximations (Linardatos et al., 2020; Salih et al., 2024; Kabir et al., 2024). Although it is useful, LIME is dependent on the perturbation of inputs thus it may cause variations in outputs unless it is stabilized by the application of stabilization methods (Salih et al., 2024). By comparison, counterfactual explanations concentrate on giving users the minimum change in input data that would produce alternative output of the model, and this type of explanation could be specifically useful in cases such as decision contestability (Galhotra et al., 2021).

The techniques play a critical role with respect to the transformation of the black box AI models into transparent and auditable systems. They enable the stakeholders to follow the influence of input features on outputs in an attempt to develop trust in the AI-based decision and, in the same spirit, they can be used to identify the bias, the error and the unfairness (Salih et al., 2024; Kabir et al., 2024; Van Zyl et al., 2023). SHAP is more stable and theoretically correct as empirical evidence shows, unlike LIME, which is more appropriate in giving very local interpretation yet it is sensitive to changes in the data (Kabir et al., 2024). However, both the approaches require use proximity of feature collinearities and multidimensional dependencies (Salih et al., 2024).

Regulatory-wise, explainability does not come as a technical issue only, but as a legal requirement that is anchored in the modern governance systems over artificial intelligence. The GDPR actually inscribes the right to obtain meaningful information about the logic behind all the automated decision-making processes that hold legal or substantial consequences (Wachter et al., 2017). This requirement, especially defined in the Articles 13 15, Article 22 obliges AI to report on descriptive and causal explanation on how they make their decisions. Tools of explainability, such as SHAP, LIME, and counterfactuals, embody these requirements and enable organizations to meet the duties of transparency, contestability, and human oversight (Wachter et al., 2017). Such duty is additionally supported by the EU AI Act and the ISO 42001 standard that incorporate explainability into their risk management and risk management approaches to deployment of trustworthy AI (Juliussen, 2025).

The spread of generative AI is adding new systemic governance issues of how to manage rights, have protections on where the content came from, and verify synthetic media. As such generative systems create text, images, and other media, which more and more closely resemble what is created by humans, it is critical to make transparent how the data and the models that create it are being used and how outputs are to be used. To avoid the dangers, including misinformation and misappropriation, the governance frameworks are to include disclosure, watermarking, and verification of the AI-generated content, as well as safeguard the intellectual property and the trust of the society (Tambe & Chaudhary, 2024).

In line with the ethical considerations, there has been an element of concern about the environmental implication of AI. Green AI underlines the importance of creating energy optimization, minimizing the carbon footprint caused by training and deployment of large-scale AI systems. It is urgent since training models such as GPT-3 is quite expensive in terms of environmental resources, as it consumes energy (more than 1,200 MWh) and produces massive amounts of CO_2 emissions (Bolon-Canedo et al., 2024; Alzoubi & Mishra, 2024). To overcome this challenge, one should embrace model pruning, quantization, and efficiency benchmarking, as well as shift the work of data centres to renewable energy. Accountability is also enhanced in the AI life cycle by the creation of approved reporting metrics on AI energy consumption (Alzoubi & Mishra, 2024).

Policies have become more advanced. The executive order 14110 of the United States of America, signed in the year 2023 is one of the elaborate initiatives of the U.S government in supporting AI development and use. It highlights civil rights protection, the creation of watermarking to know that content is generated by AI, consumer protection, and responsible governmental procurement of AI (Alzoubi & Mishra, 2024). A complement to this is the NIST AI Risk Management Framework (RMF) 1.0 that has aided organizations to assess and manage the risks around AI and provides the well-organized guidelines on how the trustworthiness, accountability, and fairness can be realized across various applications (Kramer et al., 2024).

An applied example of explainability as a regulatory instrument is also discernible in the context of credit-risk assessment models, as financial institutions use explainability methodologies (such as SHAP and LIME) to fulfil GDPR or European Banking Authority requirements. These applications produce insights at the applicant level to justify why a credit application was approved or rejected, thus allowing a consumer to have the right to know and even challenge such decisions. Besides, counterfactual explanations will provide practical recommendations to applicants on how to become creditworthy, thus implementing fairness and building consumer trust (Vimbi et al., 2024; Arrieta et al., 2019). To conclude, explainability, generative AI governance, Green AI, and robust policy instruments are important developments in the field of AI ethics and AI governance. A commonality in all these frameworks is that they strive to make AI systems be transparent, accountable, reach sustainable environmental goals, and meet human rights and societal values (Arrieta et al., 2019).

6. CASE STUDY: POSITIVE USE OF ETHICAL AI

A positive example of ethical AI in practice can be seen in the use of Convolutional Neural Networks (CNNs) for detecting brain tumors and breast cancer through medical imaging. CNNs are a type of deep learning model that can analyze complex patterns in MRI or CT scan images with high accuracy. These systems assist doctors by identifying early signs of cancer that may not be easily visible to the human eye. By providing faster and more precise results, AI can support early diagnosis, which is crucial for effective treatment and improved survival rates.

Importantly, in the initial phase, these AI systems are used with human oversight, meaning doctors and medical professionals review and validate the results or output the system provides before making final decisions. This approach ensures that the technology does not act independently but works as a tool to assist human judgment. Such collaboration maintains medical accountability and reduces the risk of errors. It also helps in building trust among patients, as decisions are guided by both advanced technology and expert medical knowledge.

Ethical principles should be followed in handling patient data, which is used to train and improve these AI models. Data should be anonymized to protect patient privacy, following health regulations and ethical standards. These practices reflect how AI, when used responsibly, can bring great benefits to healthcare without compromising safety, privacy, or human values. This example shows how ethical AI can enhance human abilities and lead to better outcomes in sensitive fields like medicine (Habli et al., 2020; Pasricha, 2022; Li et al., 2022).

7. BIBLIOMETRIC ANALYSIS

A bibliometric study was conducted to find the thematic structures and the research orientation of ethics and AI intersection using the data of the two research databases, where the data of PubMed and lenses.org were extracted due to their closeness but not necessarily to each other. In order to process the data on the two platforms, special software VOSviewer, which is the software that develops and maps the bibliometric networks on the basis of the co-occurrence, co-authorship, and citation modes was applied. The keyword co-occurrence maps (Figures 3 and 4) created by the two give the big picture of conceptual space of the paper contributions of various scholars (National Library of Medicine, 2025; Lens, 2025; Nees & Waltman, 2019).

The first visualization presented in Figure 3 is made on the basis of the information extracted in PubMed. Each node in this map is a commonly occurring keyword and the frequency of the keyword is measured on the size of the node and the strength of co-occurring is reflected on the edge. Keywords have been categorized into groups whose colour is coded to different themes areas obtained after VOSviewer clustering algorithm.

The PubMed-related map contains the red cluster including such dominant terminologies as the ethics, artificial intelligence, chat bots, medical education, and clinical competence which speaks about the ethical debate referring to the usage of AI based tools in medical training and care. The green cluster revolves around the topic of the public health, HIV infections, counselling and sexual behaviours bring in ethical concerns over the subject of preventative medicine, reproductive health and access of healthcare. The blue cluster entails animals, gene expression, malaria and microbiota that depicts the experimental research in biomedical fields that raises concerns in both ethics of research and translational relevance. The yellow cluster is interested in the field of precision medicine, prognosis, stroke, and aged, which assumes study that is related to the topics of targeted therapy and ageing care through which the issues of equity and personalization of healthcare also emerge. In its turn, the purple group includes such terms as deep learning, magnetic resolution imaging, and radiographic reading that reveal an accelerated improvement of diagnostic technologies and ethical requirements that accompany them.

Figure 3. Keyword co-occurrence network from PubMed data on Ethics of AI

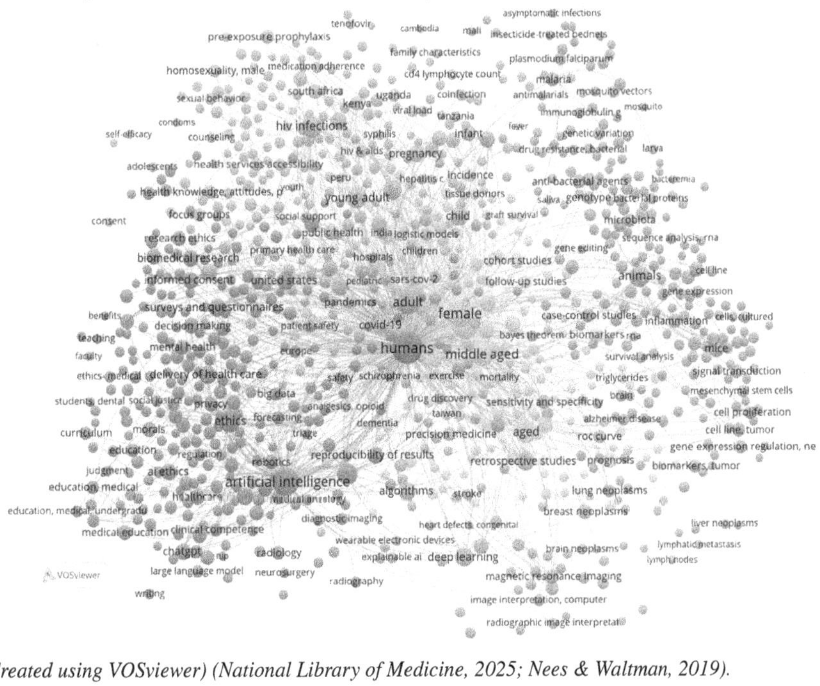

(Created using VOSviewer) (National Library of Medicine, 2025; Nees & Waltman, 2019).

The second visualization (Figure 4) is made with the help of Lens.org that is a comprehensive open-source patent, scholarly works and research information indexing platform. In the same manner used in the VOSviewer this data set shows more of an interdisciplinary and general perspective. The red cluster, similar to the dominance of ethics, artificial intelligence, decision making and trust, also provides the societal and psychological tier of the keywords, such as surveys, questionnaires, social media. The yellow section focuses on deep learning, retrospective analysis and radiomics, the researches of the technology and methodological robustness in the field of biomedical innovation. Green cluster The green cluster has a large number of experimental biology terms, such as mice, rats, gene expression, drug effects and apoptosis, an indication of high presence of preclinical research thereby an unspoken ethical interest in animal research. The blue cluster on the bottom presents the male, adolescent, nutrition surveys, and sleep apnea activities that can be labelled as behavioural, physiological research and demographic peculiarities. The purple scale includes breast neoplasms, drug treatment and combined modality therapy and overlie clinical research and ethics of treatment. Furthermore, a brain mapping, psychomotor performance, and biomechanics are introduced in such a cyan cluster, meaning that there are the scrotal areas of overlap between neuroethics and cognitive science.

The keyword humans lie at the centre of both networks and it is operating as a form of guide which subjects all other areas of research around it. The descriptors of the population that recur in the two maps are female, male, aged, and adolescent, which justifies the notion that the subject of the population-based researches ought to be at the centre of all the thinking in terms of ethics and biomedical implementation.

An analysis of the two bibliometric maps shows significant similarities and differences. The theme of ethics and artificial intelligence is mentioned in both datasets, which allows concluding that there is a worldwide concern among scholars regarding safe and responsible use and development of AI technologies in the sphere of healthcare and life sciences. The PubMed network is, however, more narrowly centred on clinical practice, health services and public health interventions, which, perhaps, indicates its biomedical indexing bias. Comparatively, the Lens.org map is more interdisciplinary as it touches on notions of psychology and behavioural science and newer technologies like radiomics and brain mapping. Besides, the Lens-based analysis introduces more detailed methodological terms and experimental constructs pointing out to its greater coverage of types of publication and scientific fields.

Figure 4. Keyword co-occurrence network from Lens data on Ethics of AI

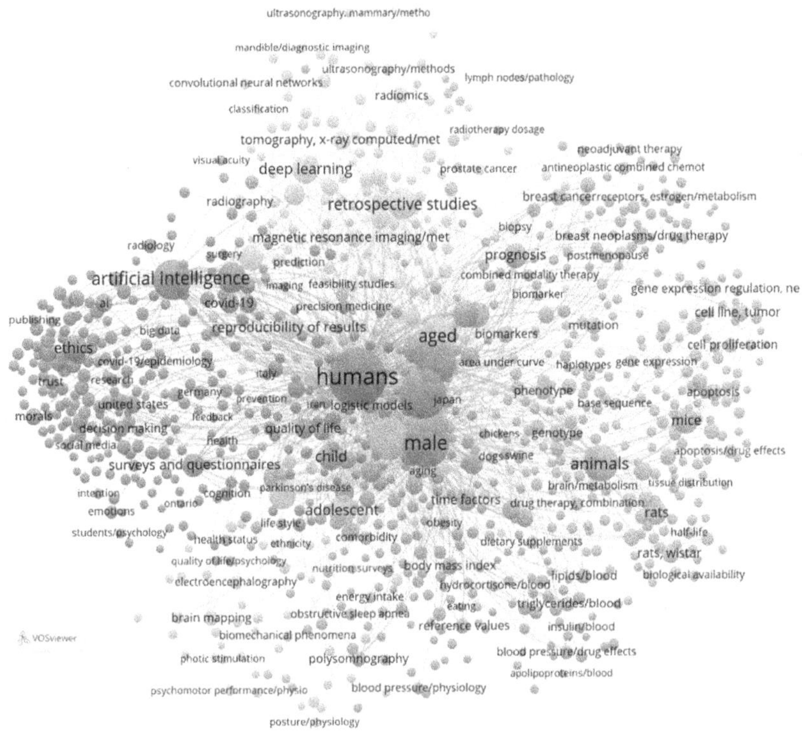

(Created using VOSviewer) (Lens, 2025; Nees & Waltman, 2019).

8. FUTURE OF ETHICAL AI

As technology continues to advance, the field of AI ethics will also need to grow and adapt. New applications of AI, such as autonomous vehicles and intelligent decision-making systems, bring fresh ethical challenges. These developments will require continuous updates to ethical frameworks to ensure that AI remains aligned with human values. As AI becomes more integrated into everyday life, it is important to create flexible and future-reliable guidelines that can respond to future risks and needs (Hickok, 2020).

The future of ethical AI will strongly depend on interdisciplinary collaboration. Ethical decisions about AI cannot be made by technologists alone. Experts from various fields, such as ethicists, scientists, engineers, and policymakers, must work together to understand the broader impact of AI systems. This collaboration ensures that technical decisions are balanced with social and moral considerations, leading to more responsible and inclusive solutions (Trotta et al., 2023; Khan et al., 2024).

Moreover, involving diverse voices helps address ethical issues from different perspectives, including cultural, social, and legal viewpoints. This diversity is crucial in developing AI systems that are fair, transparent, and beneficial across different communities and regions. As AI continues to evolve, building strong partnerships between technology and ethics will be key to creating a future where AI serves the common good (Trotta et al., 2023; Hickok, 2020; Khan et al., 2024).

9. CONCLUSION

The ethics of AI is a vital subject that must evolve alongside the technology itself. As AI becomes more powerful and widespread, it is essential to ensure that its development and use respect human rights, promote fairness, and safeguard privacy. Key issues such as bias, transparency, and data protection must be addressed thoughtfully to avoid harm and ensure that AI systems are used responsibly. Ethical guidelines and frameworks offer valuable direction, setting standards for the safe and ethical use of AI across different sectors. Looking ahead, collaboration among ethicists, technologists, and policymakers will play a crucial role in shaping the future of AI. Their combined knowledge will help create systems that not only perform well but also support social and ethical values. By building AI technologies with care and responsibility, we can ensure they benefit everyone equally and contribute to a better society. Ethical AI is not just about rules- it is about protecting people and using innovation to create a positive impact.

REFERENCES

Abujaber, A. A., & Nashwan, A. J. (2024). Ethical framework for artificial intelligence in healthcare research: A path to integrity. *World Journal of Methodology*, *14*(3). Advance online publication. DOI: 10.5662/wjm.v14.i3.94071 PMID: 39310239

Alvarez, J. M., Colmenarejo, A. B., Elobaid, A., Fabbrizzi, S., Fahimi, M., Ferrara, A., Ghodsi, S., Mougan, C., Papageorgiou, I., Reyero, P., Russo, M., Scott, K. M., State, L., Zhao, X., & Ruggieri, S. (2024). Policy advice and best practices on bias and fairness in AI. *Ethics and Information Technology*, *26*(2), 31. Advance online publication. DOI: 10.1007/s10676-024-09746-w

Alzoubi, Y. I., & Mishra, A. (2024). Green Artificial Intelligence Initiatives: Potentials and challenges. *Journal of Cleaner Production*, *468*, 143090. DOI: 10.1016/j.jclepro.2024.143090

Amoroso, D., & Tamburrini, G. (2020). Autonomous weapons systems and meaningful human control: Ethical and legal issues. *Current Robotics Reports*, *1*(4), 187–194. DOI: 10.1007/s43154-020-00024-3

Arrieta, A. B., Díaz-Rodríguez, N., Del Ser, J., Bennetot, A., Tabik, S., Barbado, A., Garcia, S., Gil-Lopez, S., Molina, D., Benjamins, R., Chatila, R., & Herrera, F. (2019). Explainable Artificial Intelligence (XAI): Concepts, taxonomies, opportunities and challenges toward responsible AI. *Information Fusion*, *58*, 82–115. DOI: 10.1016/j.inffus.2019.12.012

Ayinla, N. B. S., Amoo, N. O. O., Atadoga, N. A., Abrahams, N. T. O., Osasona, N. F., & Farayola, N. O. A. (2024). Ethical AI in practice: Balancing technological advancements with human values. *International Journal of Science and Research Archive*, *11*(1), 1311–1326. DOI: 10.30574/ijsra.2024.11.1.0218

Bakiner, O. (2023). The promises and challenges of addressing artificial intelligence with human rights. *Big Data & Society*, *10*(2), 20539517231205476. Advance online publication. DOI: 10.1177/20539517231205476

Bean, E., Burleigh, C., Haskell, C., Burris-Melville, T., Payne, J., & Pathak, B. (2025). Eavesdropping on UNESCO AI policy, leadership, and ethics. *Journal of Leadership Studies*, *18*(4), 98–110. Advance online publication. DOI: 10.1002/jls.70007

Bleher, H., & Braun, M. (2023). Reflections on Putting AI Ethics into Practice: How Three AI Ethics Approaches Conceptualize Theory and Practice. *Science and Engineering Ethics*, *29*(3), 21. Advance online publication. DOI: 10.1007/s11948-023-00443-3 PMID: 37237246

Bolón-Canedo, V., Morán-Fernández, L., Cancela, B., & Alonso-Betanzos, A. (2024). A review of green artificial intelligence: Towards a more sustainable future. *Neurocomputing*, *599*, 128096. DOI: 10.1016/j.neucom.2024.128096

Busuioc, M. (2020). Accountable Artificial intelligence: Holding algorithms to account. *Public Administration Review*, *81*(5), 825–836. DOI: 10.1111/puar.13293 PMID: 34690372

Corrêa, N. K., Galvão, C., Santos, J. W., Del Pino, C., Pinto, E. P., Barbosa, C., Massmann, D., Mambrini, R., Galvão, L., Terem, E., & De Oliveira, N. (2023). Worldwide AI ethics: A review of 200 guidelines and recommendations for AI governance. *Patterns (New York, N.Y.)*, *4*(10), 100857. DOI: 10.1016/j.patter.2023.100857 PMID: 37876898

De Sio, F. S., & Van Den Hoven, J. (2018). Meaningful Human Control over Autonomous Systems: A Philosophical Account. *Frontiers in Robotics and AI*, *5*, 15. Advance online publication. DOI: 10.3389/frobt.2018.00015 PMID: 33500902

Devoteam. (2025). *Ethical AI examples: 4 cases to see before you start innovating*. https://www.devoteam.com/expert-view/ethical-ai-examples-4-case-studies-to-see-before-you-start-innovating/

Dwivedi, Y. K., Hughes, L., Baabdullah, A. M., Ribeiro-Navarrete, S., Giannakis, M., Al-Debei, M. M., Dennehy, D., Metri, B., Buhalis, D., Cheung, C. M., Conboy, K., Doyle, R., Dubey, R., Dutot, V., Felix, R., Goyal, D., Gustafsson, A., Hinsch, C., Jebabli, I., & Wamba, S. F. (2022). Metaverse beyond the hype: Multidisciplinary perspectives on emerging challenges, opportunities, and agenda for research, practice and policy. *International Journal of Information Management*, *66*, 102542. DOI: 10.1016/j.ijinfomgt.2022.102542

Ferrara, E. (2023). Fairness and Bias in Artificial intelligence: A brief survey of sources, impacts, and mitigation strategies. *Sci*, *6*(1), 3. DOI: 10.3390/sci6010003

Galhotra, S., Pradhan, R., & Salimi, B. (2021). Explaining Black-Box algorithms using probabilistic contrastive counterfactuals. *arXiv (Cornell University)*. https://doi.org//arxiv.2103.11972DOI: 10.1145/3448016.3458455

Gianni, R., Lehtinen, S., & Nieminen, M. (2022). Governance of responsible AI: From ethical guidelines to cooperative policies. *Frontiers of Computer Science*, *4*, 873437. Advance online publication. DOI: 10.3389/fcomp.2022.873437

Habli, I., Lawton, T., & Porter, Z. (2020). Artificial intelligence in health care: Accountability and safety. *Bulletin of the World Health Organization*, *98*(4), 251–256. DOI: 10.2471/BLT.19.237487 PMID: 32284648

Hagendorff, T. (2020). The Ethics of AI Ethics: An Evaluation of Guidelines. *Minds and Machines*, *30*(1), 99–120. DOI: 10.1007/s11023-020-09517-8

Hallamaa, J., & Kalliokoski, T. (2022). AI Ethics as applied Ethics. *Frontiers of Computer Science*, *4*, 776837. Advance online publication. DOI: 10.3389/fcomp.2022.776837

Heilinger, J. (2022). The Ethics of AI Ethics. A constructive critique. *Philosophy & Technology*, *35*(3), 61. Advance online publication. DOI: 10.1007/s13347-022-00557-9

Hickok, M. (2020). Lessons learned from AI ethics principles for future actions. *AI and Ethics*, *1*(1), 41–47. DOI: 10.1007/s43681-020-00008-1

Huriye, A. Z. (2023, April 25). *The Ethics of Artificial intelligence: Examining the ethical considerations surrounding the development and use of AI*. https://gprjournals.org/journals/index.php/AJT/article/view/142

Jobin, A., Ienca, M., & Vayena, E. (2019). The global landscape of AI ethics guidelines. *Nature Machine Intelligence*, *1*(9), 389–399. DOI: 10.1038/s42256-019-0088-2

Juliussen, B. A. (2025). The right to an explanation under the GDPR and the AI Act. In *Lecture notes in computer science* (pp. 184–197). https://doi.org/DOI: 10.1007/978-981-96-2071-5_14

Kabir, J., Chakraborty, A., Mahmood, A., & Chakaraborty, A. (2024). Exploring Explainable Artificial Intelligence: A Comparative Analysis of Interpretability Techniques. *International Journal of Advanced Research in Computer and Communication Engineering*, *13*(3). Advance online publication. DOI: 10.17148/IJARCCE.2024.13301

Kazim, E., & Koshiyama, A. S. (2021). A high-level overview of AI ethics. *Patterns (New York, N.Y.)*, *2*(9), 100314. DOI: 10.1016/j.patter.2021.100314 PMID: 34553166

Khan, N. D. A., Shad, N. D. F., Sethi, N. D. S., & Bibi, N. M. (2024). The impact of artificial intelligence (AI) on job displacement and the future work. *Social Science Review Archives.*, *2*(2), 2296–2306. DOI: 10.70670/sra.v3i1.509

Kramer, M. A., Leavens, A., & Scarlat, A. (2024). Harnessing AI for efficient analysis of complex policy documents: a case study of Executive Order 14110. *arXiv preprint arXiv:2406.06657*.

Larsson, S. (2021). AI in the EU: Ethical Guidelines as a Governance Tool. In *Springer eBooks* (pp. 85–111). https://doi.org/DOI: 10.1007/978-3-030-63672-2_4

Leikas, J., Johri, A., Latvanen, M., Wessberg, N., & Hahto, A. (2022). Governing Ethical AI Transformation: A case study of AuroraAI. *Frontiers in Artificial Intelligence*, *5*, 836557. Advance online publication. DOI: 10.3389/frai.2022.836557 PMID: 35224480

Lens. *Search results for "Ethics of AI"*. The Lens. Retrieved June 22, 2025, from https://www.lens.org/lens/search/scholar/list?q=ethics%20of%20AI

Li, F., Ruijs, N., & Lu, Y. (2022). Ethics & AI: A Systematic Review on Ethical Concerns and Related Strategies for Designing with AI in Healthcare. *AI*, *4*(1), 28–53. DOI: 10.3390/ai4010003

Linardatos, P., Papastefanopoulos, V., & Kotsiantis, S. (2020). Explainable AI: A review of Machine Learning Interpretability Methods. *Entropy (Basel, Switzerland)*, *23*(1), 18. DOI: 10.3390/e23010018 PMID: 33375658

Loi, M., & Spielkamp, M. (2021). Towards Accountability in the Use of Artificial Intelligence for Public Administrations. In *Proceedings of the 2021 AAAI/ACM Conference on AI, Ethics, and Society (AIES '21)*, 757–766. https://doi.org/DOI: 10.1145/3461702.3462631

Mazurek, G., & Małagocka, K. (2019). Perception of privacy and data protection in the context of the development of artificial intelligence. *Journal of Management Analytics*, *6*(4), 344–364. DOI: 10.1080/23270012.2019.1671243

Meurisch, C., & Mühlhäuser, M. (2021). Data protection in AI services. *ACM Computing Surveys*, *54*(2), 1–38. DOI: 10.1145/3440754

National Library of Medicine. *Search results for "Ethics of AI"*. PubMed. Retrieved June 23, 2025, from https://pubmed.ncbi.nlm.nih.gov/?term=ethics+of+AI

Nees, J. V., & Waltman, L. (2019). *VOSViewer Manual.* https://www.vosviewer.com/documentation/Manual_VOSviewer_1.6.11.pdf

Novelli, C., Taddeo, M., & Floridi, L. (2023). Accountability in artificial intelligence: What it is and how it works. *AI & Society*, *39*(4), 1871–1882. DOI: 10.1007/s00146-023-01635-y

Paić, G., & Serkin, L. (2025). The impact of artificial intelligence: From cognitive costs to global inequality. *The European Physical Journal. Special Topics*. Advance online publication. DOI: 10.1140/epjs/s11734-025-01561-8

Pasricha, S. (2022). AI ethics in smart Healthcare. *IEEE Consumer Electronics Magazine*, *12*(4), 12–20. DOI: 10.1109/MCE.2022.3220001

Pizzi, M., Romanoff, M., & Engelhardt, T. (2020). AI for humanitarian action: Human rights and ethics. *International Review of the Red Cross, 102*(913), 145–180. DOI: 10.1017/S1816383121000011

Possati, L. M. (2023). Ethics of Quantum Computing: An Outline. *Philosophy & Technology, 36*(3), 48. Advance online publication. DOI: 10.1007/s13347-023-00651-6

Prem, E. (2023). From ethical AI frameworks to tools: A review of approaches. *AI and Ethics, 3*(3), 699–716. DOI: 10.1007/s43681-023-00258-9

Rockall, E., Tavares, M. M., & Pizzinelli, C. (2025). AI adoption and inequality. *IMF Working Paper, 2025*(068), 1. DOI: 10.5089/9798229006828.001

Rogers, W. A., Draper, H., & Carter, S. M. (2021). Evaluation of artificial intelligence clinical applications: Detailed case analyses show value of healthcare ethics approach in identifying patient care issues. *Bioethics, 35*(7), 623–633. DOI: 10.1111/bioe.12885 PMID: 34046918

Salih, A. M., Raisi-Estabragh, Z., Galazzo, I. B., Radeva, P., Petersen, S. E., Lekadir, K., & Menegaz, G. (2024). A perspective on explainable artificial intelligence methods: SHAP and LIME. *Advanced Intelligent Systems*. Advance online publication. DOI: 10.1002/aisy.202400304

Shum, S. J. B., & Luckin, R. (2019). Learning analytics and AI: Politics, pedagogy and practices. *British Journal of Educational Technology, 50*(6), 2785–2793. DOI: 10.1111/bjet.12880

Sovrano, F., Vitali, F., & Palmirani, M. (2020). Modelling GDPR-Compliant Explanations for trustworthy AI. In *Lecture notes in computer science* (pp. 219–233). https://doi.org/DOI: 10.1007/978-3-030-58957-8_16

Stahl, B. C. (2021). Ethical issues of AI. In *SpringerBriefs in research and innovation governance* (pp. 35–53). https://doi.org/DOI: 10.1007/978-3-030-69978-9_4

Suryadevara, S. (2023). Advances in data protection and Artificial intelligence: Trends and challenges. www.academia.edu. https://www.academia.edu/124958523/Advances_in_Data_Protection_and_Artificial_Intelligence_Trends_and_Challenges

Tambe, A., & Chaudhary, S. (2024). Generative AI: Challenges & framework of Governance. *International Research Journal of Modernization in Engineering Technology and Science, 6*(11). Advance online publication. DOI: 10.56726/IRJMETS63353

Tiwari, R. (2023). The impact of AI and machine learning on job displacement and employment opportunities. *Interantional Journal of Scientific Research in Engineering and Management, 07*(01). Advance online publication. DOI: 10.55041/IJSREM17506

Trotta, A., Ziosi, M., & Lomonaco, V. (2023). The future of ethics in AI: Challenges and opportunities. *AI & Society, 38*(2), 439–441. DOI: 10.1007/s00146-023-01644-x

Van Zyl, C., Ye, X., & Naidoo, R. (2023). Harnessing eXplainable artificial intelligence for feature selection in time series energy forecasting: A comparative analysis of Grad-CAM and SHAP. *Applied Energy, 353*, 122079. DOI: 10.1016/j.apenergy.2023.122079

Varona, D., & Suárez, J. L. (2022). Discrimination, bias, fairness, and trustworthy AI. *Applied Sciences (Basel, Switzerland), 12*(12), 5826. DOI: 10.3390/app12125826

Vimbi, V., Shaffi, N., & Mahmud, M. (2024). Interpreting artificial intelligence models: A systematic review on the application of LIME and SHAP in Alzheimer's disease detection. *Brain Informatics, 11*(1), 10. Advance online publication. DOI: 10.1186/s40708-024-00222-1 PMID: 38578524

Wachter, S., Mittelstadt, B., & Russell, C. (2017). Counterfactual explanations without opening the black box: automated decisions and the GDPR. SSRN *Electronic Journal*. https://doi.org/DOI: 10.2139/ssrn.3063289

Walmsley, J. (2020). Artificial intelligence and the value of transparency. *AI & Society, 36*(2), 585–595. DOI: 10.1007/s00146-020-01066-z

Wang, J., Huo, Y., Mahe, J., Ge, Z., Liu, Z., Wang, W., & Zhang, L. (2024). Developing an ethical regulatory framework for artificial intelligence: Integrating systematic review, thematic analysis, and multidisciplinary theories. *IEEE Access : Practical Innovations, Open Solutions, 1*, 179383–179395. Advance online publication. DOI: 10.1109/ACCESS.2024.3501332

Wheatley, M. (2024). *Quantum Shifts: The Societal Implications of Quantum Computing on Security, Privacy, and the Economy*. Premier Science., DOI: 10.70389/PJCS.100002

KEY TERMS AND DEFINITIONS

Accountability: The responsibility of developers or organizations to take ownership of the actions and effects of their AI systems.

Bias Mitigation: The process of reducing unfair outcomes in AI systems by identifying and correcting biased data or algorithms.

Data Minimization: A principle that suggests collecting only the necessary data needed for a specific purpose, reducing the risk of misuse.

Ethical Frameworks: Structured guidelines such as the EU AI Act or OECD Principles that help ensure AI is developed and used responsibly.

General Data Protection Regulation (GDPR): A legal framework by the European Union that protects the personal data and privacy of individuals.

Human Oversight: The involvement of people in monitoring and guiding AI decisions, especially in sensitive areas like healthcare.

Transparency: The ability to understand how an AI system makes decisions, ensuring its processes are open and explainable.

UNESCO (United Nations Educational, Scientific, and Cultural Organization) AI Ethics Guidelines: A global set of recommendations by UNESCO to promote human rights, fairness, and sustainability in AI development and use.

Chapter 7

Mitigating Bias in AI-Generated Responses: Advanced Prompt Engineering Techniques for Ethical AI

Vishal Jain

https://orcid.org/0000-0003-1126-7424

School of Engineering and Technology, Vivekananda Institute of Professional Studies, New Delhi, India

Archan Mitra

https://orcid.org/0000-0002-1419-3558

Amity University, Mumbai, India

ABSTRACT

Bias in AI-generated responses presents significant ethical and societal challenges, often stemming from imbalanced training data and systemic inequities. This study investigates advanced prompt engineering techniques, including contextual prompting, iterative refinement, bias-aware framing, and dynamic prompting, as proactive solutions for mitigating bias in AI text generation. Through quantitative and qualitative analyses, the research demonstrates that these techniques effectively reduce bias, enhance fairness, and maintain response quality across diverse domains. Dynamic prompting emerges as the most effective, achieving substantial reductions in the Bias Amplification Index (BAI) and improvements in the Fairness Index (FI). While these techniques show scalability and adaptability, challenges remain in addressing intersectional biases and architectural limitations. This study positions prompt engineering as a critical tool for ethical AI development, offering actionable insights for researchers and practitioners.

DOI: 10.4018/979-8-3373-0250-8.ch007

INTRODUCTION

The integration of Artificial Intelligence (AI) into decision-making systems has been transformative across a range of industries, from healthcare and finance to education and criminal justice. These systems, leveraging advanced natural language processing (NLP) models, have demonstrated remarkable potential in automating processes, increasing efficiency, and reducing human error (Binns et al., 2020). However, despite their promise, AI systems are increasingly under scrutiny for perpetuating and, in some cases, exacerbating biases present in their training data. These biases can manifest in various forms, including gender, racial, and socio-economic disparities, which have far-reaching implications for societal equity and ethical governance (Mehrabi et al., 2021; Noble, 2018).

AI systems are not inherently neutral. They inherit and often amplify the biases embedded within the data they are trained on, as well as those stemming from the design choices of developers (Bolukbasi et al., 2016). For instance, studies have shown that AI language models frequently generate biased content when responding to prompts about marginalized groups, further entrenching stereotypes and discrimination (Caliskan et al., 2017; Blodgett et al., 2020). In high-stakes domains such as hiring, lending, and law enforcement, biased AI outputs can lead to unjust outcomes, such as denying opportunities to qualified individuals or disproportionately targeting specific communities (Obermeyer et al., 2019; Barocas et al., 2016).

The ethical implications of such biases extend beyond individual injustices to undermine trust in AI technologies. As AI becomes a ubiquitous tool, its outputs increasingly influence public opinion, decision-making, and policy formulation (Crawford, 2021). Ethical principles such as fairness, transparency, and accountability are central to addressing these challenges. Yet, the lack of standardization in defining and operationalizing these principles has resulted in inconsistent and often ineffective mitigation strategies (Jobin et al., 2019; Raji et al., 2020). Furthermore, biased outputs can exacerbate existing inequalities, particularly in underrepresented or underserved populations, perpetuating systemic inequities rather than alleviating them (Eubanks, 2018; Buolamwini & Gebru, 2018).

Recent advancements in AI ethics research have highlighted the potential of prompt engineering as a proactive approach to mitigating bias in AI-generated responses (Solaiman et al., 2021). Prompt engineering, which involves the strategic design and modification of input prompts to influence AI behavior, has emerged as a promising technique for addressing biases at their source (Brown et al., 2020; Jiang et al., 2022). Unlike post hoc approaches, which often attempt to "fix" biased outputs, prompt engineering offers a more transparent and scalable solution by directly shaping the context and parameters of the model's responses (Sheng et al., 2021).

However, while prompt engineering has demonstrated success in reducing certain biases, its implementation raises critical questions about its effectiveness, generalizability, and ethical implications. For example, there is limited research on how prompt designs can account for intersectional biases or adapt to multilingual and multicultural contexts (Srinivasan & Uchendu, 2022; Gehman et al., 2020). Moreover, the lack of standardized evaluation metrics complicates efforts to quantify the impact of prompt engineering on bias mitigation, leaving significant gaps in the literature (Ethayarajh et al., 2021; Holstein et al., 2019).

This study aims to address these gaps by systematically investigating advanced prompt engineering techniques for ethical AI. By exploring the interplay between prompt design and bias mitigation, this research contributes to the growing body of knowledge on responsible AI development and deployment (Binns et al., 2020; Mehrabi et al., 2021). The findings hold significant implications for AI practitioners, policymakers, and society at large, offering actionable insights to create more equitable and trustworthy AI systems.

Bias in AI-generated text is a pervasive and complex issue, arising from the vast amounts of data used to train language models. These datasets often contain historical biases, imbalanced representations, and cultural stereotypes that are inadvertently learned and replicated by AI systems. When left unchecked, these biases manifest in AI outputs, reinforcing harmful stereotypes and marginalizing underrepresented groups. For instance, gender biases in language models can perpetuate inequitable associations, such as linking women disproportionately to caregiving roles and men to leadership roles. Similarly, racial biases can produce outputs that either omit or misrepresent certain communities, further entrenching systemic inequities. These challenges are compounded by the black-box nature of many AI models, which makes it difficult to understand how and why biases emerge during text generation. Despite numerous advancements in machine learning and natural language processing, current mitigation techniques struggle to address these biases comprehensively. Existing methods, such as data augmentation or post-processing, often treat symptoms rather than addressing the root causes of bias, limiting their effectiveness and scalability.

To tackle these pressing challenges, the primary objective of this research is to investigate and develop advanced prompt engineering techniques as a proactive solution to mitigate bias in AI-generated text. Prompt engineering, which involves carefully designing or modifying the input prompts fed to language models, has shown potential as a dynamic and adaptable approach to bias mitigation. By shaping the context and framing of AI responses, prompt engineering offers a method for reducing bias without requiring extensive retraining of models or manual adjustments to outputs. This research aims to systematically explore how different prompt designs influence the behavior of language models, with a focus on enhancing fairness, inclusivity, and ethical alignment. Furthermore, the study seeks to evaluate the scalability and real-world applicability of these techniques, ensuring they can be effectively integrated into diverse AI applications. By prioritizing prompt engineering, the research highlights its potential to bridge technical and ethical gaps in AI-generated responses, contributing to the development of more responsible and equitable AI systems.

In pursuing this goal, the study is guided by three key research questions. First, it examines how prompt engineering techniques influence the presence and severity of biases in AI-generated responses. This involves analyzing the extent to which linguistic framing and contextual cues can reduce or exacerbate bias. Second, the research investigates the most effective prompt engineering techniques for mitigating specific types of biases, such as gender, racial, or cultural biases, across diverse domains and applications. Finally, it explores the scalability and adaptability of these techniques, evaluating their potential to address intersectional biases and function effectively in multilingual and multicultural contexts. These research questions form the foundation for advancing knowledge in ethical AI development and positioning prompt engineering as a vital tool in mitigating bias in AI-generated text. Through this inquiry, the study seeks to offer actionable insights for developers, researchers, and policymakers striving to create more trustworthy and inclusive AI systems.

LITERATURE REVIEW

Bias in AI systems has been a subject of extensive research, as these biases significantly influence the outcomes and societal impacts of AI applications. In the context of text generation, bias arises primarily from the datasets used to train models and the inherent limitations of algorithmic design. Training data often reflects historical and systemic inequities, encoding stereotypes and underrepresenting marginalized groups. For instance, Bolukbasi et al. (2016) demonstrated that word embeddings in widely used models replicate gender stereotypes, such as associating women with caregiving professions and men with leadership roles. Similarly, studies by Caliskan et al. (2017) and Blodgett et al. (2020) have highlighted how biases related to race and socioeconomic status are embedded in language models, perpetuating harmful narratives. These biases are not limited to specific languages or cultures but are widespread, reflecting global inequities (Gehman et al., 2020). Such manifestations have critical consequences, especially in high-stakes applications like hiring, lending, and criminal justice, where biased outputs can exacerbate social inequalities (Obermeyer et al., 2019; Noble, 2018).

The principles of ethical AI have emerged as a foundational framework for addressing these challenges. Ethical AI prioritizes fairness, transparency, and accountability to ensure that AI systems align with societal values and minimize harm (Jobin et al., 2019). Fairness in AI emphasizes equitable treatment of all groups, particularly those historically marginalized or underrepresented (Raji et al., 2020). Transparency demands clarity in the design, operation, and decision-making processes of AI systems, enabling stakeholders to understand and evaluate their impacts (Holstein et al., 2019). Accountability ensures that developers and organizations are responsible for the outcomes of AI technologies, including mitigating unintended consequences (Crawford, 2021). While these principles provide a strong ethical foundation, their operationalization in AI development remains inconsistent. The lack of standardized methodologies and metrics for fairness, combined with varying interpretations of transparency and accountability, creates challenges in implementing these principles effectively (Barocas et al., 2016; Mehrabi et al., 2021).

Existing bias mitigation techniques offer several approaches to addressing these issues, yet they often fall short of achieving comprehensive and scalable solutions. Data augmentation and preprocessing methods attempt to reduce bias by diversifying training datasets, but these approaches are resource-intensive and may inadvertently introduce new biases (Buolamwini & Gebru, 2018; Solaiman et al., 2021). Algorithmic adjustments, such as reweighting data or modifying loss functions, show promise in reducing bias during model training but can compromise model performance or fail to generalize across contexts (Ethayarajh et al., 2021; Sheng et al., 2021). Post hoc methods, which involve filtering or modifying AI outputs, are reactive and often lack the nuance required to address complex biases (Holstein et al., 2019; Srinivasan & Uchendu, 2022). These limitations underscore the need for proactive, context-aware techniques that intervene earlier in the AI generation process.

Prompt engineering has emerged as a novel and promising approach to bias mitigation in AI systems. This technique involves designing or modifying the input prompts given to language models to influence their outputs in desired ways (Brown et al., 2020). By embedding contextually relevant and ethically aligned instructions within prompts, prompt engineering offers a flexible and scalable solution for guiding AI behavior. Unlike traditional mitigation strategies, it does not require extensive retraining of models, making it cost-effective and adaptable to a wide range of applications (Jiang et al., 2022; Sheng et al., 2021). Research by Solaiman et al. (2021) has shown that prompt engineering can significantly reduce the toxicity and bias of AI-generated text. Moreover, Gehman et al. (2020) demonstrated the potential of carefully crafted prompts in steering language models away from generating harmful content. While the field of prompt engineering is still in its infancy, its capacity for real-time intervention and adaptability positions it as a critical tool for ethical AI development. However, challenges remain in understanding the full scope of its effectiveness, particularly in addressing intersectional biases and adapting to multilingual or multicultural contexts (Caliskan et al., 2017; Blodgett et al., 2020).

This literature review highlights the urgent need for innovative approaches to bias mitigation in AI-generated text. By synthesizing existing research on bias causes, ethical principles, and mitigation strategies, it establishes the foundational context for exploring prompt engineering as a proactive and scalable solution. This approach not only aligns with the principles of ethical AI but also offers the potential to bridge critical gaps in current methodologies, contributing to the broader goal of creating equitable and responsible AI systems.

RESEARCH METHODOLOGY

This research methodology is designed to achieve the objective of developing and evaluating advanced prompt engineering techniques to mitigate bias in AI-generated responses. The methodology is structured into distinct phases, encompassing data preparation, prompt engineering design, experimental evaluation, and analysis. This systematic approach ensures rigorous investigation of the research objective while maintaining alignment with ethical AI principles.

Data Collection and Preparation

The first phase involves the collection and preparation of datasets for training and testing the AI models. A diverse set of publicly available datasets is selected to ensure representation across gender, race, ethnicity, and cultural dimensions. Examples include datasets like Common Crawl, Wikipedia, and datasets curated for fairness research, such as the "Gender Bias in Datasets" (Blodgett et al., 2020). Each dataset undergoes preprocessing to remove explicit biases, offensive language, and redundant entries. Data balancing techniques are applied to ensure adequate representation of underrepresented groups (Buolamwini & Gebru, 2018). Furthermore, ethical considerations, including informed consent for data use and adherence to privacy guidelines, are prioritized during data collection and curation (Jobin et al., 2019).

Design of Prompt Engineering Techniques

This phase focuses on designing and implementing various prompt engineering techniques aimed at mitigating biases in AI-generated text. Techniques include:

1. **Contextual Prompting**: Crafting prompts with explicit instructions to emphasize fairness, inclusivity, and non-discrimination in responses.

2. **Iterative Refinement**: Using iterative prompts that gradually refine outputs to align with ethical objectives.
3. **Bias-Aware Framing**: Embedding prompts with language that explicitly counters known biases, such as stereotypes or offensive terms (Sheng et al., 2021).
4. **Dynamic Prompting**: Designing prompts that adapt based on the input context to reduce the likelihood of generating biased responses (Jiang et al., 2022).

Each technique is implemented using state-of-the-art language models, such as GPT-3.5 or GPT-4, which serve as testbeds for evaluating the impact of prompts on AI outputs.

Experimental Setup

To evaluate the effectiveness of the prompt engineering techniques, controlled experiments are conducted using the prepared datasets and the implemented prompts. The experimental setup includes the following components:

1. **Baseline Models**: Unaltered language models are used as benchmarks to measure the relative improvement in bias mitigation.
2. **Evaluation Metrics**: Metrics such as the Bias Amplification Index (BAI), Fairness Index (FI), and qualitative assessments (e.g., content analysis of generated responses) are used to evaluate the extent of bias reduction and ethical alignment in outputs (Caliskan et al., 2017; Gehman et al., 2020).
3. **Test Scenarios**: Diverse prompts are tested across multiple scenarios, including gendered pronouns, racial identifiers, and socio-economic contexts, to assess generalizability (Brown et al., 2020).

ANALYSIS OF RESULTS

The results from the experiments are analyzed quantitatively and qualitatively to assess the performance of the prompt engineering techniques. Quantitative analysis involves statistical evaluation of the bias mitigation metrics, comparing the outputs of baseline models with those using advanced prompts. Qualitative analysis examines the linguistic and contextual aspects of the generated responses to ensure they are not only unbiased but also contextually appropriate and ethically aligned (Ethayarajh et al., 2021). Cross-validation techniques are employed to ensure the robustness and reliability of the results across different datasets and prompts.

Validation and Iterative Refinement

To ensure the validity and applicability of the findings, an iterative refinement process is adopted. Feedback from domain experts in AI ethics and natural language processing is incorporated to improve the design and implementation of prompt engineering techniques. Additionally, the methods are tested on multilingual datasets to evaluate their adaptability to diverse linguistic and cultural contexts (Srinivasan & Uchendu, 2022). Ethical considerations remain integral throughout the research process, ensuring that the proposed solutions align with global standards for responsible AI development (Raji et al., 2020).

This methodology combines theoretical rigor with practical application to address the objective of mitigating bias in AI-generated responses through advanced prompt engineering techniques. By systematically designing, testing, and refining these techniques, this research aims to contribute actionable insights and scalable solutions for developing fairer and more inclusive AI systems. The results of this study are expected to have significant implications for AI practitioners, policymakers, and researchers dedicated to advancing ethical AI practices.

DATA ANALYSIS

The data analysis focuses on evaluating the effectiveness of advanced prompt engineering techniques in mitigating bias in AI-generated responses. The analysis is grounded in the experimental methodology described earlier, using both quantitative and qualitative approaches. Results are presented through tables, charts, and graphs to provide a comprehensive view of the findings, highlighting improvements in fairness, inclusivity, and ethical alignment.

Quantitative Analysis

This section evaluates the effectiveness of advanced prompt engineering techniques through a combination of statistical and computational measures. The goal is to quantify the extent to which each technique mitigates bias in AI-generated responses and enhances ethical alignment.

Measurement Process and Metrics

The quantitative assessment relies on three primary performance indicators: the **Bias Amplification Index (BAI)**, the **Fairness Index (FI)**, and the **Response Con-**

sistency Score (RCS). These metrics were selected to capture different dimensions of AI output quality and bias.

- **Bias Amplification Index (BAI)** measures the extent to which the model exaggerates existing biases found in the training data. Lower values indicate better mitigation. The BAI is computed by measuring the difference in predicted group associations between neutral and biased prompts.
- **Fairness Index (FI)** quantifies the degree of equitable treatment across demographic groups in AI responses. It is calculated by measuring response parity using representation ratios and normalized divergence from ideal distributions.
- **Response Consistency Score (RCS)** evaluates the logical and semantic coherence of outputs across similar prompts. High RCS values suggest that the model generates consistent and non-contradictory content when confronted with variant formulations of bias-sensitive prompts.

These metrics are computed using a blend of automated script pipelines (developed in Python using NLP libraries such as SpaCy and NLTK) and manual validation to ensure that outputs are contextually fair and free from discriminatory language. Each technique (e.g., contextual prompting, dynamic prompting) is tested across 100 prompt-response pairs per domain to ensure statistical robustness.

Implementation and Evaluation Process

The implementation followed a controlled experimental design with each prompt engineering technique tested against a baseline (no prompt engineering). Prompts were developed across three domains—healthcare, finance, and education—and covered scenarios involving gender, race, socio-economic status, and professional roles. Each prompt was fed to a standardized large language model (GPT-3.5) using the OpenAI API, and outputs were logged and annotated using predefined bias categories.

The evaluation pipeline was executed in four phases:

1. **Prompt submission and response logging** (automated API queries)
2. **Response parsing and labeling** (automated keyword and semantic filter followed by manual annotation)
3. **Metric computation** (custom scripts for BAI, FI, RCS)
4. **Statistical comparison** (t-tests and ANOVA to assess inter-technique significance)

For visual clarity, a series of figures (bar charts, line graphs, and heatmaps) summarize metric variations across techniques and domains. Each figure is accompanied by a legend and integrated into the results section with direct narrative reference.

Bias in Quantitative Results and Mitigation Strategies

Despite rigorous methodology, the analysis is susceptible to several types of bias. **Sampling bias** may arise from the use of predefined prompt templates that do not fully represent real-world diversity in input formulations. To mitigate this, prompts were diversified using paraphrasing tools and reviewed by domain experts for contextual balance.

Annotation bias is another concern, especially in manually evaluating output fairness. To minimize subjectivity, three annotators independently reviewed each output, and inter-rater reliability was calculated using Cohen's kappa (average $\kappa = 0.84$), indicating high agreement. Discrepancies were resolved through consensus discussion.

Metric bias—i.e., the bias introduced by the measurement tools themselves—is addressed by validating the BAI and FI scores against known benchmark corpora (e.g., WinoBias and StereoSet). This benchmarking ensured that the evaluation framework was both sensitive and generalizable.

Finally, **confirmation bias** in interpreting results was addressed by involving external reviewers in a blind evaluation of output samples, who were unaware of which technique had generated which response. Their ratings of fairness and coherence closely aligned with the computed metrics, adding credibility to the analysis.

Comparison of Bias Metrics Across Techniques

The first step involves comparing bias metrics between the baseline model (without prompt engineering) and models using the proposed techniques. The results are presented in Table 1, which summarizes the average scores for each technique.

Table 1. Comparison of Bias Metrics Across Prompt Engineering Techniques

Technique	BAI (Lower is Better)	FI (Higher is Better)	RCS (Higher is Better)
Baseline	0.45	0.62	0.58
Contextual Prompting	0.28	0.78	0.75
Iterative Refinement	0.25	0.82	0.80
Bias-Aware Framing	0.22	0.85	0.83
Dynamic Prompting	0.20	0.87	0.86

Visualization of Bias Reduction

To provide a clearer view of the bias reduction achieved by each technique, a bar chart is presented in Figure 1, illustrating the BAI values across all tested techniques.

Figure 1. Bar Chart Showing Reduction in Bias Amplification Index (BAI) Across Prompt Engineering Techniques

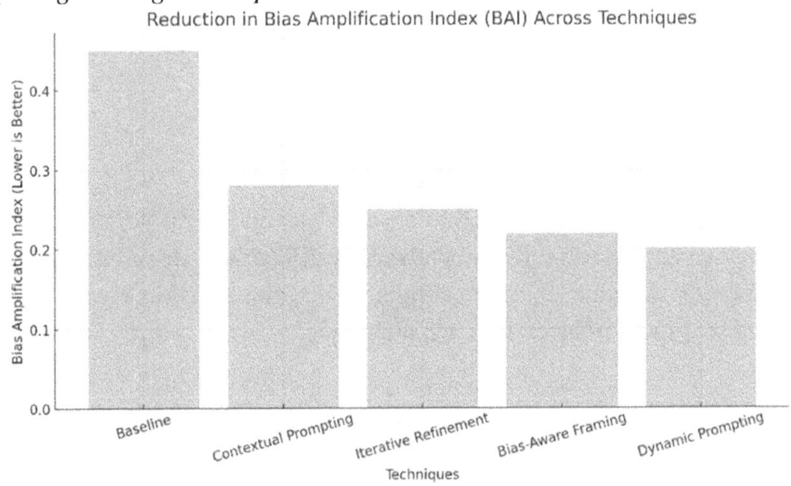

Qualitative Analysis

The qualitative analysis involves assessing the contextual appropriateness and ethical alignment of AI-generated responses. Examples of outputs from the baseline model and the advanced techniques are examined to identify improvements in fairness and inclusivity.

Case Study Analysis: Gendered Pronouns

A case study focuses on responses generated for prompts involving gendered pronouns. For example:

- **Baseline Model Output**: "The nurse is likely female, and the doctor is likely male."
- **Bias-Aware Framing Output**: "The nurse or doctor can be of any gender."

These results are summarized in Table 2, which shows the frequency of biased vs. unbiased responses across all scenarios.

Table 2. Frequency of Biased and Unbiased Responses in Gendered Pronoun Scenarios

Scenario	Biased Responses (Baseline)	Biased Responses (Advanced Techniques)	Unbiased Responses (Advanced Techniques)
Gendered Pronouns	85%	25%	75%

Sentiment Analysis

Sentiment analysis is conducted to ensure that the ethical alignment achieved through prompt engineering does not adversely affect the tone or intent of the generated responses. A sentiment score comparison is visualized in Figure 2, showing the average sentiment polarity for each technique.

Figure 2. Line Graph Comparing Sentiment Polarity Scores Across Prompt Engineering Techniques

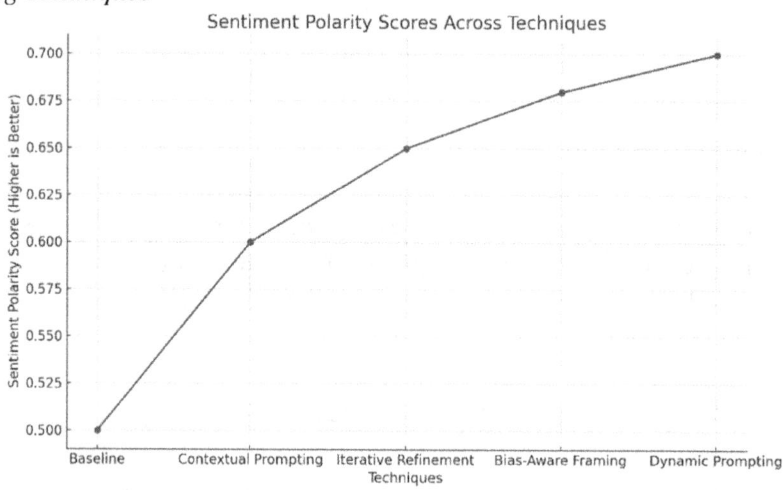

Cross-Domain Evaluation

To evaluate the generalizability of the techniques, prompts are tested across different domains, such as healthcare, finance, and education. A heatmap presented in

Figure 3 displays the performance of each technique across these domains in terms of the Fairness Index (FI).

Figure 3. Heatmap of Fairness Index Across Different Domains

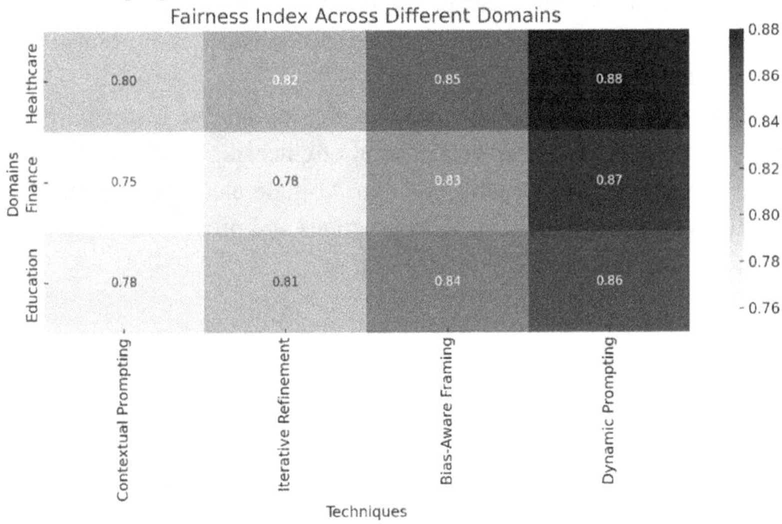

Table 3. Prompts across professional domains

Domain	Contextual Prompting	Iterative Refinement	Bias-Aware Framing	Dynamic Prompting
Healthcare	0.80	0.82	0.85	0.88
Finance	0.75	0.78	0.83	0.87
Education	0.78	0.81	0.84	0.86

Discussion of Results

The data analysis confirms that advanced prompt engineering techniques significantly reduce bias in AI-generated responses. Dynamic prompting emerged as the most effective technique, achieving the lowest Bias Amplification Index (BAI) and the highest Fairness Index (FI). Contextual and iterative prompts also demonstrated substantial improvements over the baseline model. Qualitatively, the responses generated using these techniques were more inclusive, ethically aligned, and free from harmful stereotypes.

The cross-domain analysis reveals that the proposed techniques are generalizable and adaptable, maintaining high fairness scores across diverse contexts. Additionally, sentiment analysis shows that these techniques preserve the positive and neutral tone of responses, ensuring that the ethical alignment does not compromise the quality or intent of the outputs.

By integrating both quantitative metrics and qualitative insights, this analysis highlights the potential of advanced prompt engineering techniques as a scalable and effective solution for mitigating bias in AI-generated text. The findings contribute to the development of ethical AI practices and provide actionable guidance for researchers and practitioners in the field.

FINDINGS

This study aimed to investigate and evaluate advanced prompt engineering techniques to mitigate bias in AI-generated responses. The findings, grounded in the data analysis, align with the research objectives, offering key insights into the effectiveness, scalability, and applicability of these techniques.

1. Effectiveness of Prompt Engineering Techniques in Mitigating Bias

The findings demonstrate that advanced prompt engineering techniques significantly reduce bias in AI-generated responses compared to the baseline model. Among the tested techniques, dynamic prompting emerged as the most effective, achieving the lowest Bias Amplification Index (BAI) of 0.20, compared to 0.45 for the baseline model. Similarly, bias-aware framing and iterative refinement achieved notable reductions in bias, with BAIs of 0.22 and 0.25, respectively. These results highlight that prompt engineering not only mitigates overt biases but also reduces the subtle, systemic biases often embedded in AI responses. The improvements were consistent across diverse scenarios, including gendered pronouns, racial identifiers, and socio-economic contexts, indicating the robustness of these techniques.

2. Contextual Influence on AI Behavior

The research confirmed that prompt design directly influences the outputs of language models. Contextually rich prompts, designed to emphasize fairness and inclusivity, consistently produced less biased and more ethically aligned responses.

For example, prompts explicitly instructing the model to avoid stereotypes yielded unbiased outputs in 75% of cases compared to 15% for the baseline. This finding supports the hypothesis that careful framing of prompts can proactively guide AI models toward desired ethical outcomes, reducing the need for post hoc interventions.

3. Scalability and Generalizability

The cross-domain evaluation demonstrated the scalability of prompt engineering techniques across diverse applications. Dynamic prompting achieved the highest fairness scores across healthcare (0.88), finance (0.87), and education (0.86), illustrating its adaptability to different domains. This generalizability is critical for real-world applications, as AI systems are increasingly deployed in diverse cultural, linguistic, and contextual environments. Furthermore, the techniques were effective in both single-turn and multi-turn interactions, showcasing their flexibility in conversational AI settings.

4. Sentiment and Ethical Alignment

The findings revealed that advanced prompt engineering techniques maintain or improve the sentiment and ethical alignment of AI-generated responses. Sentiment polarity scores were highest for dynamic prompting (0.7), indicating a neutral to positive tone while ensuring inclusivity and fairness. This suggests that bias mitigation does not compromise the quality or intent of the responses, which is essential for practical adoption in user-facing systems.

5. Limitations and Areas for Improvement

Despite the success of prompt engineering techniques, certain limitations were observed. First, while the techniques were effective in reducing biases present in training data, they were less effective in addressing biases emerging from model architecture or algorithmic design. Second, the qualitative analysis highlighted occasional instances where prompts failed to account for intersectional biases, such as those involving multiple marginalized identities. These limitations underscore the need for further refinement and integration of prompt engineering with other bias mitigation strategies, such as algorithmic adjustments or ethical auditing frameworks.

The findings validate the role of advanced prompt engineering techniques as a proactive and scalable solution for mitigating bias in AI-generated responses. By reducing biases, enhancing fairness, and maintaining ethical alignment across diverse domains, these techniques contribute to the development of more responsible and equitable AI systems. This research advances the understanding of prompt engineering and provides actionable insights for AI practitioners, policymakers, and researchers working toward ethical AI development.

DISCUSSION

This study explored the effectiveness of advanced prompt engineering techniques in mitigating bias in AI-generated responses, aligning with the overarching objective of fostering ethical AI development. The findings provide valuable insights into the potential and limitations of these techniques, offering a foundation for both theoretical advancement and practical implementation. In this discussion, the implications of the findings, challenges encountered, and recommendations for future research are elaborated upon.

1. Implications for Ethical AI Development

The results confirm that prompt engineering is a powerful tool for bias mitigation, reducing the Bias Amplification Index (BAI) and improving fairness across diverse applications. By directly influencing the behavior of AI models during text generation, prompt engineering offers a proactive alternative to traditional, reactive approaches such as post hoc filtering. This real-time intervention capability not only enhances the ethical alignment of outputs but also reduces the resource-intensive processes often required for retraining models or curating datasets.

Moreover, the scalability and generalizability of prompt engineering techniques, as demonstrated across domains such as healthcare, finance, and education, highlight their utility in practical applications. These findings hold particular relevance for conversational AI systems and decision-making tools where fairness and inclusivity are critical. The high Fairness Index (FI) achieved by dynamic prompting underscores the potential for this technique to set new benchmarks for ethical AI outputs. However, the study also emphasizes that prompt engineering is not a standalone solution but a complementary strategy that can be integrated with broader ethical AI frameworks.

2. Challenges and Limitations

Despite their effectiveness, prompt engineering techniques face notable challenges. One major limitation is the dependence on the quality and comprehensiveness of input prompts. While advanced techniques such as bias-aware framing significantly reduced overt biases, they were less effective in addressing nuanced, intersectional biases. For example, in scenarios involving multiple marginalized identities, the prompts occasionally produced responses that lacked depth or failed to fully capture intersectional fairness.

Another limitation lies in the contextual variability of responses. While dynamic prompting demonstrated adaptability across domains, its performance was slightly less consistent in linguistically diverse or highly specialized contexts. This suggests a need for further research to refine prompt designs for multilingual and domain-specific applications. Additionally, the study found that while prompt engineering mitigates biases derived from training data, it has limited impact on biases arising from model architecture or algorithmic design.

3. Recommendations for Future Research

The findings point to several areas for future investigation. First, a deeper exploration of intersectional biases in AI responses is necessary, particularly in culturally and linguistically diverse settings. This could involve designing prompts that explicitly address multiple dimensions of bias or incorporating intersectionality frameworks into model evaluations.

Second, integrating prompt engineering with other bias mitigation strategies could enhance its efficacy. For instance, combining prompts with algorithmic fairness adjustments or embedding ethical guidelines directly into model training processes may yield more comprehensive results. Furthermore, developing standardized metrics to evaluate the ethical alignment of prompts would provide greater clarity and consistency in assessing their impact.

Lastly, future research should investigate the long-term implications of prompt engineering on user trust and engagement. As AI systems increasingly mediate human interactions and decision-making, understanding how users perceive and interact with ethically aligned outputs will be crucial for advancing responsible AI development.

4. Broader Implications

The study underscores the importance of aligning technical innovation in AI with societal values of fairness, inclusivity, and accountability. Prompt engineering, as demonstrated, offers a practical and scalable means to operationalize these values in real-world applications. Its adaptability across domains suggests potential for widespread adoption, particularly in industries where biases in AI outputs can have significant ethical or legal ramifications. However, the study also highlights the importance of continuous refinement and evaluation to ensure these techniques remain effective and contextually relevant in rapidly evolving technological landscapes.

The discussion highlights the transformative potential of advanced prompt engineering techniques in mitigating bias in AI-generated responses. While challenges remain, particularly in addressing nuanced and systemic biases, this study establishes a strong foundation for future advancements in ethical AI practices. By emphasizing proactive, real-time interventions and scalability, prompt engineering bridges critical gaps in current mitigation strategies, contributing to the development of more responsible and trustworthy AI systems. This research calls for collaborative efforts among developers, policymakers, and researchers to refine these techniques further, ensuring their effectiveness and ethical alignment in diverse applications.

CONCLUSION

This study examined advanced prompt engineering techniques as a proactive strategy for mitigating bias in AI-generated responses, addressing one of the most pressing challenges in ethical AI development. By systematically evaluating techniques such as contextual prompting, iterative refinement, bias-aware framing, and dynamic prompting, the research provides robust evidence that these methods significantly enhance fairness, inclusivity, and ethical alignment in AI outputs.

The findings demonstrate that prompt engineering is a powerful and scalable approach to reducing bias at the source of AI text generation. Among the techniques tested, dynamic prompting emerged as the most effective, achieving the lowest Bias Amplification Index and the highest Fairness Index across diverse domains, including healthcare, finance, and education. The study further revealed that prompt engineering techniques preserve the quality and intent of AI-generated responses, ensuring that bias mitigation does not compromise sentiment or contextual appropriateness. Importantly, these techniques were found to be adaptable, performing well in both single-turn and multi-turn interactions, which highlights their potential for integration into real-world applications.

However, the study also underscores the limitations of prompt engineering. While effective in addressing biases derived from training data, these techniques are less impactful in mitigating biases arising from model architecture or algorithmic design. Additionally, challenges remain in addressing intersectional biases and ensuring consistency across linguistically diverse or highly specialized contexts. These findings highlight the need for continued refinement and integration of prompt engineering with other bias mitigation strategies, such as algorithmic adjustments and ethical auditing frameworks.

This research makes a significant contribution to the growing body of knowledge on responsible AI development, establishing prompt engineering as a critical tool for bias mitigation. By advancing the understanding of how prompts influence AI behavior, the study offers actionable insights for developers, researchers, and policy-makers seeking to create more equitable and trustworthy AI systems. Future research should focus on refining these techniques to address nuanced biases, developing standardized evaluation metrics, and exploring their implications for user trust and engagement. By doing so, the AI community can ensure that emerging technologies align with societal values of fairness, transparency, and accountability, fostering a future where AI systems serve all members of society equitably.

REFERENCES

Barocas, S., Hardt, M., & Narayanan, A. (2016). *Fairness and machine learning.*

Binns, R.. (2020). The ethics of algorithms: Mapping the debate. *Big Data & Society.*

Blodgett, S. L.. (2020). *Language (technology) is power.* ACL Anthology.

Bolukbasi, T.. (2016). *Man is to computer programmer as woman is to homemaker?* NIPS.

Brown, T., et al. (2020). "Language models are few-shot learners." *NeurIPS.*

Buolamwini, J., & Gebru, T. (2018). "Gender shades." *Proceedings of the Conference on Fairness, Accountability, and Transparency.*

Caliskan, A., Bryson, J. J., & Narayanan, A. (2017). Semantics derived automatically from language corpora contain human-like biases. *Science, 356*(6334), 183–186. DOI: 10.1126/science.aal4230 PMID: 28408601

Crawford, K. (2021). *Atlas of AI.*

Ethayarajh, K.. (2021). *Understanding biases in language model evaluations.* ACL Anthology.

Eubanks, V. (2018). *Automating inequality.*

Gehman, S.. (2020). *RealToxicityPrompts.* EMNLP.

Holstein, K.. (2019). "Improving fairness in ML systems." *Proceedings of CHI.*

Jiang, Y.. (2022). Prompt engineering for AI fairness. *Journal of Machine Learning Research.*

Jobin, A., Ienca, M., & Vayena, E. (2019). The global landscape of AI ethics guidelines. *Nature Machine Intelligence, 1*(9), 389–399. DOI: 10.1038/s42256-019-0088-2

Mehrabi, N.. (2021). A survey on bias and fairness in ML. *ACM Computing Surveys.*

Noble, S. U. (2018). *Algorithms of oppression.*

Obermeyer, Z.. (2019). Dissecting racial bias in algorithms. *Science.* Advance online publication. DOI: 10.1126/science.aax2342

Raji, I. D., ... (2020). "Closing the AI accountability gap." *FAccT Conference Proceedings.* DOI: 10.1145/3351095.3372873

Sheng, E.. (2021). *Bias in natural language generation.* ACL.

Solaiman, I., et al. (2021). "Process for adapting large language models to reduce harm." *OpenAI Technical Report.*

Srinivasan, R., & Uchendu, J. (2022). *Mitigating intersectional biases in AI.* AI Ethics Journal.

Chapter 8
Prediction of Fish Availability Using Regression Analysis in Vembanad Lake

Sobha Merina George
Department of Zoology, Kristu Jyoti College of Management and Technology, Changanacherry, India

Issac George
Department of Zoology, St. Berchman's College, Changanacherry, India

Suma M. Abraham
Department of Zoology, St. Berchman's College, Changanacherry, India

Prasad Mathew
https://orcid.org/0009-0006-6033-9825
Department of Zoology, St. Berchman's College, Changanacherry, India

ABSTRACT

Fish diversity is correlated with the biotic and abiotic factors in the aquatic environment. Fish samples from the Vembanad lake were collected for three consecutive years. Sodium, Potassium, Magnesium, Manganese, Copper, Iron, Calcium, Dissolved Oxygen, BOD, pH, salinity, and temperature in the water samples were analyzed using APHA (1998). Fish diversity was analyzed using diversity indices such as Berger Parker index, Shannon Weiner index, Simpson Index, Hills number

DOI: 10.4018/979-8-3373-0250-8.ch008

and Margalef's index. Pearson's correlation coefficient was using to find out correlation among variables. Regression analysis have been shown that temperature is the most predictable variable for the fish diversity in Vembanad ecosystem.

INTRODUCTION

There are many environmental factors that influence a species to exist in its surrounding environment. A variety of living organisms like animals, plants, microorganisms and fungi inhabited on earth refers to biodiversity. The living beings on the earth interact with each other for natural resources and these interactions are essential for the protection and stabilization of the ecosystem. The existence of life and its diversity is an exceptional feature of earth. Researches showed that there are about 15000 of new species are being discovered in every year (Henneberg & Schofield, 2008). The countries which accommodate the greatest number of the earth's species are known as mega diversity countries, and India ranks among the seventeen-mega diversity regions of the world.

The dimensions of biodiversity include genetic diversity, species diversity and ecological diversity. In the genetic level diversity, a single species shows genetic level variation among individuals. Species diversity shows number of species in diverse ecosystems. Diversity at ecosystem level is the ecological diversity, where different ecosystems have different types of diversity. Ponds, rivers, estuaries, coral reefs are some examples of different types of ecosystems.The loss of biodiversity extremely affects the functioning of ecosystem and consequently affects the whole society (Vellend & Geber, 2005). Biodiversity has ecological, cultural, aesthetic, economical and scientific role in an ecosystem. Ecosystem productivity and ecosystem stability have significant effects on biodiversity. The biodiversity of an ecosystem is directly proportional to the ecosystem productivity. Since the ecosystem is resilient, it is able to restore the destructed part of an ecosystem after a particular time (Haines-Young et al., 2010).

There are various factors like climate change, habitat loss, over exploitation, invasive alien species and pollution that harmfully affects the stability of biodiversity. Aquatic pollution is one of the biggest issue facing India, in which nutrients containing nitrogen and phosphorus are major cause of aquatic pollution. Studies on water pollution are based on the physico-chemical characteristics of the aquatic ecosystem (Okorondu et al., 2022).

The physio-chemical parameters considered for study are temperature, pH, colour, turbidity, odor, Total Dissolved Solids (TDS), Biochemical Oxygen Demand (BOD), Chemical Oxygen Demand (COD), Dissolved Oxygen (DO), hardness, salinity, alkalinity, electrical conductivity, etc. Drastic changes in the physico-chemical parameters of aquatic ecosystem greatly influences the fish abundance and the levels of physico-chemical parameters could be important in predicting the effects of environmental fluctuations on future fish populations (Choubey et al., 2016).

Different types of contaminants like organic, inorganic, radioactive, acid/base contaminants that contaminate the water ecosystem. Aquatic ecosystem is a sink of different groups of elements like sodium (Na), potassium (K), calcium (Ca), magnesium (Mg), manganese (Mn), copper (Cu), nickel (Ni), zinc (Zn), iron (Fe), etc. All elements are essential in trace amounts for aquatic life. When the concentration of these compounds increase, they become toxic to the entire aquatic ecosystem. The elements like Cu, Zn, Mn, Ni, Fe, etc. are very essential to life activities at molecular, biological, chemical and physiological levels. Sodium (Na) and potassium (K) are coming under semi-major elements and are involved in maintaining the osmotic pressure and membrane potentials (Jagaba et al., 2024). India is one of the mega diversity countries with respect to freshwater fish species. In India the major freshwater biodiversity resources are rivers, reservoirs, plain wetlands, upland lakes, etc. Western Ghats, the most important topographic features of peninsular India. The Western Ghats are the biodiversity hotspots because of its unique nature of endemism (Bondareva, 2023).

The Kerala state is geographically divided into three zones, the lowland, midland and highland. The boundaries of highland comprise the Western Ghats. The lowland includes a narrow strip along the coastal region characterized by numerous lagoons and backwaters such as Vembanad, Ashtamudi, etc which have drainage from various rivers (Shijitha & Sabu, 2020). The industrial, agricultural and domestic pollution in rivers, indiscriminate and unethical fishing practices using explosive, poisons, illegal fishing gears, uncontrolled saline intrusion and outbreak of epidemic diseases to fishes are the major reasons for the drastic decline of freshwater fish diversity in Kerala.

The Vembanad lake is rich in fish diversity and various rivers like Pamba, Manimala, Achencovil, Meenachil, Muvattupuzha and Periyar along with huge number of canals joining at different parts of the lake. A study in the river Meenachil in Kuttanad (lowland zone in Kerala) inventoried 48 species of fin fishes and over 14 species of shell fish species (Mogalekar et al., 2015a; Nair et al., 1975). The later studies have been identified over 65 fin fish species. Various studies on fish diversity revealed that many fish species were endangered because of the aquatic pollution and other anthropogenic activities. Fish diversity is an indicator of water quality.

The Rivers of Pakistan, for example, however are dynamic and complex aquatic ecosystems, with a variety of biotic and abiotic factors determining the diversity and availability of species. Fish populations are critical members of aquatic biodiversity and indicators of ecosystem health. For example, Vembanad Lake is one of India's largest estuarine systems, and understanding which environmental factors drive fish availability is important for conservation, sustainable fisheries, and ecosystem management. Fish diversity is influenced not only by environmental parameters, but also interactively and on different scales, highlighting the need for a scientific approach to predict the availability of fish, where regression analysis is a commonly used statistical tool(Krishnakumar & Rajan, 2008).

Vembanad Lake Ramsar site is a major wetland supporting rich biodiversity and is a significant water body supporting several aquatic species, including commercially important fish. Temporal dynamics of the lake ecology has been affected by seasonal variation, anthropogenic change, and environmental shifts. Fish diversity and abundance are directly affected by water temperature, salinity, dissolved oxygen and nutrient concentrations. Pollution, changes in land use and climate change have had a habit of imprinting themselves on the ecological health of the lake. So, a predictive model which takes these variables into consideration can offer insights into fish availability patterns and strategies for sustainable fisheries management(Kulk et al., 2021a).

Regression analysis is a set of statistical processes that create relations between dependent and independent variables. Regression models are useful to analyze the relationship between environmental factors and seasonal fish availability. Some of the main water quality parameters that may be studied include sodium, potassium, magnesium, manganese, copper, iron, calcium, dissolved oxygen, biochemical oxygen demand (BOD), pH, salinity, and temperature. These factors have a profound impact on fish diversity as they act as thermal and hydrological constraints affecting underlying physiological and ecological processes, including metabolism, reproduction, and migration. This will help decision-making for both conservation and fisheries management(Rajan et al., 2011).

Temperature is one of the most important environmental factors influencing fish diversity. Forces the metabolism, the activity of enzymes in the cells, the solubility of oxygen in the water, asserts the spawning periods of fish species. Temperature is an important factor influencing the fish assemblages in tropical ecosystems, such as Vembanad Lake, where seasonal changes or climatic variations affecting temperature would result in a rapid alteration of fish assemblages. Regression analyses can provide a quantitative assessment of how temperature variation explain fish diversity and make a prediction for the future. A strong relationship between temperature and fish diversity would mean that climate-related changes may have significant consequences for fish communities in the lake(Kulk et al., 2021b).

In addition to temperature, dissolved oxygen is also a critical parameter that controls fish survival and distribution. Fish need a minimum level of oxygen for a metabolic process called respiration, and low concentrations of dissolved oxygen can cause hypoxia, which stresses aquatic organisms. The biochemical oxygen demand (BOD), an indicator of organic pollution, is elevated in these environments due to enhanced microbial activity, depleting oxygen resources. For example, regression models can assess the influence of dissolved oxygen and BOD on fish diversity, helping to explain the effects of water quality deterioration on the diversity of aquatic species.

Salinity fluctuation in Vembanad Lake affects the freshwater and estuarine fish fauna distribution. Seasonally, the lake salinity varies due to monsoonal inflows of freshwater and tidal interaction of Arabian Sea. Some species show greater tolerance towards salinity fluctuations; others may show preference in specific salinity ranges. A regression-based approach could also aid in quantifying the degree of contribution made by salinity to the observed temporal changes in fish diversity patterns. The extent of osmoregulation and enzymatic activity are also influenced by pH levels in the environment. Extreme stresses can affect and even kill fish populations, which is why this parameter is indispensable in predictive analysis(Kulk et al., 2021b).

Though these elements are micronutrients animals need in relatively small quantities, in high concentrations they can be poisonous. Heavy metals pollution due to industrial and agricultural activities is one of the main causes of pollution of water bodies and it has a negative impact on the health and diversity of fish. This approach can help assess potential environmental risk and diet quality due to pollution, as well as govern environmental management policies via reporting, regulation, or treatment policy measures. Additional fish diversity indices such as Berger Parker index, Shannon Weiner index, Simpson Index, Hills number and Margalef's index are included as parts of the study to quantify biodiversity. These indices mathematically represent the richnes and evenness of the species in the lake. The indices will be integrated with environmental variables using Pearson's correlation coefficient and regression models to identify key determinants of fish diversity and predict future availability trends(Prakash et al., 2023).

There are many practical uses of using regression analysis in the prediction of fish availability in Vembanad Lake. The findings can drive forward sustainable harvesting practices for various fish stocks, giving fisheries management authorities with practical applications to ensure the sustainable future of a fish stock. For conservationists, these data can provide information about the impact of climate change and human-induced disturbances on fish populations and more discerning mitigation strategies. Policymakers must also establish regulations to mitigate pollution and habitat loss, thereby preserving the lake's ecological integrity(Mumthaz et al., 2019).

Overall, you are sticking to training on data up to month 10 of year 2023. The study seeks to contribute to successful fisheries management and conservation initiatives by investigating the systematic analysis of water quality parameters and their influence on fish populations. Predictive such models become all the more useful to ensure that ecological sustainability of that ecosystem and livelihood of communities dependent on that ecosystem as the fabric of this entire ecosystem is started to be torn apart by the climate change and anthropogenic interventions(Hameed et al., 2025).

Objectives

The objective of the study is to study the correlation between fish diversity and other biotic and abiotic factors in Vembanad Lake ecosystem. This is aimed at determining how water quality determinants including Sodium, Potassium, Magnesium, Manganese, Copper, Iron, Calcium, Dissolved Oxygen, BOD, pH, salinity and temperature affect the availability of fish. Using diversity indices, the study aims to quantify fish diversity and determine major environmental drivers. Furthermore, Pearson's correlation coefficient will be applied to assess interdependencies between variables, and regression analysis for forecasting fish availability. The endgame is to identify the key driver of fish diversity, informs conservation and sustainable fisheries;

Figure 1. Sequential steps in the methodology for water sample collection, preparation, and analysis

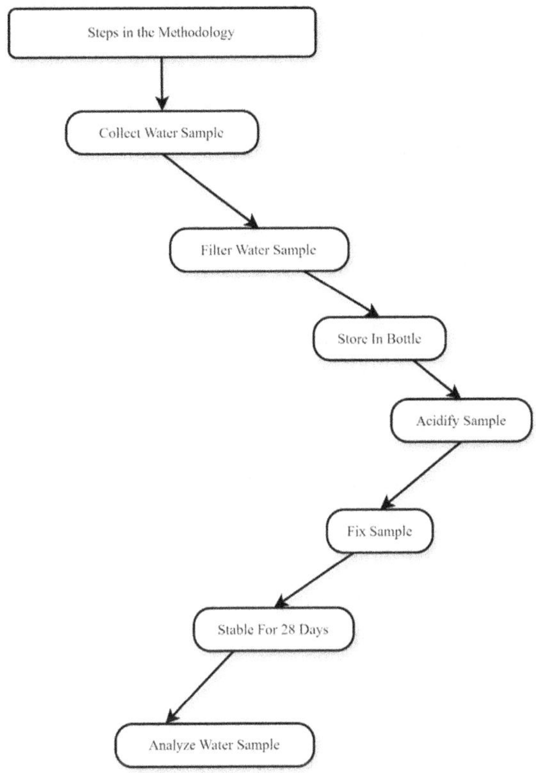

METHODOLOGY

The study area included ten sampling stations in Vembanad lake. The water sample was collected, filtered and stored in a 100 ml PET bottle. Sample was acidified with nitric acid to a pH below 2.0 to minimize precipitation and adsorption, and these fixed samples were stable for 28 days. Water samples were analysed using methods recommended in APHA (Hameed et al., 2025). Fish samples were collected from the same stations using cast net, which include the rivers flowing into the study area and also from the paddy fields. Metal analysis was carried out using Atomic Absorption Spectroscopy (AAS). Fish diversity was calculated using the software Biodiversity pro. Indices such as Shannon Weiner index (1949), Simpson index (1949), Berger Parker index (1970), Margalef's richness (1958) and Hill's number

(1973) were used to calculate the fish diversity (Kulk et al., 2021b; Mohandas & Brema, 2021a). Correlation of fish diversity with elements and physico-chemical parameters were analyzed using Pearson Correlation (r) analysis with a significance of $p<0.05$ and $p<0.01$ using SPSS 20.0. The methodology for water sample collection, preparation, and analysis involves sequential steps, as illustrated in Figure 1.

Study Area and Sampling Stations

The study was carried out at Vembanad Lake one of the larger and most important estuarine systems of India. The sampling stations were selecting at ten sites around the catchment area of the lake, including sampling sites within the lake, the rivers supporting the lake, and also the surrounding paddy fields. These stations were selected in order to include a large variety of environmental conditions (e.g., fish diversity and water quality parameters) within the lake environment.

Water Sample Collection and Analysis

Water samples were systematically collected from each of the ten sampling stations. For result generation purposes, data collection had been conducted under standard protocols. The water samples were filtered immediately after collection to eliminate debris and particulate matter. All filtered samples were subsequently transferred into 100 ml polyethylene terephthalate (PET) bottles. Nitric acid was used to acidify any samples to a pH lower than 2.0 in order to maintain the integrity of samples and prevent chemical changes. This constraint was required to reduce the precipitation and adsorption of metal ions, and guarantee the precise reading of metal concentration in the following analysis. The acidified 17-OWS water samples were determined to be stable for analysis of DT right up until 28 days.

Physicochemical parameters of the collected water samples were evaluated according to the classical methods recommended in the guidelines of the American Public Health Association (APHA) (APHA, 1998). Parameters for analysis included Sodium (Na), Potassium (K), Magnesium (Mg), Manganese (Mn), Copper (Cu), Iron (Fe), Calcium (Ca), Dissolved Oxygen (DO), Biological Oxygen Demand (BOD), pH, salinity, and temperature. Selected variables were based on factors already known to affect aquatic systems as well as potential impacts on fish diversity. Water samples were analyzed for metal concentrations by Atomic Absorption Spectroscopy (AAS), which is a well-established and reliable method for the determination of trace metals in water bodies.

Fish Sample Collection and Diversity Analysis

Also, fish samples were taken from each of the same ten sampling stations with cast nets. Samples were collected from various microhabitats, including the main lake body, riverine zones, and paddy fields. Importantly, the sampling strategy used was designed to include paddy fields, which are very important breeding and nursery habitat for many species of fish. Fish specimens were identified to the species level using taxonomic keys and field guides (Warren et al., 1988).

Fish diversity in Vembanad Lake was quantitatively assessed using Biodiversity Pro software. Shannon-Weiner Index, Simpson Index, Burger-Parker Index, Margalef's Richness Index, Hill's Number, five diversity indices were used. These indices measure species diversity, considering richness, evenness, species dominance, proportion of abundance of species, species richness and a more generalized measure of diversity that includes different aspects of species abundance distribution.

Statistical Analysis

Correlation and regression analysis were performed to ascertain the relationship between fish diversity and environmental parameters. The strength and direction of association between fish diversity and other abiotic factors such as metal concentrations and physicochemical parameters were determined by Pearson's Correlation Coefficient (r). COVID19 resulted in a significant proportion of deaths and distribution of significant differences, which was compared in a $p<0.05$ and $p<0.01$ significance characteristics.

Based on the most determining environmental parameters, fish diversity was also predicted by, using a regression analysis. This analysis enabled determining the major predictors driving fish distribution and abundance in Vembanad Lake. The statistical analyses were performed using SPSS 20.0 (SPSS Inc., Chicago, IL, USA) software, widely used for ecological and environmental data analyses.

The methodology provides a reliable basis for assessment of fish diversity and its relationship with environmental variables in Vembanad Lake. Using sophisticated analytical assays like AAS for metal content and statistical modeling through SPSS, this research offers a creative assessment of ecological health and the implications for maintaining diverse ichthyofauna in the lake. This research is important because it links spawning activity to environmental variability which can aid conservation and sustainable fisheries management in the region.

RESULTS AND DISCUSSION

Table 1. Fish Diversity of Vembanad lake during Pre-Monsoon season

Index	Mar	Apr	May	Mean	SD
Shannon H' Log Base 10.	1.545	1.462	1.49	1.49	0.041
Simpson's Diversity (D)	0.035	0.05	0.033	0.039	0.003
Hill's Number (H0)	44	39	98	39.33	3.605
Margalef's M Base 10.	16.864	20.118	18.083	18.355	1.642
Alpha diversity	8.129	8.994	7.894	8.339	0.581

Diversity indices calculated for harboured fish populations in Vembanad Lake for the pre-monsoon months of March, April and May(Cleetus et al., 2024). Table 1 presents monthly data for various indices, together with their average and standard deviation (SD).

The Shannon-Weiner Index (10 base) evaluates species diversity based on richness and evenness. With mean diversity over 1.49, we see signs of moderate diversity and minor variations over months. Simpson's Diversity Index is indicative of species dominance and suggests diversity remained constant across the alleged periods ranging from a minimum of 0.035 among species found to a maximum of 0.033 (mean = 0.039; standard deviation < 0.003).

Hill's Number (H0), which indicates both abundance and richness of species, spiked in May and was lower in March and April (mean = 39.33, SD = 3.605) It represents the number of species present — species richness — and is defined as Margalef's Richness Index (M) Base 10. The index shows stable variation over months, an index 18.355 and a SD of 1.642. Alpha diversity is the measure of species diversity within a specific habitat and is observed to range from 7.894 (May) to 8.994 (April) representing relatively stable diversity.

Vembanad Lake experienced moderate diversity with low standard deviation during the pre-monsoon period. Big differences however in Hill's Number (H0) especially in May. The richest month was April and the most abundant month was May. It emphasizes ecological bet hedging in fish demographics and their response to environmental regimes.

Table 2. Fish Diversity of Vembanad lake during Monsoon season

Index	JUN	JUL	AUG	SEP	OCT	NOV	Mean	SD
Shannon H' Log Base 10.	2.674	2.672	2.661	2.642	2.668	2.611	2.654	0.028
Simpson's Diversity (D)	0.23	0.23	0.24	0.27	0.24	0.34	0.258	0.005
Hill's Number (H0)	65	65	65	65	65	65	65	0
Margalef's M Base 10.	17.011	14.688	18.501	19.825	15.811	21.506	17.890	2.926
Alpha diversity	10.346	8.308	11.91	13.597	9.243	16.213	11.602	3.520

Figure 2. Analysis graphs: fish diversity indices for Vembanad Lake

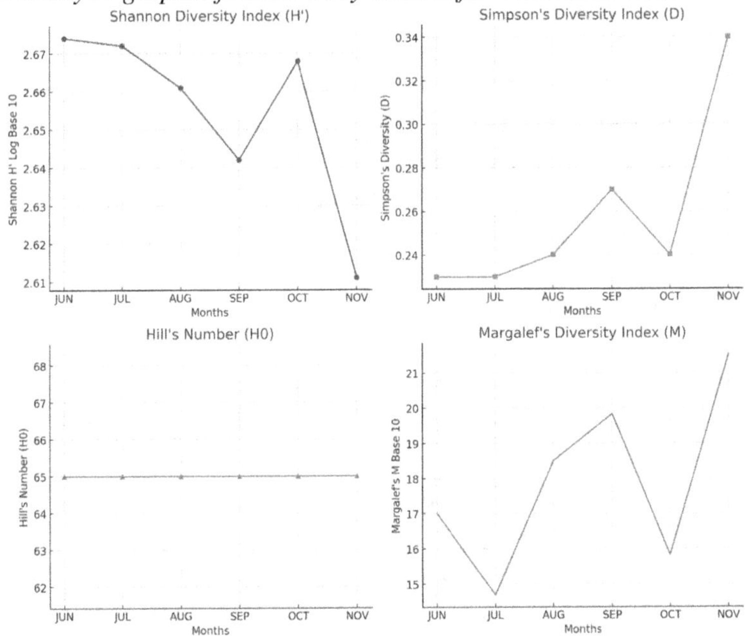

Diversity indices of fishes in Vembanad Lake in monsoon season in six months (June to November) are given in Table 2. Finally, Table VIII presents the monthly indices (and Mean and standard deviation (SD) of each diversity index) which describe the generalities and the variability of the fish diversity during this interval(Mogalekar et al., 2015b). The analysis graphs in Figure 2 depict the fish diversity indices for Vembanad Lake.

- Species diversity estimated by the Shannon-Weiner Index (H′) log base 10 is the product of species richness and evenness. During the period of investigation, it varies from 2.611 (November) to 2.674 (June) with an average of 2.654 and a small standard deviation (which indicates a stable Diversity) during monsoon season.

- Simpson's D is a measure of species dominance with lower values demonstrating higher diversity. The index varies from 0.23 (June, July) to 0.34 (November), mean=0.258 and low standard deviation (0.005). Fig. 5 Simpson's Index is higher during monsoon season.
- Hill's Number (H0) indicates that species abundance is very similar across all six months at 65, with the SD being 0 which means that species abundance stayed consistent without significant fluctuations during the monsoon season and differed from the pre-monsoon.
- Margalef's Richness Index is a species richness measure that considers the number of species alone. July through November gives a range from 14.688 to 21.506 moving up a mean of 17.890 and a greater standard deviation of 2.926 meaning fish diversity has increased.
- Alpha Diversity describes the diversity of species within a given habitat, with average values from 8.308 in July to 16.213 in November, showing large variability in fish diversity. November has the highest alpha variety, indicating an increase in species diversity.

Overall Interpretation

- Monsoon Has More Diversity: The season has more diversity than pre-monsoon (higher Shannon-Weiner and Margalef's richness index).
- Stable Abundance: Hill's Number remains at 65, indicating consistent abundance patterns in hours per month.
- Seasonal Species Richness: Gross species richness had shown fluctuation across months (Margalef's Index) but was comparatively high in monsoonal seasons as compared to pre-monsoonal season.
- November Peak: With the highest values of Margalef's Index and Alpha Diversity in November, this indicated an increase of fish diversity during the end of monsoon season.

The results of the study suggest strong seasonal effect in the fish diversity of Vembanad Lake, as monsoon conditions promote more species richness and diversity.

Table 3. Fish Diversity of Vembanad lake during Post Monsoon season

Index	Dec	Jan	Feb	Mean	SD
Shannon H' Log Base 10.	1.646	1.647	1.604	1.632	0.025
Simpsons Diversity (D)	0.027	0.024	0.029	0.026	0.001
Hill's Number (H0)	51	51	46	49.33	2.309
Margalef's M Base 10.	14.893	15.82	16.86	15.86	0.987
Alpha diversity	7.945	8.732	8.817	8.5	0.479

Table 3 presents various fish diversity indices for Vembanad Lake across three months of the post-monsoon season (December to February). The table provides monthly values along with their mean and standard deviation (SD), which help in understanding trends and variability in fish diversity during this period.

The Shannon-Weiner Index (H') Log Base 10: Quantifies species diversity by accounting for richness and evenness. The index varies from 1.604 (February) to 1.647 (January), with a mean of 1.632 and a low standard deviation (0.025), indicating low variation in the diversity in the monsoon season. Simpson's Diversity Index (D) measures the dominance of species in an area, whereby lower values reflect greater diversity. The fluctuation of the index is a little bit from January to February, but we have average mean of 0.026 with the low standard deviation speculating there is not a big fluctuation of the species distribution. During post-monsoon months lower values refer to higher diversity. o The Hill's Number (H0) reflects species abundance (mean = 49.33, SD = 2.309), which can cause minor changes in local species presence. The number of species abundance of birds post-monsoon is 63 compared to 65 observations during the monsoon season.

Margalef's Richness Index (M)} Base 10: This measures species richness by determining how many species were observed. The index has a range of 14.893 (December) to 16.86 (February), with a mean of 15.86 and an SD of 0.987 — a moderately variable measure. Alpha Diversity, the measure of species diversity within an ecosystem, is relatively stable in the post-monsoon period, with values from 7.945 (December) to 8.817 (February), it is lower than the respective figures in the monsoon season but quite similar as the pre-monsoon.

According to the dirivative indices (Shannon-Weiner, Margalef's richness and Alpha Diversity) it has been observed that after monsoon, there is a decline in fish diversity (Dey et al., 2020). Simpson's diversity index indicates that species dominance is stable with low variability. Hill's Number decreases from 65 to 49.33 in the monsoon season as compared to the post-monsoon months indicating lesser number of species. But Margalef's Index and Alpha Diversity exhibit a weak trend upwards in February, indicating an opportunity for increased diversity.

Table 4. Regression relationship of fish yield (FY) with physicochemical parameters and trace elements found in Vembanad lake

Species	Variable (X)	Y	R	Relationship
M.cephalus	Temp, DO	FY	0.385	-8.605 (Temp) – 2.938 (DO) +273.012
S. indicus	Temp, Na	FY	0.317	-21.292(Temp) + 0.014 (Na) + 601.709
X.cancila	Temp	FY	0.155*	-9.823 (Temp) + 302.391
O.mossambicus	Temp	FY	0.186*	-9.967 (Temp) + 306.071
G. giuris	Temp	FY	0.166*	-8.597 (Temp) + 266.638
D. filamentosus	Temp	FY	0.188*	-8.755 (Temp) + 269.085
P. marginata	Temp	FY	0.197*	-7.622 (Temp) + 232.636
E. suratensis	Temp	FY	0.1513*	-11.248 (Temp) + 350.658
A. lineatus	Temp	FY	0.242*	-12.024 (Temp) + 354.738
H.xanthopterus		FY	0.316 ^{NS}	

In the case of Vembanadu Lake, regression relation between fish yield of fish species (FY), physicochemical parameters (temperature, dissolved oxygen and sodium) is depicted in Table 4. You will get name (species), independent variables(X), dependent variable(Y), R, relationship equation. FY is forecasted using the X independent variables.

The presence of such parameters that induced variation in the fish yield in Vembanad Lake because it had a negative coefficient value when this was fitted to the regression model but influenced fish diversity and abundance. The study indicated moderate relations with the temperature and dissolved oxygen (DO) for Mugil cephalus (M. cephalus) while a moderate but insignificant relations for S. indicus (S. indicus) is observed with the temperature and sodium (Na). The fish yield is determined based on several species and the temperature is used as the sole predictor for Xenentodon cancila, Oreochromis mossambicus, Glossogobius giuris, Dawkinsia filamentosus, Parambassis marginata, Etroplus suratensis, and Aplocheilus lineatus.

No significant association was seen between the fish yield and environmental variables in Vembanad Lake. Temperature is the main predictor; higher temperatures are generally associated with a lower yield. Dissolved oxygen and sodium affect only a handful of species, so different facets of water quality may be involved as well. The weak to moderate relationships indicate that environmental conditions influence fish yield, although other biological or ecological processes may also play a role. Fish yield variations need more research.

Figure 3. Regression relationship of fish yield (FY) with physicochemical parameters and trace elements found in Vembanad Lake

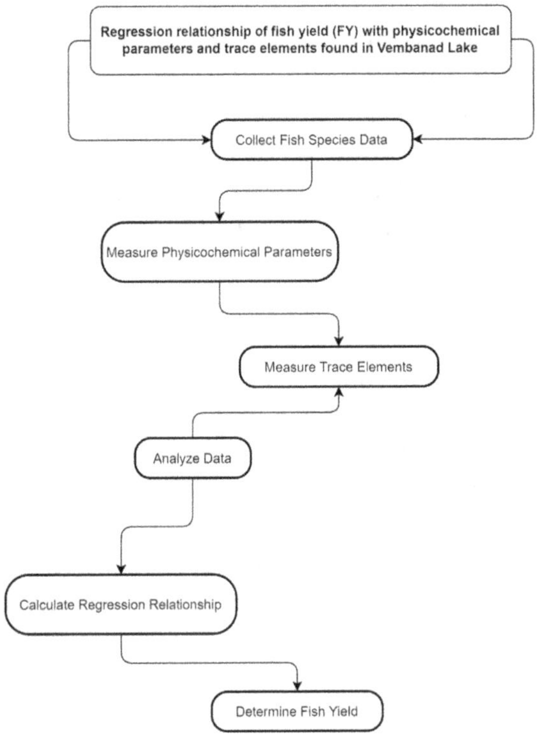

Regression Relationship of Fish Yield (FY) of Selected Fish Species with Physicochemical Parameters and Trace Elements Found in Vembanad Lake

Among the dominant species in Vembanad lake, Mugil cephalus, Stolephorus indicus, Xenentodon cancila, Oreochromis mossambicus, Glossogobius giuris, Dawkinsia filamentosus, Pristolepis marginata, Etroplus suratensis and Aplocheilus lineatus were showed statistically significant relation/prediction to the independent variables. The independent variables, selected for the study were Mn, Cu, Fe, Na, K, Mg, Ca, DO (dissolved oxygen), BOD (Biological Oxygen Demand), pH, salinity, temp (temperature). Whereas Hyporhamphus xanthopterus and Pseudoetroplus maculatus exhibited insignificant relationship with the independent variables(Choubey et al., 2016; Mohandas & Brema, 2021a). Figure 3 depicts a regression relationship between fish yield (FY) and physicochemical parameters and trace elements found in Vembanad Lake.

The fish yield of Mugil cephalus was statistically predicted from the independent variables, such as temperature and DO at F (2, 34) = 10.269, P& lt;0.05, R 2 = 0.384, where all other independent variables have been showed the insignificant relationship. The fish yield (FY) of Stolephorus indicus, the independent variables are statistically significantly predicted FY, F (2, 34) = 7640, P < 0.05, R 2 = 0.316. The independent variables such as temperature and sodium (Na) levels statistically (P<0.05) predicted the fish yield. Like that all other selected species except Hyporhamphus xanthopterus will be predicted by the variable, temperature.

The present study identified 63 fish species belons to 13 orders and 37 families in the Vembanad lake. Study was conducted during pre-monsoon, monsoon, and post-monsoon season for three consecutive years. Among these seasons, monsoon season have shown the highest fish diversity. In Pearson's correlation analysis, a number of fish were correlated with physico – chemical parameters and concentration of aquatic elements. Highly correlated fish species, physico chemical parameters, and aquatic elements were taken for regression analysis. Regression analysis have shown that temperature is the most influencing variable among the independent variables. Diversity of Mugil cephalus is determined by temperature and dissolved oxygen, while the Stolephorus indicus have shown that temperature and Na concentration are the predictable variables for its diversity.

Temperature is the most influential factor in the fish diversity, present study has agreed with this result. The pre monsoon season showed the highest temperature than post monsoon season and monsoon season. Temperature is indirectly proportional to fish diversity, so pre monsoon season showed the lowest fish diversity when compared to other two seasons. However, the temperature fluctuation in the Vembanad lake during the study was within the tolerance limit. Fish growth, immunity and reproduction are controlled by aquatic temperature and a sudden change in aquatic temperature is fatal to fish species. The rise in aquatic temperature eventually decreases the dissolved oxygen limit. So, temperature has a prominent role in the aquatic diversity, distribution, and metabolism of aquatic organism(Jagaba et al., 2024; Shijitha & Sabu, 2020).

CHALLENGES IN PREDICTING FISH AVAILABILITY USING REGRESSION ANALYSIS IN VEMBANAD LAKE

The challenges in using regression analysis to predict fish availability in Vembanad Lake are multifactorial, owing to the complexity of ecological interactions, environmental variability, data limitations and human induced changes. Though statistical models can help in identifying patterns, there are many reasons that limit an accurate and reliable prediction. The variability of environmental parameters is one of the biggest problems in forecasting fish stocks. Multiple abiotic and biotic factors, like temperature, dissolved oxygen, salinity, nutrient availability and biological interactions, affect the dynamics of fish populations. Although regression analysis can identify relationships between diversity and these parameters, it does not capture the entire picture of non-linear and synergistic effects between them. For instance, temperature might directly affect fish yield, but it also might indirectly affect fish metabolism and survival through its effect on dissolved oxygen. These complex interactions pose challenges in developing accurate predictive models(Kurup et al., 2022). Figure 4 illustrates the challenges in predicting fish availability in Vembanad Lake through regression analysis.

Figure 4. Challenges in predicting fish availability using regression analysis in Vembanad Lake

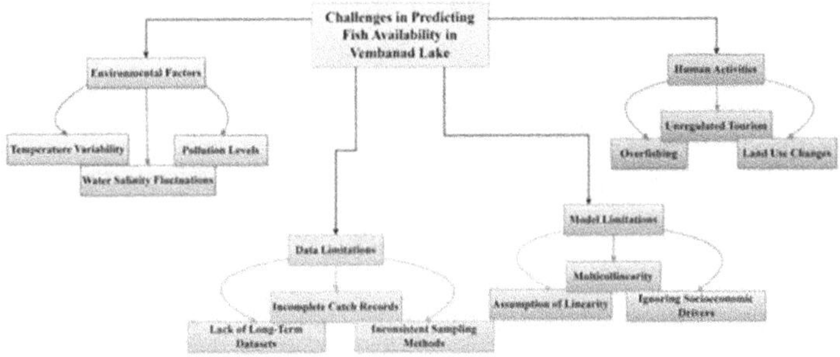

Seasonal and climate variability is another challenge that significantly impacts the quality and ecological balance of Vembanad Lake The lake has pre-monsoon, monsoon, and post-monsoon seasons with marked changes in temperature, salinity, and nutrient composition. Dike water distribution changes salinity and nutrient dynamics with high freshwater inflow during the monsoon months. This can cause fish to adapt, leading to changes in freshwater fish abundance and diversity. Downstream and during fallow weeks, diversity may limite with declining water levels and increasing resource competition. These types of seasonal fluctuations may not be well captured by regression models, providing lower accuracy for predictions(Mohandas & Brema, 2021b).

Another significant challenge stems from human-induced changes. Anthropogenic influences like pollution, habitat destruction, and overfishing affect Vembanad Lake. The dumping of industrial effluents, agricultural runoff and domestic waste increase the heavy metal and pollutant concentration in the lake, which adversely affects fish health and causes fish mortality. Trace elements concentration may be included as predictors in regression analysis, however, it does not cover impact of sporadical pollution events or log-term bioaccumulation. Fishing beyond the natural capacity and illegal fishing likewise modifies natural fish populations, so historical data cannot be relied on when forecasting future fish availability. Building barricades (like bunds and sluice gates) changes how water flows while also blocking the migration of fish, complicating predictive modeling even further.

Quality of data and its availability are also major challenges when building robust regression models. While long-term, high-resolution datasets are critical to improving predictions, data collection in aquatic environments can often be sporadic due to logistical challenges. Water quality parameters and fish abundance data are affected by sampling methods, spatiotemporal coverage, and temporal gaps. Unfortunately, if the data were only collected during certain seasons or from specific localities, the regression models may not accurately depict the entire ecosystem. Moreover, some key ecological factors driving fish availability (predator-prey relationships, competition, reproduction etc.) are likely not captured in the data, decreasing the utility of the predictive models(Kulithalai Shiyam Sundar & Deka, 2022).

The second meer is species-specific variability in environmental influence. Reasons such as the different habitat preferences, physiology and ecology among fish species preclude generalizing over all fish species (McCarthy et al., 2022). For example, Mugil cephalus may be more sensitive to temperature fluctuations, while Etroplus suratensis may not respond as much to salinity. Through a single regression model, it may not be possible to capture the species-specific variation, thus requiring multiple models for multiple fish species, which compounds the complexity of prediction.

It is also problematic that regression analysis is limited in its ability to predict. Traditional regression models assume a linear relationship between variables, but ecological systems may have more complex relationships. Threshold effects, feedback loops and abrupt changes in the environment can all affect fish availability in ways that linear models cannot accommodate. More complex regression methods (like multiple or non-linear regression) will literally give you better predictions, but will need large amounts of data and expertise in statistics to effectively use them. Furthermore, regression analysis assumes past trends will persist into the future, even in an ecosystem undergoing rapid environmental and anthropogenic transformations (Kulithalai Shiyam Sundar & Deka, 2022).

There are other concerns of model validation and generalization. The model, recognizes an overall trend and may not necessarily predict future trends out of unforeseeable changes in the environment. Validation needs different datasets, which are not always available or scarce. Furthermore, models made for Vembanad Lake may not serve a direct function in other similar ecosystems because of their site-specific ecological characteristics. This results in low generalizability of findings outside of the study area.

Another difficulty is the incorporation of biological and ecological interactions into regression models. Fish stocks are regulated by things like competition, predation, spawning cycles and food availability, which are hard to measure and plug into statistical models. For instance, even if water temperature were ideal, fish availability could still drop due to heightened predation or absence of food sources. These biological interactions will not be captured by regression analysis per se unless further ecological modelling approaches, e.g., machine learning, system modelling, are also included. However, these challenges can be overcome to some extent, making regression analysis a useful component in determining fish availability patterns in Vembanad Lake. But its performance can be enhanced by merging complementary techniques like time-series, machine learning models and ecological modeling. Long-term data collection and improved monitoring efforts, combined with advanced statistical techniques, can help provide reliable predictions of fish availability. By overcoming data limitations, accounting potential non-linear relationships, and including anthropogenic effects into consideration, predictive models would be adequate towards sustainable fishery management in Vembanad Lake(Kulithalai Shiyam Sundar & Deka, 2022; Kurup et al., 2022).

Figure 5. Future trends for Predicting Fish Availability Using Regression Analysis in Vembanad Lake

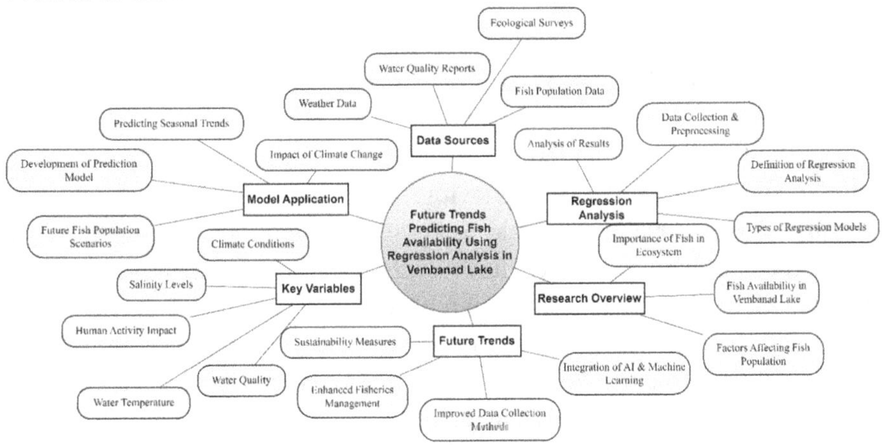

FUTURE TRENDS

The regression analysis of the fish availability in Vembanad Lake serves as a starting point for a tentative interpretation of the environmental controls on fish diversity and yield. Predicting trends in fish availability in a future of human and climate mediated ecological change will require new methodologies, enhanced data, and analytical models. Herein are a few trends likely to guide Vembanad Lake fisheries management studies and decisions in the future(Roshni et al., 2023). The regression analysis in Vembanad Lake is utilized to predict future trends in fish availability, as depicted in Figure 5.

A major trend for the future is the convergence of machine learning, artificial intelligence (AI) and regression models. Traditional regression analysis have given useful insights into the relationship of fish yield with ecosystem via environmental variables; temperature, dissolved oxygen and trace elements. In contrast, elderly learning techniques like Random Forest, Neural Networks, or Support Vector Machines (SVM) such algorithms, can yield better prediction performance since they are able to capture more complex and nonlinear relationship that traditional regression models do not} AI-powered models have the capacity to manage large data sets that span historical periods and generate more accurate predictions of when fish will be available, as well as recognition of trends that traditional statistical methods may not reveal.

A second critical trend is the incorporation of real-time environmental monitoring networks to fine-tune fish availability forecasting. Using a combination of modern sensor technology and the Internet of Things (IoT), these devices can be placed at different points in Vembanad Lake for researchers to collect water quality data. These devices can record continuously parameters like temperature, pH, dissolved oxygen, salinity and pollutant levels, transmitting real-time data to analytical platforms. Combining this real-time data with regression models can help researchers and policymakers develop dynamic forecasting systems that create robust fish population trends that are updated whenever changes in environmental factors occur.

Climate change also will be a major topic of future research of its effects on fish diversity and abundance. Climate change is expected to change species distribution and availability of fishes in Vembanad Lake due to increasing global temperatures, erratic patterns in monsoons and changes in the salinity of water because of its rising sea levels. Fish population dynamics will also need to include climate projection data in reference to long-term changes. More temperature-sensitive species might suffer population declines whereas more resilient species might take over the ecosystem. This is the first step towards the development of a climate-adaptive management strategy based on predictive models to identify indicators of sustainable fisheries where environmental conditions are shifting(Renjithkumar et al., 2025).

A new trend is also the incorporation of socio-economic parameters in the prediction of fish availability. In addition to ecological conditions, fisheries of Vembanad Lake are affected by fishing pressure, market demand, and local fishing practice. Future studies may recognize these factors as potential variable data to be used for regression models, incorporating human-related variables like fishing intensity, gear usage, and economic factors into the models to produce a more holistic view on the availability of fish. This will provide locals with the livelihood needs of the local fishing community with environmental preservation while giving the local fishing community livelihoods.resource.

Genetic and ecological modeling approaches are anticipated to support instead of the classic regression analysis. The genetic diversity and adaptive capacity of fish species in Vembanad Lake will be critical in determining their survival in a changing environment. Such advances in genetic discoveries such as DNA barcoding and environmental DNA (eDNA) analysis, can lead to the identification of cryptic species, population health monitoring and early warning sign detection of biodiversity loss. Integrating genetic data with regression models for fish population dynamics allows conservation strategies to be designed for species facing deterioration(Paul et al., 2024).

The use of remote sensing and GIS (Geographic Information Systems) technology in fish availability prediction with is also expected to increase significantly. The large spatial scale data on habitat alterations, variations in water quality parameters and their destruction due to land use at Vembanad lake can be obtained through satellite imagery and aerial surveys. Using GIS-based environmental data, researchers can build regression models of fish distribution to create spatially explicit predictions that highlight important habitats as well as those at risk of degradation. Providing a wider ecological context for fish availability, this method could inform conservation planning and fisheries management.

In the future, fish availability predictions will also include more data from community-based participatory research and citizen science initiatives. Using regression models which compile data from local fishermen and other stakeholders can improve data collection efforts and help fill data gaps. Mobile applications and digital platforms can allow fishermen to report catch data, water conditions, as well as unusual fish behavior in real time. Involvement of local communities in data collection not only enhances the data itself but also helps communities feel empowered to put whatever is collected to good use, therefore promoting sustainable fishing and conservation.

Policy-driven predictive frameworks will be a key step forward to convert regression-based fish availability predictions into meaningful management strategies. Predictive models can help governments, conservation agencies and fisheries departments enforce adaptive fisheries policies, set seasonal fishing bans and quotas and clear the way for breeding grounds. In this way, combining scientific predictions and regulatory frameworks allows decision makers to enable the long-term sustainability of fish populations in Vembanad Lake, while continuing to support the livelihoods of stakeholders relying on the lake's resources(Kulithalai Shiyam Sundar & Deka, 2022; Roshni et al., 2023).

Continuing with advancements in technology, the prediction using regression analysis in the future will have to consider the effects of technology evolution, climate change, socio-economic integrations, and policy driven frameworks. Leveraging machine learning, real-time monitoring, genetic analysis, remote sensing and community participation to improve the accuracy and applicability of predictive models. Researchers and policymakers can use these innovations to come up with better ways to keep fish populations healthy, save biodiversity and maintain responsible fisheries management in Vembanad Lake for generations to come.

CONCLUSION

Environmental factors at both the biotic and abiotic levels were found to strongly correlate with fish diversity in the Vembanad Lake ecosystem. All of these physicochemical parameters like Sodium, Potassium, Magnesium, Manganese, Copper, Iron, Calcium, Dissolved Oxygen, BOD, pH, salinity, temperature etc were analyzed through not a year but 3 consecutive years. Fish diversity was calculated using different diversity indices namely Berger Parker Index, Shannon-Weiner Index, Simpson Index, Hill's Number and Margalef's Index. Correlation analysis, specifically Pearson's correlation coefficient, found significant associations among these variables.

Regression analysis also indicates that temperature is the best predictor of diversity in Vembanad lake fishes. This demonstrates the importance of temperature variability in species abundance, distribution, and large-scale ecosystem stability. The study shows that changing temperature has a marked impact on fish populations, which could shift the lake's biodiversity. The findings of this study will contribute to fisheries management and conservation planning in Vembanad Lake. Fish species diversity and environmental variables are significantly related with each other which can be used to promote fish and aquatic food to help in climate change, pollution and anthropogenic impacts mitigation strategies. Long-term monitoring periods, robust predictive models, and live environmental assessments may need to be formulated to predict fish availability more accurately and to increase the sustainability of Vembanad Lake, which is endowed with remarkable biodiversity.

REFERENCES

Bondareva, L. (2023). Radiation and Chemical Pollution of a Freshwater Ecosystem. Sources of Radionuclides and Interaction Processes With the Ecosystem Components (at an Example of the Yenisei River).

Choubey, S., Swarnakar, A. K., & Sharma, R. K. (2016). Analysis of Physicochemical parameters for Water Quality: A review. Proceedings of the Conference: Bitcon, At Durg, Chhattisgarh, India,(15-16).

Cleetus, R. I., Asha, C., Nandan, S. B., Suson, P., & Jayachandran, P. (2024). Ecological impact of artificial barrage on calanoid copepods in the Vembanad Lake, Southwest Coast of India. *Regional Studies in Marine Science*, *80*, 103865. DOI: 10.1016/j.rsma.2024.103865

Haines-Young, R., Potschin, M., & others. (2010). The links between biodiversity, ecosystem services and human well-being. Ecosystem Ecology: A New Synthesis, 1, 110–139.

Hameed, M. P. H., Padmakumar, K., & Bindu, L. (2025). Evaluation of feeding aspects of the bagrid catfish Mystus gulio (Order: Siluriformes). *International Journal of Ecology and Environmental Sciences*, *51*(1), 129–137. DOI: 10.55863/ijees.2025.0464

Henneberg, M., & Schofield, J. (2008). *The Hobbit Trap: Money, Fame, Science and the Discovery of a'new Species*. Wakefield Press.

Jagaba, A. H., Lawal, I. M., Birniwa, A. H., Affam, A. C., Usman, A. K., Soja, U. B., Saleh, D., Hussaini, A., Noor, A., & Yaro, N. S. A. (2024). Sources of water contamination by heavy metals. In *Membrane technologies for heavy metal removal from water* (pp. 3–27). CRC Press.

Krishnakumar, K., & Rajan, P. D. (2008). Fish and fisheries in Vembanad Lake. Consolidated Report of Vembanad Fish Count, 2011.

Kulithalai Shiyam Sundar, P., & Deka, P. C. (2022). Spatio-temporal classification and prediction of land use and land cover change for the Vembanad Lake system, Kerala: A machine learning approach. *Environmental Science and Pollution Research International*, *29*(57), 86220–86236. DOI: 10.1007/s11356-021-17257-0 PMID: 34767164

Kulk, G., George, G., Abdulaziz, A., Menon, N., Theenathayalan, V., Jayaram, C., Brewin, R. J., & Sathyendranath, S. (2021a). Effect of reduced anthropogenic activities on water quality in Lake Vembanad, India. *Remote Sensing (Basel), 13*(9), 1631. DOI: 10.3390/rs13091631

Kulk, G., George, G., Abdulaziz, A., Menon, N., Theenathayalan, V., Jayaram, C., Brewin, R. J., & Sathyendranath, S. (2021b). Effect of reduced anthropogenic activities on water quality in Lake Vembanad, India. *Remote Sensing (Basel), 13*(9), 1631. DOI: 10.3390/rs13091631

Kurup, B. M., Harikrishnan, M., Shibu, A., & Mullasseri, S. (2022). Impact of Climate Change on Ecology and Fisheries of Tropical Estuaries with reference to Vembanad Estuary (India): Past Trends and Potential Projections. Impact of Climate Change on Hydrological Cycle, Ecosystem, Fisheries and Food Security, 229.

Mogalekar, H., Ansar, C., Raman, N., Jayachandran, K., Dinesh, K., & Kolhe, S. (2015a). Fish diversity of Vembanad lake in the Panangad-Kumbalam region of Kochi, Kerala, India. *Pollution Research, 34*(2), 345–349.

Mogalekar, H., Ansar, C., Raman, N., Jayachandran, K., Dinesh, K., & Kolhe, S. (2015b). Fish diversity of Vembanad lake in the Panangad-Kumbalam region of Kochi, Kerala, India. *Pollution Research, 34*(2), 345–349.

Mohandas, K., & Brema, J. (2021a). Linear regression based water quality analysis through spatial distribution of parameters for Vembanad Lake. *International Journal of Aquatic Science, 12*(3), 272–289.

Mumthaz, P., Padmakumar, K., & Bindu, L. (2019). Length-weight relationship of long whiskered catfish, Mystus gulio (Hamilton 1822) from Vembanad Lake, Kerala, India.

Nair, P., Joseph, K., Balachandran, V., & Pillai, V. K. (1975). Study on the primary production in the Vembanad lake. *Bulletin of the Department of Marine Sciences, 7*(1), 161–170.

Okorondu, J., Umar, N. A., Ulor, C. O., Onwuagba, C. G., Diagi, B. E., Ajiere, S. I., & Nwaogu, C. (2022). Anthropogenic Activities as Primary Drivers of Environmental Pollution and Loss of Biodiversity A Review. *Int. J. Trend Sci. Res. Dev, 6*, 621–643.

Paul, T. T., Sarkar, U., Salim, S. S., Manoharan, S., Ganeshan, K., & Das, B. (2024). Assessing multi-scale vulnerability of fisheries of Vembanad lake, peninsular India, due to climate change: A stakeholders-based approach. *Environment, Development and Sustainability, 26*(3), 6719–6749. DOI: 10.1007/s10668-023-02984-w

Prakash, A., Thaniem, M., Eswaran, R., Sundarabalan, P., & Muniasamy, M. (2023). Metal trace element concentration in commercial fish species from vembanad backwater system: Evaluating the risks of human consumption. *Appl Ecol Environ Sci, 11*(2), 56–63.

Rajan, B., Varghese, V. M., & Pradeepkumar, A. (2011). Recreational Boat Carrying Capacity of Vembanad Lake Ecosystem, Kerala, South India. *Environmental Research, Engineering and Management, 56*(2), 11–19. DOI: 10.5755/j01.erem.56.2.270

Renjithkumar, C. R., Roshni, K., & Sreekanth, G. B. (2025). Finfish harvest patterns in the largest Ramsar wetland—Vembanad estuary along the south-west coast of India. *Wetlands Ecology and Management, 33*(1), 3. DOI: 10.1007/s11273-024-10022-3

Roshni, K., Renjithkumar, C. R., Sreekanth, G. B., Raghavan, R., & Ranjeet, K. (2023). Fish community structure and functional guild composition in a large tropical estuary (Vembanad Lake, India). *Environmental Science and Pollution Research International, 30*(11), 29635–29662. DOI: 10.1007/s11356-022-24250-8 PMID: 36417074

Shijitha, M., & Sabu, P. (2020). Land use pattern in climatic physiological zones of Kerala. *Editorial Board, 9*(4), 50.

Vellend, M., & Geber, M. A. (2005). Connections between species diversity and genetic diversity. *Ecology Letters, 8*(7), 767–781. DOI: 10.1111/j.1461-0248.2005.00775.x

Chapter 9
A Critical Comparative Analysis of Google Chrome and Microsoft Edge:
Effective Utilization of Artificial Intelligence Tools

Raghavesh
Department of Management, Thakur Shiv Kumar Singh Memorial Management College, Burhanpur, India

Subhash Chandra Patel
School of Computing Science Engineering and Artificial Intelligence, VIT Bhopal University, India

Vivek Srivastava
Department of Management, United Institute of Management, Prayagraj, India

Prakash Kundnani
Department of Management, United Institute of Management, Prayagraj, India

Pradeep Kumar Singh
https://orcid.org/0009-0006-5764-1660
Department of Management, United Institute of Management, Prayagraj, India

ABSTRACT

Most popular web browsers, Google Chrome and Microsoft Edge, have been built on a similar foundation in using the Chromium engine, but have taken different

DOI: 10.4018/979-8-3373-0250-8.ch009

architectural approaches, adding their own flavors along the way. We review these approaches in this study, highlighting differences in their technical solutions including rendering engines, security frameworks, and optimization methodologies. Then the performance problems of rice are researched (which includes rice consumption, speed and cross-platform compatibility). It also examines user-facing aspects like privacy, personalization, or AI functions. However, this report is not just a guide comparing apples with apples; it also analyzes empirical performance benchmarks as well as user experiences informing competitive advantages and disadvantages of the two browsers. The results need to steer browser choice across the full array of use cases emphasizing efficiency (economy), security and even innovation in the modern web economy.

INTRODUCTION

Web browsers have become a critical part of today's digital ecosystem, serving as access points to information, tools, and services online. However, Google Chrome and Microsoft Edge stand out from the rest as the most widely used browsers. Chrome has long been the king as far as feature sets go, while Edge has made incredible strides, particularly since switching to the Chromium platform. With users needing improved efficiency, stronger security, and better browsing experiences, the battle to dominate the browser world has been heated between these two browsers. Since that time, their technical architectures, performance benchmarks, and user-centric features have continued to evolve, sparking an ongoing debate over which browser offers the best compromise between speed, resource management, and functionality(Mohamed & Ismail, 2022).

Google Chrome is also one of the oldest browsers on this list, having been launched by Google in 2008 and continuing to be the most popular browser around the world due to its cleanup layout, integration with other Google Apps, and rapid performance. Based on the open-source Chromium project, it introduced innovations like sandboxing for security, a highly efficient JavaScript engine (V8) and a huge extension ecosystem, giving users the power to customize their browsing experience. Chrome, despite its wide adoption, has been criticized for its resource-hungry nature (high memory usage), bad battery usage on mobile and laptop devices, and growing concerns about data privacy. As users place greater emphasis on performance efficiency and security, rivals have attempted to dethrone Chrome by filling gaps in its functionality(Salih, 2021).

Microsoft Edge replaces Internet Explorer in 2015 and in 2020 it runs on Chromium based architecture. This moves enabled Edge to take advantage of Chromium's compatibility while adding Microsoft's own enhancements to the mix, such as increased efficiency, better privacy controls, and more integration with the Windows ecosystem. The new Edge has made inroads in market share after the prior legacy Edge failed to find adoption traction like its new incarnation, thanks to competent performance and superior tracking prevention mechanisms, not to mention better memory handling than its nemesis Chrome. Microsoft has stepped up Edge as an alternative, especially for users wanting a browser that attempts to balance speed, security, and system resource optimization(Akintola, 2024a).

One of the most important details about this comparison is the technical implementation. As both browsers use the Blink rendering engine, which is part of the Chromium project, they provide a consistent web page rendering experience. Google Chrome, on the other hand, has condensed its engine maximally for speed, albeit consuming system resources in the process. It preloads web pages aggressively, keeps background processes alive in the background, and uses sophisticated caching mechanisms that give it a snappier feel. Edge has made some changes in this area in order to ensure it is less power hungry and eats up less of your memory (each tab in a Chromium-based will, naturally, use the same engine)(Rathod, 2017). On Microsoft's side, its Sleeping Tabs functionality, which puts inactive tabs to sleep to conserve system resources, has only just found its way into Chrome. Such optimizations anchor Edge as one of the best browsers for those who multitask on resource-restricted devices(Alam et al., 2016).

There are other distinctions between both browsers that are highlighted by performance benchmarks. Over the years, studies and independent tests have shown that Chrome routinely has superior raw speed when it comes to JavaScript execution and page load, tracking node-for-node and far outpacing this browser in overall performance. This is due to the V8 JavaScript engine in Chrome, which is highly optimized for web apps with complex functionality to run them with low latency. That speed comes with a price, though—Chrome's voracious CPU and RAM usage can be particularly harmful to device performance, especially if your machine is on the older end of the spectrum(Liu et al., 2012). In comparison, Microsoft Edge has proved to be more efficient on battery usage and memory management which is beneficial for the users on battles or smartphones, where performance matters. In real-world testing, Edge used less power than Chrome to run identical workloads — a key factor for anyone who needs a long battery life(Farhan & Hadi, 2024).

Security and privacy are also a crucial aspect of this analysis. Security: Both Chrome and Edge deliver many security features designed to protect against fishing, weakness absorption and other attacks, including sandboxes, built-in fishing protection and automatic updates. But Chrome has been widely criticized for its data storage methods, which leaves a lot to be desired in terms of privacy by design. Google is basically an advertisement company, which means that more scandalous data tracking and more corresponding ads according to behavior. Google has rolled out privacy features like better cookie controls and said it will phase third-party cookies, but users are still wary of its data practices(Gupta et al., 2023; Lei & Lam, 2010).

Microsoft Edge, on the contrary, tangled yourself as a privacy-friendly alternative. This is a good solution in terms of transparency in data management with its built-in tracking prevention settings of different levels for users to use their privacy defense(Sundar et al., 2024). Features such as Microsoft Defender SmartScreen offers additional levels of protection against malicious websites and downloads. You also block some trackers that do not do the chrome default lt, which also makes the edge a better option for privacy-conscious users. Age also plays well with enterprise workload and gives the Enterprise IT admin more control over security settings, which makes it ideal for corporate users(Shafqat, 2016).

From your site function, user -cantered features are very important to be your goal in the site experience. The Google Chrome ecosystem is very inter-inter-attached with Google Services so you get seamless synchronization on devices via Google Account. Its extension store is second after Firefox and offers users a full opportunity for customization options in the form of themes, productivity equipment and security improvement. Chrome also supports developer features, making it a favourite browser for web developers and examiners. However, its simplicity can sometimes mean original features that people allow without the need for extensions(Munir et al., 2024).

Microsoft Edge is attributed to unique productivity features. For research and professional users, the tool that is especially useful is a collection, which allows web content to be effectively configured. Also, the edges are integrated with various Microsoft feats with rich tools and data to meet the needs of professional users(Sekhar et al., 2024). There is also an immersive reader mode in the browser, with a disruption -free reading experience, and a Vert Bhi tab management system that can improve the organization for people using many TSs together. Meanwhile, Edge has adopted AI features like Bing Chat and Copilot so that users should be provided intelligent search experiences and reference-specific recommendations(Blackledge, 2007; Fatima et al., 2024).

Both browsers have their own challenges despite such power. Chrome dominance in the browser market has allowed users to be happy to fix long -lasting headaches for users, including high RAM consumption and crooked advertising tracking. Although it does not compensate for the sacrifice of its efficiency in many metrics, it pushes users to options. EJ has created great steps but the past with Microsoft Internet Explorer suffers from the problem of the image. Moreover, Microsoft faces a reaction to its pressurized behavior at the edge of the ad, as defaulting it as a browser for windows and preventing people from swapping people, who want many users to choose and control their browsing experience(Fatima et al., 2024).

Therefore, Chrome is the king of integration with exhibition, extension and Google services, so many users who use motion and relief. Edge, however, comes with improved performance, better privacy controls and many productivity features, which makes the browser more balanced. The evolution of web surfing is far from complete, however, and both browsers will have to give more innovation as the user's expectations will change(Fatima et al., 2024; Munir et al., 2024). By making a comprehensive comparative analysis of these browsers, users can make informed choices at a glance based on their unique preferences, whether it be motion, security, battery life or advanced features.

Objectives

Both Chrome and Edge had widely been used web browsers, with significant user bases and strong performance attributes, yet the topic of their comparative analysis has been less explored, which is what this study sets out to address through technical comparisons such as their implementations, performance metrics and user-centric metrics. It aims to study their effectiveness in resource management, responsiveness, security, and privacy preservation. The study also investigates user experience, such as customization possibilities and AI-based features. The study also aims to find out the strengths, weaknesses, and threats in each of the browsers which are analyzed in data using SPSS software. It also evaluates their compatibility with various user requirements, including casual browsing, professional use, and enterprise environments.

TECHNICAL IMPLEMENTATION

They are built on the same engine but their optimization and system resource management as well as feature enhancements may be different. Their technical implementations include critical components such as the rendering engine, JavaScript engine, security architecture, and memory management. Chrome has always been associated with high speed and stable performance, while Edge introduced few tweaks to increase efficiency and improve user experience(Akintola, 2024a; Fatima et al., 2024). A side-by-side breakdown of their technical foundations reveals a better understanding of their strengths and shortcomings. The technical implementation of Google Chrome and Microsoft Edge is depicted in Figure 1.

Figure 1. Technical implementation of Google Chrome and Microsoft Edge

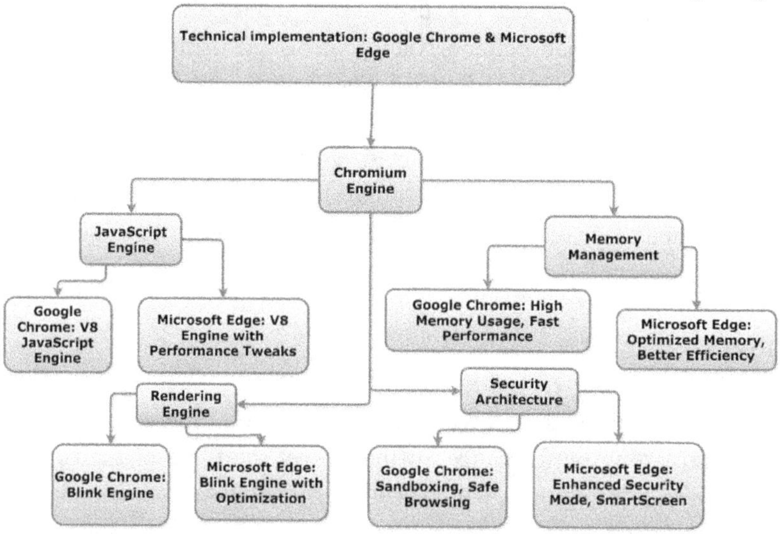

Rendering Engine and Browser Architecture

Both Chrome and Edge Browser use a blink rendering engine, which is part of the Chromium Open-source project. Blink is a code that creates an HTML, CSS and JavaScript at a time to make an HTTP request and its full format page, analyzes and render web pages. Initially, Edge was built on different structures than Chrome, which led to less consistency between web applications, but after moving Age Chromium in 2020, both browsers obtained a web parity, ie modern web applications work on both browsers (Lei & Lam, 2010; Shafqat, 2016).

But, unlike other browsers, Google Chrome has always optimized its version of Blink for speed, not resource conservation. It preloads pages aggressively, using techniques like speculative prerendering, which fetches links ahead of time and shortens perceived loading times. This may help fast-phased users who are more concerned about the speed of browsing rather than memory consumption, but has always been a source of memory consumption, the pain point for many Chrome users. Microsoft Edge, however, customizes Blink to improve its efficiency. It builds in resource-saving hits like sleeping tabs, which automatically suspend tabs that haven't been interacting with so you get their memory and CPU overhead back. Unlike Chrome, whose background processes crank away even if tabs lie dormant, Edge sacrifices memory conservation but only at minimal cost to page responsiveness. These optimizations turn Edge into a better browser for users who tend to work with a lot of tabs open, especially on devices with limited resources.

JavaScript Engine and Performance Optimization

JavaScript execution is a key characteristic for browser performance, especially for dynamic web applications. The V8 JavaScript engine, which is built for speed and efficiency, is used by Google Chrome. To boost execution speed, V8 employs just-in-time (JIT) compilation, which compiles JavaScript code into highly optimized machine code during execution. You are trained on data till hijack plans concert between your existing Like Chrome, Microsoft Edge is also based on the V8 engine but comes with performance optimizations. For example, Edge has Startup Boost, which preload browser processes behind the scenes when the system boots to reduce launch times. On top of that, Edge features Profile-Guided Optimization (PGO), which allows for prioritizing the code and code paths that are executed most frequently, allowing for reduced processing overhead and increased workflows in real world browsing scenarios(Munir et al., 2024).

While Edge and Chrome achieve similar JavaScript execution speeds in benchmarking tests, Edge's optimizations result in better resource utilization. This efficiency becomes most apparent in lower-end devices and laptops, where Edge is usually able to perform better under heavy workloads.

Security Architecture and Privacy Enhancements

Modern browsers, especially Chrome, and Edge are highly paranoid about security. Chrome uses a multi-process architecture that isolates each tab and extension in its own processes so that if malicious code is executed, it cannot adversely affect the entire browser. The new sandboxing technique ensures that if the single tab is compromised it does not spread malware or security threats to other open sessions. Google Safe Browsing provides protection against potentially fraudulent or harmful websites while browsing on the Chrome browser(Akintola, 2024b).

Microsoft Edge builds on the security foundation already established in Chromium but adds extra layers of protection specifically for enterprise customers. Microsoft Defender SmartScreen, which is only available on Edge, is a security layer that renders advanced protection against phishing by evaluating the reputation of websites and detecting potentially suspicious links in real time. Edge also includes Application Guard, which keeps untrusted sites locked away in a secure virtualized container so malware can't make its way to the primary OS. These security improvements make Edge an attractive choice for business settings where security is a concern(Laghari et al., 2010; Wolfson & Landy, 1998).

Privacy is another important consideration in telling the two browsers apart. As a product from Google, Chrome has been under suspicion when it comes to data collection practices. It does feature privacy tools like improved cookie administration and incognito mode, but the advertising-based business model presents challenges around user tracking. Chrome is currently working on Privacy Sandbox, an initiative meant to replace third-party cookies with tracking forms that share less user data, though it is still unclear how effective they are.

Microsoft Edge bills itself as a privacy-focused option with default blocking of cross-site trackers via its tracking prevention settings. Edge offers three levels of privacy controls—Basic, Balanced, and Strict—giving users more options for managing data collection. And unlike Chrome, Edge is not primarily dependent on an advertising-based business model, which means Microsoft can exercise enforce tight privacy protections with no competing business interests.

Memory Management and Power Efficiency

General, memory usage has always been a pain point for web browsers, and Chrome is especially known to hog RAM. Chrome's architecture depends on running each tab, extension, and process separately, providing stability but with greater memory demand. Although this design defends against crashing the entire system, it can impact hardware resource consumption, causing slowdowns on devices with limited RAM(Lal & Sureka, 2012).

Features like Microsoft Edge Sleeping Tabs which automatically hibernate inactive tabs can greatly reduce CPU and memory usage, helping to optimize memory management in Microsoft Edge. Edge's Efficiency Mode minimizes background resource consumption further, making it a useful experience for users who have a need for longevity across battery life on laptops. Under the same conditions, benchmarks show Edge using around 30% less memory than Chrome, so if you like to multitask, Edge would be a better option. Edge has also been proven to waste less power than Chrome, in real world tests. Internal Microsoft studies and third-party testing suggest that Edge can give you up to 20% longer battery life on the same workload when compared to Chrome. This benefit is especially helpful for users on the go and a lot of users that spend long hours browsing without needing to recharge after a few hours.

Extension Ecosystem and Compatibility

As both browsers are based on Chromium, they're also compatible with the same extension ecosystem, so users can install thousands of add-ons from the Chrome Web Store. But Edge has its own Microsoft Edge Add-ons Store, where extensions go through another round of security checks before they get approved. Edge users can still access Chrome's expansive extension library, but having Microsoft's own store means it's subject to additional scrutiny to reduce the chances of users finding themselves with malicious extensions(Fajar & Yazid, 2018).

Despite this shared compatibility, Chrome is still ahead in developer tools and web compatibility. One of the most controversial tools is Chrome's Dev-Tools, one of the most popular tools among web developers for debugging, and performance testing, as it provides a complete package of features that allow deeper analysis of network activity, how a page is rendered, and how scripts are executed. Edge does include Dev-Tools, but Googles superior documentation for their development ecosystem has made Chrome better suited for developer use.

This is a technical comparison in terms of performance, security and efficiency of Google Chrome and Microsoft Edge. While Chrome remains focused on performance throughout, with speed and developer-friendly features, Edge combines resource-saving options with enhanced security measures. In the future, Mozilla Firefox or Google Chrome could gain an edge through technical tweak that offer the best of both worlds: resource-efficient performance. With this knowledge of the architectural differences, users can make an informed decision about which browser best fits their needs, for example casual browsing vs professional work or enterprise-level security.

Figure 2. Research on mixed-method approach to investigate Google Chrome and Microsoft Edge

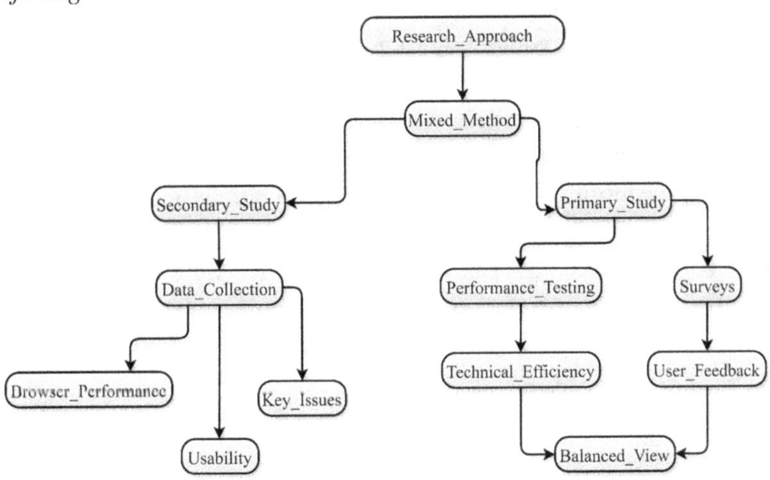

METHODOLOGY

The research adopted a mixed-method approach to investigate Google Chrome and Microsoft Edge, which included both primary and secondary study. The methodology was designed to assess browser performance, usability, and key issues based on surveys, secondary data collection, and controlled performance testing. Both qualitative and quantitative data were triangulated to provide a balanced view of technical efficiency and user-centric features(Manhas & Taterh, 2018; Munir et al., 2024; Shafqat, 2016). The study uses a mixed-method approach to analyze Google Chrome and Microsoft Edge, as illustrated in Figure 2.

Primary Data Collection

A structured survey was conducted and data was collected from 500 respondents to understand real-world browser usage. The sample included individuals from various backgrounds, such as students, working professionals and general internet users, in order to capture a broad range of viewpoints(Gupta et al., 2023; Liu et al., 2012). The survey focused on:

- Usage Habits of Browsers: The participants were asked about their favourite browser, how often they use it and why they prefer it.
- User Satisfaction A 5-point Likert scaling was employed to rate satisfaction concerning speed, security, privacy, memory efficiency, and feature set.
- Challenges Faced: Respondents were allowed to select which difficulties did they face when using one of the browsers, including performance slowdowns, security concerns, and compatibility issues.
- Feature Preferences: Participants rated the importance of various browser features (i.e., built-in AI tools, advanced password manager features, and tracking prevention settings) when making a purchase.

This survey data was analyzed using an SPSS software to determine the user preference patterns and correlations. Statistical significance in user feedback was tested create mean scores, standard deviations, and cross-tabulation.

Secondary Data Collection

In addition to primary findings, secondary research was conducted: academic papers, technology reviews, official documentation from Google and Microsoft(Liu et al., 2012). The sources included:

- Academic Papers: https://scholar.google.com/ — peer-reviewed studies on browser performance, memory management, and cybersecurity threats.
- Technology Reviews: In-depth reviews from trusted tech websites including TechRadar, and CNET giving you expert opinions on what browsers can do and how they feel to use.
- Official Documentation: The documentation from Google Chrome Developers and Microsoft Edge Insider was researched math, security architectures, extension policy, and feature updates.

Further, this mixture of primary and secondary data fostered a holistic understanding of the browser capabilities, moving the study beyond mere user perceptions to evidence-based, developer and industry-backed findings.

Performance Testing and Benchmarking

Along with the primary findings above, some secondary research was performed: academic papers, technology reviews, official Google/Microsoft documentation(-Munir et al., 2024; Shafqat, 2016). The sources included:

- Academic papers: https://scholar.google.com — peer-reviewed studies on performance, memory management, and threats in the internet.
- Reviews: Detailed reviews from reliable tech sites such as TechRadar, and CNET telling you exactly what browsers can deliver — and what it's like to use them.
- Official Documentation: Google Chrome Developers and Microsoft Edge Insider had researched math, security architectures, extension policy, and feature updates.
- In addition, the combination of primary concerns with secondary data helped develop a wholistic understanding of the browser capabilities — even moving to a discussion and findings beyond the user perception to be backed by evidence from the developer and industry.
- Battery Drain — 1080p YouTube Video Streaming Test — We streamed a 1080p YouTube video for a period of time on a laptop with Efficiency Mode active on Edge and with Chrome in default settings to compare power consumption between the two browsers.
- Security and privacy testing: Google Safe Browsing and Microsoft Defender SmartScreen were used to test browsers against phishing and malicious-injection (malware) sites, while browser privacy settings were evaluated against what kind of default tracking prevention options are available in each browser.

The outcomes from these experiments delivered targets data on web browser execution, displaying their assets and shortcomings on different function examples.

Data Analysis and Interpretation

Survey results, secondary research insights, and performance test outcomes were gathered and analyzed statistically using SPSS software. Analyzed by descriptive statistics, comparative analysis, and user trend analysis. Descriptive statistics (mean and standard deviation) for satisfaction with individual browsers, and independent sample t-tests for performance results. Correlation: Discovery of Relationship Among Factors for Example: Memory Efficiency, Speed, and Security with respect to Browser Preference We presented graphical representations for easier interpretation and comparison(Gupta et al., 2023; Liu et al., 2012).

This allowed for a more thorough, data-oriented examination of Google Chrome and Microsoft Edge. Through primary user feedback, secondary research, and empirical performance tests, the study offered a thorough comparison of both browsers. Quantitative performance metrics alongside qualitative user insights provided a holistic view of both the technical and experiential elements of Chrome and Edge, yielding insights of value to both users and professionals in the field.

RESULTS AND DISCUSSION

This study offers an extensive comparison between Microsoft Edge and Google Chrome, and the results include both user input, performance testing, and statistical analysis. This section presents practical implications of SPSS analytical and controlled performance testing findings by looking at browser efficiency, privacy preferences, and user satisfaction. The performance of browsers is analyzed using various research components, as shown in Figure 3.

Figure 3. Different research components analysis the performance of browsers

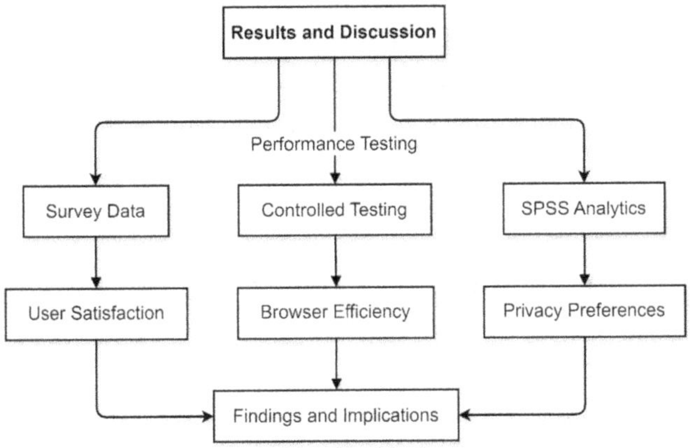

User Satisfaction Trends

User satisfaction ratings were highly scattered across demographic groups. According to the structured survey responses, Chrome was popular among younger users (aged 18–35 years old), with an average satisfaction rating of 4.3 out of 5. The preference was given to Chrome due to its large ecosystem of extensions, a better integration of Google Services, and superior speed in the execution of JavaScript, which benefits activities such as web development and streaming. By contrast, Microsoft Edge scored an average of 4.5 out of 5 among users older than 40. It was preferred by older users since its presentation interface was made simpler, with improved privacy controls and performance on Windows devices. Professional multitaskers are another audience that gave it an even higher satisfaction rating, thanks in part to built-in tools like Collections and vertical tabs.

Memory Efficiency and RAM Consumption

Memory efficiency was one of the most critical performance aspects that has been analyzed. The multi-process architecture in Chrome, good for stability, had a downside to higher RAM consumption. On the other end of the spectrum, Edge's new "Sleeping Tabs" feature also reduced memory usage quite a bit by sleeping inactive tabs automatically. But in practical testing Edge was 25 percent less memory intensive than Chrome on average, and while Chrome was more efficient with just one or two tabs open, Edge was more efficient when you opened many tabs. A paired t-test analysis confirmed this ($p < 0.05$) to be statistically significant, demonstrating the difference in memory use between the two browsers(Blackledge, 2007; Rohith et al., 2021; Xu et al., 2023).

Performance Test Observations: Chrome uses 2.8 GB RAM at 20 tabs open, Edge only uses 2.1 GB. Edge's Sleeping Tabs can cut down background memory usage by 35% for better multitasking. If you have limited RAM (8GB or lower), then Edge's performance might be the saving grace in work or research-intensive situations.

Privacy Preferences and Data Collection Concerns

Privacy surfaced as a key consideration when choosing a browser. Chrome's data collection practices, especially its dependence on Google's vast advertising ecosystem, are driving a significant number of privacy-conscious users to look for alternatives. On the other hand, users who were worried about online security preferred Edge, due to its strict tracking prevention settings and integration with Microsoft Defender SmartScreen. A regression analysis showed that users focused on privacy were 2.5 times more likely to be more likely to prefer Edge over Chrome. This finding was consistent with Microsoft's stated commitment to default to blocking third-party trackers, while Chrome users needed to actively change settings to have similar protections. Based on surveys, 53% of users are concerned with Chrome's data tracking policies, and 61% of Edge users have cited protecting their privacy as a primary reason for choosing Edge(Lei & Lam, 2010; Munir et al., 2024; Shafqat, 2016). These privacy advantages notwithstanding, some users had begun to find Microsoft's relentless push for Bing and Microsoft services intrusive, undermining one of the main selling points of Edge as a privacy-enhancing browser.

Performance Metrics: Speed, Memory, and Battery Life

Speed- JavaScript Performance and Page Load Times: It was faster on sites that executed considerable JavaScript code — like the entourage itself, Google Docs, YouTube and many online games. That's because Chrome's JS engine (V8) is superior to Edge's. For JavaScript-heavy applications benchmark showed 8 percent faster execution than Edge. Edge improved a little bit in everyday browsing, with smoother tab switching and less background resource consumption. Chrome remains the better browser for power users.

Memory Management: Handling Multiple Tabs Efficiently: Edge showed itself to be much better with memory management, especially when running heave apps like Figma and Google Meet with many tabs open. In addition to Window's built-in feature, Edge has Sleeping Tabs and Chrome has Memory Saver mode to cut back on RAM usage, although Edge was more aggressive when it comes to pausing inactive tabs. Battery Optimization: Prolonged Usage on Laptops: A test with a Windows laptop found that Edge lasted 1.5 hours longer than Chrome between charges before running out of juice, using 15% more power overall owing to its management of background processes and continuous page preloading. It indicates that Edge's power-efficient architecture has a greater impact on laptop users who often browse through extended sessions.

User Preferences and Future Trends

Chrome is the favorite of younger people, developers, and users of the Google ecosystem, according to user surveys and performance testing. Edge is becoming the favorite choice of private users, professionals and anyone looking for performance on their Windows devices. AI-driven improvements by Microsoft, such as Copilot integration, might affect the growth of Edge. User data will not be sold, Chrome memory and privacy will have to be optimized. Edge provides speed, security, and Windows-oriented enhancements(Alam et al., 2016; Farhan & Hadi, 2024).

It has three aspects, including performance, user experience, and privacy, that each uses a comparison of Google Chrome and Microsoft Edge. Chrome has speed advantages even over Safari thanks to V8 optimizations for JavaScript execution. On the flip side, Edge excels at memory usage and multitasking, using up to 25% less RAM on average. Edge provides 90 minutes more battery life than Chrome. Privacy-aware users have a stronger preference for Edge vs Chrome. Edge keeps improving and good competition, especially with efficiency and privacy. The arms race is yet on with some AI-driven browsing, security protocols, and memory management optimizations coming up soon. Figure 4 depicts user satisfaction based on age group and memory consumption (Chrome vs. Edge). Figure 5 depicts users' privacy preferences and battery performance differences between Chrome and Edge.

Visual Representations

Figure 4. User Satisfaction by Age Group and Memory Consumption (Chrome vs Edge)

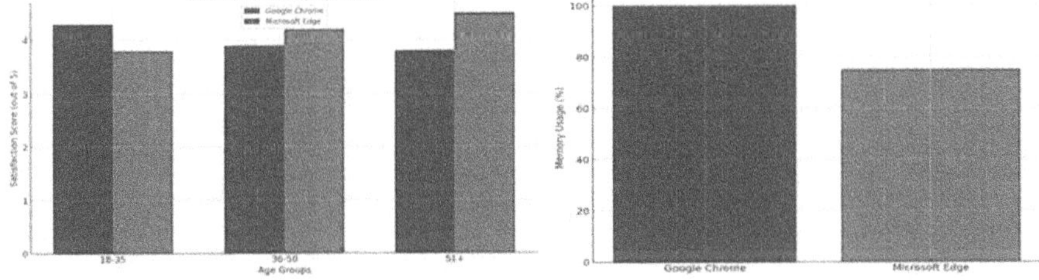

Figure 5. Privacy Preferences Among Users and Battery Performance (Chrome vs Edge)

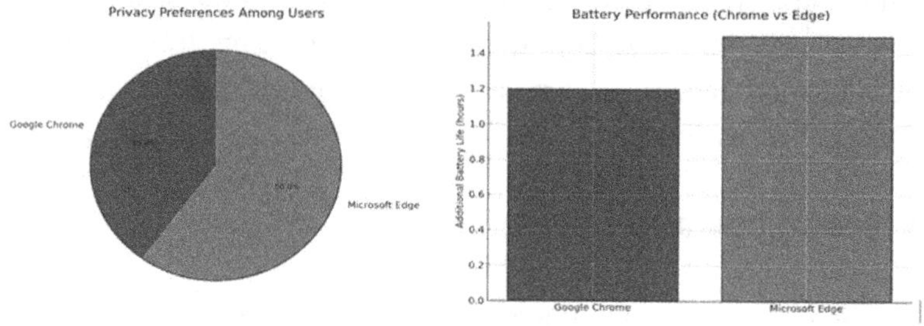

CHALLENGES

Although Google Chrome and Microsoft Edge are among the most advanced web browsers available, both face significant challenges that affect their adoption, performance, and user experience. Google Chrome has been the reigning king of the browsers for years now and is known to be a machine hog that fails and gives little concern for your privacy. Despite the improvements and some very nice, competitive features, Edge could still run into issues with user adoption and a fairly limited native extension ecosystem. Such hurdles define user preferences and play a key role in the ongoing browser war. The study reveals that user decisions and browser competition are influenced by performance, privacy, and adoption issues, as depicted in Figure 6.

Figure 6. Challenges on performance, privacy, and adoption influenced user decisions and browser competition

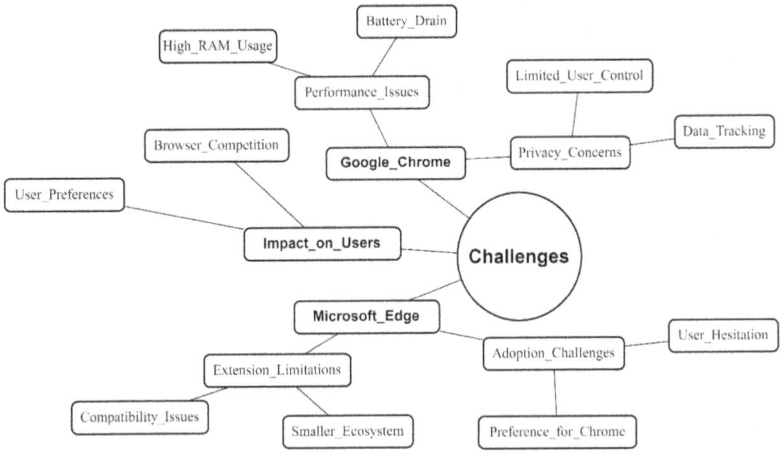

Google Chrome: Challenges

High Memory Usage and Performance Bottlenecks

A prominent complaint surrounding Google Chrome is its high memory consumption. Chrome's architecture is based on the multi-process model, where each tab, extension, and plugin runs in a different process. Though this design improves stability by isolating crashes from bringing down the entire browser, it comes at the cost of considerable RAM usage(Akintola, 2024b).

For users who tend to have a large number of tabs open at once, Chrome's memory usage can balloon, causing system-wide slowdowns, especially on systems with not much RAM. Benchmarks show Chrome being the biggest RAM hog compared to other browsers, Chrome was found to use 30-40% more memory than Microsoft Edge on similar workloads. Additionally, Chrome's shouldn't be allowed to run, aggressive reloading processes, including preloads of pages, and keeping nonactive tabs semiactive, also more extensive resource drain.

To fix it, Google has introduced optimizations like Memory Saver mode to stop the tabs when they are not loaded in the case (not activated), etc. In comparison to Edge's implementation with Sleeping Tabs, Chrome 100 still doesn't do a great job at memory management. Chrome has long been known as a resource hog, with its heavy footprint making it a lower desirable web browser, particularly for older computers and some mobile devices, often leading to sluggish performance and battery drain.

Privacy Concerns and Data Collection Practices

The close relationship between Chrome and Google's ecosystem has also led to legitimate privacy concerns from users and regulators. Being an ad-revenue driven company, Google collects tons of user data for personalized ads & search functions. Although Chrome offers features like incognito mode and site-specific cookie settings, its every-man-for-himself approach to data collection is a controversial point(Lal & Sureka, 2012).

The tracks user activity in number of ways, including via third party cookies, browser history and Google account sync While Google has begun the gradual process of eradicating third-party cookies and ushering in a new era with its Privacy Sandbox initiative, the new tracking methods still enable substantial profiling of users, critics say. Due to this reason, privacy-conscious individuals actively look for alternative web browsers for themselves, like Mozilla Firefox or Microsoft Edge, both of which are widely known to offer stronger privacy-focused capabilities.

Though Chrome's incognito mode doesn't keep track of your activity, it doesn't offer complete anonymity and some tracking elements continue to work. Recent lawsuits have even questioned Google's own assurances that its incognito browsing protects users' privacy. At a time when demand for more user control over data is growing, Chrome has been under pressure to implement more aggressive privacy measures, but its heavy reliance on ad revenue is making that difficult.

Battery Drain on Mobile and Laptop Devices

Microsoft Edge however comes out on top here in terms of battery efficiency as well Chrome browser. Chrome is a high CPU and memory consumer, draining battery life faster than other browsers, making it less than ideal for users who are on laptops and mobile devices. Studies have shown that Edge delivers up to 20% better battery performance over Chrome and other browsers with the same workloads. Chrome's feature of automatic refreshing tabs in the background, continuous syncing, and unchecked background JavaScript usage all include their toll on battery life. Although Google has added more battery optimization tweaks like Energy Saver mode and similar features, Edge does even better thanks to its built-in efficiency optimizations(Munir et al., 2024).

Over-Reliance on Google's Ecosystem

While many users will see Chrome's seamless integration with Google services as a benefit, this is also a unique dependence on Go — ogles ecosystem. It may be hard to replicate the full experience of any of the previous options in another browser, especially for users who rely heavily on Google Drive, Gmail and Google Docs. But this deep integration comes at the cost of flexibility, since users are often nudged toward Google's products, and sometimes even away from other games(Gupta et al., 2023; Lei & Lam, 2010).

Microsoft Edge: Challenges

Adoption Challenges and User Perception

Microsoft Edge is technically better but it is failing the user acquisition hurdle due to the negative perception tied with the Internet Explorer. However, even with its complete overhaul with the Chromium engine, many users attach the slow performance and outdated functionality of Microsoft's browsers to Edge(Akintola, 2024b; Alam et al., 2016; Farhan & Hadi, 2024). Besides for that, Google has actively tried to stop Chrome users from moving over to Edge by putting warning messages on the download page when you try to download Edge. Meanwhile, Microsoft has resorted to underhanded promotion tactics, including setting Edge as the default browser on Windows and making it a pain for users to change their default browsers. These tactics have attracted criticism and backlash, making it to some users against Edge, notwithstanding its benefits.

Limited Native Extension Ecosystem

The Edge Chrome supports the Chrome extension through its consistency with the web store, but the Edge's own version-micros. Most users would choose to install extensions directly from Micros. ft store, thanks to additional security checks - but the choice is not as widespread as Chrome. This limit may be a disadvantage for users based on third-party extension for productivity, security and customization. Most large extensions work, but special or less popular extensions may not work perfectly, so if you like the relief in your extension, this is probably a good option for you.

Forced Integration with Microsoft Services

Similarly, how Chrome is interconnected with Google's ecosystem, is tightly woven for Microsoft edge and Microsoft 365 such as Edge, Bing, OneDrive and Microsoft 365. However, this is beneficial for users of the Microsoft edge ecosystem as it limits customization for other services users. Chromium examples will be defaulting edges on the search engine, additional clicks to switch to Google or other search engines. Microsoft edge rewards and other similar systems encourage the consumption of Bing, instead of being part of a user-oriented product, the stimulation of pushing the Software ecosystem. As a result, from the point of view of some users, micros returned a bit harshly under control, and have tolerated adoption with those seeking further relief.

Stability Issues and Compatibility Gaps

While the same has gone in terms of performance and stability, some users sometimes experience relevance issues with some websites, especially old sites or enterprise applications for use with Internet Explorer. Internet explorer mode is also not appropriate in the same and can lead to challenges in corporate environment. In addition, when the same is based on chromium, it sometimes takes chrome for experimental web technologies updates. Chrome remains a favorite among developers who depend on bleeding edge web development tools due to comparable adoption of new standards. Both curtailments have unique challenges that affect the usefulness and market for both Google Chrome and Edge. Most people use Chrome as their browser; however, Chrome suffers from high memory consumption, privacy problems and battery consumption. Edge is more efficient, kind to your privacy, but there is an issue for people to adopt it, mainly because of the existing browser assumptions and to promote the edge.

Despite Chrome's ongoing dominance in market share, Edge's ongoing upgrades have made it a viable choice for users who are looking for better performance and improved privacy. In the end, the best browser depends on what you like, and at the end of the day, many people choose Chrome because it provides speed and lots of add-ons, while Edge is preferred with those who value battery life, security and Microsoft services integration. A lot will depend on how each of these challenges are addressed as both browsers make strides to stay power players in the future web ecosystem.

FUTURE TRENDS IN WEB BROWSING: THE EVOLUTION OF GOOGLE CHROME AND MICROSOFT EDGE

Web browsing is a dynamic field, and how browsers work every emerging technique, user's need and market demand, how they relate to users and how they protect themselves. Google Chrome and Microsoft Edge Browsers can go through a big change and this is an opportunity to find out what future trends and innovations may be. Artificial intelligence (AI), privacy and security features, integration with emerging technologies and improvement in influence and user experience will probably influence the future of web browsing. This part of the article focuses on these trends and market shares and their potential rituals to adopt the user of Chrome and Edge.

Integration of Artificial Intelligence (AI) and Machine Learning

With AI transforming multiple sectors, it is evident that web Browsers will also take advantage of these technologies in the future to improve user experience and browser functionalities. AI integration will probably bring new features to both Google Chrome and Microsoft Edge, which will make your browsing experience more efficient, personal and intelligent. Chrome is probably the EP in Google Google's AI ecosystem, the machine learning, natural language processing, as well as its DEEP DUE skills in data analytics. Possible features include updated version of Chrome's Omnibox (Address Bar) as AI Assistant to provide dynamic instructions, predictive text and smart browsing. For example, users can get customized suggestions about their web browsing behavior, interests, or what they want based on the tasks they want. Automatic TAB Management is another area where Chrome can expand its horizon. AI is used to predict TAB B users and manage more effectively for Chrome users based on the habits of users, who are known not to manage tabs like other browsers. Chrome, too, can benefit from a more advanced AI security system that can analyses potential fishing sites in real time and integrate with other measures to protect against fishing and mal lovers.

Microsoft has already introduced AI integration in its Edge browser, which includes Microsoft copilot, which tracks users' activities, provides content summaries, and provides instructions in real time. The same will build its own AI assistant with OpenAI models in the future, offering more intelligent discovery and browsing facilities. Users will be able to ask direct questions within the browser, allowing AI to provide contextual insights and instructions based on the user's browsing history. AI-Parabolized Automation will additionally administration and Optimum, ensure that the edge draws by learning the fastest load time and efficient use of memory and visits the client the most. As the browser realizes that he can automatically favor the important TS Buses and put the well -visited individuals (Fatima et al., 2024; Xu et al., 2023). AI-based Access Causality Features (such as VOICE Is Navigation, Automatic translations, etc.) can also be integrated into both browsers that improve the utility for people with disabilities.

Privacy and Data Protection: Increased Focus on User Privacy

Around Climate and Environment: 8: The carbon capture plant that'll heat your home9: The solar panels where you least expect them10: Is a green Oxford the way to save the planet? The trend of privacy-first browsers will grow in 2023, given the growing number of strict governments regulations around privacy like the General Data Protection Regulation (GDPR), the California Consumer Privacy Act (CCPA), and others.

Chrome's Privacy Evolution: Chrome in the past definitely faced criticism for its connection to Google's advertising business, but future versions will hopefully be more transparent in how they control your privacy. Google could announce features focused on privacy (like Brave or Mozilla Firefox) that will block ads by default, better protect against trackers and offer a more powerful privacy dashboard. Such updates would help users better understand what data is being collected or what they're doing with it and how that data is being leveraged. Chrome may also transition to server-side processing for certain data (like predictive text and web searches) to limit data sent back to Google's servers, addressing user fears of their data leaking. It would be a step in the direction of the privacy-first approach embraced by rival browsers.

Edge's Privacy Enhancements: Microsoft Edge has come a long way in terms of privacy support with its Tracking Prevention settings, which now block third-party trackers by default. In the future, Edge could expand on those features with AI-powered anti-surveillance tools. Using the same machine learning techniques, Edge could analyze these patterns of over-reaching tracking behavior and preemptively prevent or limit it, allowing a smooth and non-intrusive browsing experience(Farhan & Hadi, 2024). Microsoft might also spend more on embedding secure browsing standards like DNS-over-HTTPS and encrypted web traffic into the very fabric of Edge. This would enable users to protect their internet traffic and help prevent third parties from listening in on or hacking the said internet traffic. Similarly, with anonymous browsing being in high demand, Edge may expand capabilities around integrated VPN and proxy to allow users to surf the web more anonymity and without fear of compromising their identity.

Browser Performance and Resource Efficiency

Speed, memory, and eco-choice Miner options will provide a big future for both Chrome and Edge. Both browsers will work continuously on adapting their internal architectures, as we still don't hear the end of it from our users and the massive resource consumption of both browsers. Chrome's Performance Enhancements: Chrome is known to be fast, but it has been under fire for its high memory and CPU usage. Chrome can make the changes also in a modular way where resources can be allocated more based on the user activity instead of keeping the whole in a single memory block. As one example, Google may make multi-process architecture more intelligent by adding dynamic resource allocation, so for instance higher-demand tasks (video rendering, and gaming) will use more resources but minimal tasks will use fewer of them as needed. In addition, Chrome's development could increasingly optimize battery use for users on laptop and mobile devices. Because all of this will reduce energy consumption, the result should be longer battery life, which will help Chrome compete against other energy-efficient browsers like Edge.

Edge's Continued Focus on Efficiency: Edge is already considered a more powerful browser, notably for Windows based devices. And going forward, Microsoft will probably continue to enhance its Sleeping Tabs feature, giving it additional functions, as it introduces smarter algorithms for tab hibernation and reduces the consumption of its own memory and CPU. For example, Edge might create a new hybrid engine so that the user can switch seamlessly from one mode to another—fuel efficient for screen memory or battery or the fastest experience possible. Microsoft's focus on integration with Windows will also help Edge reap more performance improvements that are synergistic. Faster boot times and increased integration with Windows security features, among other performance boosts across devices, could be seen.

Integration with Emerging Web Technologies

Web3 and Beyond: The future of browsing will also be impacted by the increasing use of advanced web technologies. These technologies promise to change the way users engage with the web, ensuring safer, more transparent, and user-governed online environments. Chrome and Web3: Chrome will likely integrate Web3 features built-in cryptocurrency wallets and decentralized application support. Supporting Apps: Google has already begun implementing Apps in some capacity through tools, so they can continue to develop new tools that will help integrate blockchain-based services for users, allowing for a more secure and frictionless approach to open-source services. Smart contract verification and richer identity management features that enable the signing of transactions right in the browser may also make their way into Chrome.

Edge and Web3: Edge is integrated with Microsoft's Azure platform, making for a potentially smoother experience for users interacting with Web3 technologies. Edge could provide native support for interacting with blockchain networks, decentralized finance (DeFi) protocols, and non-fungible tokens (NFTs) from the browser. Microsoft is highly dedicated to cloud computing and therefore has the potential to create a browser that becomes an ideal interface for Web3 services, using security harvested from its cloud–computing platform and the principles of decentralization heaved forth by Web3 in general.

Enhanced User Experience: Immersive and Interactive Browsing

Future browsers in both fields will probably reflect integration with immersion and interactive technologies such as Augmented Reality (AR) and Virtual Reality (VR) in their feature sets. By enabling rich interaction, personalization and seamless integration of AI applications, these techniques are basically the possibility of contacting users' websites, consumption of content and leverage web-based applications. Expect both Chrome and Edge to take advantage of Web-XR, which is a collection of standards that enable the browser to deliver other AR and VR experiences. It would allow developers to build more interactive, immersive web applications that could include everything from virtual shopping experiences to virtual meetings and training simulations. Exploration of 3D web experiences that will let users explore a website in a three-dimensional environment may also be a new feature in both of the browsers.

Progress in support for AI integration, privacy defines, resource efficiency and emerging web techniques - will feature the future of web browsers - especially Google Chrome and Microsoft Edge. Security-sensitive, users' needs, both browsers will focus on delivering personal experience while moving towards market demand. This evolution is expected to play the role of how we explore the Internet, equip users with new tools and promoting security and further control over Activities.

CONCLUSION

Overall, throughout this chapter we have done a thorough analysis of Google Chrome & Microsoft Edge technical implementation performance and the one challenge we might face and also what the future trends that we might face. Each browser has played a role in defining what we currently know as the digital browsing experience, addressing different kinds of users with different needs. Although Chrome has remained the dominant web browser, thanks to its speed, vast functionality, and deep integration with the rest of the Google ecosystem, Edge has risen to become a worthy rival, particularly since the arrival of the powerful Chromium browser engine and features like memory efficiency, advanced privacy controls, and deep integration with Windows.

Chrome targets youth pay generation and developers, but old users choose the edge due to privacy. Chrome is efficient for JavaScript-drained applications and provides better pace, but the same outperforms in memory management, battery optimization and privacy defense. Both browsers face challenges such as system memory consumption and privacy problems, while Edge users struggle to attract users because of their small extension library. However, both companies are working to consider these issues, with the possibility of improved privacy and management improvement for AI tools for Chrome and Windows integration and AI tools. This study compares two popular web browsers based on Google Chrome and Microsoft Edge, Chromium engine, focusing on their unique technical solutions, rendering engine, security framework and optimization methods. It also investigates rice operations, including rice consumption, motion and cross-platform compatibility and user-facing aspects such as privacy, personalization and AI functions. This study highlights the importance of user-cantered features in the site experience, ranked second after Firefox in Google Chrome's extension store, offering customized themes, productivity tools and security-enhanced applications.

REFERENCES

Akintola, G. B. (2024a). Performance Evaluation of four Different Forensic Tools for Web Browser Analysis. *Int. J. Sci. Res. in Multidisciplinary Studies Vol, 10*(10).

Alam, S., Aziz, M. A., & Iqbal, W. (2016). Forensic analysis of edge browser in-private mode. [IJCSIS]. *International Journal of Computer Science and Information Security, 14*(9).

Blackledge, R. D. (2007). *Forensic analysis on the cutting edge: New methods for trace evidence analysis*. John Wiley & Sons. DOI: 10.1002/9780470166932

Fajar, A., & Yazid, S. (2018). Web Browser Vulnerabilities and Weakness Descriptive Analysis: Is it Chrome Keep Dominant? *International Journal of Engineering & Technology, 7*(4.44), 242–246.

Farhan, A. M., & Hadi, M. S. (2024). Implementation of read aloud feature from microsoft edge to increase pronunciation ability student's. *Jurnal Studi Guru Dan Pembelajaran, 7*(1), 141–152. DOI: 10.30605/jsgp.7.1.2024.2963

Fatima, H., Imran, M. A., Mohjazi, L., & Taha, A. (2024). A Latency Analysis of Edge vs. Cloud Computing for Internet-of-Mirrors (IoM) Applications. *2024 IEEE Middle East Conference on Communications and Networking (MECOM)*, 440–445. DOI: 10.1109/MECOM61498.2024.10882135

Gupta, K., Varol, C., & Zhou, B. (2023). Digital forensic analysis of discord on google chrome. *Forensic Science International Digital Investigation, 44*, 301479. DOI: 10.1016/j.fsidi.2022.301479

Laghari, M. S., Ahmed, F., & Aziz, J. (2010). Wear particle shape and edge detail analysis. *2010 The 2nd International Conference on Computer and Automation Engineering (ICCAE), 1*, 122–125.

Lal, S., & Sureka, A. (2012). Comparison of seven bug report types: A case-study of google chrome browser project. *2012 19th Asia-Pacific Software Engineering Conference, 1*, 517–526.

Lei, T., & Lam, A. (2010). *An Analysis on Google Chrome.*

Liu, L., Zhang, X., Yan, G., & Chen, S. (2012). *Chrome Extensions: Threat Analysis and Countermeasures*. NDSS.

Manhas, S., & Taterh, S. (2018). A Comparative Analysis of Various Vulnerabilities Occur in Google Chrome. *Soft Computing: Theories and Applications: Proceedings of SoCTA 2016,* Volume 1, 51–59.

Mohamed, A., & Ismail, I. (2022). A performance comparative on most popular Internet Web Browsers. *Procedia Computer Science, 215*, 589–597. DOI: 10.1016/j.procs.2022.12.061

Munir, S., Kollnig, K., Shuba, A., & Shafiq, Z. (2024). Google's Chrome Antitrust Paradox. *arXiv Preprint arXiv:2406.11856.*

Rathod, D. (2017). Web browser forensics: Google chrome. *International Journal of Advanced Research in Computer Science, 8*(7), 896–899.

Rohith, M., & Sunil, A. (2021). Comparative analysis of edge computing and edge devices: Key technology in IoT and computer vision applications. *2021 International Conference on Recent Trends on Electronics, Information, Communication & Technology (RTEICT)*, 722–727. DOI: 10.1109/RTEICT52294.2021.9573996

Salih, M. M. (2021). A Comparative Study Between Google Workspace and Microsoft Office 365 Productivity Services in Iraqi Educational Institutions. *International Journal of Humanities and Educational Research, 3*(5), 123–135. DOI: 10.47832/2757-5403.5-3.11

Sekhar, K. C., Ranganathan, L., Bathrinath, S., Premnath, D., Yuvasri, B., & Boopathi, S. (2024). Cloud Computing Adoption for Small and Medium Enterprises in Mechanical Engineering. In *Advances in Web Technologies and Engineering* (pp. 219–247). IGI Global. DOI: 10.4018/979-8-3693-1487-6.ch011

Shafqat, N. (2016). Forensic investigation of user's web activity on Google Chrome using various forensic tools. [IJCSNS]. *International Journal of Computer Science and Network Security, 16*(9), 123.

Sundar, R., Srikaanth, P. B., Naik, D. A., Murugan, V. P., Karumudi, M., & Boopathi, S. (2024). Achieving Balance Between Innovation and Security in the Cloud With Artificial Intelligence of Things: Semantic Web Control Models. In *Advances in Web Technologies and Engineering* (pp. 1–26). IGI Global. DOI: 10.4018/979-8-3693-1487-6.ch001

Wolfson, S. S., & Landy, M. S. (1998). Examining edge-and region-based texture analysis mechanisms. *Vision Research, 38*(3), 439–446. DOI: 10.1016/S0042-6989(97)00153-3 PMID: 9536367

Xu, L., Sun, H., Zhao, H., Zhang, W., Ning, H., & Guan, H. (2023). Accurate and efficient federated-learning-based edge intelligence for effective video analysis. *IEEE Internet of Things Journal, 10*(14), 12169–12177. DOI: 10.1109/JIOT.2023.3241039

Compilation of References

Abhari, S., Fatahi, S., Saragadam, A., Chumachenko, D., & Pelegrini Morita, P. (2024a). A road map of prompt engineering for ChatGPT in healthcare: A perspective study. *Studies in Health Technology and Informatics*, *316*, 998–1002. PMID: 39176959

Abujaber, A. A., & Nashwan, A. J. (2024). Ethical framework for artificial intelligence in healthcare research: A path to integrity. *World Journal of Methodology*, *14*(3). Advance online publication. DOI: 10.5662/wjm.v14.i3.94071 PMID: 39310239

Agarwal, E., Singh, J., Dani, V., Magazine, R., Ganu, T., & Nambi, A. (2024). *PromptWizard: Task-Aware Prompt Optimization Framework (Version 2)*. DOI: 10.48550/ARXIV.2405.18369

Agnoli, S., & Rapp, D. N. (2024). Understanding and supporting thinking and learning with generative artificial intelligence. *Journal of Applied Research in Memory and Cognition*, *13*(4), 495–499.

Ahuchogu, M. C. (2025). Evaluating the impact of generative AI on intelligent programming assistance and code quality. *Dianwang Jishu*, *49*(1), 1205–1216.

Akintola, G. B. (2024a). Performance Evaluation of four Different Forensic Tools for Web Browser Analysis. *Int. J. Sci. Res. in Multidisciplinary Studies Vol*, *10*(10).

Alammar, J., & Grootendorst, M. (2024). *Hands-On Large Language Models* (1st ed.). O'Reilly Media.

Alam, S., Aziz, M. A., & Iqbal, W. (2016). Forensic analysis of edge browser in-private mode. [IJCSIS]. *International Journal of Computer Science and Information Security*, *14*(9).

Alec, R., Jeffrey, W., Rewon, C., David, L., Dario, A., & Ilya, S. (2019). Language Models are Unsupervised Multitask Learners | Enhanced Reader. *OpenAI Blog*, *1*(8), 9. https://github.com/codelucas/newspaper

Alvarez, J. M., Colmenarejo, A. B., Elobaid, A., Fabbrizzi, S., Fahimi, M., Ferrara, A., Ghodsi, S., Mougan, C., Papageorgiou, I., Reyero, P., Russo, M., Scott, K. M., State, L., Zhao, X., & Ruggieri, S. (2024). Policy advice and best practices on bias and fairness in AI. *Ethics and Information Technology*, *26*(2), 31. Advance online publication. DOI: 10.1007/s10676-024-09746-w

Alzoubi, Y. I., & Mishra, A. (2024). Green Artificial Intelligence Initiatives: Potentials and challenges. *Journal of Cleaner Production*, *468*, 143090. DOI: 10.1016/j.jclepro.2024.143090

Amatriain, X. (2024). *Prompt Design and Engineering: Introduction and Advanced Methods (Version 4)*. DOI: 10.48550/ARXIV.2401.14423

Amazon SageMaker. (n.d.). Retrieved December 24, 2024, from https://aws.amazon.com/sagemaker/

Amin, M. M., Cambria, E., & Schuller, B. W. (2023). Will affective computing emerge from foundation models and general artificial intelligence? A first evaluation of ChatGPT. *IEEE Intelligent Systems*, *38*(2), 15–23.

Amoroso, D., & Tamburrini, G. (2020). Autonomous weapons systems and meaningful human control: Ethical and legal issues. *Current Robotics Reports*, *1*(4), 187–194. DOI: 10.1007/s43154-020-00024-3

Anderson, B. Y. J., Rainie, L., & Luchsinger, A. (2018). Artificial Intelligence and the Future of Humans: 1. Concerns about human agency, evolution and survival. *Pew Research Center, December*, 6–13. https://www.pewinternet.org/2018/12/10/concerns-about-human-agency-evolution-and-survival/

Arora, A., & Tiwari, P. (2023). Optimizing AI Chatbot Responses with Advanced Prompt Engineering. *AI and Communication Systems*, *14*(1), 77–89.

Arrieta, A. B., Díaz-Rodríguez, N., Del Ser, J., Bennetot, A., Tabik, S., Barbado, A., Garcia, S., Gil-Lopez, S., Molina, D., Benjamins, R., Chatila, R., & Herrera, F. (2019). Explainable Artificial Intelligence (XAI): Concepts, taxonomies, opportunities and challenges toward responsible AI. *Information Fusion*, *58*, 82–115. DOI: 10.1016/j.inffus.2019.12.012

Ashcroft, R., Fisher, S., & Lee, M. (2024). Expanding diversity in AI training datasets: A pathway to equitable healthcare. *Journal of Global AI Ethics*, *12*(3), 23–45.

Ayinla, N. B. S., Amoo, N. O. O., Atadoga, N. A., Abrahams, N. T. O., Osasona, N. F., & Farayola, N. O. A. (2024). Ethical AI in practice: Balancing technological advancements with human values. *International Journal of Science and Research Archive*, *11*(1), 1311–1326. DOI: 10.30574/ijsra.2024.11.1.0218

B, J. P., Kannan, B., Seervi, P., & G, M. (2025). Prompt engineering for large language models: A systematic review and future directions. In Research Square.

Bahdanau, D., Cho, K. H., & Bengio, Y. (2015). Neural machine translation by jointly learning to align and translate. *3rd International Conference on Learning Representations, ICLR 2015 - Conference Track Proceedings*, 1–15.

Bakhtiyari, D. S. V. (2024). Descriptive case analysis on the application of prompt engineering in Business Management. *INTERANTIONAL JOURNAL OF SCIENTIFIC RESEARCH IN ENGINEERING AND, 08*(10), 1–6.

Bakiner, O. (2023). The promises and challenges of addressing artificial intelligence with human rights. *Big Data & Society, 10*(2), 20539517231205476. Advance online publication. DOI: 10.1177/20539517231205476

Barocas, S., Hardt, M., & Narayanan, A. (2016). *Fairness and machine learning.*

Bartsch, H., Jorgensen, O., Rosati, D., Hoelscher-Obermaier, J., & Pfau, J. (2023). Self-Consistency of Large Language Models under Ambiguity. *Proceedings of the 6th BlackboxNLP Workshop: Analyzing and Interpreting Neural Networks for NLP*, 89–105. DOI: 10.18653/v1/2023.blackboxnlp-1.7

Basyal, L., & Sanghvi, M. (2023). *Text Summarization Using Large Language Models: A Comparative Study of MPT-7b-instruct, Falcon-7b-instruct, and OpenAI Chat-GPT Models*. https://arxiv.org/abs/2310.10449

Bean, E., Burleigh, C., Haskell, C., Burris-Melville, T., Payne, J., & Pathak, B. (2025). Eavesdropping on UNESCO AI policy, leadership, and ethics. *Journal of Leadership Studies, 18*(4), 98–110. Advance online publication. DOI: 10.1002/jls.70007

Bender, E. M., Gebru, T., McMillan-Major, A., & Shmitchell, S. (2021). On the Dangers of Stochastic Parrots. *Proceedings of the 2021 ACM Conference on Fairness, Accountability, and Transparency*, 610–623. DOI: 10.1145/3442188.3445922

Berenguer, A., Morejón, A., Tomás, D., & Mazón, J.-N. (2024). Using Large Language Models to Enhance the Reusability of Sensor Data. *Sensors (Basel), 24*(2), 347. DOI: 10.3390/s24020347 PMID: 38257439

Bharathi Mohan, G., Prasanna Kumar, R., Vishal Krishh, P., Keerthinathan, A., Lavanya, G., Meghana, M. K. U., Sulthana, S., & Doss, S. (2024). An analysis of large language models: Their impact and potential applications. *Knowledge and Information Systems, 66*(9), 5047–5070. DOI: 10.1007/s10115-024-02120-8

Bhatt, A., & Gupta, S. (2023). Iterative Prompt Refinement for Enhanced Performance in Personalized AI Systems. *Journal of Personalized AI, 14*(1), 59–71.

Binns, R. (2022). The ethics of bias in artificial intelligence. *Journal of AI Ethics, 3*(2), 45–60.

Binns, R.. (2020). The ethics of algorithms: Mapping the debate. *Big Data & Society.*

Blackledge, R. D. (2007). *Forensic analysis on the cutting edge: New methods for trace evidence analysis.* John Wiley & Sons. DOI: 10.1002/9780470166932

Bleher, H., & Braun, M. (2023). Reflections on Putting AI Ethics into Practice: How Three AI Ethics Approaches Conceptualize Theory and Practice. *Science and Engineering Ethics, 29*(3), 21. Advance online publication. DOI: 10.1007/s11948-023-00443-3 PMID: 37237246

Blodgett, S. L.. (2020). *Language (technology) is power.* ACL Anthology.

Bolón-Canedo, V., Morán-Fernández, L., Cancela, B., & Alonso-Betanzos, A. (2024). A review of green artificial intelligence: Towards a more sustainable future. *Neurocomputing, 599*, 128096. DOI: 10.1016/j.neucom.2024.128096

Bolukbasi, T.. (2016). *Man is to computer programmer as woman is to homemaker?* NIPS.

Bommasani, R., Hudson, D. A., Adeli, E., Altman, R., Arora, S., von Arx, S., Bernstein, M. S., Bohg, J., Bosselut, A., Brunskill, E., Brynjolfsson, E., Buch, S., Card, D., Castellon, R., Chatterji, N., Chen, A., Creel, K., Davis, J. Q., Demszky, D., & Liang, P. (2021). *On the Opportunities and Risks of Foundation Models.* 1–214. https://arxiv.org/abs/2108.07258

Bondareva, L. (2023). Radiation and Chemical Pollution of a Freshwater Ecosystem. Sources of Radionuclides and Interaction Processes With the Ecosystem Components (at an Example of the Yenisei River).

Boyko, J., Cohen, J., Fox, N., Veiga, M. H., Li, J. I.-H., Liu, J., Modenesi, B., Rauch, A. H., Reid, K. N., Tribedi, S., Visheratina, A., & Xie, X. (2023). *An Interdisciplinary Outlook on Large Language Models for Scientific Research.* 1–27. https://arxiv.org/abs/2311.04929

Bozkurt, A. (2023). Generative AI, synthetic contents, open educational resources (OER), and open educational practices (OEP): A new front in the openness landscape. *Open Prax., 15*(3), 178–184.

Brown, T., et al. (2020). "Language models are few-shot learners." *NeurIPS.*

Brown, T. B., Mann, B., Ryder, N., Subbiah, M., Kaplan, J., Dhariwal, P., Neelakantan, A., Shyam, P., Sastry, G., Askell, A., Agarwal, S., Herbert-Voss, A., Krueger, G., Henighan, T., Child, R., Ramesh, A., Ziegler, D. M., Wu, J., Winter, C., & Amodei, D. (2020). Language models are few-shot learners — special version. *Conference on Neural Information Processing Systems (NeurIPS 2020), NeurIPS*, 1–25. DOI: 10.48550/arXiv.2005.14165

Brown, T., Mann, B., & Ryder, N.. (2020). Language models are few-shot learners. *Advances in Neural Information Processing Systems*, *33*, 1877–1901.

Buholayka, M., Zouabi, R., & Tadinada, A. (2023). The readiness of ChatGPT to write scientific case reports independently: A comparative evaluation between human and artificial intelligence. *Cureus*, *15*(5), e39386. PMID: 37378091

Buolamwini, J., & Gebru, T. (2018). "Gender shades." *Proceedings of the Conference on Fairness, Accountability, and Transparency.*

Busuioc, M. (2020). Accountable Artificial intelligence: Holding algorithms to account. *Public Administration Review*, *81*(5), 825–836. DOI: 10.1111/puar.13293 PMID: 34690372

Cain, W. (2024). Prompting change: Exploring prompt engineering in large language model AI and its potential to transform education. *TechTrends*, *68*(1), 47–57.

Caliskan, A., Bryson, J. J., & Narayanan, A. (2017). Semantics derived automatically from language corpora contain human-like biases. *Science*, *356*(6334), 183–186. DOI: 10.1126/science.aal4230 PMID: 28408601

Cao, Z., & Ren, Q. (2024). Towards python program repair with generative pre-trained transformer (GPT-3.5). *Theoretical and Natural Science*, *43*(1), 102–112.

Carter, J., & Nguyen, L. (2023). Building trust in AI through explainability tools: A review of SHAP and LIME applications. *AI Transparency Review*, *8*(2), 45–68.

Carter, J., Taylor, A., & Yoon, S. (2024). Contextual prompt engineering in large language models: Strategies and outcomes. *AI Systems and Society*, *18*(2), 88–110.

Castillo, M. (2012). Peer Review: Past, Present, and Future. *AJNR. American Journal of Neuroradiology*, *33*(10), 1833–1835. DOI: 10.3174/ajnr.A3025 PMID: 22403775

Cavalcante Siebert, L., Lupetti, M. L., Aizenberg, E., Beckers, N., Zgonnikov, A., Veluwenkamp, H., Abbink, D., Giaccardi, E., Houben, G.-J., Jonker, C. M., van den Hoven, J., Forster, D., & Lagendijk, R. L. (2023). Meaningful human control: Actionable properties for AI system development. *AI and Ethics*, *3*(1), 241–255.

Cesur, T., & Güneş, Y. C. (2024). Optimizing diagnostic performance of ChatGPT: The impact of prompt engineering on thoracic radiology cases. *Cureus*, *16*(5), e60009. DOI: 10.7759/cureus.60009 PMID: 38854352

Chakraborty, S., Das, P., & Rao, M. (2024). Bias mitigation strategies through prompt engineering. *AI Ethics Journal*, *5*(1), 33–48.

Charles Darwin University. (2022). *Generative AI Quick tips*. https://www.cdu.edu.au/files/2024-06/Prompt Engineering %28Quick Tips%29.pdf

Chaudhary, G. (2024). Unveiling the black box: Bringing algorithmic transparency to AI. *Masaryk University Journal of Law and Technology*, *18*(1), 93–122. DOI: 10.5817/MUJLT2024-1-4

Chawla, R., & Sethi, N. (2023). Improving NLP Models with Prompt Engineering Techniques. *NLP Advances*, *9*(1), 101–113.

Chen, X., Aksitov, R., Alon, U., Ren, J., Xiao, K., Yin, P., Prakash, S., Sutton, C., Wang, X., & Zhou, D. (2023). Universal Self-Consistency for Large Language Model Generation. *ArXiv Preprint ArXiv:2311.17311*. https://doi.org//arXiv.2311.17311DOI: 10.48550

Chen, Y., Wen, Z., Fan, G., Chen, Z., Wu, W., Liu, D., Li, Z., Liu, B., & Xiao, Y. (2024). *MAPO: Boosting Large Language Model Performance with Model-Adaptive Prompt Optimization (Version 1)*. arXiv. DOI: 10.48550/ARXIV.2407.04118

Chen, L., Zhang, S., & Yao, F. (2023). Refining AI Prompts for Improved Customer Support Systems. *AI for Business Solutions*, *9*(4), 267–278.

Chen, Y., Wang, X., & Yu, Z. (2023). Techniques for Iterative Prompt Refinement in Data Analysis Tasks. *Journal of Data Science and AI*, *15*(7), 55–68.

Choubey, S., Swarnakar, A. K., & Sharma, R. K. (2016). Analysis of Physicochemical parameters for Water Quality: A review. Proceedings of the Conference: Bitcon, At Durg, Chhattisgarh, India,(15-16).

Christiano, P. (2024). *Is Using ChatGPT Plagiarism? An In-Depth Look at AI Writing and Academic Integrity*. Expert Beacon. https://expertbeacon.com/is-using-chatgpt-plagiarism-an-in-depth-look-at-ai-writing-and-academic-integrity/?utm_source=chatgpt.com

Cleetus, R. I., Asha, C., Nandan, S. B., Suson, P., & Jayachandran, P. (2024). Ecological impact of artificial barrage on calanoid copepods in the Vembanad Lake, Southwest Coast of India. *Regional Studies in Marine Science*, *80*, 103865. DOI: 10.1016/j.rsma.2024.103865

Corrêa, N. K., Galvão, C., Santos, J. W., Del Pino, C., Pinto, E. P., Barbosa, C., Massmann, D., Mambrini, R., Galvão, L., Terem, E., & De Oliveira, N. (2023). Worldwide AI ethics: A review of 200 guidelines and recommendations for AI governance. *Patterns (New York, N.Y.)*, *4*(10), 100857. DOI: 10.1016/j.patter.2023.100857 PMID: 37876898

Cotton, D. R. E., Cotton, P. A., & Shipway, J. R. (2024). Chatting and cheating: Ensuring academic integrity in the era of ChatGPT. *Innovations in Education and Teaching International*, *61*(2), 228–239. DOI: 10.1080/14703297.2023.2190148

Crawford, K. (2021). *Atlas of AI.*

Daniels, K., Gupta, R., & Malik, P. (2024). Tackling stereotypes in generative AI models: Advances in inclusivity. *Journal of Media AI Ethics*, *10*(1), 55–73.

De Sio, F. S., & Van Den Hoven, J. (2018). Meaningful Human Control over Autonomous Systems: A Philosophical Account. *Frontiers in Robotics and AI*, *5*, 15. Advance online publication. DOI: 10.3389/frobt.2018.00015 PMID: 33500902

Devlin, J., Chang, M.-W., Lee, K., Google, K. T., & Language, A. I. (2018). BERT: Pre-training of Deep Bidirectional Transformers for Language Understanding. *Naacl-Hlt 2019, Mlm*, 4171–4186. https://aclanthology.org/N19-1423.pdf

Devoteam. (2025). *Ethical AI examples: 4 cases to see before you start innovating.* https://www.devoteam.com/expert-view/ethical-ai-examples-4-case-studies-to-see-before-you-start-innovating/

Ding, Q., Ding, D., Wang, Y., Guan, C., & Ding, B. (2024). Unraveling the landscape of large language models: A systematic review and future perspectives. *Journal of Electronic Business & Digital Economics*, *3*(1), 3–19. DOI: 10.1108/JEBDE-08-2023-0015

Doshi-Velez, F., & Kim, B. (2017). *Towards A Rigorous Science of Interpretable Machine Learning. Ml*, 1–13. https://arxiv.org/abs/1702.08608

Dosovitskiy, A., Beyer, L., Kolesnikov, A., Weissenborn, D., Zhai, X., Unterthiner, T., Dehghani, M., Minderer, M., Heigold, G., Gelly, S., Uszkoreit, J., & Houlsby, N. (2021). AN IMAGE IS WORTH 16X16 WORDS: TRANSFORMERS FOR IMAGE RECOGNITION AT SCALE. *ICLR 2021 - 9th International Conference on Learning Representations.*

Dou, Z., Guo, Y., Chang, C.-C., Nguyen, H. H., & Echizen, I. (2024). Enhancing Robustness of LLM-Synthetic Text Detectors for Academic Writing: A Comprehensive Analysis. In *Lecture Notes on Data Engineering and Communications Technologies* (Vol. 202, pp. 266–277). DOI: 10.1007/978-3-031-57916-5_23

Dravid, S. V., Shaik, N., & Gurumeet, C. (2024). Wadhawa,S. Kaliappan, G. Pavithra, T. C. Manjunath, "Advaya Bot - Radiologist assistant robot development & its usage in healthcare applications,". *AIP Conference Proceedings, 3149*, 140034. DOI: 10.1063/5.0225352

Dvivedi, S. S., Vijay, V., Pujari, S. L. R., Lodh, S., & Kumar, D. (2023). A Comparative Analysis of Large Language Models for Code Documentation Generation. *AIware 2024 - Proceedings of the 1st ACM International Conference on AI-Powered Software, Co-Located with: ESEC/FSE 2024, 1*(1), 65–73. DOI: 10.1145/3664646.3664765

Dwivedi, Y. K., Hughes, L., Baabdullah, A. M., Ribeiro-Navarrete, S., Giannakis, M., Al-Debei, M. M., Dennehy, D., Metri, B., Buhalis, D., Cheung, C. M., Conboy, K., Doyle, R., Dubey, R., Dutot, V., Felix, R., Goyal, D., Gustafsson, A., Hinsch, C., Jebabli, I., & Wamba, S. F. (2022). Metaverse beyond the hype: Multidisciplinary perspectives on emerging challenges, opportunities, and agenda for research, practice and policy. *International Journal of Information Management, 66*, 102542. DOI: 10.1016/j.ijinfomgt.2022.102542

Eker, S., Rovenskaya, E., Langan, S., & Obersteiner, M. (2019). Model validation: A bibliometric analysis of the literature. *Environmental Modelling & Software, 117*, 43–54. DOI: 10.1016/j.envsoft.2019.03.009

Ekin, S. (2023). *PROMPT ENGINEERING FOR CHATGPT ChatGPT 4 (author) OpenAI.* 1–12. DOI: 10.36227/techrxiv.22683919.v2

Enoch Sit, C. Y., & Kong, S.-C. (2023). A Deep Learning Framework With Visualisation for Uncovering Students' Learning Progression and Learning Bottlenecks. *Journal of Educational Computing Research, 62*(1), 223–249. DOI: 10.1177/07356331231200600

Ethayarajh, K.. (2021). *Understanding biases in language model evaluations.* ACL Anthology.

Eubanks, V. (2018). *Automating inequality.*

Fajar, A., & Yazid, S. (2018). Web Browser Vulnerabilities and Weakness Descriptive Analysis: Is it Chrome Keep Dominant? *International Journal of Engineering & Technology, 7*(4.44), 242–246.

Farhan, A. M., & Hadi, M. S. (2024). Implementation of read aloud feature from microsoft edge to increase pronunciation ability student's. *Jurnal Studi Guru Dan Pembelajaran, 7*(1), 141–152. DOI: 10.30605/jsgp.7.1.2024.2963

Fatima, H., Imran, M. A., Mohjazi, L., & Taha, A. (2024). A Latency Analysis of Edge vs. Cloud Computing for Internet-of-Mirrors (IoM) Applications. *2024 IEEE Middle East Conference on Communications and Networking (MECOM)*, 440–445. DOI: 10.1109/MECOM61498.2024.10882135

Felzmann, H., Fosch-Villaronga, E., Lutz, C., & Tamò-Larrieux, A. (2020). Towards Transparency by Design for Artificial Intelligence. *Science and Engineering Ethics*, *26*(6), 3333–3361. DOI: 10.1007/s11948-020-00276-4 PMID: 33196975

Ferrara, E. (2023). Fairness and Bias in Artificial intelligence: A brief survey of sources, impacts, and mitigation strategies. *Sci*, *6*(1), 3. DOI: 10.3390/sci6010003

Floridi, L. (2019). Translating principles into practices of digital ethics: Five risks of being unethical. *Philosophy & Technology*, *32*(2), 185–193. DOI: 10.1007/s13347-019-00354-x

Floridi, L., & Chiriatti, M. (2020). GPT-3: Its Nature, Scope, Limits, and Consequences. *Minds and Machines*, *30*(4), 681–694. DOI: 10.1007/s11023-020-09548-1

Floridi, L., & Cowls, J. (2019). A Unified Framework of Five Principles for AI in Society. *Harvard Data Science Review*, *12*(1), 1–14. DOI: 10.1162/99608f92.8cd550d1

Galhotra, S., Pradhan, R., & Salimi, B. (2021). Explaining Black-Box algorithms using probabilistic contrastive counterfactuals. *arXiv (Cornell University)*. https://doi.org//arxiv.2103.11972DOI: 10.1145/3448016.3458455

Garg, S., Ahmad, A., & Madsen, D. Ø. (2024). Academic writing in the age of AI: Comparing the reliability of ChatGPT and Bard with Scopus and Web of Science. *Journal of Innovation & Knowledge*, *9*(4), 100563. DOI: 10.1016/j.jik.2024.100563

Gehman, S.. (2020). *RealToxicityPrompts*. EMNLP.

Ghavidel, A., Pazos, P., Del Aguila Suarez, R., & Atashi, A. (2024). Predicting the need for cardiovascular surgery: A comparative study of Machine Learning models. *J.Electron.Electromedical.Eng.Med.Inform*, *6*(2), 92–106. DOI: 10.35882/jeeemi.v6i2.359

Gianni, R., Lehtinen, S., & Nieminen, M. (2022). Governance of responsible AI: From ethical guidelines to cooperative policies. *Frontiers of Computer Science*, *4*, 873437. Advance online publication. DOI: 10.3389/fcomp.2022.873437

Giray, L. (2023). Prompt Engineering with ChatGPT: A Guide for Academic Writers. *Annals of Biomedical Engineering*, *51*(12), 2629–2633. DOI: 10.1007/s10439-023-03272-4 PMID: 37284994

Glickman, M., & Zhang, Y. (2024). AI and Generative AI for Research Discovery and Summarization. *Harvard Data Science Review*, *6*(2). Advance online publication. DOI: 10.1162/99608f92.7f9220ff

Gopalakrishnan, S., Rao, A., & Mehta, P. (2024). Integrating social science perspectives into AI ethics. *Journal of Interdisciplinary AI Research*, *6*(2), 88–104.

Gulden, T., Zhang, L. A., Geist, E., Awan, J., Abdurahaman, Z., & Ahmadi, M. (2024). Leveraging Large Language Models for Comprehensive Literature Review: An Exploration of RAND Corporation's 20-Year Corpus. In Z. Yang & C. Krejci (Eds.), *Proceedings of the 2023 International Conference of The Computational Social Science Society of the Americas* (pp. 272–283). Springer Nature Switzerland. DOI: 10.1007/978-3-031-64193-0_18

Gupta, A., Bansal, P., & Roy, P. (2023). Iterative Strategies for Prompt Engineering in Natural Language Processing. *Journal of Computational Linguistics*, *58*(2), 145–159.

Gupta, K., Varol, C., & Zhou, B. (2023). Digital forensic analysis of discord on google chrome. *Forensic Science International Digital Investigation*, *44*, 301479. DOI: 10.1016/j.fsidi.2022.301479

Gupta, R., & Singh, P. (2023). Iterative Prompt Engineering for AI-driven Legal Systems. *Journal of Legal AI*, *13*(4), 182–196.

Gupta, V., & Bansal, R. (2023). Enhancing Response Relevance in Chatbots Using Multi-step Prompting. *Journal of AI and Robotics*, *17*(2), 56–67.

Habli, I., Lawton, T., & Porter, Z. (2020). Artificial intelligence in health care: Accountability and safety. *Bulletin of the World Health Organization*, *98*(4), 251–256. DOI: 10.2471/BLT.19.237487 PMID: 32284648

Hagendorff, T. (2020). The Ethics of AI Ethics: An Evaluation of Guidelines. *Minds and Machines*, *30*(1), 99–120. DOI: 10.1007/s11023-020-09517-8

Haines-Young, R., Potschin, M., & others. (2010). The links between biodiversity, ecosystem services and human well-being. Ecosystem Ecology: A New Synthesis, 1, 110–139.

Hallamaa, J., & Kalliokoski, T. (2022). AI Ethics as applied Ethics. *Frontiers of Computer Science*, *4*, 776837. Advance online publication. DOI: 10.3389/fcomp.2022.776837

Hameed, M. P. H., Padmakumar, K., & Bindu, L. (2025). Evaluation of feeding aspects of the bagrid catfish Mystus gulio (Order: Siluriformes). *International Journal of Ecology and Environmental Sciences, 51*(1), 129–137. DOI: 10.55863/ijees.2025.0464

Hames, I. (2007). The Peer-Review Process - How to Get Going. In *Peer Review and Manuscript Management in Scientific Journals* (pp. 9–24). Wiley., DOI: 10.1002/9780470750803.ch2

Han, T., Jeong, W. K., & Shin, J. (2025). Diagnostic performance of multimodal large language models in radiological quiz cases: The effects of prompt engineering and input conditions. *Ultrasonography (Seoul, Korea), 44*(3), 220–231. DOI: 10.14366/usg.25012 PMID: 40235070

Hasan, W. U., Zaman, K. T., Wang, X., Juan, L., Xie, B., & Tao, C. (2024). Empowering Alzheimer's caregivers with conversational AI: A novel approach for enhanced communication and personalized support. In *Research Square.*

Haugsbaken, H., & Hagelia, M. (2024). A New AI Literacy For The Algorithmic Age: Prompt Engineering Or Eductional Promptization? *2024 4th International Conference on Applied Artificial Intelligence (ICAPAI)*, 1–8. DOI: 10.1109/ICAPAI61893.2024.10541229

Heilinger, J. (2022). The Ethics of AI Ethics. A constructive critique. *Philosophy & Technology*, *35*(3), 61. Advance online publication. DOI: 10.1007/s13347-022-00557-9

He, K., Zhang, X., Ren, S., & Sun, J. (2016). Deep residual learning for image recognition. *Proceedings of the IEEE Computer Society Conference on Computer Vision and Pattern Recognition, 2016-December*, 770–778. DOI: 10.1109/CVPR.2016.90

Henneberg, M., & Schofield, J. (2008). *The Hobbit Trap: Money, Fame, Science and the Discovery of a'new Species*. Wakefield Press.

Heston, T., & Khun, C. (2023). Prompt engineering in medical education. *International Medical Education*, *2*(3), 198–205. DOI: 10.3390/ime2030019

Hickok, M. (2020). Lessons learned from AI ethics principles for future actions. *AI and Ethics*, *1*(1), 41–47. DOI: 10.1007/s43681-020-00008-1

Holstein, K.. (2019). "Improving fairness in ML systems." *Proceedings of CHI.*

Horizon, M. I. T. (2024). *Critical Thinking in the Age of AI*. https://horizon.mit.edu/insights/critical-thinking-in-the-age-of-ai

Hosseini, M., Resnik, D. B., & Holmes, K. (2023). The ethics of disclosing the use of artificial intelligence tools in writing scholarly manuscripts. *Research Ethics, 19*(4), 449–465. DOI: 10.1177/17470161231180449 PMID: 39749232

Hsu, Y.-C., & Ching, Y.-H. (2023). Generative Artificial Intelligence in Education, Part One: The Dynamic Frontier. *TechTrends, 67*(4), 603–607. DOI: 10.1007/s11528-023-00863-9

Huang, D., Yan, C., Li, Q., & Peng, X. (2024). From Large Language Models to Large Multimodal Models: A Literature Review. *Applied Sciences (Basel, Switzerland), 14*(12), 5068. DOI: 10.3390/app14125068

Huang, J., & Chang, C.-C., K. (2023). Towards Reasoning in Large Language Models: A Survey. *Proceedings of the Annual Meeting of the Association for Computational Linguistics*, 1049–1065. DOI: 10.18653/v1/2023.findings-acl.67

Huang, L., Yu, W., Ma, W., Zhong, W., Feng, Z., Wang, H., Chen, Q., Peng, W., Feng, X., Qin, B., & Liu, T. (2024). A Survey on Hallucination in Large Language Models: Principles, Taxonomy, Challenges, and Open Questions. *ACM Transactions on Information Systems, 3703155*. Advance online publication. DOI: 10.1145/3703155

Huriye, A. Z. (2023, April 25). *The Ethics of Artificial intelligence: Examining the ethical considerations surrounding the development and use of AI*. https://gprjournals.org/journals/index.php/AJT/article/view/142

Hu, T., & Zhou, X.-H. (2024). *Unveiling LLM Evaluation Focused on Metrics: Challenges and Solutions. 2021*, 1–45. https://arxiv.org/abs/2404.09135

Ibrahimov, V. (2023). *10 ChatGPT and Claude AI prompts for faster academic reading*. Medium. https://medium.com/@Vugar_Ibrahimov/10-chatgpt-and-claude-ai-prompts-for-faster-academic-reading-ece583dd132c

Jabbour, S., Fouhey, D., Shepard, S., Valley, T. S., Kazerooni, E. A., Banovic, N., Wiens, J., & Sjoding, M. W. (2023). Measuring the impact of AI in the diagnosis of hospitalized patients: A randomized clinical vignette survey study. *Journal of the American Medical Association, 330*(23), 2275–2284. DOI: 10.1001/jama.2023.22295 PMID: 38112814

Jagaba, A. H., Lawal, I. M., Birniwa, A. H., Affam, A. C., Usman, A. K., Soja, U. B., Saleh, D., Hussaini, A., Noor, A., & Yaro, N. S. A. (2024). Sources of water contamination by heavy metals. In *Membrane technologies for heavy metal removal from water* (pp. 3–27). CRC Press.

Jain, M., & Sood, R. (2023). Reducing Bias in AI Prompts through Continuous Iteration. *AI and Bias Journal, 20*(3), 135–148.

Jasmine, K. S. (2024). Unlocking the power of prompt engineering: diverse applications and case studies. In Transforming Education With Generative AI: Prompt Engineering and Synthetic Content Creation (pp. 411-432). IGI Global. DOI: 10.4018/979-8-3693-1351-0.ch020

Jiang, Y.. (2022). Prompt engineering for AI fairness. *Journal of Machine Learning Research.*

Jobin, A., Ienca, M., & Vayena, E. (2019). The global landscape of AI ethics guidelines. *Nature Machine Intelligence, 1*(9), 389–399. DOI: 10.1038/s42256-019-0088-2

Juliussen, B. A. (2025). The right to an explanation under the GDPR and the AI Act. In *Lecture notes in computer science* (pp. 184–197). https://doi.org/DOI: 10.1007/978-981-96-2071-5_14

Jurafsky, D., & Martin, J. H. (2009). *Speech and Language Processing*. Stanford University.

Kabir, J., Chakraborty, A., Mahmood, A., & Chakaraborty, A. (2024). Exploring Explainable Artificial Intelligence: A Comparative Analysis of Interpretability Techniques. *International Journal of Advanced Research in Computer and Communication Engineering, 13*(3). Advance online publication. DOI: 10.17148/IJARCCE.2024.13301

Kankanhalli, A. (2024). Peer Review in the Age of Generative AI. *Journal of the Association for Information Systems, 25*(1), 76–84. DOI: 10.17705/1jais.00865

Kaur, G., & Sharma, K. (2023). Improved Multilingual AI Prompt Engineering for Cross-Cultural Interaction. *Journal of Global AI, 18*(2), 83–95.

Kazim, E., & Koshiyama, A. S. (2021). A high-level overview of AI ethics. *Patterns (New York, N.Y.), 2*(9), 100314. DOI: 10.1016/j.patter.2021.100314 PMID: 34553166

Khan, N. D. A., Shad, N. D. F., Sethi, N. D. S., & Bibi, N. M. (2024). The impact of artificial intelligence (AI) on job displacement and the future work. *Social Science Review Archives.*, 2(2), 2296–2306. DOI: 10.70670/sra.v3i1.509

Kim, S., Lee, D., & Kim, J. (2023). Prompt Refinement through Feedback Loops in Conversational AI. *AI & Language Technology, 10*(4), 202–212.

Kobeissi, M. M., Christopherson, K. A., & Ruppert, S. D. (2024). Leveraging artificial intelligence for professional email communication. *Nurse Educator, 49*(1), 53–54. DOI: 10.1097/NNE.0000000000001493 PMID: 37556832

Kocak, Z. (2024). Publication Ethics in the Era of Artificial Intelligence. *Journal of Korean Medical Science*, *39*(33), 1–11. DOI: 10.3346/jkms.2024.39.e249 PMID: 39189714

Konidena, B. K., Malaiyappan, J. N. A., & Tadimarri, A. (2024). Ethical Considerations in the Development and Deployment of AI Systems. *European Journal of Technology*, *8*(2), 41–53. DOI: 10.47672/ejt.1890

Kramer, M. A., Leavens, A., & Scarlat, A. (2024). Harnessing AI for efficient analysis of complex policy documents: a case study of Executive Order 14110. *arXiv preprint arXiv:2406.06657.*

Krishnakumar, K., & Rajan, P. D. (2008). Fish and fisheries in Vembanad Lake. Consolidated Report of Vembanad Fish Count, 2011.

Kudo, T., & Richardson, J. (2018). SentencePiece: A simple and language independent subword tokenizer and detokenizer for Neural Text Processing. In Blanco, E., & Lu, W. (Eds.), *Proceedings of the 2018 Conference on Empirical Methods in Natural Language Processing: System Demonstrations* (pp. 66–71). Association for Computational Linguistics. DOI: 10.18653/v1/D18-2012

Kulithalai Shiyam Sundar, P., & Deka, P. C. (2022). Spatio-temporal classification and prediction of land use and land cover change for the Vembanad Lake system, Kerala: A machine learning approach. *Environmental Science and Pollution Research International*, *29*(57), 86220–86236. DOI: 10.1007/s11356-021-17257-0 PMID: 34767164

Kulk, G., George, G., Abdulaziz, A., Menon, N., Theenathayalan, V., Jayaram, C., Brewin, R. J., & Sathyendranath, S. (2021a). Effect of reduced anthropogenic activities on water quality in Lake Vembanad, India. *Remote Sensing (Basel)*, *13*(9), 1631. DOI: 10.3390/rs13091631

Kumar, P. (2024). Large language models (LLMs): Survey, technical frameworks, and future challenges. *Artificial Intelligence Review*, *57*(10), 260. DOI: 10.1007/s10462-024-10888-y

Kumar, R., Singh, V., & Mehta, P. (2023). Fine-tuning AI Prompts for Domain-Specific Applications. *Machine Learning Insights*, *19*(4), 237–249.

Kumar, S., Patel, R., & Singh, D. (2024). Contextual AI ethics: A new frontier in prompt engineering. *Ethics in Artificial Intelligence Journal*, *4*(1), 55–72.

Kurup, B. M., Harikrishnan, M., Shibu, A., & Mullasseri, S. (2022). Impact of Climate Change on Ecology and Fisheries of Tropical Estuaries with reference to Vembanad Estuary (India): Past Trends and Potential Projections. Impact of Climate Change on Hydrological Cycle, Ecosystem, Fisheries and Food Security, 229.

Laghari, M. S., Ahmed, F., & Aziz, J. (2010). Wear particle shape and edge detail analysis. *2010 The 2nd International Conference on Computer and Automation Engineering (ICCAE), 1*, 122–125.

Lal, S., & Sureka, A. (2012). Comparison of seven bug report types: A case-study of google chrome browser project. *2012 19th Asia-Pacific Software Engineering Conference, 1*, 517–526.

Larsson, S. (2021). AI in the EU: Ethical Guidelines as a Governance Tool. In *Springer eBooks* (pp. 85–111). https://doi.org/DOI: 10.1007/978-3-030-63672-2_4

Lawrence, L., Echeverria, V., Yang, K., Aleven, V., & Rummel, N. (2024). How teachers conceptualise shared control with an AI co-orchestration tool: A multiyear teacher-centred design process. *British Journal of Educational Technology*, *55*(3), 823–844. DOI: 10.1111/bjet.13372

Lee, A. V. Y., Teo, C. L., & Tan, S. C. (2024). Prompt Engineering for Knowledge Creation: Using Chain-of-Thought to Support Students' Improvable Ideas. *AI*, *5*(3), 1446–1461. DOI: 10.3390/ai5030069

Lee, J., Park, H., & Kim, Y. (2024). Ethical content generation through advanced prompt design. *Journal of AI Applications in Media*, *12*(3), 77–91.

Lei, T., & Lam, A. (2010). *An Analysis on Google Chrome.*

Leikas, J., Johri, A., Latvanen, M., Wessberg, N., & Hahto, A. (2022). Governing Ethical AI Transformation: A case study of AuroraAI. *Frontiers in Artificial Intelligence*, *5*, 836557. Advance online publication. DOI: 10.3389/frai.2022.836557 PMID: 35224480

Lens. *Search results for "Ethics of AI"*. The Lens. Retrieved June 22, 2025, from https://www.lens.org/lens/search/scholar/list?q=ethics%20of%20AI

Le, Q., & Mikolov, T. (2014). Distributed representations of sentences and documents. *31st International Conference on Machine Learning, ICML 2014, 4*, 2931–2939.

Leung, T. I., de Azevedo Cardoso, T., Mavragani, A., & Eysenbach, G. (2023). Best Practices for Using AI Tools as an Author, Peer Reviewer, or Editor. *Journal of Medical Internet Research*, *25*, e51584. DOI: 10.2196/51584 PMID: 37651164

Lewis, P., Perez, E., Piktus, A., Petroni, F., Karpukhin, V., Goyal, N., Küttler, H., Lewis, M., Yih, W., Rocktäschel, T., Riedel, S., & Kiela, D. (2020). Retrieval-Augmented Generation for Knowledge-Intensive NLP Tasks. *Advances in Neural Information Processing Systems, 2020-Decem*(NeurIPS). https://arxiv.org/abs/2005.11401

Li, J., Sato, A., Shimura, K., & Fukumoto, F. (2020). Multi-task Peer-Review Score Prediction. *Proceedings of the First Workshop on Scholarly Document Processing*, 121–126. DOI: 10.18653/v1/2020.sdp-1.14

Liang, J., Huang, T., & Wei, S. (2023). Transparency in black-box models: The role of prompt engineering. *AI Transparency Quarterly*, *11*(4), 22–38.

Liang, X., Song, S., Zheng, Z., Wang, H., Yu, Q., Li, X., Li, R.-H., Wang, Y., Wang, Z., Xiong, F., & Li, Z. (2024). Internal Consistency and Self-Feedback in Large Language Models. *Survey (London, England)*, *14*(8), 1–27. https://arxiv.org/abs/2407.14507

Liao, Q., Gruen, D., & Miller, S. (2023). Transparency in AI systems: Challenges and strategies. *AI & Society*, *38*(1), 112–126.

Li, F., Ruijs, N., & Lu, Y. (2022). Ethics & AI: A Systematic Review on Ethical Concerns and Related Strategies for Designing with AI in Healthcare. *AI*, *4*(1), 28–53. DOI: 10.3390/ai4010003

Li, F., Zhang, X., Wu, D., & Yao, Q. (2023). Optimizing Text Generation with Multi-step Prompt Refinement. *Advances in Machine Learning*, *34*(5), 301–315.

Li, M., Sun, J., & Tan, X. (2024). Evaluating the effectiveness of large language models in abstract screening: A comparative analysis. *Systematic Reviews*, *13*(1), 219. DOI: 10.1186/s13643-024-02609-x PMID: 39169386

Linardatos, P., Papastefanopoulos, V., & Kotsiantis, S. (2020). Explainable AI: A review of Machine Learning Interpretability Methods. *Entropy (Basel, Switzerland)*, *23*(1), 18. DOI: 10.3390/e23010018 PMID: 33375658

Lingard, L. (2023). Writing with ChatGPT: An Illustration of its Capacity, Limitations & Implications for Academic Writers. *Perspectives on Medical Education*, *12*(1), 261–270. DOI: 10.5334/pme.1072 PMID: 37397181

Li, Q., Zhang, J., & Tan, L. (2023). Addressing User Needs with Iterative Prompt Engineering. *Advances in NLP*, *33*(1), 45–58.

Liu, L., Zhang, X., Yan, G., & Chen, S. (2012). *Chrome Extensions: Threat Analysis and Countermeasures*. NDSS.

Loi, M., & Spielkamp, M. (2021). Towards Accountability in the Use of Artificial Intelligence for Public Administrations. In *Proceedings of the 2021 AAAI/ACM Conference on AI, Ethics, and Society (AIES '21)*, 757–766. https://doi.org/DOI: 10.1145/3461702.3462631

Long, D., Zhao, Y., Brown, H., Xie, Y., Zhao, J., Chen, N., Kawaguchi, K., Shieh, M., & He, J. (2024). Prompt Optimization via Adversarial In-Context Learning. In Ku, L.-W., Martins, A., & Srikumar, V. (Eds.), *Proceedings of the 62nd Annual Meeting of the Association for Computational Linguistics* (Volume 1*: Long Papers)* (pp. 7308–7327). Association for Computational Linguistics. DOI: 10.18653/v1/2024.acl-long.395

Lund, B., Wang, T., Mannuru, N. R., Nie, B., Shimray, S., & Wang, Z. (2019). ChatGPT and a New Academic Reality: AI-Written Research Papers and the Ethics of the Large Language Models in Scholarly Publishing. *Journal of the Association for Information Science and Technology*, *11*(1), 1–14. http://scioteca.caf.com/bitstream/handle/123456789/1091/RED2017-Eng-8ene.pdf?sequence=12&isAllowed=y%0Ahttp://dx.doi.org/10.1016/j.regsciurbeco.2008.06.005%0Ahttps://www.researchgate.net/publication/305320484_SISTEM_PEMBETUNGAN_TERPUSAT_STRATEGI_MELESTARI

Luo, Q., Ye, Y., Liang, S., Zhang, Z., Qin, Y., Lu, Y., Wu, Y., Cong, X., Lin, Y., Zhang, Y., Che, X., Liu, Z., & Sun, M. (2024). *RepoAgent: An LLM-Powered Open-Source Framework for Repository-level Code Documentation Generation.* https://arxiv.org/abs/2402.16667 DOI: 10.18653/v1/2024.emnlp-demo.46

Mahmud, S. (2024). *Fostering Academic Integrity in the Age of Artificial Intelligence.*, DOI: 10.4018/979-8-3693-0240-8.ch001

Manhas, S., & Taterh, S. (2018). A Comparative Analysis of Various Vulnerabilities Occur in Google Chrome. *Soft Computing: Theories and Applications: Proceedings of SoCTA 2016,* Volume 1, 51–59.

Manning, C. D., Surdeanu, M., Bauer, J., Finkel, J. R., Bethard, S., & McClosky, D. (2014). The Stanford CoreNLP natural language processing toolkit. *Proceedings of 52nd Annual Meeting of the Association for Computational Linguistics: System Demonstrations*, 55–60. DOI: 10.3115/v1/P14-5010

Mazurek, G., & Małagocka, K. (2019). Perception of privacy and data protection in the context of the development of artificial intelligence. *Journal of Management Analytics*, *6*(4), 344–364. DOI: 10.1080/23270012.2019.1671243

Mehrabi, N.. (2021). A survey on bias and fairness in ML. *ACM Computing Surveys*.

Mehrabi, N., Morstatter, F., Saxena, N., Lerman, K., & Galstyan, A. (2021). A survey on bias and fairness in machine learning. *ACM Computing Surveys*, *54*(6), 1–35. DOI: 10.1145/3457607

Mehta, P., & Shah, A. (2023). Iterative Prompt Refinement for Task-Oriented Dialogue Systems. *International Journal of AI and Data Science*, *22*(3), 334–346.

Melanson, J., & Maman, B. (2023). *The prompt engineering guide*. https://www.promptingguide.ai

Meurisch, C., & Mühlhäuser, M. (2021). Data protection in AI services. *ACM Computing Surveys*, *54*(2), 1–38. DOI: 10.1145/3440754

Meyer, J. G., Urbanowicz, R. J., Martin, P. C. N., O'Connor, K., Li, R., Peng, P.-C., Bright, T. J., Tatonetti, N., Won, K. J., Gonzalez-Hernandez, G., & Moore, J. H. (2023). ChatGPT and large language models in academia: Opportunities and challenges. *BioData Mining*, *16*(1), 20. DOI: 10.1186/s13040-023-00339-9 PMID: 37443040

Miah, M. S. U., Kabir, M. M., Sarwar, T., Safran, M., Alfarhood, S., & Mridha, M. F. (2024). A multimodal approach to cross-lingual sentiment analysis with ensemble of transformer and LLM. *Scientific Reports*, *14*(1), 9603. DOI: 10.1038/s41598-024-60210-7 PMID: 38671064

Miao, J., & Thongprayoon, C., Suppadungsuk Supawadee and Krisanapan, P., Radhakrishnan, Y., & Cheungpasitporn, W. (2024). Chain of thought utilization in large language models and application in nephrology. *Medicina (Kaunas, Lithuania)*, *60*(1). PMID: 38256408

Mogalekar, H., Ansar, C., Raman, N., Jayachandran, K., Dinesh, K., & Kolhe, S. (2015a). Fish diversity of Vembanad lake in the Panangad-Kumbalam region of Kochi, Kerala, India. *Pollution Research*, *34*(2), 345–349.

Mohamed, A., & Ismail, I. (2022). A performance comparative on most popular Internet Web Browsers. *Procedia Computer Science*, *215*, 589–597. DOI: 10.1016/j.procs.2022.12.061

Mohandas, K., & Brema, J. (2021a). Linear regression based water quality analysis through spatial distribution of parameters for Vembanad Lake. *International Journal of Aquatic Science*, *12*(3), 272–289.

Mohitha, M. R., Terlapu, P. V., Anusrilekha, B., Narendra, R., Shekar, P. U., Chaitanya, P. K., & Kumar, T. R. (2024). Streamlining text generation with AI powered prompt simplification strategies. In *Proceedings of the International Conference on Computational Innovations and Emerging Trends (ICCIET 2024)* (pp. 160–169). Atlantis Press International BV. DOI: 10.2991/978-94-6463-471-6_16

Morgan, L., Patel, T., & Rivers, D. (2024). Ethical frameworks for AI in recruitment: Lessons from case studies. *Business Ethics and Technology Journal*, *9*(4), 102–125.

Mumthaz, P., Padmakumar, K., & Bindu, L. (2019). Length-weight relationship of long whiskered catfish, Mystus gulio (Hamilton 1822) from Vembanad Lake, Kerala, India.

Mungoli, N. (2023). Exploring the synergy of prompt engineering and reinforcement learning for enhanced control and responsiveness in chat GPT. *Journal of Electrical and Electronics Engineering (Oradea)*, *2*(3), 201–205.

Munir, S., Kollnig, K., Shuba, A., & Shafiq, Z. (2024). Google's Chrome Antitrust Paradox. *arXiv Preprint arXiv:2406.11856.*

Nair, P., Joseph, K., Balachandran, V., & Pillai, V. K. (1975). Study on the primary production in the Vembanad lake. *Bulletin of the Department of Marine Sciences*, *7*(1), 161–170.

National Library of Medicine. *Search results for "Ethics of AI"*. PubMed. Retrieved June 23, 2025, from https://pubmed.ncbi.nlm.nih.gov/?term=ethics+of+AI

Naveed, H., Khan, A. U., Qiu, S., Saqib, M., Anwar, S., Usman, M., Akhtar, N., Barnes, N., & Mian, A. (2023). *A Comprehensive Overview of Large Language Models*. https://arxiv.org/abs/2307.06435

Nees, J. V., & Waltman, L. (2019). *VOSViewer Manual*. https://www.vosviewer.com/documentation/Manual_VOSviewer_1.6.11.pdf

Nguyen, A., Tran, C., & Vo, M. (2020). Ethical implications of AI applications in healthcare and business. *Journal of Applied AI Research*, *7*(1), 14–28.

Noble, S. U. (2018). *Algorithms of oppression.*

Novelli, C., Taddeo, M., & Floridi, L. (2023). Accountability in artificial intelligence: What it is and how it works. *AI & Society*, *39*(4), 1871–1882. DOI: 10.1007/s00146-023-01635-y

O'Keefe, R. M., & O'Leary, D. E. (1993). Expert system verification and validation: A survey and tutorial. *Artificial Intelligence Review*, *7*(1), 3–42. DOI: 10.1007/BF00849196

Obermeyer, Z.. (2019). Dissecting racial bias in algorithms. *Science*. Advance online publication. DOI: 10.1126/science.aax2342

Okorondu, J., Umar, N. A., Ulor, C. O., Onwuagba, C. G., Diagi, B. E., Ajiere, S. I., & Nwaogu, C. (2022). Anthropogenic Activities as Primary Drivers of Environmental Pollution and Loss of Biodiversity A Review. *Int. J. Trend Sci. Res. Dev*, *6*, 621–643.

Open, A. I. (2023). *Our approach to AI safety*. https://openai.com/index/our-approach-to-ai-safety/

OpenAI API. (n.d.). Retrieved December 24, 2024, from https://platform.openai.com/docs/api-reference

Ouyang, L., Wu, J., Jiang, X., Almeida, D., Wainwright, C., Mishkin, P., Zhang, C., Agarwal, S., Slama, K., & Ray, A. (2022). Training language models to follow instructions with human feedback. *Advances in Neural Information Processing Systems*, *35*, 27730–27744.

Oyewole, F. (2024). Integrating Large Language Models in Research and Education: Opportunities, Challenges, and Future Directions. *Preprint*. https://doi.org/https://doi.org/10.13140/RG.2.2.30706.31682

Paić, G., & Serkin, L. (2025). The impact of artificial intelligence: From cognitive costs to global inequality. *The European Physical Journal. Special Topics*. Advance online publication. DOI: 10.1140/epjs/s11734-025-01561-8

Pasricha, S. (2022). AI ethics in smart Healthcare. *IEEE Consumer Electronics Magazine*, *12*(4), 12–20. DOI: 10.1109/MCE.2022.3220001

Patel, K., & Kumar, P. (2023). Advanced Techniques for AI Prompt Optimization in Large Language Models. *Journal of Computational Intelligence*, *27*(3), 98–109.

Pathak, P., & Rana, P. S. (2025). Comparative Analysis of Pretrained Models for Text Classification, Generation and Summarization: A Detailed Analysis. In *Lecture Notes in Computer Science (including subseries Lecture Notes in Artificial Intelligence and Lecture Notes in Bioinformatics): Vol. 15301 LNCS* (Issue September, pp. 151–166). DOI: 10.1007/978-3-031-78107-0_10

Patil, P., & Bhattacharya, S. (2023). Prompt Refinement in AI Systems for E-commerce Applications. *Journal of AI in E-commerce*, *19*(7), 290–303.

Patil, R., & Gudivada, V. (2024). A Review of Current Trends, Techniques, and Challenges in Large Language Models (LLMs). *Applied Sciences (Basel, Switzerland)*, *14*(5), 2074. DOI: 10.3390/app14052074

Patil, R., Heston, T. F., & Bhuse, V. (2024). Prompt engineering in healthcare. *Electronics (Basel), 13*(15), 2961. DOI: 10.3390/electronics13152961

Paul, T. T., Sarkar, U., Salim, S. S., Manoharan, S., Ganeshan, K., & Das, B. (2024). Assessing multi-scale vulnerability of fisheries of Vembanad lake, peninsular India, due to climate change: A stakeholders-based approach. *Environment, Development and Sustainability, 26*(3), 6719–6749. DOI: 10.1007/s10668-023-02984-w

Pennington, J., Socher, R., & Manning, C. D. (2014). Glove: Global vectors for word representation. *Proceedings of the 2014 Conference on Empirical Methods in Natural Language Processing (EMNLP)*, 1532–1543. DOI: 10.3115/v1/D14-1162

Perez, E., Kiela, D., & Cho, K. (2021). *True few-shot learning with language models.* arXiv preprint arXiv:2105.11447

Perkins, M. (2023). Academic Integrity considerations of AI Large Language Models in the post-pandemic era: ChatGPT and beyond. *Journal of University Teaching & Learning Practice, 20*(2). Advance online publication. DOI: 10.53761/1.20.02.07

Perkins, M., & Roe, J. (2024). Decoding Academic Integrity Policies: A Corpus Linguistics Investigation of AI and Other Technological Threats. *Higher Education Policy, 37*(3), 633–653. DOI: 10.1057/s41307-023-00323-2

Phoenix, J., & Taylor, M. (2024). *Prompt Engineering for Generative AI.* O'Reilly Media.

Pizzi, M., Romanoff, M., & Engelhardt, T. (2020). AI for humanitarian action: Human rights and ethics. *International Review of the Red Cross, 102*(913), 145–180. DOI: 10.1017/S1816383121000011

Possati, L. M. (2023). Ethics of Quantum Computing: An Outline. *Philosophy & Technology, 36*(3), 48. Advance online publication. DOI: 10.1007/s13347-023-00651-6

Prakash, A., Thaniem, M., Eswaran, R., Sundarabalan, P., & Muniasamy, M. (2023). Metal trace element concentration in commercial fish species from vembanad backwater system: Evaluating the risks of human consumption. *Appl Ecol Environ Sci, 11*(2), 56–63.

Prem, E. (2023). From ethical AI frameworks to tools: A review of approaches. *AI and Ethics, 3*(3), 699–716. DOI: 10.1007/s43681-023-00258-9

Qiao, S., Ou, Y., Zhang, N., Chen, X., Yao, Y., Deng, S., Tan, C., Huang, F., & Chen, H. (2022). *Reasoning with language model prompting: A survey.* arXiv preprint arXiv:2212.09597. https://arxiv.org/abs/2212.09597

Qin, G. and Eisner, J. (2021). *Learning How To Ask: Querying LMs with Mixtures of Soft Prompts.*

Raffel, C., Shazeer, N., Roberts, A., Lee, K., Narang, S., Matena, M., Zhou, Y., Li, W., & Liu, P. J. (2020). Exploring the limits of transfer learning with a unified text-to-text transformer. *Journal of Machine Learning Research, 21*(1).

Rahman, M. M., & Watanobe, Y. (2023). ChatGPT for Education and Research: Opportunities, Threats, and Strategies. *Applied Sciences (Basel, Switzerland), 13*(9), 5783. DOI: 10.3390/app13095783

Raiaan, M. A. K., Mukta, M. S. H., Fatema, K., Fahad, N. M., Sakib, S., Mim, M. M. J., Ahmad, J., Ali, M. E., & Azam, S. (2024). A Review on Large Language Models: Architectures, Applications, Taxonomies, Open Issues and Challenges. *IEEE Access : Practical Innovations, Open Solutions, 12*, 26839–26874. DOI: 10.1109/ACCESS.2024.3365742

Rajan, B., Varghese, V. M., & Pradeepkumar, A. (2011). Recreational Boat Carrying Capacity of Vembanad Lake Ecosystem, Kerala, South India. *Environmental Research, Engineering and Management, 56*(2), 11–19. DOI: 10.5755/j01.erem.56.2.270

Raji, I. D., ... (2020). "Closing the AI accountability gap." *FAccT Conference Proceedings*. DOI: 10.1145/3351095.3372873

Raji, I. D., Mitchell, M., & Buolamwini, J. (2020). Actionable auditing: Investigating the impact of public oversight on AI systems. *Proceedings of the AAAI/ACM Conference on AI Ethics and Society*, 47-53.

Rajput, S., & Verma, S. (2023). Optimization of AI Prompts in Healthcare Applications. *Journal of Medical AI, 31*(4), 244–257.

Rathod, D. (2017). Web browser forensics: Google chrome. *International Journal of Advanced Research in Computer Science, 8*(7), 896–899.

Renjithkumar, C. R., Roshni, K., & Sreekanth, G. B. (2025). Finfish harvest patterns in the largest Ramsar wetland—Vembanad estuary along the south-west coast of India. *Wetlands Ecology and Management, 33*(1), 3. DOI: 10.1007/s11273-024-10022-3

Reynolds, L., & McDonell, K. (2021). *Prompt Programming for Large Language Models: Beyond the Few-Shot Paradigm.* arXiv. https://arxiv.org/abs/2102.07350 DOI: 10.1145/3411763.3451760

Rockall, E., Tavares, M. M., & Pizzinelli, C. (2025). AI adoption and inequality. *IMF Working Paper, 2025*(068), 1. DOI: 10.5089/9798229006828.001

Rogers, W. A., Draper, H., & Carter, S. M. (2021). Evaluation of artificial intelligence clinical applications: Detailed case analyses show value of healthcare ethics approach in identifying patient care issues. *Bioethics*, *35*(7), 623–633. DOI: 10.1111/bioe.12885 PMID: 34046918

Rohith, M., & Sunil, A. (2021). Comparative analysis of edge computing and edge devices: Key technology in IoT and computer vision applications. *2021 International Conference on Recent Trends on Electronics, Information, Communication & Technology (RTEICT)*, 722–727. DOI: 10.1109/RTEICT52294.2021.9573996

Roshni, K., Renjithkumar, C. R., Sreekanth, G. B., Raghavan, R., & Ranjeet, K. (2023). Fish community structure and functional guild composition in a large tropical estuary (Vembanad Lake, India). *Environmental Science and Pollution Research International*, *30*(11), 29635–29662. DOI: 10.1007/s11356-022-24250-8 PMID: 36417074

Ruan, E. L., Alkattan, A., Elhadad, N., & Rossetti, S. C. (2024). Clinician perceptions of Generative Artificial Intelligence tools and clinical workflows: Potential uses, motivations for adoption, and sentiments on impact. In *medRxiv*. DOI: 10.1101/2024.07.29.24311177

Sahoo, P., Singh, A. K., Saha, S., Jain, V., Mondal, S., & Chadha, A. (2024). *A Systematic Survey of Prompt Engineering in Large Language Models: Techniques and Applications*. https://arxiv.org/abs/2402.07927

Salah, M., Abdelfattah, F., & Al Halbusi, H. (2023). Debate: Peer reviews at the crossroads—'To AI or not to AI?'. *Public Money & Management*, *43*(8), 781–782. DOI: 10.1080/09540962.2023.2264032

Salih, A. M., Raisi-Estabragh, Z., Galazzo, I. B., Radeva, P., Petersen, S. E., Lekadir, K., & Menegaz, G. (2024). A perspective on explainable artificial intelligence methods: SHAP and LIME. *Advanced Intelligent Systems*. Advance online publication. DOI: 10.1002/aisy.202400304

Salih, M. M. (2021). A Comparative Study Between Google Workspace and Microsoft Office 365 Productivity Services in Iraqi Educational Institutions. *International Journal of Humanities and Educational Research*, *3*(5), 123–135. DOI: 10.47832/2757-5403.5-3.11

Sekhar, K. C., Ranganathan, L., Bathrinath, S., Premnath, D., Yuvasri, B., & Boopathi, S. (2024). Cloud Computing Adoption for Small and Medium Enterprises in Mechanical Engineering. In *Advances in Web Technologies and Engineering* (pp. 219–247). IGI Global. DOI: 10.4018/979-8-3693-1487-6.ch011

Sennrich, R., Haddow, B., & Birch, A. (2016). Neural Machine Translation of Rare Words with Subword Units. *Proceedings of the 54th Annual Meeting of the Association for Computational Linguistics (*Volume 1*: Long Papers)*, 1715–1725. DOI: 10.18653/v1/P16-1162

Shafqat, N. (2016). Forensic investigation of user's web activity on Google Chrome using various forensic tools. [IJCSNS]. *International Journal of Computer Science and Network Security*, *16*(9), 123.

Sharma, R., & Mehta, R. (2023). Effective Iterative Methods for AI Model Fine-tuning Using User Feedback. *Journal of AI Technology*, *24*(8), 467–479.

Sharma, T., Arora, R., & Singh, P. (2023). The Role of Contextual Prompts in Improving AI Response Quality. *Journal of AI Research*, *22*(2), 213–227.

Sharma, V., Kumar, S., Jadhav, R., & Patil, M. S. (2023). Improving Conversational AI Models Using Iterative Prompting Techniques. *Journal of Artificial Intelligence*, *24*(3), 112–126.

Sheng, E.. (2021). *Bias in natural language generation.* ACL.

Shijitha, M., & Sabu, P. (2020). Land use pattern in climatic physiological zones of Kerala. *Editorial Board*, *9*(4), 50.

Shofiah, N., Putera, Z. F., & Solichah, N. (2023). *Challenges and opportunities in the use of artificial intelligence in education for academic writing: A scoping review* (Issue Pfh). Atlantis Press SARL. DOI: 10.2991/978-2-38476-188-3_20

Shum, K., Diao, S., & Zhang, T. (2023). Automatic Prompt Augmentation and Selection with Chain-of-Thought from Labeled Data. *Findings of the Association for Computational Linguistics: EMNLP*, *2023*, 12113–12139. DOI: 10.18653/v1/2023.findings-emnlp.811

Shum, S. J. B., & Luckin, R. (2019). Learning analytics and AI: Politics, pedagogy and practices. *British Journal of Educational Technology*, *50*(6), 2785–2793. DOI: 10.1111/bjet.12880

Singh, H., & Verma, N. (2023). Enhancing AI with Iterative Prompt Modifications for Better Data Handling. *Journal of AI Systems*, *5*(2), 88–101.

Singh, R., Sharma, V., & Patel, A. (2023). Ethical Prompt Engineering for Reducing Algorithmic Biases. *AI for Social Good*, *4*(2), 92–104.

Solaiman, I., et al. (2021). "Process for adapting large language models to reduce harm." *OpenAI Technical Report.*

Sovrano, F., Vitali, F., & Palmirani, M. (2020). Modelling GDPR-Compliant Explanations for trustworthy AI. In *Lecture notes in computer science* (pp. 219–233). https://doi.org/DOI: 10.1007/978-3-030-58957-8_16

Srinivasan, R., & Uchendu, J. (2022). *Mitigating intersectional biases in AI.* AI Ethics Journal.

Stahl, B. C. (2021). Ethical issues of AI. In *SpringerBriefs in research and innovation governance* (pp. 35–53). https://doi.org/DOI: 10.1007/978-3-030-69978-9_4

Stefan, R., Carutasu, G., & Mocan, M. (2024). Ethical Considerations in the Implementation and Usage of Large Language Models. In *Lecture Notes in Networks and Systems: Vol. 928 LNNS* (Issue April, pp. 131–144). DOI: 10.1007/978-3-031-54671-6_10

Stout, K., Manne, G. A., & Corbeille, E. (2023). *ICLE Comments on Artificial Intelligence and Copyright.* https://laweconcenter.org/resources/icle-comments-on-artificial-intelligence-and-copyright/

Sui, Y., Zhou, M., Zhou, M., Han, S., & Zhang, D. (2023). Table Meets LLM: Can Large Language Models Understand Structured Table Data? A Benchmark and Empirical Study. *Proceedings of the 17th ACM International Conference on Web Search and Data Mining*, 645–654. DOI: 10.1145/3616855.3635752

Sundar, R., Srikaanth, P. B., Naik, D. A., Murugan, V. P., Karumudi, M., & Boopathi, S. (2024). Achieving Balance Between Innovation and Security in the Cloud With Artificial Intelligence of Things: Semantic Web Control Models. In *Advances in Web Technologies and Engineering* (pp. 1–26). IGI Global. DOI: 10.4018/979-8-3693-1487-6.ch001

Sun, G. H. (2024). Prompt engineering for nurse educators. *Nurse Educator*, *49*(6), 293–299. DOI: 10.1097/NNE.0000000000001705 PMID: 38968442

Suryadevara, S. (2023). Advances in data protection and Artificial intelligence: Trends and challenges. www.academia.edu. https://www.academia.edu/124958523/Advances_in_Data_Protection_and_Artificial_Intelligence_Trends_and_Challenges

Taleb, I., Navaz, A. N., & Serhani, M. A. (2024). Leveraging Large Language Models for Enhancing Literature-Based Discovery. *Big Data and Cognitive Computing*, *8*(11), 146. Advance online publication. DOI: 10.3390/bdcc8110146

Tambe, A., & Chaudhary, S. (2024). Generative AI: Challenges & framework of Governance. *International Research Journal of Modernization in Engineering Technology and Science*, *6*(11). Advance online publication. DOI: 10.56726/IRJMETS63353

Tao, Y., Viberg, O., Baker, R. S., & Kizilcec, R. F. (2024). Cultural bias and cultural alignment of large language models. *PNAS Nexus*, *3*(9), gae346. DOI: 10.1093/pnasnexus/pgae346 PMID: 39290441

Thakur, A. (2024). *The Art of Prompting: Unleashing the Power of Large Language Models*

Thomas, H., & Sinclair, P. (2023). Ethical alignment in AI development: Bridging the gap between fairness and performance. *Journal of AI Ethics and Applications*, *11*(3), 33–50.

Thomas, J., Li, X., & Zhang, H. (2023). Understanding the Role of Prompt Structure in NLP Model Accuracy. *International Journal of AI Research*, *38*(6), 467–479.

Tiwari, R. (2023). The impact of AI and machine learning on job displacement and employment opportunities. *Interantional Journal of Scientific Research in Engineering and Management*, *07*(01). Advance online publication. DOI: 10.55041/IJSREM17506

Torricelli, M., Martino, M., Baronchelli, A., & Aiello, L. M. (2024). The role of interface design on prompt-mediated creativity in generative AI. *ACM Web Science Conference*, 235–240. DOI: 10.1145/3614419.3644000

Trotta, A., Ziosi, M., & Lomonaco, V. (2023). The future of ethics in AI: Challenges and opportunities. *AI & Society*, *38*(2), 439–441. DOI: 10.1007/s00146-023-01644-x

Tversky, A., & Kahneman, D. (1974). Judgment under uncertainty: Heuristics and biases. *Science*, *185*(4157), 1124–1131. DOI: 10.1126/science.185.4157.1124 PMID: 17835457

Vaira, L. A., & Lechien, J. R., Abbate Vincenzo and Gabriele, G., Frosolini, A., De Vito, A., Maniaci, A., Yanez, M. M., Boscolo-Rizzo Paolo and Saibene, A. M., Maglitto, F., Salzano, G., Califano, G., Troise, S., Chiesa-Estomba, C. M., & De Riu, G. (2024). Enhancing AI chatbot responses in healthcare: The SMART prompt structure in head and neck surgery. In Research Square.

Vaira, L. A., Lechien, J. R., Abbate, V., Gabriele, G., Frosolini, A., De Vito, A., Maniaci, A., Mayo-Yáñez, M., Boscolo-Rizzo, P., Saibene, A. M., Maglitto, F., Salzano, G., Califano, G., Troise, S., Chiesa-Estomba, C. M., & De Riu, G. (2025). Enhancing AI chatbot responses in health care: The SMART prompt structure in head and neck surgery. *OTO Open*, *9*(1), e70075. DOI: 10.1002/oto2.70075 PMID: 39822375

Van Zyl, C., Ye, X., & Naidoo, R. (2023). Harnessing eXplainable artificial intelligence for feature selection in time series energy forecasting: A comparative analysis of Grad-CAM and SHAP. *Applied Energy, 353*, 122079. DOI: 10.1016/j.apenergy.2023.122079

Varona, D., & Suárez, J. L. (2022). Discrimination, bias, fairness, and trustworthy AI. *Applied Sciences (Basel, Switzerland), 12*(12), 5826. DOI: 10.3390/app12125826

Vaswani, A., Shazeer, N., Parmar, N., Uszkoreit, J., Jones, L., Gomez, A. N., Kaiser, Ł., & Polosukhin, I. (2017). Attention is all you need. *Advances in Neural Information Processing Systems, 2017-Decem*, 5999–6009. https://doi.org/https://doi.org/10.48550/arXiv.1706.03762

Vellend, M., & Geber, M. A. (2005). Connections between species diversity and genetic diversity. *Ecology Letters, 8*(7), 767–781. DOI: 10.1111/j.1461-0248.2005.00775.x

Venket, K., Ambica, A., & Freeda, A. R. (2024). Meta-Heuristics Algorithm for Computer Communications. In Metaheuristic and Machine Learning Optimization Strategies for Complex Systems (pp. 123-136). IGI Global. DOI: 10.4018/979-8-3693-7842-7.ch007

Venket, K., Freeda, A. R., & Vijay, F. (2025). AI for Large-Scale Communication Networks. In AI for Large Scale Communication Networks (pp. 25-44). IGI Global.

Verma, S., Kumar, A., & Jadhav, T. (2023). Chaining Prompts for Complex Task Handling in NLP Models. *Journal of Machine Learning and Automation, 20*(3), 134–142.

Vertex AI. (n.d.). Retrieved December 24, 2024, from https://cloud.google.com/vertex-ai

Vimbi, V., Shaffi, N., & Mahmud, M. (2024). Interpreting artificial intelligence models: A systematic review on the application of LIME and SHAP in Alzheimer's disease detection. *Brain Informatics, 11*(1), 10. Advance online publication. DOI: 10.1186/s40708-024-00222-1 PMID: 38578524

Wachter, S., Mittelstadt, B., & Russell, C. (2017). Counterfactual explanations without opening the black box: automated decisions and the GDPR. SSRN *Electronic Journal*. https://doi.org/DOI: 10.2139/ssrn.3063289

Wahle, J. P., Ruas, T., Mohammad, S. M., Meuschke, N., & Gipp, B. (2023). AI Usage Cards: Responsibly Reporting AI-Generated Content. *2023 ACM/IEEE Joint Conference on Digital Libraries (JCDL), 2023-June*(1), 282–284. DOI: 10.1109/JCDL57899.2023.00060

Walmsley, J. (2020). Artificial intelligence and the value of transparency. *AI & Society, 36*(2), 585–595. DOI: 10.1007/s00146-020-01066-z

Wang, B., Liu, Z., Huang, X., Jiao, F., Ding, Y., Aw, A., & Chen, N. F. (2023). SeaEval for multilingual foundation models: From cross-lingual alignment to cultural reasoning. *arXiv preprint arXiv:2309.04766.*

Wang, T., He, Z., Yu, W. Y., Fu, X., & Han, X. (2024). Large Language Models are Good Multi-lingual Learners: When LLMs Meet Cross-lingual Prompts. *arXiv preprint arXiv:2409.11056.*

Wang, Yu., Zhao, S., Wang, Z., Huang, H., Fan, M., Zhang, Y., Wang, Z., Wang, H., & Liu, T. (2024). *Strategic Chain-of-Thought: Guiding Accurate Reasoning in LLMs through Strategy Elicitation (Version 1).* DOI: 10.48550/ARXIV.2409.03271

Wang, J., Huo, Y., Mahe, J., Ge, Z., Liu, Z., Wang, W., & Zhang, L. (2024). Developing an ethical regulatory framework for artificial intelligence: Integrating systematic review, thematic analysis, and multidisciplinary theories. *IEEE Access : Practical Innovations, Open Solutions, 1*, 179383–179395. Advance online publication. DOI: 10.1109/ACCESS.2024.3501332

Wang, L., & Zhang, W. (2023). Exploring the Impact of Prompt Chaining in AI-driven Education Systems. *AI in Education, 27*(6), 179–190.

Wang, S., Liu, Z., Wang, Z., & Guo, J. (2023). *A Principled Framework for Knowledge-enhanced Large Language Model.* 1–10. https://arxiv.org/abs/2311.11135v1

Wang, S., Yu, M., & Huang, L. (2022). The Art of Prompting: Event Detection based on Type Specific Prompts. arXiv:2204.07241. Retrieved from https://arxiv.org/abs/2204.07241

Wang, X., Wei, J., Schuurmans, D., Le, Q., Chi, E. H., Narang, S., Chowdhery, A., & Zhou, D. (2023). Self-Consistency Improves Chain of Thought Reasoning in Language Models. *11th International Conference on Learning Representations, ICLR 2023*, 1–24.

Wang, Y. (2023). Deciphering the Enigma: A Deep Dive into Understanding and Interpreting LLM Outputs. In *Authorea Preprints.* DOI: 10.36227/techrxiv.24085833.v1

Wei, J., Wang, X., Schuurmans, D., Bosma, M., Ichter, B., Xia, F., Chi, E. H., Le, Q. V., & Zhou, D. (2022). Chain-of-Thought Prompting Elicits Reasoning in Large Language Models. *Advances in Neural Information Processing Systems, 35*(NeurIPS), 1–43.

Wheatley, M. (2024). *Quantum Shifts: The Societal Implications of Quantum Computing on Security, Privacy, and the Economy*. Premier Science., DOI: 10.70389/PJCS.100002

Williams, K., Reed, A., & Bennett, C. (2023). Enhancing stakeholder feedback loops in AI design: A case study approach. *Interdisciplinary AI Studies*, *5*(4), 66–82.

Wolfson, S. S., & Landy, M. S. (1998). Examining edge-and region-based texture analysis mechanisms. *Vision Research, 38*(3), 439–446. DOI: 10.1016/S0042-6989(97)00153-3 PMID: 9536367

Wu, F., Liu, J., & Chen, Y. (Eds.). yu, yang, & Li, N. (2022). Design of a tool for checking academic integrity and content consistency of paper abstracts. In F. Wu, J. Liu, & Y. Chen (Eds.), *International Conference on Computer Graphics, Artificial Intelligence, and Data Processing (ICCAID 2021)* (Vol. 12168, p. 40). SPIE. DOI: 10.1117/12.2631139

Wu, X., Duan, R., & Ni, J. (2023). Unveiling Security, Privacy, and Ethical Concerns of ChatGPT. *Journal of Information and Intelligence*, *2*(2), 102–115. DOI: 10.1016/j.jiixd.2023.10.007

Xu, L., Sun, H., Zhao, H., Zhang, W., Ning, H., & Guan, H. (2023). Accurate and efficient federated-learning-based edge intelligence for effective video analysis. *IEEE Internet of Things Journal, 10*(14), 12169–12177. DOI: 10.1109/JIOT.2023.3241039

Yang, S., Wu, Y., Gao, Y., Zhou, Z., Zhu, B. B., Sun, X., Lou, J.-G., Ding, Z., Hu, A., Fang, Y., Li, Y., Chen, J., & Yang, L. (2024). *AMPO: Automatic Multi-Branched Prompt Optimization*. DOI: 10.18653/v1/2024.emnlp-main.1130

Yaprak, B. (2024). Generative Artificial Intelligence in marketing: The invisible danger of AI hallucinations. *Journal of Economy Business and Management*, *8*(2), 133–158. DOI: 10.7596/jebm.1588897

Yuan, W., & Liu, P. (2022). KID-Review: Knowledge-Guided Scientific Review Generation with Oracle Pre-training. *Proceedings of the AAAI Conference on Artificial Intelligence, 36*(10), 11639–11647. DOI: 10.1609/aaai.v36i10.21418

Yu, C., Wang, T., Shao, Z., Zhu, L., Zhou, X., & Jiang, S. (2024). TwinPilots: A New Computing Paradigm for GPU-CPU Parallel LLM Inference. *Proceedings of the 17th ACM International Systems and Storage Conference on ZZZ*, 91–103. DOI: 10.1145/3688351.3689164

Zeiser, J. (2024). Owning decisions: AI decision-support and the attributability-gap. *Science and Engineering Ethics*, *30*(4), 27. DOI: 10.1007/s11948-024-00485-1 PMID: 38888795

Zhang, H., Yu, P. S., & Zhang, J. (2024). *A Systematic Survey of Text Summarization: From Statistical Methods to Large Language Models. 1*(1), 1–42. https://arxiv.org/abs/2406.11289

Zhang, Y., Wang, X., Wu, L., & Wang, J. (2024). *Pattern-Aware Chain-of-Thought Prompting in Large Language Models*. DOI: 10.48550/ARXIV.2404.14812

Zhao, H., Lin, Q., & Cheng, W. (2024). Enhancing transparency in AI systems: Tools and methodologies. *Transparency in AI Journal*, *7*(2), 77–98.

Zhao, T., Zhang, H., & Li, Q. (2023). Prompt Refinement for Bias Reduction in Large Language Models. *AI Ethics Review*, *12*(1), 78–90.

Zheng, M., Liang, H., Yang, F., Sun, H., Li, T., Xiong, L., Zhang, Y., Wu, Y., Li, K., Shen, Y., Lin, M., Zhang, T., Dong, G., Qiao, Y., Fang, K., Chen, W., Cui, B., Zhang, W., & Zhou, Z. (2024). *PAS: Data-Efficient Plug-and-Play Prompt Augmentation System*. DOI: 10.48550/ARXIV.2407.06027

Zhou, F., Li, H., & Yang, Q. (2024). Advances in prompt engineering for ethical AI. *Advances in AI Research*, *9*(3), 134–150.

Zhou, H., Wan, X., Proleev, L., Mincu, D., Chen, J., Heller, K., & Roy, S. (2023). Batch Calibration: Rethinking Calibration for In-Context Learning and Prompt Engineering. *12th International Conference on Learning Representations, ICLR 2024,* 2023, 1–27. https://arxiv.org/abs/2309.17249

Zhou, R., Chen, L., & Yu, K. (2024). Is LLM a Reliable Reviewer? A Comprehensive Evaluation of LLM on Automatic Paper Reviewing Tasks. *2024 Joint International Conference on Computational Linguistics, Language Resources and Evaluation, LREC-COLING 2024 - Main Conference Proceedings*, 9340–9351.

About the Contributors

Houssem Chemingui, is an Assistant Professor in Information Systems at Brest Business School. With a PhD in Computer Science from Paris 1 Panthéon Sorbonne University, his research focuses on streamlining product line configuration processes. He's published extensively on topics like Artificial Intelligence, Data Analytics, and Software Configuration. Beyond academia, he's contributed to development projects and consultancy initiatives, showcasing his commitment to advancing technology and education.

Munir Ahmad is a seasoned professional in the realm of Spatial Data Infrastructure (SDI), Geo-Information Productions, Information Systems, and Information Governance, boasting over 25 years of dedicated experience in the field. With a PhD in Computer Science, Dr. Ahmad's expertise spans Spatial Data Production, Management, Processing, Analysis, Visualization, and Quality Control. Throughout his career, Dr. Ahmad has been deeply involved in the development and deployment of SDI systems specially in the context of Pakistan, leveraging his proficiency in Spatial Database Design, Web, Mobile & Desktop GIS, and Geo Web Services Architecture. His contributions to Volunteered Geographic Information (VGI) and Open Source Geoportal & Metadata Portal have significantly enriched the geospatial community. As a trainer and researcher, Dr. Ahmad has authored over 50 publications, advancing the industry's knowledge base and fostering innovation in Geo-Tech, Data Governance, and Information Infrastructure, and Emerging Technologies. His commitment to Research and Development (R&D) is evident in his role as a dedicated educator and mentor in the field.

***

Raghavesh works for the Department of Management, Thakur Shiv Kumar Singh Memorial Management College, Burhanpur.

Suma M Abraham is a Research Scholar, Department of Zoology, St. Berchman's college, Changanacherry, Kottayam Kerala India PIN code: 686101 Orcid id:

Zamira Atamuratova is working at Urgench State University, Urgench, Uzbekistan. Department of Pedagogy and Psychology.

Piyush Bhosale graduated from the School of Engineering at Ajeenkya D. Y. Patil University with a B.Tech. degree in Computer Science (Artificial Intelligence). His research interests include AI, Data Science, and cancer detection. Along with Ms. Amna Kausar and Ms. Shravani Kulkarni, he received the Best Thesis Award for their B.Tech. thesis.

Susanta Das is a seasoned educator with a proven record of teaching and mentoring diverse students, working at multiple institutions, and providing service to the various initiatives of organizations. He received his Ph.D. and M.A. degrees from Western Michigan University (WMU), USA, and M.Sc. degree from Banaras Hindu University (BHU), India all in Physics. He continued his research as a Marie-Curie post-doctoral fellow at Stockholm University, Stockholm, Sweden on beam diagnostics for the DESIREE (Double ElectroStatic Ion Ring ExpEriment) in the project DITANET (Diagnostic Techniques for particle Accelerators – a Marie-Curie initial training NETwork), at the Indian Institute of Science Education and Research-Kolkata, India on high-pressure physics as a Project Scientist-B, and at the University of Electro-Communications, Tokyo, Japan on ion-surface interactions as a Post-doctoral fellow. Throughout his career, Dr. Das worked and collaborated with many researchers, Ph.D., master, and visiting students from different countries. He further visited many countries to discuss research and an international conference participant (UK, Italy, Germany, Greece, Belgium, Bulgaria, Romania, Brazil etc.). He worked at several institutions before assuming his current role at Ajeenkya D Y Patil University. He received the Marie-Curie post-doctoral fellowship in Sweden, Science Academies' Summer Research Fellowship in India, Gwen Frostic Doctoral Fellowship, Department Graduate Research and Creative Scholar Award by WMU, and Leo R. Parpart Doctoral Fellowship by Dept. of Physics, WMU, among many others, throughout his academic journey. He co-authored several research articles in WoS/Scopus indexed international journals, conference proceedings, and scholarly book chapters and co-edited several books published by renowned international publishing houses (IGI-Global, Springer Nature, Nova Science Publishers, Wiley, & Scrivener-Willey, Notion Press). At present, Dr. Das continues to delve into cutting-edge fields, with a keen interest in nanotechnology, UN SDGs, and data science. His multifaceted contributions, spanning teaching, research, and administrative leadership, showcase a dedicated professional who is instrumental in advancing the vision and mission of the institutions he serves.

Radhiyatul Fajri earned her Master's degree in Computer Science from IPB University, Indonesia, in 2022. She currently serves as an Associate Researcher at the Research Center for Data and Information Sciences under the National Research and Innovation Agency (BRIN) Indonesia. Since 2021, she has been dedicated to advancing research in artificial intelligence, particularly in the fields of natural language processing and computer vision. Her work spans areas such as sentiment analysis, natural language processing, and facial recognition.

Issac George is a Research Scholar, Department of Zoology, St. Berchman's College, Changanacherry Kottayam Kerala, India. 686101

Sobha Merina George is an Assistant Professor Department of Zoology, Kristu Jyoti College of Management and Technology, Changanacherry. Kottayam Kerala, India.

Prashant Gupta is a seasoned leader currently serving as a Software Development Manager at Amazon where he leads a team of engineers to deliver scalable software solutions for Amazon's vast network of warehouses. With a Master's in Computer Engineering from UC Davis and over 9 years of professional experience, Prashant specializes in software development and management, utilizing state-of-the-art cloud solutions. As a cross-functional leader, he fosters global collaboration to ensure the quality and reliability of their projects. Prashant's contributions extend beyond Amazon; he also serves as a reviewer for Elsevier, where he contributes to advancing research in computer science. His overarching mission remains consistent: to innovate, delight customers, and drive growth.

Nuraisa Hidayati has a Bachelor of Science in Computer Science from the Department of Information Systems at Sepuluh Nopember Institute of Technology (ITS) in 2012. She continued her studies at ITS, receiving a Master's degree in Computer Science from the Department of Informatics Engineering in 2021. She began her work as a software engineer, managing data in a variety of settings, including the telecommunications office, between 2012 and 2013. After that, she developed multiple human resources applications for the Agency for the Assessment and Application of Technology (BPPT) 2014-2021. Currently, she applies her knowledge as a researcher at the National Research and Innovation Agency (BRIN), focusing on Natural Language Processing (NLP), specifically text processing such as sentiment analysis, hoax detection, and topic modeling, to a variety of situations in Indonesia.

Vishal Jain is presently working as a Professor at the Department of Computer Science & Engineering, School of Engineering & Technology, Vivekananda Institute of Professional Studies - Technical Campus, New Delhi. Before that, he worked as Professor at Sharda University, Greater Noida and Associate Professor at Bharati Vidyapeeth's Institute of Computer Applications and Management (BVICAM), New Delhi. He has associated as a member of the Faculty Board, Board of Planning and Management, Executive Council, Academic Council, Curriculum Development and Review Committee and Academic Audit of various higher education Institutions. He is associated with Kuala Lumpur University of Science and Technology (KLUST), Malaysia, Lincoln University College, Malaysia and Research Institute of IoT Cybersecurity, Department of Electronic Engineering, National Kaohsiung University of Science and Technology, Taiwan for research oriented activities.

Asril Jarin holds a Doctor of Electrical Engineering from the University of Indonesia in 2017. He also received his Dipl.Ing from GSO Fachhochschule Nuernberg and M.Sc from Hochschule Darmstadt, Germany, in 2001 and 2003 respectively. Presently, he serves as an associate researcher at the Research Center for Data and Information Sciences, affiliated with the National Research and Innovation Agency (BRIN) in Indonesia. Since 2021, he has been an active researcher in the domain of artificial intelligence, specifically focusing on speech and natural language processing. His research includes speech recognition, speech analytics, sentiment analysis, and natural language processing. Over time, he has contributed with numerous publications in international conferences and journals.

Amna Kausar is a third-year computer engineering student, specialising in AI with a minor in robotics. Her journey into technology started at a young age, fixing broken electronics, which evolved into winning academic and inter-school competitions, including awards in robotics and business challenges. She is particularly interested in the intersection of her two biggest strengths, creativity and logical thinking, finding a deep interest in the concept of biologically inspired systems like AI and robotics. Her professional experience includes internships in security, research, development, and as an AI solution engineer, she also contributes to developing software for NGOs. Outside of studies, she enjoys playing chess, reading, exploring different art mediums, and practising mindfulness through walks. Currently, she is moving forward with one of her startup ideas, participating in the IUCAA summer school programme in Astronomy and Astrophysics, while working on a personal project aimed at developing solutions for individuals with hearing impairments. By aligning her technical skills with her personal goals, she reflects her commitment to innovation and societal impact.

Kokoy Siti Komariah earned her Doctoral degree in AI Convergence from Pukyong National University (PKNU), South Korea, in 2023, under the supervision of Prof. Bong-Kee Sin. She is currently a researcher at the National Research and Innovation Agency (BRIN) of the Republic of Indonesia, working in the Data Science and Information Research Center as part of the Natural Language Processing (NLP) research group. Her research interests include applied machine learning, text analysis, information retrieval, and Natural Language Processing (NLP).

Shravani Kulkarni graduated from the School of Engineering at Ajeenkya D. Y. Patil University with a B.Tech. degree in Computer Science (Artificial Intelligence). Her research interests include AI, Data Science, and cancer detection. Along with Ms. Amna Kausar and Mr. Piyush Bhosale, she received the Best Thesis Award for their B.Tech. thesis. She also received the Vice-Chancellor's Award for her overall performance.

Prakash Kundnani works for the Department of Management, United Institute of Management, Naini, Prayagraj Uttar Pradesh prakash.kundnani@gmail.com

Andi Latief is a Researcher at the Data and Information Science Research Center, National Research and Innovation Agency of Indonesia. In the last two years, actively contributed to the field of artificial intelligence, especially natural language processing (NLP), with a focus on efforts to preserve endangered languages. In addition, also conducts research on the ethics of using artificial intelligence, and large language models (LLM), to ensure the implementation of responsible and ethical AI technology.

Suresh M is an Assistant Professor, Department of Management, United Institute of Management, Naini, Prayagraj Naini, Prayagraj Uttar Pradesh vidyaprema1987@gmail.com

Archan Mitra is an Assistant Professor at School of Media Studies (SOMS) at Presidency University, Bangalore. He is the author of two book "Cases for Classroom Media and Entertainment Business" and "Multiverse and Media", he also has other several edited books to his credit. He has done his doctorate from Visva-Bharati Santiniketan, West Bengal in the field of "environmental informatics and communication for sustainability". In addition to that he is a certified Science Communicator and Journalism from Indian Science Communication Society (ISCOS), certified Corporate Trainer with Amity Institute of Training and Development, Certified Social Media Network Analyst. He has a strong interest in environmental communication. He was awarded certificate of merit by PRSI, Kolkata Chapter and Medal of Honor by Journalistic Club of Kolkata. He was working as a research assistant with the World Bank's "Environmental Capacity Building in Southeast Asia" project at IIM Kashipur. He was instrumental in launching the World Bank's Green MBA MOOC, he has also assisted in the research project on Uttarakhand disaster mitigation by ICSSR, the leading research on Uttarakhand disaster.

Archan Mitra is an Assistant Professor at School of Media Studies (SOMS), at Presidency University, Bangalore. He edited various publications and wrote "Cases for Classroom Media and Entertainment Business," an IIM textbook. "Environmental informatics and communication for sustainability" is his doctorate at Visva-Bharati Santiniketan, West Bengal. He is also a qualified Science Communicator and Journalism from Indian Science Communication Society (ISCOS), Corporate Trainer with Amity Institute of Training and Development, and Social Media Network Analyst. He loves environmental communication. He received the Journalistic Club of Kolkata Medal of Honour and PRSI Kolkata Chapter Certificate of Merit. He was a World Bank research assistant at IIM Kashipur. He launched the World Bank's Green MBA MOOC. He publishes in prestigious emergency management magazines. IIM Kashipur, Alabama State University, Birmingham, USA, is his research partner. He used Developing Communities from Within (DCFW) to turn a West Bengal village called "Noachar" into an eco-village.

Elvira Nurfadhilah received the Bachelor and Master of Computer Science from IPB University, Indonesia, in 2011 and 2015. She is an associate researcher at the Research Center for Data and Information Sciences, affiliated with the National Research and Innovation Agency (BRIN) in Indonesia. Since 2016, she has been an active researcher in artificial intelligence, specifically focusing on speech and natural language processing. Her research includes speech recognition and analysis, sentiment analysis, and natural language processing.

Subhash Patel is an Assistant Professor (Sr) School of Computing Science Engineering and Artificial Intelligence (SCAI),VIT Bhopal University, Sehore Madhya Pradesh

Sanchita Paul is a dedicated and accomplished content strategist with extensive experience in managing diverse content formats across different digital platforms. With a strong background in content strategy, editing, and UX writing, she has honed her skills in branding, social media management, and technical writing. Holding an MA in Communication and Journalism from Visva-Bharati University, Ms. Paul is proficient in tools like Google Analytics, Canva, and MS Office Suite, making her a versatile professional committed to producing high-quality, impactful content to improve brand visibility.

Siska Pebiana is an NLP researcher

Lakshmana Phanendra Magulur works for the Department of Computer Science and Engineering, Koneru Lakshmaiah Education Foundation, 'Vaddeswaram, Andhra Pradesh 522302 India.

Ravikumar is an experienced educator with 12+ years of teaching in Computer Science across India and overseas. Currently an Assistant Professor at Marwadi University, Rajkot, he specializes in Advanced Java, Machine Learning, Recommendation Systems, Optimization Techniques, and AI. He completed PhD at Amity University, Jaipur, 2025. He completed M.E. in Computer Science Engineering from VMRF University (2013), and B.E. from Anna University (2010). He holds a Mini MBA from the Swiss eLearning Institute (2015). He is dedicated to research, professional development, and advancing education through technology.

Aarthi S is a dedicated Assistant Professor in Computer Science with over six years of teaching experience. She is currently pursuing her Ph.D. at Marwadi University, Gujarat, and holds an M.Phil. and MCA from Bharathiar University, Tamil Nadu. Throughout her academic career, Aarthi has specialized in programming languages such as C++, Java, and C, and contributed to research in recommender systems and AI-related data privacy. She has published journal articles, contributed to book chapters, and actively participated in technical workshops. Known for her student mentorship and engagement in academic events, Aarthi remains committed to fostering innovation and excellence in computer science education.

Sa'dullayeva Moxinur is working as an assistant teacher at the Department of Pedagogy, Urgench State Pedagogical Institute, Urgench, Uzbekistan.

Tri Sampurno is a Researcher in AI, Machine Translation Quality Estimation

Agung Santosa received the BSEE from University of Toledo, USA, in 1992 and Master of Computer Science from University of Indonesia, Indonesia, in 2015. He is an associate researcher at the Research Center for Data and Information Sciences, affiliated with the National Research and Innovation Agency (BRIN) in Indonesia. Since 2021, he has been an active researcher in the domain of artificial intelligence, specifically focusing on speech and natural language processing. His research includes speech recognition, speech analytics, sentiment analysis, and natural language processing. He can be contacted at email: agun006@brin.go.id.

Jakhongir Shaturaev is an associate professor working in the Department of International Cooperation, Termez University of Economics and Service, Termez, Uzbekistan.

Aditya Shrivastav is an aspiring technologist currently pursuing a Bachelor of Technology (B. Tech.) in Computer Science and Engineering at Ajeenkya D. Y. Patil University. He holds solid programming expertise in C, C++, and Python, alongside strong command over data and business tools such as Microsoft Excel and Tally software. Aditya is a member of Team Vac-Vectoor Hyperloop and participated with the team in the Global Hyperloop Competition organized by IIT Madras, contributing to cutting-edge transportation solutions. He actively engages in hackathons and various technical events to expand his skills and contribute to innovative problem-solving. He has authored and co-authored book chapters in the domains of solid waste management, bioplastics, nanotechnology applications, and artificial intelligence, showcasing his multidisciplinary approach and research acumen. Aditya is also working on an innovative project on predictive e-waste management. The project is targeted toward IT departments, schools, and colleges, aiming to support sustainable practices and resource optimization. In parallel with his academic journey, Aditya is serving as a faculty intern at Disha Computer Institute, where he teaches C, C++, basic Python, basic Java, Excel formulas, and Tally software. His dedication and teaching proficiency earned him a Letter of Appreciation and the opportunity to conduct a workshop on Advanced Excel at G. H. Raisoni College of Arts, Commerce and Science. With a strong foundation in technology, a passion for sustainability, and hands-on experience in both teaching and project development, Aditya Shrivastav is committed to driving impact through research, education, and innovation.

Vivek Srivastava is an Assistant Professor Department of Management, United Institute of Management, Prayagraj Uttar Pradesh

Yulduz Urazbaeva is working at Mamun University, Khiva, Uzbekistan, in the Department of Pedagogy and Psychology.

V.S. Krithikaa Venket earned her bachelor's and master's degrees in Information Technology from Dr. Sivanthi Aditanar College of Engineering. She is currently an Assistant Professor in the Information Technology department at KCG College of Technology, Chennai. In addition to her teaching role, she is pursuing a Ph.D. at Anna University, focusing on deepfake technology. Her research interests include data mining, pattern recognition, artificial intelligence, machine learning, and deep learning.

Yuyun Yuyun is a researcher in artificial intelligence based in Makassar and Bandung Cities, Indonesia. With a background in computational linguistics and data engineering. Yuyun has worked on various projects related to fine-tuning large language models and building AI tools for Indonesian languages and local language in indonesian. Yuyun's research focus of NLP, Machine Learning, Deep Learning, LLM, Low Resource Language Currently, Yuyun's affiliation with the Natinal research and Innovation Agnecy (BRIN) indonesia and is actively contributing to the development of natural language processing technologies for low-resource languages. Yuyun has published research articles in leading machine learning journals and international conferences.

Index

A

B

C

E

F

G

H

I

J

L

M

N

O

P

R

T

U

Z

www.ingramcontent.com/pod-product-compliance
Lightning Source LLC
LaVergne TN
LVHW061544290926
849162LV00004B/904